Jim Ford was born in 1965 a<u>1</u>
his parents unexpectedly upp
farm in the Brecon Beacons. R   ....~ ..uu to be more
to life than just sheep and wellies, he eventually moved
down to the south coast in order to further his education.
Once he'd graduated in 1986, he toiled for three years in the
back offices of two large American banks, before the travel
bug ultimately came to his rescue, finally snapping him out
of his senses and removing him from the office environment
once and for all. Or so he thought! Having since joined the
ranks of the self-employed, he now lives happily in West
Sussex with his partner, Sam; their new born daughter and
their mad but lovable Springer Spaniel. *Don't Worry, Be
Happy* is his first book.

JIM FORD

Don't Worry, Be Happy

Beijing to Bombay
with a Backpack

Matador
9 De Montfort Mews
Leicester LE1 7FW, UK
Tel: (+44) 116 255 9311 / 9312
Email: books@troubador.co.uk
Web: www.troubador.co.uk/matador

ISBN 1 905237 22 7

Cover illustration: Simon Abbott

Typeset in 11pt Stempel Garamond by Troubador Publishing Ltd, Leicester, UK
Printed by The Cromwell Press, Trowbridge, Wilts, UK

Matador is an imprint of Troubador Publishing Ltd

For Nanny Jess, Queen of Chuckles.

CONTENTS

Maps   x
Introduction   xiii

PART 1   CHINA

1	Getting to Grips	3
2	At Home with the Danes	38
3	Shansh Maanee	54
4	Invisible Gorges and Trying Travellers	60
5	Chinese Secrets	71
6	Shangri-La	77
7	Royal Blood	91
8	A Chinese Christmas	105
9	New Friends	119
10	Chamber of Horrors	133
11	Back to the Future	144
12	Life's a Beach	164

PART 2   AUSTRALASIA

13	Under a Southern Sky	175
14	Visiting the Relo's	194
15	Petrolheads	200
16	The Hustler	212

17	Crocs and Rocks	223
18	Hula Hula Time	229
19	An Australian Christmas	244
20	The Old Stomping Ground	249
21	A Hitchhiker's Guide	260
22	Culture Shock	282

PART 3　　　INDIA

23	Welcome to India	295
24	Orange, Pineapple, Watermelon... You Like?	307
25	Saddam Hussein & the Dali Lama's Sister	320
26	Oh, Pretty Woman	328
27	City of Joy	341
28	The Strange Case of a Man Called MacGregor	357
29	Friends Reunited	374
30	Rip-offs, Rakshi & Rhinos	384
31	Burning the Candle Both Ends	398
32	An Odd Place for Dolphins	417
33	Just Gotta Get Out of this Place	431
34	Desert Delight	447
35	Chunglee Singh	458
36	Maugham Heaven... And Then I See the Headlines	470

Afterword	493

DON'T WORRY, BE HAPPY

BEIJING TO BOMBAY
WITH A BACKPACK

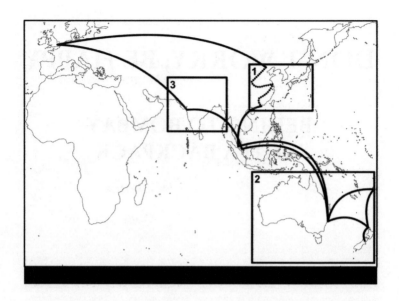

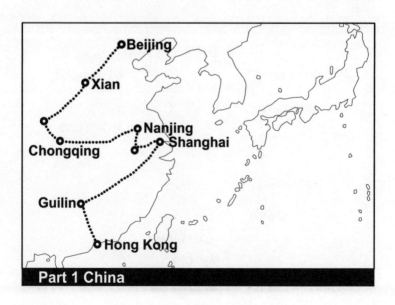

Part 1 China

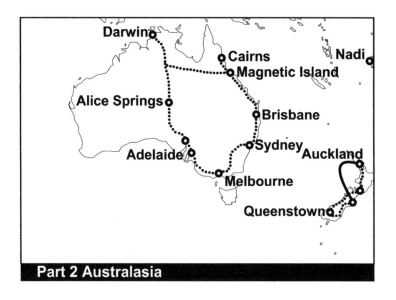

Part 2 Australasia

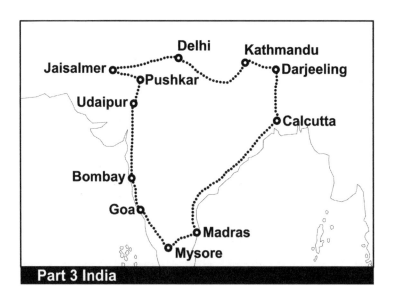

Part 3 India

INTRODUCTION

7th January 2001

8.15pm. Grimacing at the Tupperware box, I rub my stubbly chin. Is it *really* the time to be doing this? Earlier in the afternoon, as I was preparing the Sunday roast, I was wondering whether it'd be better to leave it a while longer, but then I remembered how depressing it gets this time of year. Opening it now would surely provide the distraction I need to shake off the January blues.

My eyes return to the box. Perhaps I'm kidding myself? It'll probably be a complete waste of time. As I sit there jigging my foot under the lounge table, my thoughts drift back in time and for a few moments I picture myself sitting on the plane back from Thailand in '86. Even before that wondrous fortnight, I'd had a yearning to go to the east; I'd been transfixed by China ever since I'd seen *The Last Emperor* at the cinema and I was just as desperate to travel around India to finally find out for myself exactly what this baffling country was really like. But sitting on that plane reflecting on the two weeks that had just passed—that was when I'd made up my mind once and for all.

I laugh to myself now, thinking how naive I was in assuming two family holidays a year in Europe would've prepared me for Thailand. How wrong could I have been? I was left stirred by the sounds, intoxicated by the smells and spellbound by the sights. A different continent perhaps, but to me, a different world. And it wasn't only that. The more I spoke to my travelling friends, the more I became excited by the whole backpacking phenomenon: arriving in strange places, striking up friendships with other young travellers and observing cultures of countries so different to ours. They were in Thailand in the middle of their travels; I was just there for a fortnight's holiday and now that I'd had a sniff, I wanted a piece of the action. It was time for me to plan *my* trip.

Peeling the lid slowly off the box, I stare down at the tapes. There are more inside than I remember; all meticulously filed in number order and each labelled with relevant locations and dates. The first one I pick up is marked 'London Nov 89'.

I had to move to London; there was no way I could have saved enough money on my paltry salary in Bournemouth, even with all the overtime. And just as I was beginning to despair after months of fruitless job-hunting, I struck lucky and was offered a post working for a rival American bank in the City. The salary was substantial, I accepted immediately and then, just a day later, I received the phone call from a friend informing me a room had come up in their house in Muswell Hill, rent a meagre £50 a week. Things were finally looking up, but my God, those six months that followed were difficult. There were my flatmates, gallivanting every night in bars, restaurants and nightclubs, enjoying the London Scene to the full and there was I, either working late or sat in front of the telly on a Friday or Saturday night, being forced to sacrifice my social life completely, in this, one of the most sociable cities of all. But then if I hadn't, I'd never have been able to go that November.

I empty the tapes out onto the table. There are twenty-six in all. That's twenty-six one-hour tapes, more than a whole day of me babbling on non-stop in my dull monotone voice: 'I arrived here, I went there, I did this, I did that.' But then as I gaze at the labels one by one, those stirring memories start flooding back: Darjeeling and the bizarre episode of the man on the bus, the surreal boat trip down the Yangtze River, the extraordinary events that compelled me to leap off a 140-foot tower in Queensland, my first experience of hallucinogens at a full moon party in Goa and the tragic assassination of Rajiv Gandhi just days before I returned. Leaning over the table, I grab hold of the first tape, carefully insert it into the recorder and very purposely, press down the large silver button marked 'Play'.

PART 1

CHINA

PART

CHINA

CHAPTER 1

BEIJING

GETTING TO GRIPS

21st–30th November 1989

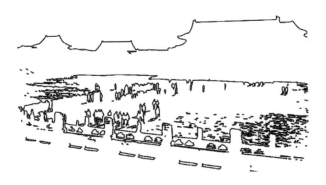

Keeping a beady eye on the twinkling lights below, I finally settled back into my seat. I still felt drained after the last seven days, although the emotional roller coaster had begun weeks before on a dreary Friday morning in the City.

'So tell me,' said my boss, carefully placing the receiver back on the cradle. 'What is it you're doing again?'

I took another deep breath and gulped. 'Going over to work on my auntie's sheep farm,' I repeated from the other side of his desk. 'She's been struggling to cope ever since my uncle's heart attack last year,' I added, trying to make it sound a little more plausible.

'Well, what can I say?' he sighed, scratching his furrowed brow. 'It's a great shame you know, you've been making some real inroads recently.'

'Mmm,' I mumbled, lowering my eyes.

'Never been to Australia myself. Supposed to be wonderful. The land of opportunity, or so they say.'

'Mmm,' I muttered again, blankly staring down at the piles of beige folders and memos strewn across the desktop.

'Well, I'll let Personnel know straight away. Hope it all works out well for you. Still, great shame, though.'

Standing up, I shook his outstretched hand and doing my utmost to remain po-faced, made the long walk back to my desk at the other end of the office. The fact that my uncle had died ten years ago and my auntie was a tiny frail lady in her eighties living in a bungalow in a quiet suburb of Melbourne didn't seem to matter. All that did was that my boss had appeared to believe the story.

I guess my final week in London was always going to be frenetic. There were still purchases to be made, farewell parties to attend and hours of packing to be done, all before my parents came to pick me up on the weekend. Yet somehow, by Sunday, I was all but ready. I'd even finally taken the plunge and splashed out on a £70 pair of walking boots. I glanced down at the list one more time and sure enough, every line of writing had a barbed wire scribble through it. Then my mother phoned.

'I'm not going to be able to come,' she said in a deadpan voice.' I think your father's got pneumonia. I just can't leave him as he is.'

Brilliant, bloody brilliant! What was I going to do now? There was no way I'd be able to lug all my stuff back to Wales on the train.

'Is he okay?' I asked after an uncomfortably long pause.

'Well, we've had a rough twenty-four hours. He was up all night with a soaring temperature. I've just called the doctor now, it looks like he might have to go down to hospital.'

Hospital? It sounded a little extreme. Everybody gets pneumonia, so what was all the fuss about? I had pneumonia two weeks ago. He couldn't be that bad, surely?

'But listen,' she added. 'I've just spoken to Janet. She and John are going to pick you up instead.'

4

Three hours later we were tearing down the M4 in my uncle's plush Mercedes. As I fidgeted about on the shiny leather back seat, surrounded by all my boxes and bags, they started telling me all about their recent holiday in Thailand.

'China should be fascinating,' commented John, twenty minutes later. 'There was an article in *The Bangkok Post* which said very few tourists are going there after Tiananmen.'

'Oh, really?' I replied, my thoughts by now a million miles away from China.

When we arrived back at my parents' farm, all my mounting fears were realised. My father lay on their bed, eyes closed, his face pale and gaunt. The doctor, who'd just arrived, immediately called for an ambulance to take him down to infirmary. Later that afternoon he underwent a series of x-rays. The radiotherapist conferring with hospital doctor then called my mother into his office. The pictures had revealed a shadow on one of his lungs. They suspected it was a cancerous growth. I accompanied her down to the hospital every morning and evening for the next three days to visit my ailing father who rapidly losing weight, was looking ghastlier by the hour. I also contacted both my travel agent and insurance company to advise them of these circumstances, informing them I'd almost certainly need to cancel my trip.

The following afternoon, my mother received a call from the hospital. The results from their tests weren't as bad as first thought. The shadow they'd identified on the lung was now believed to be pleurisy and although my father perked up over the weekend, I was still adamant I should postpone my flight. Constant reassurances from the rest of my family, however, finally persuaded me otherwise.

Then there was my last night when worries of another kind were occupying my mind. I had spent the early part of the evening with a group of old college mates in an Ealing pub. It was supposed to be a big final night send-off but as the night wore on, I was becoming increasingly concerned. I could tell from all the giggles and whispering each time I emerged from the toilet they had something in store for me. That I was sure, the problem was trying to guess what. Unable to contain their excitement any longer, they finally unveiled my designated means of torture over the traditional end of night curry. It came in the form of a padlocked plastic latticed toy (similar in appearance to a shuttlecock), which, I learnt, was to be fastened onto my penis. And no, they wouldn't be presenting me with the key as a leaving present either. Ten minutes later out in the street, they put the plan in motion although they encountered some unexpectedly fierce resistance. There was one reason in particular why I was putting up so much of a fight and the consequences of this didn't bear worth thinking about. Indeed, as I lay on the pavement, throwing my arms and frantically kicking my feet, desperately trying to push them off, the nightmare scenario kept flashing through my mind.

'Pete... Pete, come in here a second, you're not gonna believe this one.'

'Wey hey, what we got here then?'

'Reckons his mates put it on him last night. Says they threw away the key.'

'Threw away the key? C'mon now Stanley. You're not trying to tell me he can't get it off?'

'Ay, says he needs the key to unfasten it.'

'Bloody 'ell, I've seen it all now. Wait 'til I tell the missus about this one. Where's he travelling to?'

'Beijing.'

'Beijing? Bloody Hellfire! Can't have him travelling there like that. Better take him down to the medical room, then. They'll have to cut it off. Some mates you've got there, son.'

At this late stage, however, I was determined that nothing whatsoever was going to stand between me and my departure, so as soon as I managed to grab hold of the codpiece, I threw the others off, and leaping to my feet, hurled it high into the night sky, watching it land over a hedge into the safety of some poor unsuspecting person's front garden.

Twelve hours later at Heathrow, a group of customs officers idly chatting amongst themselves were congregated around the scanner. Retrieving my daypack from the conveyer belt, I looked over and grinned. If only they could have known why.

I was setting off alone not entirely by choice. The truth of the matter was nobody wanted to come with me. Naturally, it would have been nice to depart in the company of a mate or a loved one to share all those illuminating experiences en route but the opportunity simply hadn't presented itself and I could no longer let this stand in the way. I was, after all, reaching the ripe old age of twenty-five.

Unlike many others, I'd purposely decided *not* to embark on a full round-the-world trip as that would inevitably entail travelling back through the States and this was not something that enthused me in any way, shape or form. Not that I had anything against America in particular but when it came to places to visit, virtually every other country in the world seemed more interesting. I'd booked three flights in all, the first to Beijing, where I'd spend my first week visiting the city's sights — Tiananmen Square, the Forbidden City, the Great Wall — slowly acclimatising and trying to adjust to the backpacking routine. Then, when I was confident I'd found my feet, I'd leave the capital to start the long six-week overland trek southwards to Hong Kong. After that I'd make a brief stopover in Kuala Lumpur and then fly on to Sydney. I was setting off with around £4000 worth of savings although I'd taken the added precaution of obtaining a 12-month working visa for Australia just in case I needed to supplement these funds before travelling back through India. I was also curious to see if Australia was all it was cracked up to be. When I was three years old, my mother, leaving me in the capable hands of doting grandparents, had embarked on a twelve-month teaching exchange in New South Wales. She came back extolling the virtues of the country and for many months after, seriously contemplated moving back there for good. Not entirely sure I wanted to settle in the UK, I was thus keen to test the water myself.

But aside from this there was no apparent mission or quest. I wasn't following in anybody's footsteps, I wasn't travelling on a camel or with a fridge or television crew, I was just heading off into, what for me at least, was uncharted territory. Sure, travelling through China and India was never going to be easy, though this was just part of the challenge. More and more people were setting off on similar trips and travelling now at such an impressionable age seemed the obvious thing to do. Yet almost without exception all these friends and relatives were going off in pairs or small groups whereas I was setting off alone. So the big question was how would I cope travelling by myself. I'd always thought myself strong-minded and independent but this would surely be the ultimate test, and in truth, I couldn't wait for it to begin. That said, there was a certain point to prove and that was the small matter of silencing the critics.

'So let's get this right,' people would say before I left. 'You're travelling through China all by yourself? Surely you must be worried?'

'Oh, I'll be fine,' I'd glibly reply. 'You don't have to worry about me.'

But I'd be lying if I said I wasn't worried. Of course I was worried. In the months leading up to my departure I'd been worrying my little head to death. I was worried about meeting people, I was worried about not meeting people, I was worried about being ripped off, I was worried about getting lost, I was worried about losing my money, my passport, my rucksack, I was worried about falling ill, contracting diarrhoea, dysentery, malaria, hepatitis, or even worse, the dreaded Aids. I was worried about being hospitalised, I was worried about being drugged, being accosted, being kidnapped, I was worried about drowning, about being burnt alive, about falling off a cliff. You name it, I was worried about it: wars, military coups, revolutions, typhoons, earthquakes, volcanoes, cyclones, bus crashes, train crashes, plane crashes, the list went on and on. Quite simply, when it came to worries, I had more things to worry about than Mr Worry himself, though I was damned if I was gonna let anybody else know this.

And not only did I want to silence all the doubters, I wanted to confound them as well, by proving that the advantages of travelling alone—not having to continually rely on others all the time, not having to forever discuss which places to visit, which routes to take, which places to stay, which places to eat— actually outweighed those of travelling with friends or partners. I had no restrictions as such, there was nothing I needed to get back for: no children, no job and no girlfriend, and herein lay the beauty and excitement of it all. I could feasibly go where I wanted, stay where I wanted and return when I wanted, money and health permitting. In my eyes, travelling solo effectively meant the world was my oyster and the fact I was ultimately responsible for my destiny counted for everything. As far as I was concerned, so long as this was the case, all the worries would duly take care of themselves. Right from the outset, all I'd wanted to do was to set off and just see what happened. Okay, I'm not saying I didn't have this rough itinerary mapped out in my mind, but I didn't necessarily have to follow it. I was at the helm, I was in command, I was behind the controls just as those two cheery middle-aged men in uniform were currently sitting behind that cabin door a mere fifteen feet ahead of me. Now at long last I was finally on my way. Now it was time to start looking ahead.

What, I wondered, could I expect of China, a country that had still only recently opened its doors to outsiders for the first time? Would the nation have recovered from the tragic events of Tiananmen Square? What, if any, were the likely chances of repercussions? Would I be prevented from travelling to certain places? Would it be safe? Would the locals be friendly or would they be hostile? How would I get by with no grasp of their language? Would it be an easy language to pick up? What kind of other travellers would I meet? Now there was a thought! What kind of other travellers *would* I meet? Here I was three hours into my Scandinavian Airlines flight to Beijing, idly staring down at the flickering Russian streetlamps below and my long awaited adventure had already begun. Leaping up in a flash of optimism, I lurched down the aisle towards the toilet, carefully surveying all the other passengers in the hope I'd come across a gorgeous young nubile Swedish backpacker to befriend. Slipping inconspicuously back into my seat a few minutes later, I reached for the plastic ice filled beaker in front of me, knocked back the remaining contents, then switched off the overhead light. Moments later, I was out for the count.

Having picked up my rucksack from the sparse baggage hall, my second priority after flight SK995 touched down was to exchange some of my hard earned travellers cheques into Foreign Exchange Certificates or, as the tourist money in China is more commonly known, yuan. The third, ten minutes later, was to book a taxi to the city centre. That done, I tentatively stepped outside of the terminal building and found to my astonished delight I'd been blessed with a glorious autumnal morning. The air was crisp, the deep blue skies were unblemished, sparrows merrily chirped from bare branches of trees and laser-like shafts of sunlight blazed into my eyes. Without further ado, I jumped into my designated cab, eager to gauge my first impressions of the city from the back seat. For the first ten minutes, though, I had my work cut out. The roads close to the airport were riddled with large stones and potholes and as we careered along these bumpy tracks, weaving precariously between donkey drawn carts, scrawny flocks of sheep and seemingly oblivious cyclists, I continually found myself being unceremoniously jolted up and down from my seat. Clutching onto the handrail above the window, my whole body juddering like a pneumatic drill, I spotted the driver squinting at me in his mirror.

'Very bumpy,' I yelled.

He nodded his head and chuckled.

With the ice broken, I leant forward. 'How long to Beijing?'

This time there was a shake of the head.

I tried again. 'Err...Bay-Jing...very far?'

He continued to shake his head so, sitting back into my seat, I gazed out of the window.

Surprisingly, there was very little squalor on the streets and this was largely down to the scores of workers lining the pavements. Wrapped up in long quilted coats, fur-lined hats and boots, most were going about their routines impassively, picking up leaves and the odd scraps of paper with their hands or sweeping the roads and gutters assiduously with twig-clustered brushes. Each time I was spotted staring out of the window, though, they'd stand there open-mouthed for a few seconds, then raising a hand to their lips, grab hold of a colleague and quickly point to the car, grinning and waving excitedly. Their reaction was greatly encouraging, as I had been fearing I'd encounter a city of mournful faces after the momentous events that had recently beset their city. Fifteen minutes later, passing through the drab concrete tenement blocks of the outlying suburbs with the city centre still nowhere in sight, I realised I'd completely underestimated the size of the capital. It was clearly one of those large sprawling cities which, over time, had mushroomed out from the centre like a spilt pot of paint. Yet just as I was beginning to suspect my driver was taking me on a longer route to increase his fare, we emerged onto a busy thoroughfare and suddenly the amount of cars on the streets noticeably increased. Quickly sitting up in my seat, we turned onto another long orderly avenue. Lined with tall stately poplars, it was bordered on either side by lush green lawns and fountains. As we sat in silence waiting for a set of traffic lights to change, I peered out of the other window. In the distance, clusters of half-built tower blocks—offices, high-rise apartments, hotels, it was difficulty to tell—blotted the horizon, each encircled by a motley collection of gargantuan mechanical cranes. Seeing me gaping out of the window in their direction, the driver, wiggling a pointed finger, spontaneously burst into sermon. Of course, not knowing a single word of Chinese, I had no idea what he was raving about, but not wishing to offend, I nodded in agreement. Then, just a couple of minutes later, after catching my first breathtaking glimpse of the distinctive pale yellow pagoda roofs so synonymous with the imperial city of Beijing, we pulled up outside the hotel.

I'd decided for my first night to book into a large and relatively expensive establishment close to the centre of the city. This made the embarrassingly indifferent welcome I received on checking-in all the more perplexing. There were no smiles, no bowing of heads and certainly no greetings of, 'Ah, welcome to China, Mis-ta Ford. Is this your first visit to our fine city?' Instead, the receptionist held out her hand, barked, 'Pass-pot,' and irritably shoved some registration forms across the counter. Perhaps I was still weary from the long flight, for when I got to my room, I fell into a deep sleep on my bed and didn't stir until late afternoon. When I eventually came to, I wandered over to the window, pulled back the curtains and rubbing my eyes, stared down at the long avenues beneath me. Earlier on, they'd been virtually empty. Now they were awash with bicycles and buses. It was time to venture out onto the streets for the first time.

Noticing a tube station on the other side of the street, I decided to take a short ride on the Beijing underground towards the city centre. After waiting at a set of traffic lights for the swathes of cyclists to grind to a halt, I briskly crossed over, made my way down the crowded steps and duly paid the standard 10 fen (20 pence) fare at the ticket window. Hearing the sound of a rumble from below, I quickly trotted down a second flight of steps towards a bright airy platform. Separated by a gleaming row of granite pillars, two long orderly lines of passengers stood either side of the tracks on a spotless marble floor. Almost simultaneously, two blue and white trains thundered through each of the tunnels and with no time to work out which direction of the city they were heading, I jumped aboard the busier of the two. Three stops down the line I emerged from another immaculate station just as darkness was falling. The pavements were packed with pedestrians, street stalls were setting up on the roadsides and glorious savoury smells of stir-fry cooking wafted in the air. It felt as if the city was just springing to life, but this was the heart of the chaotic evening rush hour and the stirring spectacle of a sea of cyclists surging down the wide avenues like the marathon runners on Pall Mall completely took my breath away. And so it was, with the incessant sounds of bicycle bells ringing in my ears, that I wandered indiscriminately up and down these busy streets for twenty, thirty, perhaps even forty minutes and so pleased was I to finally find myself in Beijing after all the months of waiting, I could have quite happily carried on walking until midnight. But the fact of the matter was my tummy was starting to rumble. In fact it was positively gurgling. Hopeful of phoning down for some dinner, I scurried back to the hotel, my mouth watering at the prospect of wolfing down a chicken chow mein or sweet and sour pork in front of the television. When I returned, my dour-faced friend was there to greet me in reception. I say 'greet me' but such was the look of utter indifference etched onto her face, I reckon I could have walked through the foyer wearing nothing but a Chairman Mao mask and she still wouldn't have batted an eyelid. And whilst I was determined not to let her detracted manner influence my mood, her continual shaking of her head in the protracted discussions that followed told me all I needed to know: namely that room service wasn't quite the truly global wonder I'd taken it to be. So shrugging my shoulders, I plodded up to my room, plonked myself down on the bed and now feeling all the more grateful to my grandmother for instilling in me the inherent value of doggy bags, reached into my day pack and settled on a soggy ham roll I'd saved from the flight.

Late the next morning, after booking into a smaller and infinitely more receptive establishment, I made my way on foot to Tiananmen Square. Just a few months before, Chinese tanks and troops had descended on the square and indiscriminately opened fire on thousands of students protesting for democracy. Pictures of the peaceful demonstrations had been broadcast live on the BBC news for days leading up to the 4th June and I, like millions of others, had avidly followed the coverage with an increasing sense of foreboding. All the speculation had indicated that the troops would eventually be sent in to disperse the crowds; the only question was when. But when that fateful night finally arrived, the armed forces didn't hold back and several hundred (some say thousands) of protesters lost their lives in the bloodbath that ensued. Visiting the site of this brutal massacre so soon after it had happened was clearly going to be an emotional affair.

13

The first thing noticeable on approaching the expansive flat square were the numerous troops of armed soldiers who, dressed in olive green uniforms, were marching in procession across the concrete like demented clockwork toys. The second thing apparent was the lack of other people in the vicinity. I'd read that the square was one of those great gathering places, where people would often arrange to meet, where families would come to fly kites on weekends, where students would sit around and while away long summer evenings discussing Mao, the Cultural Revolution, the Gang of Four and various other political issues of the day, but aside from the soldiers and a few indiscriminate parties of camera toting tourists, the vast playground-like arena was curiously bereft of civilians. It was only when I wandered over to the manning post and was asked to produce my passport did it occur to me why: local people weren't being allowed inside the perimeter. In spite of the recent turmoil here, I still found this staggering. Well, I say 'staggering' but in truth I was appalled. How could the authorities be so insensitive? Surely, this wasn't the right way to deal with the aftermath? If anything, prohibiting locals from the square was only likely to cause further resentment. Such an intolerant attitude simply beggared belief. Yet, there again, who was I to argue? I was merely a visitor to the country and how this tyrannical regime chose to deal with their turbulent past was solely down to them.

Shaking my head disconsolately, I slowly made my way across the square. It was much bigger than expected and bordered on either side by huge and imposing concrete monoliths: the Great Hall of the People, the Chinese History Museum, the Mao Mausoleum, Qianmen Gate and the Museum of the Chinese Revolution. Equally as striking to the north was the vermilion pagoda-topped Tiananmen Gate, but the thing that struck me more than any of these truly magnificent buildings was the silence. The square itself was such a vast area—nearly 100 acres in fact, as I went on to discover—but given there were so few people wandering about, the quietness was quite chilling. Foolishly, I stared down at the flat concrete paving stones half expecting to come across at least one piece of evidence left over from the horrific events of June but of course, there was nothing. Not a single bloodstained spot, not one revealing cracked tile, not even the trace of a piece of faded graffiti daubed into the concrete.

As I continued to stand in silence, desperately trying to take it all in, I recalled a drizzly morning back in October when I'd attended a series of events and speeches in London's Chinatown marking the 100-day anniversary of that ignominious day here in Beijing, remembering, as I'd stood amongst a crowd of muted onlookers, how the dank depressing conditions seemed to perfectly sum up the sombreness of the occasion. The first of the guest speakers called to the platform was BBC correspondent John Simpson, who'd just happened to be in Beijing covering President Gorbachov's visit to the city days before the Tiananmen demonstrations began. After making his way to the makeshift stage, he cleared his throat, paused for a moment and then started to speak, slowly and deliberately in his inimitable calm and reassuring voice.

'In the hundred days that have passed since those events in Tiananmen Square, a lot of people have died in a lot of countries. Some of them have been killed by their governments, some of them have been killed by terrorists, some of them have even been killed in crime. What makes the events of a hundred days ago stand out in the memories of those of us who saw it is that these weren't just meaningless deaths, these were the deaths of people who knew that they might very well die and turned out simply because they wanted more freedom. And they were killed simply because they challenged the government that refused to give them more freedom. So that is the symbol, that is the importance, it seems to me, of remembering a hundred days later what happened then.'

He then went on to talk about the ardent non-violence of the students, describing how he'd seen many instances of students rescuing the lives of soldiers, the very people who had been sent in to kill them and how he'd earlier stood watching the statue of the Goddess of Democracy being pulled down by tanks.

15

'Even then,' he concluded 'even before the troops moved in, I remember thinking to myself, "we mustn't allow this to be forgotten" and that's the only purpose of turning out here, we mustn't allow it to be forgotten.'

Still rooted to the spot, I stood on the centre of the square alone and pensive, recalling his last words. Just for the time being, I was plainly one who hadn't.

Dining alone can be an intimidating experience, especially for the uninitiated who've still to overcome the embarrassment that comes when asking for a table for one. So when I left my hotel early that evening to eat out for the first time, it was with a certain feeling of trepidation. The choice over what cuisine to opt for was a simple one: it had to be Peking duck, the local speciality. Which duck restaurant to try, however, was another matter altogether, for all the streets in the Qianmen district were lined with a mind-boggling selection of eating houses, dining halls and snack bars. Timidly, I peered into many of the open fronted restaurants looking for the busiest on the assumption that this would serve the best food, but all the smoke-filled canteens were spilling over with early evening diners. Finally deciding on a particularly crowded establishment, I approached the steps leading down to the dining area only to be stopped in my tracks by a barrage of Mandarin. It came from the mouth of a sturdy doorman who was stood in front of me with his hand outstretched like a police officer stopping traffic. Peering over his shoulder, I tentatively pointed to a couple of empty tables at the back of the restaurant. Firing off another salvo of the local vernacular, he then shouted over to a colleague who on seeing me standing somewhat gingerly on the steps, yelled something back and grinned. I pointed to the empty tables again, this time to his colleague, and now the doorman started laughing too. Shaking his head, he again tried to explain assuming by some miracle I'd suddenly understand him. He did, though, point to another restaurant on the other side of the street, so with a rueful smile, I nodded my thanks and turned around to leave.

Crossing over the road, I was again met at the entrance, this

16

time by an extremely stern looking waitress who pointed upstairs to a section of the establishment set aside for foreigners. 'Oh God,' I groaned, 'not again.' This time, however, I shook my head and insisted on a table on the packed ground floor. After a moment's hesitation, she reluctantly consented and muttering something under her breath, led me to a table where she stood hovering over me, impatiently tapping her pen against her pad as she waited for me to place my order, which would have been relatively straightforward had the entire menu not been written in Pinyin. After much gesticulating and pointing to my phrasebook, though, a whole roasted honey-glazed duck duly arrived on a plate a few minutes later and assuming the waiter would come back with a carving knife to slice up the meat in front of me, I sat in my seat waiting for him to return. He never did, so finally giving up the ghost, I slowly began to prod and jab at the duck with my chopsticks, trying to separate the succulent meat from the bone, which was impossible to do without picking it up and covering my fingers in grease. Not entirely sure this was the correct etiquette, I glanced around to see how the locals were tackling their dishes, but surprisingly nobody else seemed to be eating duck or anything else off the bone for that matter. I tried to persevere for a while but before long, I was drooling and slobbering like a rabid dog. Each time, after I'd finally grabbed onto a piece of meat, I'd roll it into the rice, dip it in the sauce, then carefully lift it up to my face only to watch it all agonisingly fall between my chopsticks a few tantalising centimetres away from my mouth. As I say, the obvious thing to do would have been to prise the meat off the bones with my hands, but I was desperate not to draw undue attention to myself from the other people in the restaurant. The only other alternative was to ask for a knife and fork but in China that would have been sacrilege. I felt like putting my hand up to the waitress and saying: 'Miss, Miss, can't do this one.'

Just then, a couple of bleary-eyed young soldiers who'd staggered in a few minutes earlier were served with the same dish and promptly began to attack their duck with scant regard to anyone around them. Now I had the cue to ransack the remains of the food with my hands, which in true Henry the Eighth style, is precisely what I did. A quarter of an hour later, feeling ten times better, I glanced down at the tablecloth and very nearly fell off my chair in the process. Looking like something out of a First World War battlefield, it was covered in fragments of bone, numerous dark brown stains, tiny remnants of duck flesh and countless grains of rice. By contrast, every other table around me was totally spotless and to make matters worse, every time I looked up, all the diners in close proximity seemed to be guffawing in my direction. Wishing the ground would swallow me up, I slowly slid further and further into my seat. Eventually a waitress, who'd obviously drawn the short straw amongst the restaurant staff, came over to put me out of my misery and although I tried to apologise and make light of the mess, she cleared up my dishes with a detached air of nonchalance. With the coast seemingly clear, I hastily pulled out a cigarette to calm my nerves only for the waitress to return a few moments later. Pulling the tablecloth with a whoosh from beneath me, she bundled it up in a ball and stormed off back to the kitchen, probably for all I knew to drop it into the incinerator. Still, after paying the 17 yuan (£3.40) bill, I strolled back to the hotel feeling rather pleased with myself, another little hurdle safely negotiated.

As I wandered the streets of Beijing early the next morning, the sheer volume of cyclists plying the streets continued to astound. At busy junctions, cute-faced infants lovingly wrapped up in red hooded 'Santa Claus' coats sat impassively on the back of their parents' seats; on dusty back roads, spindly men on hefty tricycles, carting insurmountable loads of coal, straw, paper and cardboard boxes stacked high on their trailers, struggled along unabated, whilst in the overflowing bike parks that popped up all over the city, hundreds and hundreds of regulation black cycles stood dormant, deserted by their owners until later in the day. Yet even though the early morning rush hour had long since subsided, there was still little respite from the continual tinkling of bicycle bells which, for the time being at least, made a refreshing change from the reverberating car engines, spluttering exhausts and beeping horns of London.

Although I wasn't travelling with a specific agenda, one thing I did know before I'd set off was that I wanted make an ongoing account of my travels to keep as a lasting memento. Envisaging myself frequently turning up at places late at night tired and dishevelled, I didn't suspect I'd have the discipline to maintain a diary. Consequently, prior to my departure I'd decided to invest in a Dictaphone recorder instead. After three or four hours tramping around the extensive and breathtakingly resplendent palatial grounds of the Forbidden City—so extensive in fact that the large rectangular compound housed over 800 buildings in all—I was feeling dead on my feet so spotting an empty bench in a neighbouring park, I plonked myself down and prepared to make my opening recording recounting my first few days away. A group of children dressed in bright blue 70s style tracksuits happened to be playing nearby and it wasn't long before a couple of them spotted me talking into my strange machine. With the curiosity getting the better of them, they eventually built up the courage to come over, so after demonstrating how the recorder worked, I happily took a back seat, content just to soak up some of the afternoon sun and watch them amuse themselves. They started off by screaming and howling into the machine and when they first heard the recorded sounds of their own voices they were beside themselves, looking on open-mouthed and staring at each other incredulously. Before long, though, they were experimenting with other noises. At the end of every go, they'd conduct their own little conference to decide what sound to make next, then collectively, they'd 'moo' or 'baah' into the machine, squealing in delight each time the tape was played back. After coming up with every single sound of the entire animal kingdom, they moved on to impersonating humans (parents, siblings, friends, teachers—I could only guess) but whichever person they mimicked it only seemed to send them further into raptures. They'd jump up and down excitedly, clapping their hands, then stand around with their palms behind their heads trying to regain their composure before they conferred again. Twenty delightful minutes later, I finally got up and bade them a reluctant farewell and after calling in at the post office to despatch my first letters and postcards, made a quick telephone call home to find out the official result of my father's biopsy. His illness, I discovered, had now been officially diagnosed as pleurisy and such was the relief coming through in my mother's voice as she told me he was now well on his way to a full recovery, I was struggling to hold back the tears myself. Little was I to know that in just a few months' time, I'd shamelessly be using his sudden illness as a means of digging me out of another hole.

I woke at the crack of dawn again the next morning. Whether it was my body still adjusting to the eight hour time difference or simply the blinding beam of light piercing the gap in the curtains, I don't know but with another glorious sun-drenched day beckoning, I hastily got dressed and headed out into the cold for an early morning walk. Covered with glass-like layers of ice, the roads and paths were treacherously greasy, as I quickly found out to my cost so, sticking to the brittle slabs of frost-encrusted grass, I proceeded to make my way instead across a series of parks where, breathing out wafts of the cold morning air, large groups of elderly locals wrapped up in hats and mittens were already out practising tai chi. Stood in long lines with their hands arched high above their heads, they stealthily leant over to their sides, first one way, then the other, all in strict synchronisation, their wrinkled sinewy faces betraying no signs of emotion.

By way of contrast, the locals in a bustling indoor market I passed through shortly after were engaged in some particularly vociferous haggling. I was in Wangfujing, one of the city's main shopping districts and everywhere I looked, men and women of all ages were frantically waving their hands in the air at traders and shrieking and hollering at the top of their voices. As I battled my way through the frenzied crowds, up and down the packed central aisles, I suddenly felt relieved that I'd gone for my banquet when I did, for all the stalls seemed to be selling the same thing: ducks. Everywhere I looked were hundreds and hundreds of the things. Naked, pink and hapless, they hung in bundles in mid-air, their yellow webbed feet tantalisingly close to the metallic trays full of already severed limbs that lay beneath them on the white tableclothed benches. Looking to the sky in salvation, their necks were grossly elongated like ostriches, for their heads had been pierced in the area between eye and beak by jagged hooks from which they were all suspended. Their reactions to the final moments of their meaningless lives were all too visible. Some had surrendered, their wings upright and crossed like a woman trying to cover her breasts, whilst the wings of others flapped down in right angles, giving the impression they'd stood there with their hands on hips in a final moment of defiant exasperation. How exactly they'd met their fate, I wasn't too sure but it wasn't something I particularly wanted to dwell on. I needed some fresh air.

Back outside in the adjacent parks, the early morning exercise classes had finished and groups of elderly men dressed in dark blue Mao suits and flat caps were now sitting around on benches playing cards, and board games: chess, draughts and Mah Jong. I desperately wanted to frame this wonderful scene but no matter how hard I tried I just couldn't bring myself to do so. Pulling out my camera and indiscriminately snapping away somehow just didn't seem right. These venerable old men, happily sitting there whiling away the morning, looked so contented and I feared any such intrusion would only break the spell. A short while later, though, passing another roadside bike-park where hundreds of cycles were jammed together side by side, I *did* reach for my camera. Now this had to be worth a photograph. As I peered through the viewfinder, trying to adjust the focus, I felt a tap on my back. Facing me as I spun around was a young woman, probably no more than twenty years of age. Dressed in a shabby beige wrap, her face was smeared in what looked like soot and cradling a sleeping baby against her shoulder, she was glowering at me intently. Jigging the infant up to free one of her arms, she pointed first at the camera and then back to herself, tapping her finger impatiently on her shawl. Shaking my head, I quickly bundled the camera back into my daypack but as I briskly trotted off down the pavement, I could already hear some kind of commotion developing behind me. Glancing back over my shoulder a few seconds later, I noticed a small group of people had gathered around the protesting mother. They stared back disdainfully so I moved on again stepping up my pace.

I spent the remainder of what turned out to be a rather troublesome day trying to change some of my tourist money (yuan) for some local currency (renminbi). Most of the negotiations over exchange rates, conducted in shady side streets and dark alleyways with a series of middle-aged men in grimy dark woollen jackets, were prolonged and abortive but after eventually agreeing to a mutually favourable rate with a spirited spiky-haired youth, I finally emerged with a wad of dirty notes and hurried back to my hotel for some much needed sustenance.

'Oh Jim, you should see your face.'

I tried to force a smile, but it wasn't easy. 'Do you think we're ever gonna see this wall?' I replied dourly.

Michelle looked at her watch. 'God, it's nearly three o'clock!'

'I know,' I groaned under my breath. 'That's what I keep trying to tell you.'

'Quick, looks like we're going,' cried Nicole as the engine of the bus spluttered back to life.

I'd met the two English girls the previous afternoon at the China International Travel Service (CITS) Office when I'd been booking a trip up to the Great Wall. In their early thirties, they'd been working in Hong Kong as nurses and were here in Beijing on vacation. On discovering we'd just reserved seats on the same trip we'd agreed to share a taxi to the Jianguo Hotel from where the tour began, so early that morning they met me outside my hotel. Our bus eventually departed an hour later but just after ten, we stopped at a place called the Ming Tombs.

Opting not to go down into any the excavated burial sites where the tombs of thirteen Ming Emperors were housed, I passed the time instead wandering along the picturesque Avenue of Animals, lined with various stone statues of mythical creatures and beasts. Soon after, though, we made another unscheduled stop at some other temple and as we idly wandered about, I found myself becoming increasingly frustrated by the whole 'package trip syndrome.' It seemed that we were being herded around like a flock of sheep, and as our group of twenty or so frantically tried to keep up with our guide, I suspected I wasn't the only one wondering what had happened to the Great Wall. Thirty minutes later we re-boarded the bus, but soon after, we piled back off it again, this time to stop for lunch. After being shown to a long trestle table, one of many in an airy courtyard surrounded by a large rectangle of food stalls, the small talk that often accompanies these kinds of trips dutifully commenced.

'So where did you stay in Singapore, then?' asked a middle-aged woman sitting next to me, rather haughtily.

'Ah, we stayed in the Excelsior,' replied the lady opposite in the obscenely large pair of Prada glasses. 'We liked Singapore, but we much preferred Bali.'

'Oh, Peter and I went to Bali last year,' exclaimed my neighbour, dismissively pushing aside her bowl of noodles. 'We bought a lovely table and had it shipped back home.

'Did you?' huffed the larger lady again. 'Some friends of ours did that too. They had terrible problems, you know. Had to wait for four months and when it arrived, there was a huge great crack down the side. So have you been to the Summer Palace yet?... Oh, you haven't? We went yesterday. Oh you must go, it's simply divine.'

I tried to reason with myself. I'd booked onto this trip simply for convenience and even if I had taken a taxi up to Badaling, I'd still have been faced with the throngs of other visitors that would doubtlessly already be there.

So when we clambered aboard our vehicle around mid-afternoon and were at last informed we'd now be making our way up to the Great Wall, a somewhat ironic round of applause resonated from the back. As the bus slowly began its ascent up the steep mountain road, the gearbox screeching with high-pitched displeasure, I sat in my seat straining my ears as our tourist guide, Chang, began to deliver his customary address over the microphone:

'It is a distance of errr... seventy-five kilometres Norse West of Beijing, Norse West of Beijing, seventy-five, seven five from the centre of the city, it is errr... a distance of, a distance, I apologise, it is about some eight hundred metres above sea level, Beijing city only forty-five or forty-seven metres above sea level... Constwuction of the wall first began during the period of four hundwed and seventy-six to two hundred and seventy first BC... It was built for protection... in two hundwed and twenty first BC after the Ching Dynasty, the first Emperor of the Ching Dynasty unify whole of China... he decided to link up warious sections of the wall with one million people... It is six to seven metres high and in old days some materials, constwuction materials were carried up the mountains from end to end, some were carried in buckets by donkeys and cows up to the wall... Several renowations have taken place since nineteen forty-nine, since nineteen forty-nine... Here we are, I think you are lucky to see the best part of the wall, okay? Any questions to ask about the wall? If you want to know more about the wall, you can get the book, the guidebook on the wall... Thank you.'

Half a dozen perplexed looking passengers quickly filed off the bus, presumably to buy the guidebook, whilst the rest of our party assembled in the car park, contemplating which section of the wall to scale. The vast majority of visitors piling off the other coaches were all heading towards the east but after a brief discussion with Michelle and Nicole, we decided we'd take the alternative western route. This was made on the basis that the sun would be behind us which should improve any photographs we wanted to take. Leaving the rest of our group behind, the three of us scurried off, eager to commence our ascent. The air was thin and the wall, in places, inordinately steep, so the forty-minute climb up the huge steps was exhausting yet we dared not grumble for we'd been blessed with near perfect conditions; indeed, so deep and clear was the vast cobalt canopy above us that I was beginning to wonder whether clouds actually existed in China. Stopping every few minutes to catch our breath, we repeatedly peered back at the view behind us and despite the fact it was lined with vast processions of tourists, the sight of the turreted wall snaking itself over an undulating barren terrain as far as the eye could see was still mightily impressive. Up and down it went, over hills and down into valleys, meandering, curving, and bobbing along relentlessly like some never-ending inverted cresta run. (It was only the next day that I discovered it once stretched for 2400 miles: virtually the equivalent length of the entire English coastline!) Reaching the highest watchtower we could get to before the wall descended, the three of us paused long and hard for breath again, and then simultaneously exchanging cameras, took it in turns to pose for the obligatory photo album snapshots. By the time we'd eventually returned to the car park some thirty minutes later, the sun had disappeared behind the mountains and the temperatures had plummeted and although we were left to stand around in the biting cold for a while waiting for our driver to return this no longer seemed to matter. We were all still exhilarated by the experience and the long wait to cast our own eyes on the Great Wall had, after all the hours of waiting, finally been worthwhile.

Arriving back at the Jianguo early evening, the three of us stopped off for a reviving cup of hot chocolate in the hotel lounge. The contrast between the two girls couldn't have been more marked. Michelle was diminutive, red haired and not at all frightened to speak her mind whereas the much larger Nicole was quieter and thoughtful and talked in length about her laudable plans to work in the hospitals of Calcutta. But although they were good company they were only in Beijing for a few more days before they went their separate ways: Michelle heading home to London on the Trans-Siberian Railway and Nicole back to Hong Kong to continue her nursing. After a while we were joined by a couple of Brummie lads who the girls had apparently met a few days before. They'd been selling spectacles all around Asia, and of similar height and build, both were wearing thick-rimmed glasses. The resulting banter was initially light-hearted as the bespectacled 'twins' readily cracked quips and jokes. Before long, though, I found myself shifting uncomfortably in my seat.

'So how was your day today?' said one.

'Oh, you've been to see the wall haven't you?' said the other. 'How was it because I thought walls were just for pissing against?'

'Shit,' said the first again, 'You'd need a bloody lot of beer to piss all the way along that thing!'

'What about the Chinks, though? I bet they can't even see when they're having a piss!' said the other, making reference to their slanted eyes.

Without further ado, I got to my feet.

'You heading off, Jim?' asked Nicole, looking somewhat surprised.

'Yeah, I'm knackered,' I sighed, feigning a yawn.

Michelle, reaching into her bag, quickly scribbled something on a scrap of paper. 'We're probably gonna meet up again tomorrow night for a few drinks if you fancy coming along.'

'Oh right,' I muttered. 'That'd be good.'

'Here, take this,' she said, handing me the note. 'Give us a call in the afternoon.'

Not through any fault of the girls, however, I knew I'd be giving the rendezvous a wide berth so as soon as I got outside, I scrunched the paper up and tossed it into a bin.

Having conquered the Great Wall, the Forbidden City and Tiananmen Square, the three attractions I'd been so keen to see, I spent all the next morning sat on my bed planning the route I'd take through the rest of China. My second flight from Hong Kong to Malaysia was scheduled for the 9th January, giving me six weeks in which to travel overland down to Hong Kong. The rough itinerary I decided on would take me initially southwest

26

to Xian (pronounced *she-an*), then further south through Chengdu to Chongqing from where I'd travel along the Yangtze River back to Shanghai on the east coast. After that, I'd make my way inland again towards Guilin, hopefully stopping off to climb the sacred mountain of Huang Shan on the way, before cutting back across to Guangzhou and then down to Hong Kong. The only two things I wasn't too sure about were firstly, whether I'd have enough time to visit the vibrant city of Kunming, some 600 kms west of Guilin and close to the Burmese border, and secondly, where I'd end up for Christmas. Still, there was plenty of time to dwell on these finer points yet.

With the next few weeks mapped out in my mind, I set off to book my train ticket to Xian. The main rail station wasn't difficult to find, in fact it was impossible to miss. The huge concourse outside was amassed with touts, snack sellers, beggars, cyclists as well as dozens of waiting passengers huddled around trunks, bags and suitcases underneath the rather grandiose station hall. After joining a lengthy queue in the booking lobby, I sidled up to the ticket desk and made the reservation without any of the complications I'd been expecting but, to my horror, when the ticket was finally handed to me, it looked nothing at all like the specimen rail ticket illustrated in my guidebook. Another backpacker, presumably spotting the look of bewilderment etched upon my face, quickly came to my rescue. Inspecting the ticket, she proceeded to explain all the symbols and numbers and assured me everything was in order. My saviour was a Canadian girl also travelling solo who was somewhat taken aback when she learnt I was planning to backpack around China alone without any grasp of the local dialect. She'd just returned from Datong, a city some seven hours west of Beijing close to the Inner Mongolia border. Complaining of the 'real negative vibes,' she went on to describe how unnerving and frustrating it was to find people continually staring at you. I'd already received quite a few stares from locals myself in the short time I'd been in the capital and although it wasn't something that was bothering me yet, I suspected after a while this would gradually wear me down too. Just then, another backpacker came striding towards us.

'G'day,' he chirped, stretching out a hand. 'Need any help? I'm Kev by the way.'

The girl, who seemed an enterprising character, shook her head and glancing down at her wrist, said she had another train to catch so I quickly thanked her for her help. Perhaps she knew something that I didn't for Kev proceeded to bore me senseless. His obsession for haggling the lowest prices was of little interest to me although he insisted on describing in great detail how he'd adamantly been refusing to pay anything more than the local Chinese ever since he arrived in China six weeks ago. He asked me how much I was paying for my room.

'Aw, I'm not sure...about forty yuan,' I muttered although the actual rate was 60.

'Geez, how much?' he exclaimed. 'I'm paying fifteen.'

One of the things I'd promised myself at the outset was that I wouldn't fall into the trap of wasting unnecessary time in the eternal quest of securing the cheapest prices for hotels, train fares and food unless circumstances dictated otherwise, ie. I ran out of money. Bartering for goods, not paying over the odds and not being stitched up, of course, but arguing over fen, cents and paise...forget it. So after eventually escaping his clutches, I heaved a huge sigh of relief and quickly headed back to my room.

When I returned, there was a message waiting for me in reception to phone Michelle. My first reaction was not to return the call. A few minutes later, though, I picked up the receiver and tentatively dialled the number.

'Michelle?'... 'Hi, it's Jim.'... 'Yeah, not too bad. Just booked a ticket to Xian. How about you?'... 'You're going out tonight?'... 'So, who's going exactly?'... 'I see.'... 'But you're sure there'll be a few other people there.'... 'Okay, and where is it you're meeting?'... 'Right, the Lido at nine, I'll see you there.'

It was just after eight when I left my hotel and even then, I still wasn't sure if I was doing the right thing. The evening was bitterly cold, the darkened streets were already deserted and the Lido Hotel, situated close to the airport in the far north of the city, now seemed an awfully long way away. Surely I'd be better off lazing away the evening back in my room, I kept thinking, yet if I did turn back I'd only be cutting off my nose to spite my face, for it wasn't every day you get the opportunity to socialise in Beijing. Taking a tube to the main railway station, I waited outside for an airport bus but after a standing around for a while, stamping my feet and blowing into my hands, a passer-by informed me this service had stopped hours ago. Another forty-five minutes passed before I managed to flag down a taxi willing to take me so far out of town at this time of night, so by the time I eventually arrived at the Lido, it was a full hour and a half after our arranged meeting time. Jumping out of the cab, I hastily paid the driver his fare, and dashing up the carpeted steps past the waiting concierge, barged my way through the revolving doors. When I emerged on the other side my eyes nearly popped out of my head. In the foyer, a crystal glass chandelier that must have measured forty feet in length hung from the ceiling. As I stood there staring up in amazement, the concierge appeared beside me.

'You like?' he asked.

'Yes,' I gasped. 'It's magnificent.'

'Please, welcome to the Lido Holiday Inn. You are meeting friends?'

'Yes,' I said now turning my gaze to the uniformed man. 'How d'you guess?'

'And your friends, they are staying here in the Lido?'

'No,' I chortled. 'I don't think so.'

'Please, you'll need to sign in, then.'

Following his eyes over to the side of the lobby, I nodded cordially and crept over to the reception desk, my trainers squelching noisily on the polished marble floor. On top of the counter, a leaflet listed the hotel's facilities: a beauty salon, a swimming pool, a gymnasium, a sauna, a Jacuzzi, a steamroom, a health club, a bank, a post office, a full size bowling alley, a disco, a gift shop, three separate bars and no less than eight restaurants. Next to me, a party of KLM airline staff in pristine bright blue uniforms were busily filling out registration forms.

Feeling rather out of place in my jeans and pullover, I quickly peered around at the other guests in the foyer; predominantly elderly foreigners, they were all in dinner suits or evening dresses.

It was far too late, though, to be worrying about attire now so after establishing from one of the receptionists that the main bar was located on the first floor, I dashed up the stairs and spotted the girls immediately. Sat on a plush leather sofa at the far end of the lounge they were flanked by three males, two of who were unmistakably wearing glasses. With a sinking heart, I slowly made my way over to join them and as I got nearer, I could see Michelle visibly tapping her watch.

'Jim! Where've you been?'

'Don't ask,' I replied, shaking my head. 'It's a long story.'

She introduced me to the others, firstly to Mark, a tall and studious looking journalist, perhaps not too much older than myself, who'd apparently been based in China for the last three years, and then to the 'Speccies' again who, I learnt to my horror, were in fact staying here at the Lido. Where was the justice in that? Whilst Michelle got up to get a round of drinks in, I sat there with gritted teeth trying to make small talk with the pair, now fuming in the knowledge I'd been dragged across half the city on their behest. To add insult to injury, it appeared they hadn't even recognised me from our previous encounter for they proceeded to bombard me with the very same questions about my trip they'd perfunctorily asked back in the Jianguo. Happily, though, when Michelle returned a few minutes later carrying a tray of Tsingtao beers, we all shuffled around and I managed to enter into a much more engaging dialogue with Mark. He told me he'd been teaching English for six months in Beijing when he was offered a job at a news agency. I asked him what the position entailed.

'Well, basically,' he said, sitting back in his chair, 'I was responsible for coming up with photographs of any significant news events that broke around the country.'

'Lots of travelling then,' I remarked.

'Mmm, too much sometimes. China's such a vast country.

Do you know, even now, I'm still only one of four western journalists based here on a permanent basis? And this in a country that accounts for twenty per cent of the world's population.'

'God,' I said scratching my jaw, 'that's staggering. So what's it like living here?'

Shaking his head, he exuded an ironic smile. 'It can be extremely difficult at times.'

'In what way?'

'Well, the people really.'

I looked at him quizzically.

'No matter what you do in China,' he explained, 'you will always be a foreigner. In other countries you can learn the local language, adopt the local lifestyle and in time you will generally be embraced and taken in by the people as one of them but in China you will always remain a foreigner.'

It was really enlightening to hear firsthand the views of someone who'd actually been living in China, especially somebody who'd been here in June, so the very least I could do was buy him a drink. Unfortunately, my round necessitated buying beers for my irreverent friends too, but it was a small price to pay for the absorbing conversation I was having with Mark. After returning from the bar, I asked him what he thought about the political state of the country.

He sighed. 'Under the surface, there's a melting pot just waiting to explode again. The people of Beijing are still seething over what happened here, but those in charge of the armed forces are desperate to re-impose their authority on the country. If they're unable to maintain the economy, then there'll probably be another uprising.'

Although I was a bit hesitant, I felt obliged to ask him about the events of June. 'So,' I said clearing my throat, 'what did you make of Tiananmen?'

'Yep, good photos,' he replied in an instant. Breaking off for a few seconds he glanced over his shoulder, his eyes darting circumspectly around the room. With the coast seemingly clear he reached for his beer, took a large sip, then licking his lips, purposefully leant forward. 'Did you see that picture of the dead body on the cover of *Time* magazine?' he whispered.

I hadn't, but nodded my head all the same.

'It was one of mine.'

This was not said as a boast but more as a statement of a fact. He carried on as if he was relieved to be getting it all off his chest.

'My only surprise is that the guards didn't come in earlier and that there weren't more people killed. One of the problems that the Chinese people had was they didn't have a defined set of rules.'

I frowned.

'Well,' he continued, 'when the demonstrations at Tiananmen started, there were two rival factions in the government. It was only when victory prevailed on one side that the decision was made to send in the troops and that was when all the trouble started. Only when Deng Xiaoping and his other fuddy duddies pop their clogs, which'll probably be in the next couple of years, will we see the next period of change and instability in the country.'

'And then what?'

He shrugged. 'Who knows? Watch this space I suppose,' he replied with a rueful smile.

I asked him about his future plans. Leaning back with his hands behind his head, he told me he was now working for one of the big photograph agencies. They paid him well, provided him with his own car and apartment as well as a generous expense account, and without all the distractions of the West, he was able to put a lot of money away in the bank.

'Sounds like you've got a good life here,' I said. 'Do you think you'll go back to the States?'

He shook his head. 'Got everything I need here. Perhaps in a couple of years I'd consider a similar vacation in somewhere like, er, I dunno, Vietnam maybe.'

'Vietnam?'

'Mmm, not sure why. Just like to go and see it. Anyway, that's enough of me,' he said, downing the rest of his beer. 'What places are you planning to visit?'

32

I gave him my planned itinerary, explaining my dilemma about whether or not I'd have the time to travel down to Kunming.

'Oh you must,' he enthused. 'Kunming's a fascinating place, especially the area close to the border.'

Hearing this only made it a bigger quandary.

With the bar about to close, the Speccies suggested we move on to the hotel disco, so after paying the £5 entrance fee, the six of us made our way inside the dimly lit room and planted ourselves down on some leather chairs in a corner. There weren't many other people inside; just a few businessmen perched on stools around the circular bar. The chequered neon-lit dance floor was empty and barring a late rush of guests looked like it would remain so all night which made the outrageously loud music pulsating through the room all the more bewildering. We tried in vain to converse over the constant drumbeat but it was difficult enough just to think, let alone talk, against such a racket. The only consolation were the five pretty bar girls congregated at the side of the bar so, having given up on the shouting, I sat there ogling for a while, trying to pick out my favourite and rank the other four in order of looks. Soon after, the others got to their feet, and deciding to call it a day, we headed off, the Brummies back to their luxurious room, the rest of us wrapping up to brave the freezing cold night. Outside, Mark kindly offered to drop us back at our hotels and it was only when I noticed the clock on the dashboard that I realised it was 2am. How time flies in Beijing, I thought, now all the more glad I hadn't turned back after all.

Buoyed on by such an enjoyable evening, I made my way after breakfast the following morning to a bike hire stall. My plan was to cycle up to the Summer Palace in the north west of the city, a distance of approximately eight miles. Braving the streets of Beijing for the first time on two wheels was simply exhilarating. Finding my way to the Summer Palace was a different matter altogether.

My bike was the regulation prototype: a black, unwieldy, heavy model, no different to all the other bicycles I'd seen in

Beijing. I'd purposely waited for the early morning rush hour to subside before I left but I still set off a little apprehensively, rigorously sticking to the designated cycle ways that existed on the side of virtually every road. The locals, however, seemed to be paying scant regard to the cycle lanes. As I turned onto the first busy avenue, they were cycling five abreast across the entire width of the road without a care in the world. Every so often, a car would approach from behind beeping its horn and they'd all move over to let it through. Surely, it wouldn't be like this on the way back? I thought. By then, the late afternoon rush hour would be beckoning and straying from the cycle lanes then would be an infinitely more precarious pursuit. In spite of the continual sunshine it was still a bitterly cold morning and as I took a turning to the left at the next junction, the icy north wind bit into my face. Before long, I could barely feel my fingers on the handlebars, the mucus streaming down from my nostrils was already beginning to cake and my toes were so cold they were positively aching. Notwithstanding this, the sheer thrill of joining the masses of people out on their bikes gave me a huge rush of adrenaline. It seemed as if I'd finally crossed the line and by joining the locals cycling the streets, I'd somehow ingratiated myself into their society. Now and then one or two would glance over in surprise at my bright red jogging trousers or green bomber jacket and, spotting a western face, would double take before affording me a wry grin or a nod. One man in particular was so startled that he swerved abruptly, crashed into a female cyclist and was almost beaten up on the spot by his atoner. But with my confidence growing, I began whistling and humming to myself. This was what travelling was all about! How many of those tourists up at the Great Wall would be doing this now? Not many, I suspected. They'd probably be passing me this very moment in their air-conditioned coaches as they were whisked off to some other palace or temple across the city.

Having crossed Changan, the main road that bisects the centre of Beijing in an east-west direction, I headed further north for ten or fifteen minutes. By now, the streets were much quieter and I was passing through a series of virtually deserted residential areas. Slightly perturbed, I continued for another ten minutes up a long gradual incline but two-thirds of the way up the hill, I was eventually forced to dismount. Huffing and puffing, I pushed the bike the rest of the way to the top, then resting it against a lamppost, reached for my guidebook to try to work out how far I'd got. The pattern of the roads I'd followed, though, bore little resemblance to the lines on the map. Undeterred, I decided to carry on, following my northerly instincts a little further. Twenty minutes later, the map was out again. Every route I'd taken to the north had quickly veered off to the east or west yet the map clearly indicated that the road leading all the way up to the Summer Palace was as straight as an arrow. It had seemingly disappeared off the face of the earth; either that or it had never existed in the first place. Staring at the map indignantly, I set off once again, but fifteen minutes later found myself back at exactly the same place again. Somehow, all I'd done was go around in a big circle. This time I was forced to admit defeat. I was lost, trapped somewhere in an infuriating maze of some quiet and undistinguished suburb and to make matters worse, there was still nobody about to ask for directions. Sighing heavily, I decided to cut my losses and headed back towards the city centre, abandoning all hopes of the reaching the Summer Palace for the day. Returning my bike an hour later, I trudged back to the hotel, clammy with sweat, vowing to try to make it up there again the next morning. This time, though, I'd go by bus. When I got back after dinner the phone in my room was ringing. I picked up the receiver. It was Michelle.

I don't know if you've ever watched Dennis Norden's *It'll be Alright on the Night* series. I'm not a great fan myself but one clip in particular remains lodged in my mind. It's the one where a reporter is seen standing in the pouring rain outside 10 Downing Street. The camera focuses in on the bedraggled correspondent who finishes yet another 'take' with the words to the effect of: 'This is Joe Nicholson, reporting for the *ITN Six*

O' Clock News, tired, bored, frustrated, hungry, pissed off and desperate to get home.' When I found myself lost again on the way to the Summer Palace the following morning, I immediately thought of this clip and related to the forlorn reporter. My frustration was compounded by the hangover I'd been nursing from the previous night—I'd met the girls and their seemingly unshakable friends in the lobby of another plush hotel in order that we could have a few toasts to celebrate Michelle's last night. The Speccies, I'm loath to admit, were both entertaining and amusing all evening (although this might have had more to do with the number of Tsingtaos that were being rapidly consumed) reciting stories of various culinary disasters they'd experienced in Asia such as the occasion when they were—or so they said—served up a dish of Alsatian in a Mongolian *Yurt.*

So the morning had not got off to a good start. My head was pounding, I'd already waited over an hour for a number seven bus that had failed to show up and after taking the tube as far to the north west of the city as I could, I'd walked for a further thirty minutes with the sun beating down on my back only to find myself back in another bleakly nondescript suburb. I was clearly lost again and it was then I thought of that poor reporter. Yet just as I was wondering if I was destined never to make it the Summer Palace, my luck finally turned. Glancing up from my map, I noticed an elderly pedestrian walking along the other side of the road so I dashed over to ask him for help. In fact, I charged over the road so quickly that I think the poor man thought he was about to be accosted for his face was consumed with a look of startled terror. Quickly opening my guidebook, I pointed to a picture of the Summer Palace. He nodded excitedly and after much turning of the heads and pointing into the distance, I managed to establish that I'd been walking in completely the wrong direction. Seconds later, the old man quickly grabbed my arm and, pointing at a passing bus, held up seven fingers. That I already knew, but the number seven bus had already proved elusive. Miraculously, just a few minutes later, one turned up.

The Summer Palace was the residence used by the Empress Dowager Cixi at the end of the last century to escape from the oppressive heat of the city. She was supposed to have spent weeks on end here and after finally passing through the entrance gates, it didn't take long to see why. Bordering a large tranquil lake, the extensive grounds contained numerous temples and pavilions, all set amongst immaculately maintained flowerbeds and gardens. I whiled away a few hours wandering indiscriminately along the quiet secluded paths, breathing in the glorious scent of freshly mowed lawns, admiring the splendidly restored Marble Boat where the Empress used to dine and climbing the aptly named Longevity Hill from where the views of the shimmering steely blue lake on another glorious Beijing afternoon were dazzling. All my efforts to get here now felt worthwhile and just like the Great Wall and the rendezvous at the Lido, it seemed my perseverance had again been rewarded. Indeed, this was to become a recurring theme over the weeks that followed, although I wouldn't always get my just rewards, as I'd discover in just 72 hours' time at the Tomb of Qin Shihuang.

CHAPTER 2

XIAN

AT HOME WITH THE DANES

30th November–5th December 1989

There were three main classes of travel available when I'd booked my ticket to Xian: hard seat, hard sleeper and soft sleeper. The choice had not been difficult. Two years before, I'd met up in Thailand with Gibbo, a friend from college; Pat, his schoolmate pal and Caroline, Gibbo's girlfriend, who'd joined the two of them in Australia. They were in the middle of their own 'round-the-world trip' and I'd flown over for a two-week holiday. On our first night in Bangkok, they asked me what I wanted to do. We could either travel south to the islands or head north to Chang Mai to go trekking in the mountains. To try to do both in a fortnight, they informed me, would be nigh on impossible. It took me about two seconds to decide so the next day we travelled down the gulf of Thailand to the beautiful (and then) blissfully unspoilt island of Koh Samui. After a glorious week lazing on the beaches, snorkelling in the shallow emerald seas, gorging ourselves on dishes of freshly cooked snapper or catfish and whiling the evenings away over an endless stream of ice cold Singhas, we briefly crossed over to the west coast before heading back to Bangkok where we'd spend my last few days. But although we'd made a reservation for this return journey, we somehow conspired to miss our connection. There was only one more train heading up to the capital that night and when it eventually pulled into the station late in the sweltering evening, each compartment was crammed with Thais returning to Bangkok to celebrate the *Songkran* (the Thai New Year) with their families. Following the crowds of waiting passengers along the platform, we hurriedly clambered aboard and making our way down the stifling and airless carriages, tried in vain to find a place to stand but it was hours into the journey before a couple of seats became available. When they finally did, they afforded little in the way of comfort and by then, we'd already made the fatal mistake of purchasing a couple of bottles of Mekong whisky to try to make the journey pass quicker. Instead, the sickly tasting spirit sent us into a two-folded state of dehydration and delirium and by the time we'd eventually arrived back in the capital early the next morning, absolutely shattered after a long and sleepless night, I had vowed never to make such a long journey in basic class again. Consequently, the hard seat option for the nineteen-hour passage to Xian had never been in the running. Soft sleeper class was also out of the question simply due to costs and I'd therefore opted instead for a hard sleeper ticket at 100 yuan (£20).

As I made my way to the station the following afternoon for the 1200 km journey to Xian, I was, I have to admit, feeling pretty chuffed with myself. My first week in Beijing had passed without any real hiccups and all in all, I doubted I could have picked a better place to start my travels. With its surfeit of cultural riches, Beijing had lived up to all prior expectations and ten consecutive days of brilliant clear blue skies and sunshine had only enhanced my enjoyment of the city's sights. The hotel I'd been staying at was probably a little overpriced although my room had been comfortable enough and whilst the majority of people I'd come across in the capital had been curiously indifferent, they'd still been courteous and civil. Now, though, I was heading back into the unknown again and as I approached the station, I was tingling with nervous excitement.

If I had any misgivings about the train journey itself, however, they were to prove totally unfounded. Making my way along the crowded platform, I duly presented my ticket to a guard who, waving me up the steps of the waiting train, led me through three or four carriages to my designated compartment. Comprising six bunk beds—three on each side—the door-less cubicle wasn't particularly spacious but I was immediately put at ease by the three Chinese men sitting on the lower bunks who, offering me cigarettes and tea from their flasks, promptly invited me to join them in a game of cards. There was a nice convivial feel in the compartment for lying on the top bunks were two other young backpackers, whom once the train set off, jumped down and joined us.

'So, where're you heading?' yawned one, rubbing the sleep from his eyes with the palms of his hands.

'Xian,' I replied, 'and you?'

'Ya, Xian too.'

'Been here long?' I enquired.

Frowning, he glanced at his friend and then peered curiously around the compartment.

'No, no, sorry,' I said waving my hand. 'I mean here, in China.'

'Ah,' said the other, rocking back his head. 'We thought you meant how long have we been on de train.'

Puffing his cheeks, the first one turned to his friend again. 'So, when *did* we get here now?'

'Last week,' said the other, nodding thoughtfully.

'And you?' asked the first again.

'Yeah, about the same. Got here last Tuesday.'

'Tuesday? Hey, us too,' said the other excitedly. 'Maybe we were on de same flight.'

'You fly SAS?' blurted the first.

'Yes,' I exclaimed, 'I did! Had to change at Copenhagen.'

'Ah, we fly from dere too. Dat's where we're from'

'What, Copenhagen?'

'Ya, we are from Denmark,' he proclaimed, his face now beaming.

'Sorry, I haven't introduced myself,' I said, stretching out my hand. 'I'm Jim by the way.'

'Ah, I'm Jesper,' said Jesper prodding his chest, 'and this,' he said, pointing to his friend, 'is Piere.'

It turned out that not only had we shared the same flight, we'd visited pretty much all the same places in the capital too, so we proceeded to chat at length about our respective first impressions of China. Indeed, two or three hours later, these fervent conversations were still going on in earnest, when a rather grouchy guard came around and popping his head into the compartment, crossly tapped his watch and muttered something to our card playing colleagues. Pointing up to the beds, they hastily abandoned their game and tottered off down the corridor with toothbrushes in their mouths. Exchanging perplexed glances, the three of us reluctantly hauled ourselves up onto our bunks. When the guard returned five minutes later to switch off the lights, it was still only ten past eight.

The train was still trundling through the countryside when I woke the next morning and glancing at my guidebook, it began to dawn on me just how vast this country really was. We'd been travelling now for over sixteen hours yet we'd barely moved a centimetre on the map. A journey of this duration back home would have taken me the entire length of the country; yet here, a sixteen-hour train journey was nothing. Passing through a succession of terraced yellow-earthed river valleys a couple of hours later, the scenery began to take on quite a surreal feel. We were crossing the Loess Plateau, where for hundreds of years whole communities of peasants and farmers had been living almost in oblivion in cave dwellings dug out of the surrounding soil. And watching these seemingly contented folk—groups of whistling men busily carting huge mounds of earth in barrows up and down the chalky irrigation channels and smiling mothers sat cross-legged drying clothes over fires as half naked children shrieking in delight ran around chasing pigs—it seemed that in these parts, time had indeed stood still.

Arriving in Xian at lunchtime, I gratefully took up the offer from the Danes to find some accommodation together. As soon as we set foot outside the train station, a dirty-faced hawker approached, promising us 'very good hotel, very cheap price.' I was a little sceptical although Jesper and Piere seemed quite happy to go along with the scrawny man, so nodding our heads we followed him through the streets to a guesthouse a short distance from the centre of the city. It was pretty basic but it turned out to be more than adequate. It was also very cheap, just 15 renminbi a night for a three-bedded room compared to the 60 I'd been paying in Beijing.

Most people who visit Xian do so primarily because of the Tomb of Qin Shihuang. Located some twenty-five miles to the east of city, the Tomb is the home of the legendary six thousand terracotta soldiers. The story has it that the life-size clay models, which had lain undisturbed for more than two thousand years, were unearthed in 1974 when a local farmer, digging a well in his field, inadvertently struck one of the buried heads with his pickaxe. The resulting discovery attracted worldwide attention and I still remember staring in awe at the television screen all those years ago when the first dramatic pictures of the warriors were unveiled to the British public on *John Craven's Newsround*.

So it'd be fair to say that when the three of us boarded a tourist bus the next morning for a guided tour to the Tomb and the accompanying Huaqing Springs we had high hopes for the day ahead. What I certainly wasn't expecting to see as I stared morosely out of the window waiting for the bus to depart was a group of Swedish lads staying in the same guesthouse who, charging across the tarmac with cans of Carlsberg in their hands, were screaming and shouting at the top of their voices. Now I, just like the next man, enjoy the odd glass of ale or two, but at ten o'clock in the morning this was pushing the boat out a little. At first, I wondered whether it could just be my old age setting in but when the Danes, clocking their Scandinavian neighbours as they bundled their way down the aisle, started shaking their heads as if to say, 'That's the Swedes for you,' I began to fear the day wasn't going to pan out exactly as planned.

By the time we pulled up at the site, it was fast approaching midday, and already, scores of other tourist buses stood empty in the car park. But before we were allowed to set eyes on the vault, our guide insisted on ushering us through all the various food and souvenir stalls surrounding the museum. Just like the Great Wall, it seemed, we were going to be kept in suspense. It was a full hour, in fact, before we were finally allowed to join the lengthy queue that had formed outside the 'hangar' and as we inched our way to the front, the finger-wagging attendants, repeatedly pointing at our cameras, reminded us time and time again that photography inside the building was strictly forbidden. Although I'd read about this beforehand — apparently the Chinese authorities were convinced that flash photography could damage the statues — this still came as a great disappointment, especially when we stepped inside forty minutes later and finally cast our eyes on the vast lines of moustachioed stone figures that stood four abreast in the huge pit beneath us like a lost sea of souls. Equally as disconcerting as the 'no photography' rule, though, was the layout of the museum, which offered little chance for the visitor to inspect the soldiers close-up. I had assumed that there would at least be a small section cordoned off somewhere for us wander down to but sadly this was not the case. (Such privileges it seemed were only made for royal dignitaries such as the Queen who'd come here just two years before.) Instead, we were made to follow the walkways that skirted the edge of the crater and as we shuffled around in muted silence, I found myself peering around at all the other people in the hall and placing bets with myself as to who'd be the first to try to take a sneaky picture. The stern-faced attendants, however, were not to be crossed and I ended up deriding just as much pleasure from watching the futile protests of a party of American tourists across the other side of the hall as I did from the warriors themselves.

Our afternoon visit to the Huaqing Springs could well have made up for the anti-climactic morning had it not been for our lively group of Swedish friends. The extensive grounds, set under the shadow of the looming Li Mountain, were shrouded in a permanent veil of mist, which ordinarily, would have made a leisurely stroll around all the pavilions, gardens and lakes a relatively pleasant and calming experience. The boisterous Swedes, though, seemingly had other ideas, for it was through this mist that the three of us wandered for over an hour, repeatedly running for cover like the ghostly figure in Munch's *The Scream* whenever we heard in the distance the raucous cries of the unruly gang approaching. Indeed, so eerie was the backdrop to this impromptu game of hide and seek, that by the time we eventually returned to the bus, I'd decided I'd rename them the 'Haunting Springs' instead.

Late in the afternoon, after being dropped off at the train station, the three of us hung around for a while, waiting for a bus to take us back to our hotel. When it eventually pulled in there was the usual frantic scramble to get on board. This had already happened on a number of occasions in the short time I'd been in China and I was continually struggling to comprehend why people simply couldn't wait for passengers to alight before they tried to climb onto the vehicle. Once aboard, we were crammed like sardines and I quickly lost sight of the Danes. As the bus passed down the main street of the city a few minutes later, many of the passengers disembarked and I managed to claim a seat near the front. At the next stop, a tiny bow-legged old lady came tottering up the steps. Being the noble sort, I tried to offer her my seat, but because there were five or six other people stood between us, my well-intentioned signals went unnoticed. Placing the basket down on the floor, the old woman grabbed onto the handrail and, with that, the bus set off again back into the chaotic late afternoon rush hour. A few minutes later, though, something out of the corner of my eye caused me to glance back down at her feet. A single brown feather had fallen from the basket and, caught in a slipstream from the unventilated doors, was slowly being whooshed up the dirty aisle. Just then the bus

44

stopped abruptly, the doors sprang open and the feather was lost amidst another scramble between those passengers trying to alight and those surging aboard. As we set off once again the old woman picked up her bag and placed it on her other side. It was then I noticed something in the bag move. I wasn't sure at first but staring at the basket intently as I was, I spotted another rocking movement a few moments later. Slightly bemused I glanced up at the wrinkly-faced woman, searching for some clues as to what it could be but, staring impassively out of the window, she seemed a million miles away. And then, protruding from the top and spinning around staccato-like, I saw its pink tousled head followed seconds later by a pair of beady eyes that, blinking inquisitively, were now staring straight back at me. It was a bloody chicken and almost in acknowledgement of being recognised, it suddenly let off a loud cluck. No one else aboard batted an eyelid but I sat in my seat bolt upright, refusing to take my eyes off the creature for a single second.

Although we were still careering along a busy highway, many of the passengers who were standing in front of me were now anxiously pushing and shoving their way down the aisle; the next stop was clearly going to be a busy one. This sudden movement obviously unsettled the chicken for, without warning, it decided this was a good a time as any to make its escape. The old lady was totally oblivious but I quickly spotted the impending danger, realising that if the bird launched itself towards the front, it could easily distract the driver and the consequences of this didn't bear thinking about. But it was too late. Amidst a flurry of feathers, the squalling bird had already taken flight and as the startled driver swung around, the bus lurched across the street. In a flash, I leapt from my seat and somehow managed to grab hold of the bird in mid-air as the driver, wrestling with the steering wheel, tried to regain control of the vehicle. With my hands outstretched and my eyes closed, I stood there for a few seconds with the chicken secure in my grasp, as the driver, slowly applying the brakes, pulled over to the side of the road. As soon as we stopped, I turned around slowly and carefully handed the bird back to the old lady.

Nodding and grimacing, she muttered something, which I took to be a thank you, then, calmly taking the bird off me, placed it back in its basket and just peered out of the window again as if nothing had happened.

I, though, was still shaking my head five minutes later. Just what was it with chickens and me recently? Four weeks before, when my father was ill in hospital, one of the chickens on my parents' farm had become sick. In fact, it was so poorly it could barely walk any more. To save the bird from further distress, my mother calmly asked me in the kitchen one evening to put it out of its misery. From her tone she might as well have been asking me to fill up the kettle with water, but I'd never harmed an animal in my life and I was now being asked to kill one.

'Don't look so worried,' she said, pouring me out a healthy measure of whisky a couple of minutes later. 'All you have to do is go down to the shed, pick the thing up and wring it by its neck. You might even get down there and find its already dead.'

It wasn't. Slamming the empty tumbler down on the table, I marched down to the yard, pushed open the creaking door of the coop, poked my head in and flashing the torch around, spotted the chicken in question lying on a small clump of straw in the corner. Blinded by the spotlight, the dying bird raised its head straight away.

Wondering just what on earth I'd done to deserve this, I crawled back out and pacing around the yard, tried to summon up the courage to do what was required. But it was no good. Whilst my mother's sentiments had never come into question, I simply knew I didn't have it in me to kill the bird in the method she'd prescribed. Although it was undoubtedly the time-honoured tradition out here in the country and quite possibly the most humane way to put it out of its misery, simply picking the chicken up and snapping its neck in half seemed to me so heartless. Yet the longer I left it, the worse it got and ten minutes later, I was truly on the verge of despair. Just as I was about to run off into the twilight, shaking my hands above my head never to be seen again, the kitchen door slammed and I heard my mother's footsteps coming down the path, so after a couple of final deep breaths, I barged my way back into the coup, quickly bundled the poor creature into a sack and, with tears of torment rolling down by face, slammed it repeatedly against an upturned boulder.

Xian itself was a damn sight warmer than Beijing and, situated at the end of the Silk Road, the city had a fantastic imperial feel to it. A seemingly impenetrable city wall twelve metres high and twelve metres wide with gateways, towers and ramparts still surrounded parts of the city centre. Inside these walls at the very centre of the city stood a huge and imposing bell tower nestled on top of a vast plinth of concrete and just to the west of this was the Great Mosque that marked the entrance to the city's Muslim quarter. The people here seemed different too, darker in colour and certainly friendlier than their Beijinese counterparts. Everywhere I walked, I'd be greeted with broad beaming smiles whereas in the capital all I seemed to get were long inquisitive stares.

Still only a week or so into my trip, I'd already started to appreciate the importance of setting aside days for doing very little. After tiring train journeys, arduous sightseeing tours and harrowing bus trips, it was nice to take some time out to recharge the batteries. The following day had been designated as just one of those days. In the morning, we lounged about until lunchtime watching a South American football game on the television in our room and later on, I wandered into town and picked up some detergent to wash some of my clothes in the bath. After hanging them up to dry in the hotel garden, I returned to the room and, while Jesper and Piere had gone out, got out all my guidebooks and maps and went over my route again for the next few weeks.

By now, I was quite warming to the Danes. Friends since school, the bond that existed between them had a certain air of the 'Starsky and Hutch' about it. They exuded the same kind of self confidence, they frequently teased and chaffed one another in the playful banter that comes naturally to trusted friendships, they even bore a striking resemblance to their illustrious crime

47

fighting counterparts: Jesper the taller of the two with a friendly amenable face and a shoulder length mane of straw coloured hair; Piere, a little more circumspect by nature with a head of tight brown curly locks. Travelling as a pair, they seemed far more disposed to deal with all the vagaries that China was throwing up too. Whether this contributed to the fact they were both so extraordinarily laid-back and managed to take everything in their stride, I wasn't too sure; perhaps this was just the Scandinavian psyche. But as likeable as they were, I was already looking forward to heading off the next day and getting my own space back.

Late in the afternoon, I took another stroll into Xian and, passing through a park backing onto a section of the City Wall, came across a large crowd. Wondering what could be causing such a stir, I asked a passer-by what was happening. Apparently it was a Chinese Opera and as I wandered over, an expectant audience of perhaps two or three hundred locals stood in a semi-circle patiently waiting for the production to commence. For a few minutes, I bobbed up and down at the back of these crowds, dancing on tiptoe and craning my neck desperately trying to peer towards the front when out of the blue, a female member of the cast appeared in front of me. Dressed in a purple silk gown, her face was powdered white, like a Geisha, her eyelashes were smothered in mascara, her lips were as red as blood, whilst protruding through her bun of raven hair was one of those long ornate wooden sticks. She was also talking nineteen to the dozen. For a few seconds I just stood there shrugging my shoulders. Shaking her head, she promptly grabbed my hand and led me through the crowds to the very front. Sitting me down on a stool right next to the five-man ensemble, she handed me a cup of green tea and then charged me ten yuan for the privilege which, for the best seat in the house, seemed pretty reasonable. Moments later the production commenced: firstly, a rousing crashing of cymbals and drums, followed by the screeching sounds of a fiddle-like instrument. This soon gave way to a piercing wail which, much to my surprise, came from the mouth of the frightening woman who'd brought me to my seat before a battle ensued with her high pitched warbling just managing to outdo the persistent din of the fiddle. But not to be outdone, the cymbals and drums then returned to the foray and we now had complete musical anarchy—a cacophony of sounds without apparent harmony, rhythm or melody, an uncoordinated mass of noise that I could make little sense of. Not wishing to offend my hosts, I sat there for as long as I could, but before long the music was becoming so harsh on my ears that I seriously thought my head was going to explode. The audience, however, appeared thoroughly engrossed in the matinee and finding myself surrounded by such a transfixed crowd, I desperately wanted to capture their spellbound faces on film. Having been sat in such a prominent position, though, this would have been far too disrespectful so, in between acts, I eventually crept over to the side and quickly reached into my bag for my camera. This was one photo opportunity I wasn't going to let pass me by.

Back in our room later that evening, I sat on my bed writing some letters whilst the Danes, lying on theirs, whiled away another few hours in front of the television. Later on, we started chatting about the respective countries we were planning to visit after China. They, like me, were embarking on a Grand Tour and after running through their itinerary, I was somewhat interested to note their next destination after Hong Kong was Bangkok. Mentioning I'd been there myself a couple of years ago, they proceeded to ply me with questions, picking my brains on prospective sights to visit in the capital. Glad to be of help, I started to scribble down the names of a couple of guesthouses on Khao San Road and, as I was doing so, couldn't help noticing they'd started to whisper to each other across their beds in their native tongue.

'Here you go,' I said to Piere handing him the piece of paper a few moments later.

Overcome by a sudden coughing fit, he nodded his thanks, then cleared his throat.

'Um, Jim, I think Jesper has something he wants to ask you.'

'Fire away,' I said, glancing across to the other bed.

Jesper, now rubbing the back his head, was looking decidedly sheepish. 'Well, we were wondering if er... you know, well er....' He turned to his friend: 'No, you ask him, Piere.'

'What?' I said, holding out my upturned palms like a shirking Italian. 'What d'you want to know?'

'Well,' blurted Piere, 'we were wondering if you went to the red-light area?'

'Sure,' I said nodding my head. 'Two or three times actually.'

In a flash, he leapt up and dashed over to the television set. As he did, Jesper raised his eyebrows. 'And did you...?'

'God, no,' I said shaking my head.

'That's better,' said Piere, diving back onto his bed. 'Couldn't hear a thing with that noise. So come on,' he pleaded, rubbing his hands expectantly, 'tell us what it's like.'

'Well,' I said lowering my voice, 'the place you need to go to is Patpong.'

'Patpong?' frowned Jesper.

'Yeah, just ask a tuk-tuk driver, he'll know it all right.'

'So what's it like?' repeated Piere, now sitting bolt upright.

'Well, it's a small sidestreet in the centre of Bangkok lined with girlie bars.'

They both started giggling.

'And do you have to pay to go in?' asked Piere, raising a hand to his mouth to suppress his titters.

'No, not that I can recall,' I replied. 'The drinks aren't cheap, though.'

'And what goes on inside?' asked Jesper, his eyes widening by the second.

'Well most of the bars have a stage in the centre where all the girls stand. Some have shows...'

'What kind of shows?' asked Piere, open-mouthed.

'Well,' I said, now desperately trying to keep a straight face myself. 'The best one of all is the ping-pong balls.'

'Ping-pong balls?' they both said at once.

As I went on to describe all the salacious acts, they sat there agog like two kids watching a Disney film.

On the way over to Beijing, I'd come across a rather intriguing article in the in-flight magazine on genes and sleep patterns. What first drew my eye to the feature was a somewhat bold statement at the top of the passage that claimed the entire human race could be divided up into two categories: early birds or night owls. Whilst many people don't come alive until later in the day, I'm definitely of the former category, much more active, resourceful, buoyant and receptive in the mornings but as the day progresses, I tend to slowly wilt. When I got up early the next day to walk into Xian to post some letters, I found myself contemplating this very subject. It was only just gone eight but already the place was buzzing with activity. Market stalls were hastily being erected, cyclists ferried fruit and vegetables back and forth across the square, grinning apron-clad women shouted across balconies to each other as they hung out their laundry, old men on pavements sat on stools studiously digesting the contents of the morning papers, whilst down in the alleyways skull-capped worshippers briskly made their way to early morning prayers. All of this plotting, planning and preparing for the day ahead only confirmed in my mind how this time of day is always the most invigorating. Yet in spite of this I found myself feeling rather perturbed. I *had* been under the impression that Jesper and Piere were planning to stay in Xian for another day or so, although when I'd told them the previous night I'd be heading off today, they'd both looked surprised. Earlier on, though, I discovered that they'd decided to move on as well, so it looked like the three of us would be leaving Xian together to travel southwest to Chengdu. Still, there was no point fretting about it; I'd just have to wait a little longer to get my own space back.

The twenty-hour journey later that afternoon passed quickly enough, and although we woke up to find Sichuan Province bound in fog, rather impairing our enjoyment of the passing scenery, we arrived at our destination just after lunchtime still in good spirits. When we ran into the six Swedish lads outside the station a few minutes later, however, my jaw dropped to the floor. Bumping into the unruly gang again in Chengdu certainly wasn't on the agenda. Jesper and Piere exchanged a few words with their Scandinavian neighbours who recommended that we book ourselves into the Black Coffee Hotel. I remembered reading about this hotel on the train and reaching for my *Lonely Planet* again as we set off in the back of a taxi, my fears were confirmed:

> '*The Hei Kafei Fandian (Black Coffee Hotel), a few minutes walk east of the Jinjiang Hotel, is a bomb shelter which has been converted into an underground hotel. Unless you like living in a rat-hole, this place won't appeal. Doubles cost Y16; a bed in a four bedroom costs Y5. In the dank maze of rooms, all sorts of things go on: disco dancing, snogging, furtive fumbling and even prostitution.*'

Even with this description fresh in my mind, I was still shocked to the bone when we arrived. Two floors underground were a series of freezing cold and seemingly never-ending dimly lit passageways, which on first sight looked more like the corridors of a medieval torture chamber. Immediately thinking fire risk, big fire risk, I began to envisage myself being chased down the tunnels by a huge ball of flames and the conspicuous lack of extinguishers hanging on the walls did nothing to allay these fears. Not having eaten for twelve hours, Jasper and Piere were keen to get some food so as soon as we located our room, we dumped our rucksacks on the beds and, marching back up the steps, headed straight back out, which was fine by me because all I was concerned about was seeing daylight again. Yet when we got outside, I realised it wasn't only claustrophobia I was feeling. Whether it was the hotel and the thought of being burnt alive, the need to be alone again or just an instinct to keep on moving, I don't know, but although we'd only been in Chengdu for less than an hour, I'd already developed an acute urge to get out of the place. So after telling the Danes I was going for a wander, I sneakily jumped in a cab and returned to the station, praying there'd still be seats available on the overnight train to Chongqing. When I arrived at the ticket office late afternoon, the woman behind the counter confirmed that there were seats available in hard sleeper class. After tentatively producing my white youth hostel card (very similar looking to the Chinese student identity cards), she then charged me a reduced fare for the journey, which saved me nearly £20. Elated, I hurried back to the hotel and explained to Jesper and Piere that I was travelling onwards that evening. Indeed, such was my relief to be moving on that I insisted on giving them my share of the money for the hotel room for that night, even though I wouldn't be staying there. Giving them both a hug, I wished them well for the rest of their travels, and picking up my rucksack heaved it onto my back.

'Perhaps we'll bump into each other again,' said Jesper, pensively rubbing his chin.

'Yeah, who knows,' I replied rather unconvincingly. Hurrying down the passageway, I reached the stairs at the end of the corridor and turning back, shouted: 'Oh, and have a great time in Bangkok!'

Sitting on the bus as I made my way back to the station, the city, which had been shrouded in fog all afternoon, felt like Christmas. Darkness was falling, shoppers were emerging from department stores laden with goods, the long avenues lined with fir trees twinkled with fairy lights and I was just content in the knowledge that I was moving on again, alone.

CHAPTER 3

CHONGQING

SHANSH MAANEE

6th–7th December 1989

The first thing I saw as I looked out of the window the next morning was a sprawling muddy brown river that I mistakenly took to be the Yangtze. The twelve-hour 500km journey southwest from Chengdu was nearing its end and I again found myself thinking about my travel plans for the next few weeks. By now, I'd resigned myself to the fact that Kunming was too far out of reach and, if I was to continue with my desired route, it was beginning to dawn on me that even getting to Hong Kong for Christmas would be difficult.

The train pulled into the port of Chongqing around ten and it was nothing like I imagined. With the Jialing River to the north and the Yangtze to the south, the city was a steep sided peninsula struggling, like a boxing referee separating two sparring fighters, to keep the waters at bay until they eventually converged at the eastern tip. The train station was situated on the southern shore, right alongside the water's edge and although there was a cable car that ran to the top, I decided to walk up the steep steps through the bustling indoor fruit market instead. Ten minutes later, I reached the top exhausted and then, partly because of the fog that seemed to have followed me down from Chengdu, was unable to locate the bus stop. Undeterred, I carried on walking in the direction of the Renmin. The hotel had been described as a palace. Twenty minutes later, I turned a corner and saw why.

Up until this moment, Chongqing had been a series of windy steps, narrow grey alleys and dreary dilapidated houses and here, out of the blue was an enormous futuristic hotel that at first sight looked like something out of an episode of *Dr Who*. The sheer size of the building, which was completely incongruous to the rest of the city, stopped me in my tracks. A huge concert hall, modelled on the Temple of Heaven in Beijing, (recognisable as the picture that often adorns the lids of tiger balm tins) sat proudly in the middle of a colossal building flanked by two vast concrete wings containing hundreds of rooms. Utterly transfixed, I stood at the gates for a few more moments, half expecting a troop of Daleks to come whizzing down the path to escort me up to the building. I'd read that there were dormitory rooms available in the hotel for as little as five yuan and, never having slept in a palace before, I felt quite excited about securing a luxurious bedroom, so without further ado I scurried down the path through the spacious tree-clad gardens towards the hotel steps. When I got to the reception, though, the girl behind the counter informed me the cheapest room available was 100 yuan, which was way out of my price range. The receptionist, picking up on my despair, directed me to a cheaper establishment and this marked the start of an intensely frustrating wild goose chase that took me around almost every single fogbound street of Chongqing. Consequently, by the time I finally walked into the reception of the recommended hotel an hour and a half later, shattered and filthy after forty-eight hours of travelling, I was virtually at my wits' end, so when the man behind reception informed me that the rate for a single room was an exorbitant 110 yuan a night, I was totally lost for words.

'A hundred and ten yuan?' I remonstrated after I'd picked myself up from the floor a few seconds later. 'Don't you have any sharing rooms or dormitories?'

He nodded his head although the rate was still an unaffordable 50 yuan. I asked if he could give me any discount. In fact, I pleaded with him. 'Oh come on, surely you must have something cheaper?'

'Would you take a room without air conditioning?' he casually enquired.

Without air conditioning? It was the first week of December, for heaven's sake. Why on earth would I want air conditioning?

'Of course,' I replied, and not even bothering to ask about the price, I set about completing the paperwork. Five minutes later after he'd handed me the key, I rushed up the stairs and when I reached the room and opened the door, my mouth fell open; in front of me was a plush motel style suite with a deep navy shagpile carpet, two great double beds, a television set and an en-suite bathroom. Not even the Renmin could have had rooms of this calibre and if I hadn't felt so tired, I swear I'd have got on my knees and kissed the ground. Instead, I heaved my rucksack off my back onto the floor and collapsed onto one of the beds.

Now the obvious and certainly most sensible thing to do at this point would have been to crash out and catch up on some much-needed sleep but I had a bee in my bonnet. The only reason I'd come to Chongqing was because this was the port where my planned boat trip along the Yangtze River began and I was keen to commence this journey in a couple of days' time. So ten minutes later, after a reviving shower, I headed back out to the booking office. Whilst I'd been checking-in earlier, the receptionist had quoted fares of 50 yuan, third-class, and 100 yuan, second-class, for the three-day journey to Wuhan, so I was somewhat taken aback when the booking clerk informed me that the fares had increased to 212 and 400 yuan respectively. As a foreigner in China I'd already become accustomed to paying considerably more than locals for train fares and accommodation but this was verging on the ridiculous. Either inflation in Chongqing was spiralling horribly out of control or I was blatantly being ripped off. Nevertheless, I booked the ticket on the spot, as I simply couldn't face the thought of any more traipsing around trying to find a place selling cheaper tickets. That said, I knew there'd be very few passengers, if indeed any, who would have paid anything like 400 yuan for their tickets but 'c'est la vie.'

Not entirely sure how efficient the postal service was in China, I spent the remainder of the evening back in my room writing out Christmas cards to send back home and, as I scribbled away, my thoughts again turned to where I should spend my first festive season away from my family. Hong Kong had effectively been ruled out and now Guangzhou, the biggest city closest to the border, was also looking unlikely if I was to persist with my planned route. I didn't really know what I was expecting Christmas to be like in China, but if I wanted to afford myself some kind of luxury for 24 hours, then I certainly didn't want to end up stuck in the middle of nowhere on Christmas Day. Shanghai was now looking the obvious choice.

Chongqing was still grey and shrouded in fog when I woke the next morning. Feeling ten times better after a decent night's sleep, I spent a couple of hours exploring the city in a far more relaxed frame of mind, which was just as well really for as I wandered the streets, all I heard were the incessant cries of, 'Shansh maanee, shansh maanee, hello, shansh maanee.' For some untold reason, the business of changing money on the black market in Chongqing seemed rife. Others came bounding up to me asking if they could practise their English. This I didn't mind so much, they were just being inquisitive, and quite often one or two would tag along for a few minutes invariably bombarding me with the same questions: 'What is your name?' 'Which country you from?' and 'How long you stay in Chongqing?'

A few hours later, with my patience wearing a bit thin, I decided to seek refuge in the indoor market. Heading up the hill like the 'Pied Piper of China', I noticed a large crowd had gathered at the top of the market steps. This time, there were no sounds of screeching fiddles or wailing voices resonating from beyond so, with my curiosity eventually getting the better of me, I wandered over and peeped into a gap at the side to find out what was attracting so much attention.

Shackled to a fence by two clanking iron chains were a couple of scrawny looking monkeys. So thin, in fact, were their torsos that each time they raised their arms to scratch their armpits and exposed their carcass-like ribcages, I had to look away. As well as malnutrition, it appeared they were suffering from alopecia too—at least that was what I hoped it was—for blotched sporadically amongst their bodily hair were seven or eight discernibly large and unsightly patches of bright pink flesh. Leaning languidly against the railings on either side were two middle-aged men, both with shabby jackets draped over their shoulders, who every now and then, squinting through a haze of blue cigarette smoke, would bark orders to the screaming creatures. Cowering for a few seconds, with their heads buried in their hands, the monkeys would eventually peer up, and on seeing these scowling faces hissing down at them, quickly jump up and down performing somersaults to the delight of the onlooking crowd. It was probably the reaction of this hastily convened audience more than the two grubby-faced men themselves that made me realise I'd finally seen enough, for when the monkeys, after each being handed a lit cigarette, deftly started blowing smoke rings into the air, the crowd went ballistic, whistling and cheering at the top of their voices.

Yet in spite of this and the 'Shansh Maanee' brigades, I was quite taken by Chongqing, with its mountainous terrain, waterside proximity and long winding roads. It was no Monte Carlo, admittedly, but it did retain a certain charm.

Early evening, I wandered down to the dockside to check where my boat would depart from in the morning. With the night drawing in, the surrounding mountains finally unveiled themselves from the mist that had been hugging onto them for the past two days, and all around, blinking light bulbs flickered into action like an array of flashing paparazzi cameras. When I saw my boat in dock, I suddenly became quite excited and was further heartened when I noticed a number of other Westerners milling around the waterside, including a couple of Australian blokes I recognised from our guesthouse in Xian. Soon after, I returned to my room. The boat was leaving at 7am, so after pulling out my travel clock, I diligently set my alarm for 5.30 and turned in for an early night. If I knew what lay in store over the next few days, I would have happily left it at the bottom of my rucksack.

CHAPTER 4
THE YANGTZE RIVER
INVISIBLE GORGES AND TRYING TRAVELLERS
8th–12th December 1989

It was, at first, quite refreshing to hear 'English' being spoken again (albeit English with a nauseating twang) but after spending the morning in the company of twenty or so excitable teenagers who'd set up camp in the boat's lounge, the novelty had quickly worn off. The only other Westerners on board were a couple of pairs of travellers, two of whom went on to inform me that the party of students were from Chicago and here in China on a cultural exchange. In their late twenties, Bob and Dave were also American and both had travelled extensively. Bob, who'd been studying in Taiwan, just happened to be travelling around China in June and, as a result of the authorities panic in the wake of Tiananmen, was unceremoniously kicked out of the country. He was back here now to travel to the remaining places he'd been unable to see and had been joined for a few weeks by his old college friend, Dave.

The other pair of travellers were the two guys I'd mistakenly taken to be Australians. Yaan turned out to be Finnish and his friend, also American, and I knew in an instant I was going to find it extremely difficult to spend three days in their company. The alarm bells started ringing the moment they cracked open a beer each in the cabin just after 9am and as they lay on their bunks reciting stories of their recent travels in Thailand, I began to fear the worst. Both were scruffily dressed, Yaan in particular who, judging by his Mohican haircut, long woollen pullover and baseball boots, was still clearly living in the punk-era. Later in the morning they were slouched in the lounge with their feet up on the tables, still drinking beer like there was no tomorrow. Admittedly, there wasn't a great deal else to do as dense fog was obscuring all the surrounding scenery, but it wasn't long before I found myself sitting through another rendition, this time for the sake of Dave and Bob, of how they'd spent their time on Koh Samui.

'Yeah,' droned Yaan, 'we go to da beach and we get out da bong and we sit by da bong and we smoke and we 'ave goot food in de sun and we sit on da beach and we smoke from de bong.'

In fact, all he seemed capable of speaking about was Thailand and for the first time in my life, I found myself experiencing pangs of despair for a place that remained dear to my heart. Thailand had been the first country I'd visited outside Europe and from start to finish, it had been a totally captivating experience—the spluttering tuk-tuks on the congested frenetic streets of the capital, the blissfully unspoilt sandy palm fringed beaches of Koh Samui, the endearing hospitality of the forever smiling Thais—and although I had no right to, I felt particularly possessive about the country as a result. Listening to Yaan going on and on about it now, I was slowly beginning to realise that if I ever returned there, it would never quite be the same second time around.

Later in the afternoon, I was stood at the back of the boat, with my hands deeply entrenched in my trouser pockets. There was not much to see around me; the clouds were still as low and grey as they had been ever since we'd set off and it was bitterly cold. I was hoping, praying even, these conditions would clear by the morning when we were due to pass through the Three Gorges, apparently the most scenic part of the trip. There wasn't a lot going on aboard the boat either. The restaurant, by all accounts, had been packed out at midday by Chinese and nobody else was able to get a look-in, so much to the amusement of the locals, the five of us managed to concoct a lunch of noodles in one of the corridors from some provisions Bob and Dave had brought with them. The others had made a reservation in the restaurant for dinner, although I was pinning my hopes on the boat docking later in the evening when we'd hopefully be able to disembark and sample some local dishes.

By the time we finally dropped anchor for the night at the port of Wanxian, though, it was getting on ten and my stomach was so hungry it was hurting. After being advised that we could disembark for three hours, the five of us—Bob, Dave, Yaan and his Californian travelling partner, Robert—quickly strode up the 400 steps to the darkened town in search of a beer. A small group of locals met us at the top and informing us there was a power cut, led us along a winding candlelit cobbled street to a small open-fronted bar. Pulling up some chairs, Bob immediately started chatting to the owner in Mandarin. Moments later, five bottles of Tsingtao arrived at the table and shortly after, we were served up a terrifically fiery dish of spicy goat meat and potato stew. Not having had any dinner, the food was a godsend and judging by the huge grin on his face, the chef seemed delighted to have us as diners. It wasn't until our eyes had become accustomed to the dim light twenty minutes later that we happened to notice the series of porcelain sinks and mirrors all along the wall and only then did it dawn on us we were actually sitting in a barber's.

Mellowed by the food, we sat around the table chatting for a while. The conversation initially centred on the Japanese—their lifestyles, their threat to the West, their immense power as a race and their strange customs—although for large parts, I just sat there quietly listening in, becoming increasingly in awe of Bob and Dave. The more they spoke, the more I realised how knowledgeable they were, I could only assume as a consequence of their travels. They both spoke fluent Chinese, Bob perhaps a little better than Dave, and I couldn't help reflecting on how much I was missing out by not being able to converse with local people accordingly.

'So,' said Bob eventually, looking at his friend with a mischievous twinkle in his eyes as Yaan returned from the toilet. 'Are you gonna tell them the thing about the Japanese boys, then?'

Dave, sat in his seat with his arms folded, tilted his chair back and glanced around the table. 'You know they won't believe it,' he smirked.

'Believe what?' barked Yaan.

'You think I should?' asked Dave, still smiling at Bob.

'Yeah, go on, it's funny as hell, they'll enjoy it.'

'Yeah, come on,' implored Robert, 'if you've got a story then let's hear it,'

'Well,' said Dave, 'it's like this. You know most Japanese men work very long hours?'

We all nodded.

'Well, I bet you didn't know that in Japanese households, the sons quite often end up sleeping with their mothers.'

While Bob chuckled, the three of us stared at Dave incredulously.

'What, you mean share the same bed?' asked Yaan.

'No,' said Dave rubbing his chin. 'I mean they actually have sex.'

'Come on, that's ridiculous,' cried Robert, taking the words right out of my mouth

Dave, puckering his lips, opened his outstretched hands. 'It's true, I swear'

Bob was nodding his head in agreement

'What, the son and the mother have sex?' I enquired.

Now it was Dave's turn to chuckle.

'Why?' I asked, shaking my head.

'Well, they're not really given that much choice'

'What, you're trying to tell us that the mothers force them to have sex with them?'

'It happens, I tell you.'

I looked around at the others. Now Robert was nodding his head too. It seemed for a moment that he was prepared to believe this preposterous story. Even Yaan had a knowing look on his face. 'Wouldn't surprise me dat much,' he said. 'Nothing about dose people would. De're crazy people, de lot of dem.'

Dave tried to offer an explanation. 'What you've got to realise is that Japan is a very different society to ours. The mothers are fiercely protective of their sons. They don't want them wandering the streets late at night and sleeping with other girls.'

'Yeah but...'

Bob then interjected. 'Hey Jim, I was just the same as you when Dave first told me but I was in Tokyo myself earlier this year and I heard the same story. It does goes on, honestly. You should try and go there on your travels, it's a really interesting country.'

Shaking my head still, I sat in my seat for a full five minutes chewing the cud, much to the amusement of the Americans. After that, the conversation moved on to linguistics, and when Yaan let on that he was fluent in four other languages, I began to feel that I'd perhaps misjudged him. By contrast, Robert, his companion, proceeded to plunge into depths of indignity from where there could be no return. He continually badmouthed the people and the country, complaining, 'they talk behind our backs, they rip us off... Yeah, fuck the Chinese, China's a shithole!' On the way back down to the boat, he urinated in the middle of the street then repeated the dubious feat on the quay. When we re-boarded sometime after midnight and returned to our cabin, Yaan took up the mantle, complaining about the habits of the Chinese in our quarters, in particular, their chain-smoking and incessant spitting. I felt like telling him to remember that we were in another country that we'd chosen to visit and whilst these habits were no doubt disgusting and took a lot of getting used to, we didn't necessarily have the right to criticise, but at the same time, the evening had been one of the most enjoyable nights I'd had on my trip so far. A magical night like this—sat around in a barber's on the banks of the Yangtze exchanging stories over a few beers with a group of fellow travellers I'd only just met – was exactly the kind of experience I'd been hoping for from the outset, so I held my tongue and let it pass.

The fog still hadn't cleared the following morning, if anything it had got thicker. Whilst I was lying on my bunk after breakfast vacantly staring up at the ceiling, Yaan came bursting in with the news that a skinned dog had been found on deck. 'C'mon' he cried 'You must come and have a look.' I refused to budge, one, because I didn't particularly want to see such a gruesome sight and two, because I suspected he was just pulling our leg but when the others returned rather ashen-faced a few minutes later, I realised it wasn't a sick joke after all. I spent the remainder of the day passing the time playing chess, Mastermind and cards with the other guys but by late afternoon, the wretched dog had become the major talking point in the lounge as the students, at various intervals, crept up on deck in twos and threes to inspect the corpse. The only respite came mid-afternoon when we emerged from the three gorges and passed through the massive gates of the Gezhouba Dam.

Later in the evening, still in the lounge, Dave, Yaan and Robert started making plans to meet on Koh Samui at Christmas. For over an hour they went on and on about how brilliant it was all going to be; sunshine, cocktails, girls, palm trees, dance parties, sandy beaches, beautiful food, it was never-ending. At one stage, I even considered making drastic changes to my travel plans but I then tried to reason with myself. In five weeks' time, I'd be arriving in Sydney and what's more, I'd probably never get another chance to visit all the remaining places I wanted to see in China. Yes, they would be cold and no, I wouldn't be partying on a beach over Christmas like the others but these were my travel plans that I'd taken months to work out and if I didn't persist with them, I'd only regret it in the future. To cap it all, one of the female stewards came in later in the evening and announced that she'd be closing the lounge an hour earlier than planned. Although a half-hearted attempt to try to find somewhere else to while away a few more hours followed, we eventually returned to our cabins for an early night.

Early the next morning, I did something quite odd. For some reason, I decided to hurl my new walking boots into the Yangtze. I'd only bought them four weeks ago, and that was after months of deliberation, but my feet were already severely blistered. They were also taking up far too much room in my rucksack so, in a moment of madness, over the side they went. It wasn't like me to be so irrational but maybe that was what this infernal river did to people.

Back in the lounge later on, I pulled out an aerogramme and started to write a letter to my parents:

> I've now been on this wretched boat for 48 hours and I'd be lying if I said that this trip has been anything else than a huge disappointment. The weather has been bitterly cold, and thick fog and mist has obscured most of the gorges. The boat itself is cold, dreary, damp and lacking in any proper facilities and the only consolation of the trip is that I've been accompanied by a party of Westerners who've had to suffer the same bad experience as myself. We were due to arrive in Wuhan about four this afternoon but we've just received an announcement over the boat's tannoy to say that because of the fog, we won't be able to dock until 2am tomorrow morning. This is not good news. Our agony, it seems, is only going to be prolonged.

Around 6pm, we received a second announcement advising us that the conditions had deteriorated so badly that we wouldn't be able to travel any further that night. Consequently, our revised arrival time in Wuhan was now 4pm the next day. The cards, Mastermind and chess sets were hastily unpacked again but when, an hour later, our female steward returned to the lounge and asked us all to leave, all hell broke loose. The excitable students hollered in protest while Yaan and Robert leapt to their feet and yelled at the steward. Bob and Dave diplomatically stepped in and conversed in Chinese with the steward to find out why we were being evicted. The looks on their faces changed, firstly from annoyance to incredulity, and then to amusement. It emerged that we, as a group, were collectively being blamed for somebody crapping in the bottom of one of the showers. A heated row ensued although the steward and another member of the boat's staff stood firm. With no obvious signs that it could be resolved, the Captain was eventually summoned and although he banned all drinking and smoking, he finally restored order by allowing us to remain in the lounge until 10pm. It subsequently came to light that one of the Chinese on board had spotted Bob coming out of the shower in question earlier that morning. Bob was adamant, though, that the lump of pooh was already in there, so he'd decided to make a hasty retreat from the cubicle. What was most interesting in this little incident, however, was the reaction of all concerned. Bob, just shrugging his shoulders, came out with the adage: 'This is China, it's one of the things you just accept and laugh about as this is China.' Dave's bottom line was, 'Yep, just remember, it's us who've got the passports here.' Yaan and Robert pleaded with Bob and Dave to hurl back abuse at the female steward who, in turn, suffered the ultimate Chinese indignity of losing face when the Captain finally overruled her decision. Significantly, it was not she who came back to close the lounge at the agreed time of 10pm but another member of staff instead. When we returned to our cabin, Yaan and Robert began another ranting tirade against China: the people, the place, the habits, the climate, the culture, you name it. Pulling out my Walkman, I turned over on my bunk and tried to immerse myself in the Australian travel book I'd just started to read.

The next morning, the fog had disappeared and the Yangtze

River had swollen to a width of half a mile. We were now passing through much flatter terrain and Wuhan was in touching distance. I'd been on this boat for nearly fifty-seven hours and ultimately Yaan's lumbering droll voice had proved to be the killer. For the rest of the day, he just went on and on and on about Thailand, the beaches, and stories of his experiences there with Robert, and by the end, I felt like throttling him. Indeed, if I'd heard, 'We go to da beach and we get out da bong...' one more time, I seriously think we could have had a potential man overboard problem on our hands. Compounding my misery was the realisation I'd developed the full-blown symptoms of a cold: sore throat, aching bones, blocked up nose and general fatigue.

When we finally docked in Wuhan late afternoon, I had the same feeling I'd had when I'd arrived in Chengdu to just keep moving on. Besides, Wuhan didn't look a particularly appealing place, so I made my way straight to the booking office and bought an onward ticket to Nanjing on another boat departing just two hours later. Bob also happened to be travelling to Nanjing later that evening so when he learnt there was another service departing earlier, he managed to change his reservation in order that we could travel together. So, after a departing meal with the others, who were travelling south together the next day towards Hong Kong, we quickly made our farewells and dashed off to board our new vessel.

The new boat was better than the last—faster, quieter and cleaner—and although we were the only Westerners on board, Bob was the consummate travelling companion. His extensive knowledge of China was extremely useful and throughout the course of the next two days, I continued to pick his brains about anything I could think of—prospective places to visit, types of dishes he could recommend and various Chinese words and phrases that could help me on my way. He even told me how to get locals to buy my train tickets for half the price. His ability to converse in Mandarin also made the journey much easier for me as I had someone to tell me exactly how long we'd got in a port each time the boat docked, at what time we could expect to arrive in Nanjing and so forth. The only downside was Bob's insistence on speaking to everybody on board in Chinese. Feeling totally inadequate, all I could do each time this happened was look on, smile, and dumbly nod my head.

Late afternoon, we managed to sneak into the first-class lounge at the front of the boat. The only other passenger in the lounge was an elderly, silver haired man in a beige suit who was sat in a wicker chair reading a book. Bob introduced himself and predictably started chatting in Mandarin again with the man who, I was reliably informed, was the manager of the port of Wuhu, a small town on the south of the Yangtze. Soon after, another gentleman dressed in full military regalia wandered in and pulled up a seat. As the conversation unfolded, Bob discovered that the new arrival appeared to command a very high ranked position in the Chinese army. If this wasn't enough to make me feel completely out of my depth, the Captain of the boat then emerged through another door and promptly sat down to join us. Bob was in his element and I was out on a limb and all I could do was sit there and grin with gritted teeth. So when, twenty minutes later, three white-coated waiters carrying trays of food trooped in and started placing the dishes down on a long dinner table behind us, it would be fair to say I was somewhat relieved. But before we knew it, the Captain had invited us to join the esteemed trio in a sumptuous Chinese banquet and whilst the food—lavish platters of chicken with capsicum, fish in chilli sauce, pork with lychees and crispy fried beef—was easily the best I'd had since I arrived in China, I doubt I've ever put so much concentration into eating as I did around the table that afternoon.

All I kept thinking about was spilling food all down my jumper and, surrounded by such distinguished company, this was totally unthinkable. In spite of the fact I'd now been in China for three weeks, my skills in the chopstick department still left a lot to be desired, so the choices over what dishes I tried were made purely on the basis of 'sloppability.' Sweet and sour pork, for example, was fine so long as I didn't dip the meat into the sauce. The crispy beef was okay but noodles were a definite no-no. Rice was a tricky one. Foregoing it altogether, I suspected, could easily be construed as deeply insulting, yet I'd never fared well with rice in previous meals, so I eventually opted for the smallest of portions in order just to cover the base of my bowl. The biggest dilemma was whether to risk the fish in chilli sauce. Bob, who was sitting next to me, said he'd never tasted a better dish in all the time he'd been in China and I simply adore spicy food, but it was served in a tantalisingly runny brown sauce. After finally deciding to err on the side of caution, I somehow managed to get through the meal unscathed but the rice wine that accompanied the food went straight to my head and for a while I just quietly sat there smiling inanely.

When the dishes were eventually cleared away, I tried to think of a way I could express my gratitude to the Captain and suddenly remembered the photographs sitting in the side pocket of my rucksack. (I had read before I'd left home that giving out postcards and pictures of your country and family to local people was a gesture that would nearly always be welcomed. Consequently, I'd taken a series of photographs of my parents' farm in Wales and had a number of copies developed to bring away with me.) I asked Bob if he thought that presenting each of them with one of the pictures was a good idea.

'Jim, I think that's a mighty fine idea,' he whispered, now looking decidedly glassy-eyed, so I scurried back to the cabin and returning a few minutes later, handed them each a photo. Nodding their heads respectfully, they seemed suitably pleased. Just then, one of the waiters reappeared with a bottle of Johnnie Walker, and not wanting to outstay our welcome, we hastily got to our feet. Then, after shaking hands with the three men across the table, we left them to carry on their animated conversations and as soon as we closed the cabin door behind us, I drew a huge deep breath, my relief all too palpable.

CHAPTER 5

NANJING

CHINESE SECRETS

13th–15th December 1989

Lying on my bunk, I peered around the darkened dormitory thinking how wonderful it was to wake up and realise I was finally back on dry land. Still feeling run down, I decided the best thing to do was to stay here for a couple of days to recuperate. I was in the industrialised city of Nanjing where our boat had finally docked late the previous night. The city itself, a strategic trading port on the Yangtze, was the fifth largest in China and home to three million people. Earlier in the year, Bob had studied at the university here for six weeks. He'd told me that it wouldn't be a problem securing some accommodation on the site so, as soon as we'd stepped off the boat, we'd taken a taxi straight to the campus where, true to his word, we were offered a room for a couple of nights.

    With Bob still asleep, I started to read up on the history of

Nanjing. And what an extraordinarily turbulent history it was, for when it came to catastrophes, the city appeared to be in a league of its own. Nanjing had seemingly seen it all: floods, fires, plagues, famines, typhoons, peasant rebellions not to mention constant attacks from rival factions. For thousands of years, as successive dynasties fought for control of the city, it had found itself embroiled in some particularly barbarous battles. Disconcertingly, though, the worst of these atrocities, the infamous 'Rape of Nanjing', had occurred in relatively recent times, as recent as 1937, in fact, when an estimated 300,000 Chinese lost their lives in six weeks of horrific and gratuitous violence that followed the Japanese capture of the city. Bob had been at pains to explain all this the previous day on the boat but sometimes you actually need to be in a place before you can even begin to take these kinds of things on board. As he stirred from his lower bunk, I poked my head down and said cheerily, 'I see what you mean now when you were talking about Nanjing.'

Taking breakfast in the university canteen later in the morning, we got chatting to some other American students, one of whom kindly offered to lend us her bike, so an hour later, I found myself sitting rather uncomfortably on the back of the bicycle as Bob pedalled us through the busy streets on a whistle-stop tour of the city.

Surprisingly, the main attraction wasn't the city walls that had so valiantly defended Nanjing in many of its bloody battles, or the heavily fortified Zhonghau City Gate, which in its time could accommodate up to 3000 armed guards. It wasn't even the mightily impressive three-mile long Yangtze River Bridge at the north of the city, widely regarded as the biggest two-tier bridge for road and rail traffic in the world. No, the prime tourist site, judging by the hordes of Chinese stood outside its gates excitedly posing for photographs, was the monstrous 36-storey Jingling Hotel, a huge and imposing concrete monolith which looked as if it had just been directly transported from downtown Manhattan and plonked down directly in the centre of the city. As we made our way towards the foyer, Bob pointing up to the skies said, 'C'mon, there's a revolving restaurant at the top.' Gulping, I warily followed him through the reception to the lift. (I have never been good with heights. In fact I'm so terrified of them I once suffered the humiliation of having to crawl around the upper level of the Eiffel Tower on my hands and knees.) So when, thirty minutes later, Bob headed off to break off his relationship with a Chinese girlfriend, I happily trotted back to our room, thoroughly relieved just to have my feet firmly back on the ground.

Reconvening early evening back at the Jingling, I was somewhat surprised to notice Bob contentedly lounging on one of the leather sofas in the reception with a smiling young girl on his arm. Chong Lee (name changed for reasons that will later become obvious) was not at all how I'd imagined. Instead of the long-legged, tall and glamorous girl that Bob had described, she was big boned, portly and round-faced by comparison, but in no way did this detract from her obvious beauty. Her complexion was smooth, her white teeth dazzled and her long raven hair shimmered under the bright foyer lights. More importantly, she was both charming and vivacious. Perhaps sensing my discomfort earlier on, Bob suggested we take dinner in the ground floor lounge, which was probably just as well, for there was no way in the world I was going all the way back up to that restaurant again. An hour or so later, just as we were just finishing our coffees, Bob was greeted by Lu Fang, a chubby and affable middle-aged television producer he'd met the previous summer. He introduced us and then the three of them started chatting for a while. About what, I couldn't tell you as they were talking nineteen to the dozen in Mandarin. So, shortly after, when Bob became engrossed in a conversation with Chong Lee, I was still sat there twiddling my thumbs, wondering if I'd be better off heading back to our room again.

'Wan a secret?' asked Lu Fang eventually, leaning over the table.

'A secret?' I replied, somewhat surprised.

'You ha a secret I want...umm. I wan a secret of yours'

'Well, I'm sorry,' I chuckled, 'I haven't got a secret...I

mean...a secret? No, no. I definitely haven't got a secret.'

What on earth was he going on about? Screwing up my face, I peered over to Bob for help. 'I don't know what he's asking me but I think he wants me to tell him a secret?'

Bob frowned for a few seconds and was just about to say something when Lu Fang, producing a packet of 'Kents' from his pocket, pulled out one of the cigarettes and waved it in front my face. 'You ha a secret?' he repeated.

'Ah, a secret!' I replied, before reaching into my bag and handing him an unopened box of Marlboros.

A short while later, Bob disappeared to the toilet and after another obvious lull in the conversation, Lu Fang picked up his glass and went to make a toast.

'Cheer up,' he said.

Cheer up? I might have seemed a little detached, but I certainly hadn't thought it was that obvious.

'Cheer up, Jim, cheer up,' he repeated, clinking my glass.

Then the penny dropped. 'It's cheers...not cheer up,' I said. 'Cheer up means something different.'

'Ah, cheers Jim, cheers.'

'Yep, cheers, Lu Fang, all the best!'

Later the next day, I tried to turn my thoughts towards my planned trip to Huang Shan where I was hoping to scale the 3000-foot Lotus Flower Peak. (Although it wasn't strictly on the designated tourist trail, I was damned if this was gonna stop me veering off the beaten track.) To get to Huang Shan, I needed to make a ten-hour overnight train journey to the old trading town of Tunxi. From there, I'd be able to pick up a bus that would take me the final thirty or so miles to the base of the mountain, so early afternoon, I called into the booking office at the train station. Unfortunately, there were only hard seats available which was not good news. If I was to make what would be a potentially exhausting climb to the summit, the last thing I needed the night before was a long train journey that offered little chance of sleep. Later on in the afternoon, more bad news followed. Chong Lee told me she thought the mountain might be closed, something the authorities apparently did quite a lot in the winter when the weather deteriorated. As the temperature in the city dropped to well below freezing that night, the whole trip I'd been quietly looking forward to for so long appeared to be in serious jeopardy.

Mid-morning the following day, I was sitting in an eating-house in the south of the city gorging myself on noodles. Out on the large square, three or four couples were playing badminton, old people were chatting feverishly outside open fronted shops, and dozens of cyclists were weaving in and out of cars and oncoming pedestrians. The sun had returned, raising my spirits and it looked like I'd finally managed to get over the cold that had been plaguing me for days. I was sure being based in one place and taking things at a leisurely place for forty-eight hours had helped in this regard.

When I'd woken up I had also found all my resolve had returned, so I'd decided to persist with my original plans. The only alternative at this stage would have been to travel on with Bob and Chong Lee but I wasn't quite sure what was going on there. If Bob was trying to terminate the relationship he was certainly going about it in a funny way. Whether he was having second thoughts or was still trying to pluck up the courage, I'm not entirely sure, because the two had remained virtually inseparable. The prospect, therefore, of playing gooseberry for a few more days really left me with no choice and, besides, I was keen to get back to travelling alone. When I made my way back to the train station at lunchtime, I discovered there was, in fact, an option of travelling soft sleeper class to Tunxi later that evening. I'd not travelled soft sleeper class yet (the equivalent to first class) and the cost was an expensive 60 yuan. Still, I made the reservation nonetheless and then bade farewell to Bob and Chong Lee who were also heading south later that night.

My train wasn't leaving until nine, so I whiled away a couple of hours stocking up on some provisions. Walking along Zhongshan Lu, Nanjing's main street early evening, I peered up at the fluffy cotton wool clouds chugging across the sky. If only I knew what kind of conditions these cloud patterns signified.

The weather was likely to be such an important factor over the next couple of days in determining whether my trip to Huang Shan would be a success or not, just as it had been with the trip down the Yangtze. After packing my rucksack, I then made my way to the station and, thinking back on the last week as I was doing so, I knew I'd got a lot to be thankful for to Bob, for showing me aspects of life in China that I'd otherwise have been deprived of if I'd been travelling alone. And in the process, he'd unwittingly dispelled my long held beliefs that all our American cousins were loud, brash and obnoxious.

CHAPTER 6
HUANG SHAN
SHANGRI-LA
15th–17th December 1989

Whilst I'd been in Nanjing, I'd borrowed one of Bob's books, *Riding the Iron Rooster*, by Paul Theroux. In the book, the author, who'd travelled extensively around China by train just the previous year, had found himself followed, somewhat against his wishes, by a Chinese official called Mr Fang. An hour into the journey to Tunxi, I wondered if the authorities had despatched another Mr Fang to keep an eye on me too.

I'd boarded the train just after 9pm and, after being shown to my soft-sleeper cabin, it didn't take long to see what I'd been missing out on. For a start, there were only four bunks instead of the usual six in hard sleeper, which immediately made the compartment feel more spacious, and the décor was infinitely more homely: the floor was fully carpeted, the walls were panelled with wood, lace curtains hung from the window, there was even a complimentary tea set sitting on the window table beside a rather ornate reading lamp. The two Chinese men lying flat out on their beds looked as if they were ready to turn out the lights and go to sleep there and then, but I wanted to bask in my new luxurious surroundings for a while longer so, sitting on my lower bunk, I'd purposefully reached into my daypack for a book.

Not long after the train departed, however, a whistling round-faced man in a shirt and tie walked past our compartment. Spotting a foreigner in the cabin, he turned on his heels and, somewhat to my surprise, promptly invited himself in, plonking his large frame down next to me on the bed. Now up until this point, all the conversations I'd had with local people had, without exception, followed the same standard pattern... Where are you from? Why have you come to China? Do you like England? Which places will you visit in China? So when this grinning middle-aged man started asking me loaded questions on what were potentially very sensitive subjects, I naturally became a little suspicious and began to think that I was being closely monitored too.

'What is your opinion of what has happened in East and West Germany with the Berlin Wall?' he asked. 'Do you think the same thing will happen in other Eastern European countries?' 'What do you think will become of Russia?' and more pertinently, 'What do you think about what happened in Tiananmen Square?'

These, as I say, were certainly not the run-of-the-mill questions I'd been accustomed to. In each instance, I tried to avoid giving opinionated answers and did my utmost to skirt around the issues. In reply to his question on what I'd thought about what had happened back in June, for example, I stated that as a foreigner this was not something I felt I should really be commenting on. His response to this was just the same as it had been to all the others: after looking deep into my eyes during the course of my reply, he left a long uncomfortable gap between this and his next question. He also had a calculated look on his face. It was a look that said, 'We know all about you, don't worry, we know where you've been, we know what you're doing and we're watching you all the time.' It was a look that I found most unnerving. Still fidgeting about nervously on my bunk ten minutes later, I finally managed to interrupt him by asking if he had any details on buses from Tunxi to Huang Shan. This information wasn't strictly that important but I was hoping that a change of subject would at least bring the interrogation to an end. Raising his eyes for a moment, he shook his head. The two men on the upper bunks were now beginning to stir in their beds, so I pointed up at them, indicating to my friend that it was probably time to turn out the lights. Slowly getting to his feet, he clasped my hand, shook it firmly and, whistling again, wandered back out of the cabin, the interrogation evidently over. Closing the compartment door quickly behind him, I gestured to the two men again, switched off the light and hurriedly jumped into bed.

The train pulled into the sleepy town of Tunxi around daybreak. There were no buses or taxis waiting outside the desolate station so, after twenty minutes, I asked a man waiting at the bottom of the station steps if he knew when the next bus to Huang Shan was due. He told me I needed to take a bus to the main station in the centre of Tunxi and pointed at a battered rusty vehicle on the other side of the road. Boarding the empty bus, I sat in a seat and waited for a while. A few more passengers got aboard but fifteen minutes later there was still no sign of the driver. Before long all the other locals, fed up with waiting, had got up and left so I jumped off too and set off in search of the bus station on foot with two lean, unshaven men who'd been studying a map a couple of seats in front of me. It emerged the men were related—uncle and nephew, I think—and they too were heading for Huang Shan. When we found the bus station ten minutes later, we discovered to our collective disbelief that there were only two daily bus services to Huang Shan. The first had left just twenty minutes ago and the second wasn't departing until 1pm. This was a bitter blow as it effectively meant I wouldn't be able to climb the mountain that day. I simply didn't know what do, so without rhyme or reason, I followed the two men back to the train station. In front of the station steps, a minibus was now stood with its engine running. The nephew marched up to the driver, enquired where the vehicle was going and returned a few seconds later with a beaming grin on his face. Miraculously, it was heading to Huang Shan. It turned out that the driver had been waiting there in the hope that a few more passengers would turn up before it departed. Someone up in the heavens must have been looking down on us favourably.

Quickly jumping aboard, I discovered the fare was an incredibly cheap 6 yuan. I continued to be amazed by the prices of things in China. More often than not, I'd been exasperated by the increases in travel costs compared to the prices quoted in my guidebook, yet every now and then, a fare for a journey was quoted which was five or ten times less than expected. Even then, I still suspected that there'd been some kind of misunderstanding and that the fare charged when we arrived at Huang Shan would be 60 yuan and not 6 yuan for the thirty-mile trip, but I was to be pleasantly mistaken. We set off almost straight away and the rural scenery on the way was captivating; yellow and white dry arid mountains, dams, reservoirs, lakes, rivers and streams with the clearest waters I think I'd ever seen. Passing through a succession of remote villages, I stared out of the window watching men in short sleeves chopping wood and loading carts, frothy-mouthed pigs roaming carefree in the streets, dogs yelping at the side of the road and a lone woman marching a procession of thirty ducks or more along the bank of a canal. After an hour or so, the bus made an unscheduled stop to pick up an elderly couple standing on the roadside. Although our driver was unable to start the bus up again, I was still so relieved just to be on a minibus to Huang Shan that I could only smile at this latest predicament. Eventually, we all piled out to help push the vehicle out of the roadside ditch and mercifully, just a few moments later, the engine started up and we were off again.

As soon as we arrived at the base of the mountain another hour later, I deposited my rucksack at the office of the mountain police and then, at precisely ten-thirty, began my 7km ascent to the top of the mountain. Two paths led to the peak and I opted for the easier and supposedly more scenic eastern route. Thankfully, the weather gods had come up trumps as I'd been blessed with a glorious warm sunny morning. Tying my coat around my waist, I followed the crowds through a narrow wooded valley before arriving at the foot of a long concrete staircase that gradually tapered off into the distance hundreds of feet above. The steps were inordinately steep and before long I was gasping for breath with many of the elderly locals who'd temporarily stopped to rest on their walking sticks. If this was the easier route, I dreaded to think what the west steps were like. Removing my jumper, I soldiered on but the climb was exhausting and after a couple of hours, my brow was dripping with sweat. Eventually, I decided to stop for some lunch with the provisions I'd picked up in Nanjing, well, a few cans of Coke and a couple of ham rolls. The special celebratory can of Guinness would have to wait until I reached the top. But even at this height, the scenery was delightful. Already beneath me, I could just make out the tiny ant-like figures of people setting off at the foot of the mountain whilst all around, craggy rocks clothed in ancient pines jutted up to the sky like giant stalagmites. It was the steps themselves, though, that left me dumbfounded. I doubted there could be another race in the world that would even contemplate, let alone construct, a continual flight of steps all the way up to the top of this mountain and I could only admire the Chinese for their doggedness and ingenuity. After sitting down for so long, my legs were already stiff and aching but knowing I still had a long way to go, I slowly got back to my feet and wearily continued my ascent. The number of people climbing the steps seemed to be getting less and less the higher I got, although a procession of Chinese porters, all carrying extraordinary loads on their backs continued to dash by at regular intervals. Ten minutes later, stopping again to pause for breath, I bumped into a couple of backpackers on their way back down.

'G'day,' said one, rubbing his forehead. 'How you doing?'

'Bloody knackered,' I replied. 'Any idea how much longer to the top?'

'Aw, cripes, you've got a good few hours to go yet,' grinned the other, much to my consternation. 'It'll be well worth it, though,' he added. 'The sunrise over the mountains is amazing.'

We sat on the steps and chatted for a while, talking about the respective places we'd visited and, after discovering they were planning to spend Christmas in Shanghai too, I set off again in much better spirits. Three gruelling hours later, I finally reached the top, where perched on an expansive plateau was a lone but large concrete guesthouse. Stumbling through the empty courtyard, I made my way into the reception and then waited for a full ten minutes in silence. The place felt deserted. When a man finally appeared through one of the doors clutching a pile of papers, he gave me such a contemptuous look I wondered what on earth I could have done to offend him. I asked him for a room for the night but he instantly shook his head. He told me there was no accommodation available and directed me to another guesthouse a further 3kms away. It was patently obvious that the guesthouse wasn't full but what could I do? I protested, I offered him more money, I even put on my most sorrowful face but the owner was having none of it and after some further futile remonstrations, I eventually walked out disconsolate. By now, it was nearly 6pm, the temperatures were plummeting and the daylight was fading quickly. The walk to the other guesthouse was a long one.

On my arrival at the reception of the second guesthouse, I encountered a few more difficulties completing the check-in formalities with the girl behind the desk. A group of three Chinese had just arrived, the eldest of whom came to my rescue. He was a podgy middle-aged man with a cheery face and after explaining that the receptionist wanted to see my passport, I irritably obliged. As I pulled out another can of Coke, the man shook my hand and introduced himself as Mr Fang.

'Oh Christ, not another one,' I muttered, frantically wiping myself down with a tissue after the sickly-sweet liquid had embarrassingly shot up my nostrils and sprayed my face. His companions were a quiet and unassuming couple in their early twenties who, I discovered, had met Mr Fang on the way up the mountain. As we set about completing the paperwork, I was surprised to notice that the others appeared to have been charged the same rate for the room. As a foreigner in China, I'd already become accustomed to paying three or four times more for everything than locals, although unlike many other travellers, this was something that really wasn't bothering me too much. If that was what the Chinese wanted to do, it was fine by me. Charge us ten times more for all I care. Frankly, as far as I was concerned, all those who didn't agree with the policy should shut up or just bugger off someplace else. But amidst the ensuing conversation, the receptionist then handed over some screwed up notes back to the others when she thought I wasn't looking. Why did they have to go so such lengths to conceal this? I felt like saying to her: 'Look, you don't have to hide it. Charge me more, honestly, I don't care.' Paying more was one thing; being taken for a complete imbecile was another matter altogether.

The girl was then shown to a separate room while we were taken our own male quarters. After dumping our bags, the three of us wandered back out into the corridor in search of an evening meal. The dinner hall, when we found it, was cold and sparse; in the corner of a large dimly lit room stood three empty tables whilst across the concrete floor, a corrugated iron sliding door was wide open to the starlit sky. Mr Fang manfully pulled one of the tables over to the middle of the hall under the single bare light bulb whilst the young man and I grabbed a few rickety chairs and sat ourselves down. As the girl rejoined us, I looked around hopefully for a menu or a member of staff. Mr Fang, again seizing the initiative, got up and boldly walked over to a door at the opposite corner of the room. When he returned from the kitchen a few minutes later, he informed us that there were three dishes available. After asking him to repeat the choice slowly, he said again, 'Dog, cow and pig.'

'Not dog,' I replied with a wavering voice. 'Please, not dog...umm...I think I'll go for the beef.'

But if I thought things couldn't possibly get any worse, then I was sadly mistaken. Whilst waiting, rather nervously, for the food to be served, something shuffling across the floor caught the corner of my eye. Glancing across the hall, I then watched in dismay as a huge slimy grey rat scurried nonchalantly from the open door straight into the kitchen where our food was now being cooked. I was hoping, praying even, that my eyes had deceived me when, seconds later, another one followed his mate straight into the kitchen. The others were in the middle of a conversation and worried that I'd already offended them over my persistent questioning of dog use in casseroles, I decided to say nothing. Our communal dish was served up ten minutes later and I desperately tried to reassure myself that the food in the hotpot was purely beef and they'd not thrown in an assortment of other 'meat' just for the heck of it. Deep down, though, I knew that if I was ever going to pick up an illness in China, such as the dreaded hepatitis, then this would be the meal to do it. The accompanying dish of rice was full of dirt, the cabbage the meat was served with was raw and the beef, if it really was beef, was virtually solid gristle.

It was only just gone eight when we returned to our dank squalid room for the night. My clothes were still wet and cold from the day's climbing and my feet were freezing. The young man climbed into his bed straight away and with nothing better to do, I followed suit and jumped into mine. Reaching into my bag, I pulled out the book I was currently reading—Howard Jacobson's *In the Land of Oz*—and took solace from the author's indignation on arriving with his wife in a sweltering Darwin after a 24-hour flight from London only to discover that their baggage had inadvertently been redirected to Bali. Mr Fang, however, was restless. Hearing the sound of a television movie playing down the corridor, he got up to see if he could invite himself in to watch the film, but returned soon after. The two Chinese police officers in the room had apparently not been very hospitable, so sighing heavily, he too retired to his bed.

After being woken at 5am by Mr Fang, the four of us, along

with another party staying in the guesthouse, set off in the dark to wait for the much-heralded sunrise. Passing through a landscape of upturned boulders and rocks clad in miniature trees, we meandered with chattering teeth, up and down a series of sandy tracks for a while, but after much deliberation as to the correct whereabouts of the lookout terrace, we eventually gave up the search. The consensus was that if we spent any more time wandering around, we would be in danger of missing the sun come up altogether, so we settled on climbing a long flat craggy rockface instead. After making our way to the top, we stood around for an age, clapping our hands and banging our feet together, trying to keep warm. Half an hour later, a bright stripe of orange had lit up the horizon although mysteriously, the sun itself was still nowhere to be seen. Mr Fang and a couple of the other party began to murmur and it was decided that one of the group should wander off on a recce. Our designated surveyor returned fifteen minutes later with the news we'd all been fearing. Not only had we been stood in the wrong place but we'd also been pretty much facing the wrong direction as well. This was becoming all too clear, for the now indigo sky had revealed the darker shadowy outline of a large peak directly in front of us that would have obscured the sun even if we had been looking directly to the east. Still, all was not lost. Apparently, the Fresh Breeze Terrace was not that far away and if we were quick, our reconnoitre assured us the views out to the horizon would still be spectacular. When we arrived there ten minutes later, dozens of people armed with cameras and binoculars were congregated on the terrace but this mattered little, for he'd been dead right in his assertion. As we looked out from the balcony, a vast cream sea of fluffy clouds, enshrouding the tops of the highest peaks below us, floated out way into the distance and beyond. It was a picture of complete serenity, so calm and so peaceful that it almost made you want to leap off the balcony to be swathed in these imaginary gigantic rolls of cotton wool that lay before our eyes. Such a breathtaking sight more than made up for our initial disappointment.

Soon after, I stopped for a rather muted breakfast with my

friends who, it seemed, were still feeling guilty about missing the sunrise. I sensed their embarrassment had only been exacerbated by my presence. 'What will this foreigner think of us now?' they seemed to be saying, but as far as I was concerned they had done nothing wrong. It was just one of those things and indeed, I'd hardly helped the cause by remaining quiet and impassive throughout. Trying to make light of it, I kept saying that it really didn't matter, yet in spite of my reassurances, they continued to shake their heads and apologise. Finally, I got to my feet and after thanking them and making my farewells, headed off to make my descent.

The steps seemed even steeper on the way back down the mountain and my heart went out to all the people I passed slowly trudging their way up. An hour or so later, perhaps halfway down, I caught up with two elderly Chinese men who were keen to converse in English. They were of equal build and height and dressed similarly. They told me their names, which I forgot in an instant, so I dubbed them Chang and Cheng accordingly. In the course of the many conversations we had on the remainder of the way down, they helpfully provided me with details of respective train times out of the area. With tiredness finally taking its toll, we eventually decided to make the final journey to the bottom of the mountain by bus and then stopped on a bridge in the warm midday sun to exchange addresses before they departed.

I was still on this bridge, crouched over and fiddling about with my bag, when I heard the words: 'You have just climbed de mountain?' I looked up and there, stood in front of me, was a woman in a long dark fur-trimmed coat and monkey boots. Her hair was blonde and greasy, her yellow teeth were grotesquely tobacco stained and a dinky little black leather handbag hung from her shoulder. She must have been in her late forties and if it wasn't for the fact that we were standing at the foot of an 1800 metre mountain in a relatively remote part of China, I would have probably mistaken her for a prostitute. I nodded my head in reply to her question. 'Actually,' I said, 'I've just got back down.' She proceeded to tell me that she'd travelled to the area the previous day and had spent the night in accommodation nearby. It couldn't have been that close, though, as she went on to inform me it had taken her two hours to reach the base camp on a local bus and a further two hours to get to the bridge.

'Yes,' she then proclaimed, 'I am going to climb to de top now.'

I looked at her incredulously.

She frowned. 'Dis is not possible?'

'Well, it's a very long way; it'll take a good five or six hours. You could take the bus, though,' I added. 'It'll take you half the way up so you'll at least be able to have a look around.'

Taking a step closer, she narrowed her eyes, squinted at me for a few seconds, not unlike a witch, and then said, 'You're from Australia, ya?'

'No, I'm from England, actually,' I replied. 'And you?'

'I am from Helsinki.'

In a split second, I thought of Yaan, the other Finn I'd had to endure on the Yangtze boat trip. If a scenario ever existed where the nationalities of people you met were to determine the countries you could choose to visit, then Finland would now be vying with the States for last place. Staring up to the mountain steps rather unconvincingly, she glanced back at me again, and fearing she was about to ask me to accompany her back down to the base of the mountain, I told her I had to train to catch.

'You're leaving?' she replied, looking somewhat startled.

'Yeah, better dash,' I said, picking up my shoulder bag, 'and enjoy the climb.' And with that, I was gone.

When I arrived back to the office of the mountain police early afternoon, the same guard from the previous day was sat in a chair with his feet on his desk and a newspaper on his lap. Muttering to himself, he wearily got to his feet and yawning, rummaged around for a while searching for the key to the luggage room. After a few minutes, he looked at me blankly, scratching his head. Great, I thought, I was now going to have to sit and wait here all afternoon until a colleague arrived with another key. The officer obviously had other ideas, though, because without warning, he picked up a torch and promptly proceeded to smash the outside window in front of my very eyes. After carefully removing the shards of glass remaining in the frame, he then clambered through the tiny hole, so his backside was hanging out like Winnie the Pooh, and disappeared into the dark room. A couple of seconds later, he proudly emerged with my trusted rucksack in his hand and a huge smile beaming across his face. I duly thanked him and handed him some extra currency for his troubles. This place was getting weirder by the minute!

I turned up at the station thirty minutes later in the nick of time, as a bus to Tunxi was just about to leave and, just like the outward trip, the journey back through the villages was again delightful. Children played happily amongst chickens, pigs and water buffalo that freely roamed the streets, mothers contentedly hung out washing in the late afternoon sun and, time and time again, excitable kids sprinted after the bus, their screaming voices only muted by the glass windows. Life here in the countryside seemed so uncomplicated and peaceful compared to the hustle and bustle of the cities I'd previously restricted myself to and I vowed to return to Huang Shan one day, promising to allow myself more time to explore this lovely area when I did.

When the bus arrived late afternoon, I bumped into Chang and Cheng again outside the station. They informed me that contrary to their earlier advice, there was, in fact, an overnight train heading back to Nanjing at 1am, so I quickly made a reservation and then strolled into Tunxi to get some food. As I was ambling down the street, contemplating how I was going to while away the rest of the evening before the train departed, a scrawny young man beckoned me into his eating establishment. Although there was nobody else in there, the black and white television playing in the corner of the bar looked quite inviting and the man seemed friendly enough, so I ordered some food and treated myself to a well-deserved cold beer. Tucking into a fantastic dish of spicy beef and vegetables a few minutes later, I toasted the success of my trip to Huang Shan. Inside, I was glowing with pride. In truth, I should have been exhausted from my exertions, but instead, I was bursting with energy and confidence. My decision to set off alone and veer off the beaten track had now been fully vindicated and what's more, I'd proved to myself that I *could* actually get by without any grasp of the language, so all in all, I couldn't have felt more pleased. After all the trials and tribulations of that infernal trip down the Yangtze, Huang Shan, it seemed, had finally come up trumps and suddenly everything was rosy again in the Garden of Eden.

Still faced with a wait of over five hours until the train arrived, I idly wandered back to the station. Spotting Chang and Cheng sitting in the corner of the waiting room, I went over to join them. Although their grasp of English was good, we'd already been through all the ritual questions earlier that afternoon so, before long, I reached into my rucksack for my book again, and as I did, spotted my travel Mastermind game amongst my belongings. Taking it out, I pointed to the box to see if they were interested in playing. Although not familiar with the game, they nodded excitedly, so after doing my best to explain the object of the game, we sat down to play. Immediately, five or six men gathered around to look on. To their credit and my surprise, Chang and Cheng picked up the rules in no time at all, quickly establishing the significant differences between a black peg, a white peg and no peg at all. After an hour or so, I sat back and let them play each other. By now, the crowd around us had swelled considerably. In fact, we were surrounded by a circle of onlookers three to four deep who continued to watch on intently as each game unfolded and such was the excitement that, after a while, many of the crowd were arguing amongst themselves as to who was going to play next. I was amazed that the game had sparked off such a reaction. The time flew by after that, and over the ensuing hours, people who were continuing to arrive at the station kept wandering over to see what all the fuss was about. Some even looked genuinely disappointed when they realised that they had to leave the waiting room to board their trains. When midnight arrived, the games were still going on in earnest and by the time our train pulled in half an hour later, all but the finer details of the letter I'd be writing to Waddingtons had been drafted in my head. I had a marketing proposition for the manufacturers which, if they liked the sound of, could just mean I might find myself back in Huang Shan sooner than I'd anticipated. All I'd need was a bigger rucksack to accommodate all the games.

CHAPTER 7

THE GRAND CANAL

ROYAL BLOOD

18th–21st December 1989

As soon as the train pulled into Nanjing mid-morning, I met Chang and Cheng on the platform and, after thanking them for all their help, duly presented them with the Mastermind game. They were reluctant to take it at first but I insisted and they were overjoyed. They told me there was a train to Wuxi leaving in ten minutes so we quickly made our farewells and I dashed off to get a ticket. Tearing back to the platform minutes later, I just managed to board the departing train in time and then slept for the entirety of the three-hour journey.

Judging from my guidebook, there didn't seem a lot to see or do in Wuxi. In fact, I'd only come here in order to take a five-hour trip down the Grand Canal to Suzhou and hoping to make this trip the very next day, I decided to book a ticket there and then. After finding a hotel, I'd then be able to spend the remainder of the day wandering around Wuxi at leisure. So I marched over to the China Travel Service just outside of the station only to discover they didn't make boat bookings. When I asked the girl about hotels, she quoted an exorbitant 410 yuan a night for the Liangxi Hotel (my guidebook gave a rate of 67 yuan for a double room in the same hotel and then went on to state that there was certainly cheaper stuff available). 'Is there anything cheaper?' I asked. She shook her head and walked off. Undeterred, I wandered over to the CITS office on the other side of the station. The clerk here was far more helpful and although they too didn't make bookings for boats, the man kindly told me that a no. 20 bus would get me to the booking office on the other side of town. The bus arrived shortly afterwards, but as soon as I got on board, I felt a sharp pain in my stomach. Quickly jumping off, I realised I needed to get to a toilet...and fast. Rushing back into the station, I made a beeline for the waiting room where I was sure there'd be a loo, but the attendant refused to let me in without a ticket. Hurrying back to the CITS office, I told my friend, the booking clerk, of my predicament. Walking me back across the waiting room, he explained my plight to the attendant who reluctantly let me through the gate. Scurrying down the steps, I threw down my rucksack, barged into the cubicle and unfastening my trousers just in the nick of time, sat there ignominiously emptying my bowels as the tears of relief rolled down my cheeks.

With this little crisis averted, I waited outside again for another no. 20 bus. However, when I got to the booking office alongside the canal fifteen minutes later, I discovered they only issued tickets for trips to Hangzhou, another town at the southern end of the Grand Canal. I asked where I could book a ticket to Suzhou and was told that the booking office was back at the train station. Consulting my guidebook, I discovered there was a second ticket office in the centre of Wuxi. When I got there half an hour later, I was again told they didn't issue boat tickets to Suzhou. They too directed me back to the train station and when the bus eventually pulled up outside the steps nearly two hours after I'd first arrived, my frustrations finally caught up with me and for the very first time in this trip, I lost my temper, thus committing the cardinal Chinese sin.

Before I could disembark, a throng of passengers tried to clamber past me to board the bus, as seemed to be the custom here in China. Picking up my rucksack and grunting with clenched teeth, I abruptly barged three or four oncoming passengers back onto the pavement, and as I alighted, a predictable commotion ensued. Hurling my rucksack to the ground, I rested my backside on my pack and, closing my eyes, sat on the pavement with my head in my hands. Of course, I really shouldn't have let something as petty as this bother me. I mean, at this precise moment, people all over the world were being killed, tortured, raped and heaven only knows what else, but as the lone backpacker can all too easily testify, when you find yourself with so much time on your hands, testing little challenges such as these often take on the utmost importance, and when they ultimately get the better of you, you can't but help to take them to heart. When I looked up some moments later, a group of over twenty Chinese were staring at me inquisitively. One of the onlookers approached and before he had chance to open his mouth, I explained to him very very slowly that I needed a boat ticket to Suzhou for the following morning. He informed me foreigners couldn't purchase tickets from this office and pointed to another booking office in the train station. 'I DON'T WANT A TRAIN!' I screamed. The young man swiftly stepped back a few paces. Pulling out my phrasebook, I quickly leafed through the pages looking for the Chinese word for boat but couldn't find it, so on a scrap of paper, I drew a child's picture of a ship instead, and then beckoned the man back over. Seeing the picture, he nodded excitedly. Minutes later, I was following him back through the streets to yet another booking office. When we got there at just after 4pm, I realised it was the first office I'd tried three hours ago. And to make matters worse, it was now closed. The young man, looking around in desperation, grabbed the arm of the first person he could see, a small wrinkled-faced man dressed in a navy tunic and flat cap who was shuffling along the side the canal. After interrogating him for a couple of minutes, he turned to me smiling. It appeared that the old man was a fisherman, who reckoned that I'd be able to buy a ticket for the boat to Suzhou from the dockside in the morning. 'But the boat leaves at six-thirty,' I cried. They conferred again and the young man assured me it would be no problem: the fisherman was getting the boat himself so he'd be there in the morning to help me out. Still not entirely convinced, I thanked the two of them for their help and trudged off to find a room for the night. When I got to the Liangxi Hotel, the receptionist informed me that the rate was 110 yuan. Immediately, I remonstrated with her over the price. She told me I could get a discount if I took a room in the older building.

'How much would it be with discount?' I asked.

'Seventy yuan,' she replied.

'Done,' I said slamming my hand down on the counter.

After the 24-hour journey from Tunxi, I was totally shattered but when I was shown to my room, my eyes lit up, for sitting on a set of drawers in front of the window was a television set. By now, it was late afternoon and although all my plans for a leisurely walk around Wuxi had effectively been dashed, I suddenly realised that for the first time in more than ten days, I'd finally got my own space back. After six days on the Yangtze, three days in Nanjing with Bob, a night on the mountain and another on the train, I now had the luxury of my own room, and furthermore, a room with a television set. Coming across the unopened can of Guinness at the bottom of my day-pack, I decided that after the afternoon from hell, this would be a good a time as any to celebrate, so I quickly pulled back the ring only for it to snap off in my hand with can still intact. Sighing heavily, I reached for my towel, took a quick shower and was about to go back out to get some food when I noticed the curtains hadn't been drawn. I reached up but they wouldn't pull together, so I yanked out a chair to stand on and as I did, caught the lead from the television set, which jerked out of its socket. I tried to switch the set on but now that didn't work either. And the curtains still wouldn't close. Then to cap it all, as I reached down for my trainers, I stubbed my toe on the foot of the chair. Deciding to cut my losses, I promptly jumped into bed, concluding this was plainly not my day. The only thing to do was to bring it to an end and start afresh in the morning.

The alarm on my travel clock was bleeping. I fumbled around for the switch on the bedside light and reluctantly pulled back the covers. It was 5.15am. Ten minutes later, heaving my rucksack onto my back, I made the short walk back to the canal. Much to my relief, the fisherman, instantly recognisable by his flat cap, was standing outside the booking office. After helping me purchase my ticket, he then led me to our boat, which we boarded just as the sun was coming up. The boat itself was small and dingy. Indeed, all the descriptions I'd read of the boats hadn't been that favourable and whilst I agreed with one traveller's comments that the windows were both filthy dirty and low to the surface, I saw no real reason to complain when the fare for the five-hour trip was a paltry $2\frac{1}{2}$ yuan (50 pence).

No sooner had we sat down in the squalid vessel, the old man brought out of his pocket a crumpled bag of nuts, which he placed on the table between us. He gestured for me to help myself and whilst the nuts were addictive, the cigarettes he insisted I took each time he lit up were not, and left me coughing and spluttering, much to his amusement. Although we tried to converse, his knowledge of English was as limited as mine of Chinese so we settled on nods, grins and chuckles. Before long, four or five others joined us around the table but the language barriers persisted, so after a while, I delved into my rucksack for the pile of photographs I'd brought with me to give out to people I met. In with the pictures, I happened to come across half a dozen postcards of London that I'd completely forgotten about up until now. I handed the man one of the cards, a lovely picture of the Royal Family laughing on the balcony at Buckingham Palace. The man, staring at the picture for an eternity, eventually handed it back to me but I gestured to him that it was his to keep. He was beside himself

and sat there with a beaming smile on his face, banging his fist
against his heart. As he passed the card around the table to the
others, I pointed to one of the figures on the front and said:
'Charles.'

'Sharl?' repeated the man.

I nodded and smiled. 'Chaaarrrles,' I said again.

'Shaarles?...Shaaaarl?' He pointed to another figure.

'Elizabeth...Liz-a-buth,' I said, pointing to the Queen.

'Lisbuh?'

'Yep, that's it, you've got it'

Then, one by one, he pointed at the others.

'Ann...Aaaaann,'

'Aaann?' He pointed back to Charles.

'Chaaarles,'

'Shaaarles?'

'Di-a-nu.'

'Di-a-nu? ... Shaarles?' The others looking on were now
whispering excitedly.

'Oh God, umm, lets see now...um...Jook-ov-ed-in-bu-ruh.'

'Ed-in-bu?'

'Jook-ov-ed-in-bu-ruh.'

Then abruptly reversing the roles, the old man said: 'Acun.'

Ac-our?' I replied, looking around wondering just who or
what 'acour' was.

'Ac-un,' he repeated.

'Ac-oon?'

'Ac-un,'

'Ac-un?'

For a few seconds, the man conferred with his colleagues
and then with a glint in his eyes said: 'Shik-en-ze-ba-ba.'

Now they were getting difficult. 'Ba-ba?'

'Ba-ba,'

'Cheek-ee-ze-ba-ba?'

'Shik-en-ze-ba-ba,'

'Ba-ba?' I said again, totally nonplussed as the others
collapsed into fits of giggles around me. 'No, I'm afraid I don't
know ba-ba.'

'Ba-ba,' he repeated a final time before closing his eyes, as if bringing the lesson to an end. Slowly leaning back in his seat, the old man continued to stare at the picture and every so often, glanced up at me and then returned to the postcard, smiling endearingly. After a few minutes it dawned on me that he thought it was me in the picture. I was not sure whom exactly, although I guessed it had to be Edward. I quickly pointed to the picture again. 'No, you see this lady here, she is the Queen.'

'Aaaarh...Keen,'

'No, no, she is the Queen of England...you know, Queen of Eng-er-land? That man there, he isn't me. That is one of her sons, err...babies? You know, um...bambinos?'

But it was no use. Try as I did, he just continued to stare at the picture and smile at me and the others were clearly none the wiser. As the boat chugged its way merrily down the Grand Canal, I wondered just what on earth I'd done. I looked at the old man, who would no doubt go home and tell his family that he had met someone on the boat. He'd show them the postcard, which somebody would eventually recognise as the Royal Family, and the man would point at the picture and tell them it's me, the Prince he'd met on the boat, and I knew that there was absolutely nothing I could do about it.

Suzhou had been described as 'the Venice of the East.' It was famous for its production of silk and the Italian traveller Marco Polo was said to have been very taken with the city when he'd arrived here in 1276. So, for that matter, was I, well at least on first impressions. Passing a succession of narrow canals lined with graceful willow trees, cobbled streets full of pretty whitewashed houses, and picturesque bridges that spanned the quaint waterways, Suzhou indeed looked an enchanting place and a suitably nice one to while away a few days. Jumping off our boat, I quickly said goodbye to my friends and set off to find a hotel.

An hour later, after procuring a room, I took an early afternoon stroll and as I was passing along one of the main streets, a young Chinese student came bounding up to me on the pavement. Holding out his hand, he promptly introduced himself as Lu Xiao (pronounced *Loo Sheeow*) and then asked me where I was going. After informing him I was planning to spend the afternoon wandering around Suzhou, he asked if he could accompany me so that he could practise his English. In truth, I was quite glad of the company and hoping he'd be able to tell me a little bit about the city, I nodded my head. He turned out to be an enterprising character and his English was already surprisingly good. He was also very enthusiastic.

'You want to buy some silk?' Lu Xiao enquired seven seconds later. 'Suzhou very famous for silk,'

'Yes, maybe,' I replied.

'Come on, I take you to shop.'

'What now?'

'Yes, it is near.'

'Woah, woah, woah, hang on a minute!'

'You not want to go?'

'Well, no, not today, maybe tomorrow.'

I then made the foolish mistake of asking if he could recommend a barber's in Suzhou. Again, he tried to take me to one there and then, and again, I tried to explain that I didn't want to go immediately. A few minutes later, passing through a local market, I stopped to ogle a vast plate of freshly cooked dumplings sitting on a table on one of the stalls. They smelt delicious and my mouth was already watering so I impulsively reached down for my money belt only to hear: 'No, no, you should not eat this food, this food is dirty.' Reluctantly, I refrained and moved on.

Lu Xiao proceeded to lead me on a leisurely two-hour tour around Suzhou, over bridges, along canals and through the city's many gardens and he didn't stop talking and asking questions throughout. When we eventually came across a barber's, I finally had the excuse I needed to part company from Lu Xiao who, by now, I thought would go on talking to midnight. He asked if we could meet again the next day. Although he was a bit overbearing, he certainly meant well, so we arranged a time and place to meet, then I thanked him for showing me around, he thanked me for helping him with his English and I hastily retreated into the barbers.

Ten minutes and the equivalent of fifty pence later, I emerged sporting a severe crew cut and made my way back to my guesthouse. When I got to my room, I met the ironically named Marco. 'Not Polo?' I jested when he told me his name but choosing to ignore the remark, he stood there in silence and the joke was lost. Marco was a Canadian in his mid-thirties. He was tall and emaciated with a receding hairline and big beady eyes that were superfluously magnified to almost frightening proportions by the thick lenses of his glasses. He also looked terribly ill and shameful though this was, I couldn't help wondering if he'd contracted Aids and was here on some kind of final swan song. Just as the perfunctory small talk was petering out, the dormitory room swung open and in burst Mark.

Marco jumped up from his bed. 'Haaaaayy, welcome back Mark!'

Mark was shaking his head 'Wuxi, God, what a terrible place. I couldn't get a hotel room anywhere, what a fuckin' place! What a nightmare!'

I knew exactly how he felt after my trials and tribulations there the previous day. Mark was a backpacker from New Zealand who'd stayed in the dormitory the previous night. He'd headed off to Wuxi earlier that morning, but unable to find a room, he'd decided to cut his losses and had returned to Suzhou this afternoon by train.

'Fuckin' Wuxi, fuckin' place, fuckin' nightmare.'

He was also lanky and bespectacled, with a mop of long curly hair but in spite of his current disposition, seemed a far more laid-back character than the up-tight Marco.

Just then, came another knock at the door. Marco got up and welcomed in a couple of young Chinese students he'd apparently met earlier that morning. Quite why he'd invited them back here, I wasn't too sure and I was rather uncomfortable with the way he was leering at them as they sat on his bed swinging their legs. It was the kind of look that the evil child catcher gave the kids in *Chitty Chitty Bang Bang*. After sitting around for a while in awkward silence, Mark suggested we venture out for some food. He was keen to return to an eating-house that he and Marco had frequented the previous evening, but after putting on our coats and traipsing around the streets for twenty minutes, we were unable to find it so Mark left it to Marco and his two friends to find somewhere else—his only requirement was that it served beer. Marco also had a stipulation; it had to serve vegetarian food. I was ravenous and just wanted to find somewhere to eat as quickly as possible while the two Chinese just shrugged their shoulders. When we somehow managed to stumble across a vegetarian beer-serving restaurant a few minutes later, the waiter tried to usher us upstairs but Marco insisted on a table on the ground floor. The Chinese students conversed with the staff and then explained that they only served vegetarian food on the first floor, and for a while total confusion beckoned. Eventually, we were given a table on the ground floor and whilst Mark took charge of the drinks, Marco ordered the food. I was not that impressed when it arrived. It was the first time I'd tasted bean curd and I wasn't at all comfortable digesting these strange chewy tablets, so when he wasn't looking, I deftly lifted up my boiled cabbage with my chopsticks, and hid them in with the rice.

As the others carried on eating, I couldn't help noticing the faces of the two Chinese students, who'd been knocking back their beers surprisingly quickly, were now visibly flushed. Slightly perplexed, I made some comment about this to Mark who was sitting next to me.

'Mmm,' he replied, lowering his voice. 'I've seen this happen a number of times with the Chinese. I'm told it has something to do with their metabolism.'

Marco, who'd been listening in on the conversation, peered over to the students and grinned. 'Gee boys, is it only your cheeks that go red when you drink beer?'

I glanced at Mark in astonishment. Shaking his head ruefully, he raised his hand in the air, caught the waiter's attention and promptly ordered another round of beers.

After all the plates were cleared from the table, the conversation returned to the rather familiar subject of Japan. Marco, who'd recently been teaching English in Tokyo, was now in his element. 'Well,' he chirped, 'people ask me why I went to Japan and I tell them "Money," it's as simple as that,' his eyeballs just about to pop right out of their sockets. A few minutes later, I recited the story Dave had told back in Wanxian of how Japanese sons often ended up sleeping with their mothers, but Marco said that in all the eight years he was there, he had never heard of anything like that. He did, however, use this as a cue to then describe a series of other dubious sexual practices in excessively lurid detail.

Mark, to my relief, preferred to talk travellers' stories and before long, we were taking it in turns to describe various characters we'd met on our travels. He told us his account of meeting a legendary Australian who had supposedly been travelling all over the world non-stop for twenty years. Apparently, this fabled wanderer had claimed to have visited every country in Asia and Africa and was now planning to do the same in South America. His intention was to carry on travelling until he'd visited every country in the world.

'God, how depressing,' I cried. 'How on earth is he going to settle down if he ever returns to Australia? Where, for a start, would he go for his holidays?'

It was a sobering thought and for a few moments we all sat around in contemplative silence. 'Anybody come across any Finns on their travels?' I eventually asked, in a light-hearted attempt to get the conversation up and running again.

'Finns?' exclaimed Mark. 'Mad as hatters, the lot of them.'

'Oh gosh, yes,' said Marco, 'I met quite a few in Tokyo. They don't half like their drink, you know.'

'What about that one in the dormitory last week? Remember her?'

'Oh, you mean the woman who was walking around Suzhou barefoot?'

'Yeah, her, that's the one. I met another a couple of weeks ago in Shanghai. He wore one of those long Chinese army coats.

Never took it off, wherever he went. Even wore it to bed. Completely off his trolley he was...' and for the next twenty minutes, I could barely get a word in edgeways.

After the meal, the students headed off and the three of us, returning to the hostel, retired to our beds. Sometime around midnight, though, I was woken when another backpacker came into the dormitory to claim the fourth remaining bed. He fumbled around in the dark, continually tripping over the belongings that were scattered around the floor, and when he decided to make a couple of calls in fluent Mandarin from the phone in the room, I could see the other two visibly stirring in their beds. Just as I was wondering why he hadn't bothered to turn the light on, the new arrival found his voice. 'Hey, anybody mind if I just turn the light on a minute?' He was American.

Just after 7am, he did a repeat performance. Evidently not satisfied with his previous night's efforts, he clumsily stomped around the dormitory room for an eternity, repeatedly banging into things, dropping objects on the floor and yanking all kinds of things from his rucksack before cramming them back into different compartments. Eventually, he stood up, heaved his rucksack onto his back, looked back to his bed for a last time to make sure he'd left nothing behind and, as he walked out, slamming the door behind him, I could almost hear the collective sigh of relief.

Mark and Marco were leaving later in the day, so I was wondering whether I'd have the room to myself that evening, but when I got back from a morning wander, I was somewhat surprised to discover that the bungling American had returned. He introduced himself as Richard from San Francisco. He, like Marco, had been teaching English to students and he too was tall and effeminate. He also carried a little shoulder bag with him around the room and even took it with him into the bathroom when he went for a shower. He, though, had a far more genial demeanour than his Canadian counterpart.

Early in the evening, Lu Xiao phoned. I had arranged to meet him earlier in the afternoon at Zhouzheng, a renowned

Suzhou garden, but after standing around in the cold for over thirty minutes, he hadn't shown up, so I'd whiled away some time instead leant over a bridge watching a group of a dozen or so men, stood foot deep in basketball-sized cabbages, unloading consignments from boats on the river below. As it happened, it turned out I'd been waiting for him at completely the wrong gate. He asked if I wanted to go out now so we arranged to meet for a bite to eat. When I told Richard where I was going, he looked a bit forlorn so I asked him if he wanted to come along too. When the three of us met fifteen minutes later, I realised that this was a bit of a mistake as I'd forgotten that Richard spoke Chinese, so not for the first time in China, I found myself sitting in silence as the other two happily conversed across the table. In fact, as time passed, though, it came as something of a relief not to find myself on the end of Lu Xiao's persistent questioning. Before we departed, he asked me if he could take my address so that he could write to me. At first, I was a bit reluctant to give it to him, as I knew it would be a long time before I arrived home, but a look of sadness suddenly fell across his face.

'David, my good friend,' he said in a wavering voice, desperately trying to hold back the tears, 'he come to Suzhou five weeks ago. He promise to write to me. Every day I wait for his letter but no letter arrive.'

After explaining to him that I was travelling on to Australia, I told him if he gave me his address, I would promise to write to him in due course.

Lu Xiao met me again on the platform early the following morning and, completely out of the blue, presented me with a silk purse to 'give to a girlfriend' and a Cloisonné and brass key tag shaped in the letter 'J'. Taken aback by his generosity I thanked him profusely. I was also rather surprised when he offered to purchase my train ticket for me, as he knew full well he'd be charged a cheaper price, and I *had* been under the impression that he was a very law abiding citizen. (He'd been visibly upset the day before when he'd discovered I had in my possession a wad of renminbi notes, believing that all foreigners should only be carrying the official Foreign Exchange Certificates.) I had promised myself that before I left the country, I'd make at least one 'hard-seat' train journey in China, the cheapest and most basic class of rail travel. The journey to Shanghai was just over an hour so I'd decided that this would be that journey, not exactly a hardship, I know, but I gratefully took up Lu Xiao's offer nevertheless and, sure enough, he returned a few minutes later brandishing a hard-seat ticket for just 4 yuan (80 pence). Shaking his hand as the train pulled in shortly after, I thanked him for all his help, and again promised I'd write. As soon as I slammed the carriage door shut, though, I realised I'd not got a hope in hell of getting a seat. Each carriage was hopelessly overcrowded with early morning commuters so, standing in the aisle, I quickly reached for my Walkman. Just after nine, the train pulled into Shanghai Central. Or so I thought.

CHAPTER 8

SHANGHAI

A CHINESE CHRISTMAS

21st–26th December 1989

'Shanghai, Paris of the East, Whore of China, Queen of the Orient; city of bums, adventurers, pimps, swindlers, gamblers, sailors, socialites, dandies, drugrunners. Humiliation, indignation, starvation, back-alley corpses, coolies, rickshaw drivers, deformed beggars, child prostitutes, scab-ridden infants, student activists, strikers, intellectuals, communist activists, rebels, foreign armies supporting foreign business interests. Trendsetter, snob, leader, industrial muscle, the name that keeps the Beijing bureaucrats awake at night...a hybrid of Paris and New York in the 1930s with millions trampling the streets where millionaires once trod...one way or another Shanghai has permeated the western consciousness.'

What my *Lonely Planet*, however, failed to mention was that there was a Shanghai East station where, just after nine, I unwittingly got off the train. Consequently, I spent two intensely frustrating hours roaming streets that according to my maps did not exist and although I proceeded to ask a succession of pedestrians for directions, it was to little avail. Still struggling to get my bearings, I cursed my guidebook, I cursed Shanghai and I cursed China. When I finally made the discovery that the station I'd alighted from was not in fact the Central Station at all, I didn't know whether to laugh or cry and for a few moments, I sat on the pavement picturing John Cleese in the episode of *Fawlty Towers* where he's seen hopping up and down in a frog-like squat across the hotel lobby. Slapping my forehead, I felt like doing the same.

One of the discoveries I'd made so far on this trip was that whenever I go for long periods without food, my irritability increases to frightening proportions. Throughout the train journey from Suzhou, my stomach had been reminding me, through a succession of embarrassingly loud churning noises, that I'd forgotten to take breakfast that morning so when I stopped off at the post office twenty minutes later to see if I had any mail and found myself being kept waiting for what seemed like an eternity, I began to get impatient. Indeed, by the time I was directed to a third different counter over an hour after I'd first arrived, I was close to boiling point and upon reaching the window, was all set to vent my anger at the unfortunate clerk:

'Do you know how long I've been queuing up in this office? You don't? Well I'll tell you how long. Over an hour. A bloody hour, that's how long. Half an hour being sent from counter to counter and then another thirty minutes waiting in this bloody queue. It's just not good enough, you know. Quite frankly, I've got far better things to be doing with my time than wasting half my day in here. Do you know, I haven't eaten since last night and I've still got to find a room yet, and what happens? I find myself stuck in here all morning.'

But such was the unexpected and totally endearing smile I received from the girl behind the counter, it completely took the wind out of my sails and I just stood there quietly huffing and puffing as she checked my passport photograph. Then, gaily jumping off her stool, she pulled out a pile of mail from the allotted pigeonhole, quickly flicked through the letters and postcards and skipped back to the window before calmly handing me an aerogramme with my name on. I murmured a thank you and, red faced, shuffled out of the hall. Outside, sat on the steps of the post office, I quickly tore open the letter from my mother. She had written it just after I'd phoned her from Beijing and it started off with some wise words of advice:

Dear James,

It was lovely to hear your voice this morning at 8am. You sounded so clear, confident and happy. I presume the first few days have probably been the hardest and in many respects, the most exciting when the adrenaline is at its highest. To travel so quickly from the west to the east you are plunged straight into it—the noise, smells, languages and atmosphere of a different country. I both admire and envy you, but you deserve it because you have worked so hard towards this trip. Go everywhere and try everything, you may never have the opportunity again and don't worry too much about the expense—you can make that up later in Australia.

She then went on to thank me for all of my support when my father was ill and described how proud she felt when I'd departed. All of this put my near outburst in the post office fully in perspective and I berated myself for even thinking about shouting at the clerk. Indeed, by the time I'd finished reading the letter, I felt so guilty that I marched back into the post office to apologise for my tantrum. Unfortunately, the clerk was no longer behind her counter.

Half an hour or so later, feeling ten times better after a slap-up Kentucky Fried Chicken meal, I got my first glimpse of the Bund, the long tree-lined promenade that runs alongside the murky Huangpu River. Across the busy six-laned road, facing out to the water, stood a lengthy procession of stately and grandiose buildings that immediately took my breath away. By far the two most imposing of these were The Hong Kong and Shanghai Banking Corporation Building, housing a large Roman styled dome, and The Customs House right next to it, surmounted by an equally impressive clock tower, the largest of its kind in Asia. Like so many of the buildings on the Bund, they'd been built in the 1920s and their facades were characterised by a series of huge granite pillars so prevalent in the architecture of this period. Further along were a string of other government buildings, consulates, banks and hotels, all extravagantly constructed in a variety of styles: renaissance, gothic and classical. Still startled by such opulence, I strode up the promenade whistling along to the tune of Glen Miller's *In The Mood*, finally beginning to appreciate just how decadent and exciting a city this must have been in its heyday.

Upon reaching the Pujiang, Shanghai's official backpackers' hangout, I booked in for three nights, which would take me right up to Christmas Eve. Depositing my rucksack on an empty bed, I quickly returned to the streets to check out a few of the big hotels to see where I could spend Christmas Day. (Although this wasn't entirely in keeping with the backpacking ethos, I was damned if I was going to let this stop me seeing-in the day in style.) First stop was the Shanghai Mansions, just across the road from the Pujiang. They didn't look particularly inspiring, so I wandered further along The Bund and tried the Peace Hotel. The reception here was plush: wood panelled corridors, art deco lights and a thick and inviting deep red carpet. Furthermore, the rooms were moderately priced at $35 a night and they had a big gala Christmas meal planned for Sunday evening. Now this was a bit more like it! But just to put my mind at ease, I then tried the Jinjiang Hotel, a swish and modern establishment, located some twenty minutes downtown in the city's French Quarter, but nice though the lobby looked, its marbled floors, tinted windows and recessed halogen lights didn't seem indicative of Shanghai, or China for that matter, so scurrying back across the packed streets of the city, I booked a room at the Peace Hotel including a table for the Christmas Eve meal.

The dormitory I was allotted in the Pujiang was the real type of dormitory room I'd been expecting to see when I first arrived in China but had still yet to come across: large sprawling quarters full of bunk beds, belongings scattered everywhere, and half a dozen backpackers sat around chatting. There must have been about eight or nine of these dormitories altogether, each accommodating around twenty people, so when I wandered down to breakfast the next morning and found the vast dining hall packed with other travellers, I felt like the new schoolkid walking into the canteen for the first time. My nerves were slightly eased somewhat by a few of the longer-term guests who were glancing up at the speakers on the wall and sniggering. Above the sounds of clanking cutlery and excited chatter, *Last Christmas* was being played over the hotel tannoy which, judging by the their reactions, was clearly not a daily occurrence. Helping myself to a couple of rounds of toast from the self-service, I tentatively lowered my tray onto one of the long tables and sat myself down amongst a group of western backpackers.

Encouragingly, just a couple of seats down, I happened to notice one of the two Australians I'd met on my climb up Huang Shan. As he looked up, I grinned and waved to him down the table, but to my consternation, he just stared at me blankly and returned to his corn flakes. Just then, a couple of lads from my room sat themselves down on an adjacent table. One was dressed in a long green army coat, whilst perched ridiculously on the top of his head was one of those Russian fur hats, although in truth, it looked suspiciously more like a dead cat. The other, dressed more conservatively in pullover and jeans, sported a mulleted haircut: short on top and around the ears and long at the back. It was a hairstyle that looked crass even at the height of its fashion and if either of them was in genuine need of a hat, it surely had to be him. When I heard their cockney accents ('Cor blimey, Dave, that tea is rank!'), it dawned on me. These were the two culprits who'd kept everyone awake in the dormitory the previous night. After returning at some ungodly hour, they'd sat on their beds getting noisily drunk on rice wine, irritatingly repeating over and over again that the only two words they knew in Chinese were 'rice' and 'beer', which continually sent them into fits of laughter.

As I started tucking into my toast, the conversation around the table again revolved around Japan. Just what was it with Japan? This mystifying country I knew so little about was seemingly on the tip of everybody's tongues and I was beginning to rue the fact I hadn't included it on my itinerary too. This time the subject was the role of the woman in Japanese society. An oriental American sitting opposite spoke of her time temping in Tokyo where she'd been consigned to making teas and coffees all day long for her office colleagues, something she clearly hadn't been too enamoured with. Comparisons were then made with Chinese women who, I was reliably informed, were often seen fighting in streets. Although this was news to me, everyone agreed they were not to be trifled with. When I returned to the table after a fruitless search for a sachet of jam, the conversation had moved on to hairdressers. Only then did it occur to me that my Australian friend probably hadn't recognised me because of my severe haircut in Suzhou. I quickly leant across the table again.

'You don't remember me, do you?'

He squinted at me for a few seconds.

'Huang Shan? Last week? You were on your way down?'

'Shit, yes, you've um...' then he rubbed a clenched fist over his head.

'Yeah, I went to the barbers but didn't know the Chinese word for 'stop.''

Everyone chuckled and I was chuffed.

Still keen to ensure I got to Hong Kong in time for New Year, I called in at the train station later in the morning and booked a ticket to Guilin for Christmas day night, shocked to discover that the journey time was a whopping thirty-six hours.

This translated to two consecutive nights aboard the train, which would easily make it the longest journey of the trip so far. Then, after purchasing another ticket for a day trip to Hangzhou departing the following morning, I bumped into a pony-tailed Japanese American who'd been occupying one of the bunks opposite me in the dormitory. On the way back to the Pujiang, he informed me that he'd just made a reservation for the train to Guangzhou.

'Cor, bet that's a long journey!' I said.

'Thirty-two hours,' he replied gravely.

'Booked a sleeper, though?'

'No, I'm going hard seat.'

Hard seat for a thirty-two hour journey? I stared at him in astonishment. Earlier on, over breakfast, the Australian guy had mentioned that he and his mate were travelling to Beijing the next day, a journey that would take seventeen hours. They too were travelling hard seat...Why? Were these people stark raving mad or what? I didn't understand it. Why put yourself through so much hardship? In my book, any journey over a few hours is a long one so the very least you do is afford yourself some comfort. Sod the expense!

Late afternoon, I ventured out once more, this time to the main shopping street of Nanjing Donglu. The pavements were packed with early evening shoppers, the bright lights of department stores illuminated the darkening sky and there was a real Christmas feeling in the air. As I had nothing in my rucksack suitable to wear to Sunday's Christmas meal, I purchased, after much dillying and dallying, a pair of shoes and shirt and, relieved that I'd now be able to go to the ball properly dressed, headed back for some food. Passing a narrow alleyway a few blocks on, I caught the whiff of some glorious savoury smells of stir-fried cooking. So intoxicating were they, that I had to go back and have a look. When I did, I saw, under a string of bright white light bulbs, a long row of food stalls veiled in clouds of steam and smoke rising from the blackened pans of wincing cooks who were busily conjuring up arrays of snacks – spring rolls, dumplings and pancakes – for early evening shoppers. I'd been promising myself for weeks that I would stop to eat at one of these stalls, which I'd seen in virtually every city I'd been to, and I couldn't resist any longer. So without further ado, I boldly pulled out a stool from beneath one of the tables, sat myself down and promptly ordered a bowl of steaming minced pork dumplings. And they were delicious. 'Dirty food' indeed! I knew I shouldn't have listened to Lu Xiao back in Suzhou. On the way back to the hotel, the Bund was alive with activity: flashing neon billboards rippled and pulsated, foghorns blasted from tugs on the river, the bells on the clock tower chimed seven and tomorrow was Christmas Eve. Maybe Shanghai wasn't such a bad choice after all.

By all accounts, Marco Polo was even more impressed by Hangzhou than Suzhou, for he described it as the most beautiful city in the world so when I got up the next morning at dawn, I had high expectations for the day ahead. What I was certainly not expecting to see when I wandered down to the reception of the Pujiang was the torrential rain that was cascading down outside. I waited around in the lobby for a while, hoping it was only a passing shower, but ten minutes later there was still no let up, so running out in the darkness, I made a dash for the bus stop and in seconds, I was drenched. When I reached the station twenty minutes later, it was still chucking it down remorselessly, so I quickly boarded the train, found my compartment and teeth chattering, took my seat, praying that the skies would clear. I was sharing the compartment with a Japanese family. There was a grandfather and grandmother, and a husband and wife with a son and daughter around five and two years of age respectively. Looking on in fascination at the family as we finally set off, I quickly realised they'd prepared meticulously for the journey. The father had one of those large teabag-like things that he was using to keep parts of his body warm, while the grandfather favoured a space-age metallic blanket, which was draped over his lap. They had their own state-of-the-art thermos flask and they also had a small box of toys at the ready, just in case the impeccably behaved children finally succumbed to boredom. Since they'd prepared for every eventuality, they didn't appear unduly bothered by the rain that continued to lash down outside. They seemed a very close-knit family too, continually laughing amongst themselves, which I found quite endearing. After a while, we got chatting. The grandparents told me that they had been in London just a couple of weeks ago and proceeded to reel off the sights—Westminster Abbey, St. Paul's Cathedral, Buckingham Palace—they'd visited in the two days they were there. I asked them if they liked London. They nodded excitedly. 'And Shanghai?' They nodded again, though this time not quite as enthusiastically. The children's parents, who'd been busily unwrapping some pre-made sandwiches and snacks from their bags, had just set up a little picnic on the side table, so as they all settled down to eat, I proceeded to stare out of the window at the filthy black skies as the rain continued to drum against the window. It looked like the daughter had got the right idea for she was now curled up and fast asleep, resting lovingly on her grandmother's shoulder, totally oblivious to the downpour.

When we arrived just after midday, the rain was still teeming down, so having come to the conclusion it would be futile to explore Hangzhou in such atrocious conditions, I marched straight to the ticket office to book a seat on the first train back to Shanghai. The first train heading back, though, was not leaving until 4pm, so faced with a $3^1/_2$ hour wait, I eventually decided that I should brave the wet to at least see some of Hangzhou, so the moment the conditions slightly eased, I traipsed off in the drizzle down to the famous West Lake. Just a few minutes later, though, the heavens opened again so I dashed into the foyer of a hotel to take shelter and waited for it to clear. By the time it eventually had half an hour later, I didn't really care much more for the West Lake, so I hurried back to the station and on the way there, happened to bump into my old friend again, the intrepid Finnish woman I'd met at the foot of Huang Shan. Now I don't know about you, but I greatly value my own body space. There exists around my body, especially around my head, a six-inch sacred zone and anything that tries to enter that zone without prior permission will find themselves unceremoniously pushed, swatted or shoved out of the way. As this ghastly woman proceeded to interrogate me again, I found this very space being continually encroached. It was extremely unnerving and all I could do was keep stepping back. In fact, I was retreating so quickly that if she carried on much longer, I feared that I *was* going to end up down at the West Lake after all. And since she was asking all the usual questions—how long had I been in China, which places had I visited and where was I heading—I realised that she didn't even remember me from Huang Shan. This I found even more disconcerting. Then, all of a sudden, she broke off halfway through another question, looked me up and down for a few seconds and through squinted eyes said: 'Wait a minute, I tink I know you, you're from Australia, ya?'

I checked into the Peace Hotel at 10.30 the next morning, which was just about as early as I could. After spending over an hour basking in the luxury of the room, I felt like a little boy who'd just been given the keys to a toyshop. I bounced on the bed, I flicked through all the channels on the TV, I pulled open all the wardrobes and doors, I checked out the view of the waterfront from the window, I turned on all the taps in the bathroom, I read the directory listing the hotel's facilities, I inspected the mini-bar, I even phoned down to reception and childishly hung up as soon as they answered. Suitably pleased with my new luxurious surroundings, I looked around wondering what to do next. Deciding I needed to take in some of the Christmas atmosphere, I therefore took a walk down the Bund. The streets outside, though, were hopelessly packed, so I quickly returned to my room and soaked for over an hour in a gloriously hot steaming bath. Lying on the bed in my hotel dressing gown, I then waited apprehensively for the Christmas meal wondering what I could expect. Would all the diners be Chinese or would there be foreigners there too? Would they all be old people? What would everybody be wearing? What would the food be like? Who would I be sat next to? I got up and looked in the mirror. My face was gleaming. I tried on my new shoes and then my shirt, which was somewhat on the small side, although there was little I could do about that now. I took it off again and paced around the room nervously. I had a shave. I got dressed again. I lit a cigarette. I helped myself to a beer from the mini-bar, followed by a vodka chaser and then just after 5.30, I crept down to the eighth floor.

Already, a long orderly line of Chinese dressed in dinner jackets and ball gowns were queuing in silence outside the Dragon and Phoenix Restaurant, and the large dining room, visible form the corridor, looked quite magnificent. Strategically positioned under a row of sparkling crystal chandeliers across a shiny wooden floor were twenty or so long dinner tables, all covered by pristine starched tablecloths and adorned with Christmas crackers, champagne flutes and candelabras, whilst stood in the corner was a huge fir Christmas tree, elaborately decorated with gold tinsel, burgundy baubles and foil wrapped chocolates. A few minutes later, as I was shown to my table, I glanced around at the other guests. Except for an elderly couple at the far end of the room, they were all Chinese. Taking my place at the end of the table, three middle-aged businessmen sat alongside me deep in conversation. I nodded to them briefly as I sat down. They nodded back cursorily, then quickly returned to their discussions. Just then, a couple, possibly in their late teens or early twenties, were shown to their seats opposite me. As the maître d' went around pouring out the champagne, I started chatting to the young lovers who, holding hands under the table and repeatedly gazing lovingly into each other's eyes, were quite charming. Although their English wasn't that good, I managed to ascertain that she was a flute player and, I could only assume, rather an acclaimed one at that. Right on six o'clock, a troupe of waiting staff carrying dishes of prawn cocktails emerged from the kitchen and promptly served up our first course. No sooner had we finished these, bowls of oxtail and sherry soup arrived at our table. A dish of steak and salad called Tournedos Rossini quickly followed and, concerned that the main course would soon be upon us, I glanced around wondering whether I should be ordering a bottle of wine before it arrived. Eventually managing to catch the eye of a waiter, I pointed at a carafe on a nearby table and a minute or so later, he returned with the wine list. As he waited at the end of the table, the young couple, shifting uncomfortably in their seats exchanged awkward glances. Surmising that they couldn't afford the 70 yuan being charged for a house white, I said that it would be my pleasure to order a bottle for the three of us. It was, after all, Christmas Eve, and this was a time for giving. The dishes, meanwhile, continued to arrive post-haste: the turkey was served not long after, followed quickly by a disappointingly bland Christmas pudding, an array of cakes, a selection of fruit, a large plate of cheese and biscuits, and finally a selection of coffees. In fact, by eight o'clock the meal was all but over and I couldn't help feeling that the whole thing had been far too rushed.

But as soon as the tables had been cleared, the lights were dimmed and the pulsating thud of drumbeat resonated around the hall. Spotlights from high in the gantry flashed into action, floodlighting the catwalk that ran from the stage to the centre of the hall, and many of the other diners quickly manoeuvred their seats around it, muttering expectantly to each other. Then, to rapturous whistles and applause, three stilettoed Chinese models clad in chiffon evening dresses of scarlet, emerald and azure emerged from the side of the stage. Assembling in a line side by side, they paused for a few seconds and then started to march down the catwalk, their shoulders strutting back and forth with every step. As they reached the end of the platform, I sat in my seat gaping at their beauty, their elegance and their grace. Hands on hips and heads leant back, they held their pose for a few seconds, staring out to the back of the hall as guests desperately fumbled around for their cameras and then they turned to stride back in perfect synchronization. As soon as they left the stage, three more in subtler pastel colours appeared to more gasps and cheers and, equally as stunning, glided towards us, their diamante necklaces and tiaras glistening beneath the lights. The thirty minutes that followed were simply delightful as I happily sat in my seat attempting to pick out my favourites from the twenty or so different models, trying to spot them each time they returned in a different guise, desperately hoping sooner or later I'd catch their eye. But these girls were consummate professionals and my gazes were not once returned. And besides, why for one moment would any of them be remotely interested in a stubby-fingered, five-foot seven, gawking Welshman leant back in his chair at the back of a hall in a shirt that was three sizes too small? The show culminated in a grand mock wedding finale and as the models returned to the stage for a final time to take their bows, they finally let down their guard and smiling vivaciously, waved back to the guests.

The stage was then hastily cleared to make way for the jazz band. As soon as the music started, virtually all the elderly diners got up to dance and before long, as the band alternated between old-time tunes and carols, I found myself alone on my table. The young couple—who evidently weren't staying in the hotel—had, by now, left in a taxi; the three businessmen had moved on to the downstairs bar, and whilst a few families were still sat around their tables chatting, all those who hadn't already retired to their rooms were still happily waltzing around the dancefloor like there was no tomorrow. Realising that my night had come to a premature end, I reluctantly got to my feet and as I silently wandered off and waited for the lift out in the corridor, I could already feel a headache coming on from the champagne.

I wasn't too sure what to make of Shanghai. It had been described as the 'Paris of the East' and when I'd first arrived here, I'd been tremendously excited, but it hadn't quite lived up to the initial expectations and I pictured the city more as how I'd imagined Chicago or New York to look like in the 1930s: tall grey buildings with spiralling stairwells, sinister dark alleyways, cumbersome iron bridges, incessant foghorns and a permanent mist rolling in from the water. It was also cold and cloudy and everything seemed grey—everything: the sky, the river, the buildings, the people, all grey. Perhaps I'd been expecting too much from Shanghai by comparing it to a London or a Paris. This was, as I kept being reminded, China after all.

Arriving at the train station early evening for the eight hundred mile journey south, I spotted a disgruntled European who I recognised from the Pujiang a couple of nights back. He came over and as we started chatting, he asked me what I made of Shanghai.

I wiggled my head. 'Yeah, it's okay, I suppose,' I said. 'I thought it might be a bit livelier. And you?'

'I hate dis place,' he replied before launching into a scathing verbal assault on every single aspect of the city: the people, the accommodation, the nightlife, the food, the traffic, even the dogs. He was clearly not enamoured by Shanghai. Slightly puzzled by his accent, I asked him where he was from.

'Ha, I am from Finland, ya, you know Finland?'

I didn't and judging by its people, I really didn't want to. Nodding my head nevertheless, I glanced down at my wrist and exclaimed, 'Shit, got to dash!' then legged it off towards the platform.

CHAPTER 9

YANGSHOU

NEW FRIENDS

27th–29th December 1989

At long last, we were finally approaching Guilin. In truth, the 36-hour journey from Shanghai had actually passed quite quickly, though it didn't get off to a particularly good start. Seeing as it was still Christmas Day, I'd decided soon after boarding the train to treat myself to a cup of whisky from a half bottle of duty-free I'd purchased at Heathrow. Topping it up with Coke, I settled myself down on the top bunk of the empty compartment and pulled out my Walkman, but as I went to reach for the drink, I knocked the beaker over, spilling the contents all over my jogging bottoms. To make matters worse, the sweet and sticky liquid had also slopped onto the sheets of my bed. Undeterred, I poured myself another cup and sat on the bunk below listening to some music for a while. Later in the evening, I was joined by a middle-aged couple. The man, who looked uncannily like Mike Reid (the big chirpy cockney comedian who later went on to play 'Frank Butcher' in

Eastenders), appeared besotted with his partner, although from the resulting conversations that ensued, I learnt they weren't actually married. In fact, both had children of their own which made their little affair all the more intriguing. It emerged that they were teachers on some kind of school outing and after snuggling up together, they quickly began to indulge in playful small talk. Leaving the lovebirds to it, I climbed back onto my bunk, pulled back the whisky stained sheets and rolled over for some shuteye.

I was fully expecting to be woken on Boxing Day by the blinding rays of the early morning sun but the skies were still depressingly gloomy and leaden. Still, I was adamant I wasn't going to let this get me down, so I reached into my rucksack and pulled out my Dictaphone. A couple of days before I'd left to come away, the same group of friends who'd try to stitch me up on my final night in London had driven up to my parents' farm in Wales. We'd arranged to spend the night doing a pub-crawl in one of the local towns, along with two of my brothers and younger sister. In high spirits, I'd decided to take the Dictaphone out with me, primarily to get some practice using it but also to record a few messages from my friends and family for posterity. All too predictably, very early on in the evening, my trusted and endearing mates had forced a number of foul tasting cocktails down my neck and, whilst I'd spent much of the subsequent evening throwing up in pub toilets, the others decided the farewell messages could still be recorded without me. I had the tape of this night with me and decided that this would be a perfect time to play it back for the first time. Within seconds, I was having a real job to contain my hilarity and by the time I reached the end of the recording, which culminated in a rousing high-pitched a-cappella rendition of an old college drinking song, tears of laughter were rolling down my cheeks. I was even compelled to pass the recorder over to my bemused fellow passengers so they could have a listen too.

After a couple of hours' reading, I spent the afternoon lying on my bunk planning my itinerary for the next few days trying to decide whether or not I should make a dash to Hong Kong to arrive there in time for New Year. I dozed for an hour or so, then, around teatime, a guard wandered into my compartment and rattled off a series of questions in Chinese. I looked at him dumbly so he wandered back out scratching his head. He returned a few minutes later and ushered another young traveller into the compartment.

'Hi, I'm Tony,' said Tony in an Australian accent.

I jumped down from my bunk and shaking his outstretched hand, introduced myself. The guard then said something to Tony, who nodded his head thoughtfully. 'He wants to know if you want to book a table in the dining carriage tonight.'

'No, I'm all right,' I replied, 'I've brought some food with me.'

Tony translated this to the guard who then wandered back out again.

'Heading to Guilin?'

I nodded. 'And you?'

'Mmm, me too. I'm with my folks actually.'

Tony, it emerged, was a student from Melbourne University who'd been studying in Shanghai. He was travelling with his parents who had decided to come up from Australia to pay him a Christmas visit.

'Yeah,' he sniggered, tilting his head backwards, 'we're all back there in hard seat,'

I looked at him a little puzzled, failing to see what was tickling him so much. He went on to tell me they'd all booked hard seat from Shanghai, but his father hated smoking and the constant sight of Chinese people spitting repulsed his mother so they'd managed to upgrade to soft seat while Tony had remained where he was. I got the feeling his parents hadn't heeded their son's advice when they'd made the reservation, which seemed to explain why Tony was so amused. I thanked him for his help and offered him my copy of *The Hong Kong Standard*, which he gratefully took back with him to his smoke-filled carriage.

Early in the evening, I took a stroll up the train to stretch my legs. When I returned, there were several new faces in the compartment. One was an old man sitting opposite, wearing a pair of thick-rimmed spectacles. His eyes seem sad and I couldn't help but wonder why. Of course, there could have been a whole multitude of reasons, but the one thought that kept coming back to me was how unfair it was that most Chinese were prohibited from travelling overseas. Here was I, freely ambling around this man's country without a care in the world and there was he, virtually imprisoned in his own back yard. The man sitting next to him, meanwhile, perhaps in his early sixties, was dressed in a shirt and tie and possessed the most extraordinarily long fingernails that my eyes constantly returned to. He was travelling with a colleague, slightly younger but also smartly dressed. When the pair returned from the dining carriage later in the evening, the older man asked me what my profession was. I told him I'd been working for an American bank in London.

'And how much money did you earn?' he asked.

Up until now, I'd been reluctant to divulge details of my earnings when I'd been asked this question. Nevertheless, I calculated my salary into a daily rate and informed him and the other passengers that were now listening in, that I'd been earning around 70 dollars a day. As soon as this was translated, there were looks of astonishment and bewilderment all around. One middle-aged man who worked in a silk factory quickly worked out that his daily salary came to no more than two dollars. I tried to justify the differences in the relative prices of houses and commodities yet even allowing for this, I realised, somewhat to my embarrassment, that the gaps in the respective incomes were still vastly disproportionate. Somebody then asked what my father's occupation was. I explained he owned a small farm and proceeded to make a series of 'baah' and 'mooing' noises to describe the livestock he kept. They then asked me about the rest of my family. My oldest brother happened to work in the sports department of the BBC. Not quite sure how to explain this, I scribbled out a football pitch on a piece of scrap paper. Faced with perplexed looks, I thought of China and drew a table tennis bat and ping-pong ball instead. In a split second, one of the passengers excitedly grabbed the arm of the sad-faced old man I'd been thinking about earlier. 'This man here, he is...err... ping-pong champion.'

'Noooaaah,' I teasingly replied.

'He is, he is, he is very, very good ping-pong!'

'Noooaaah, I don't believe you.'

'He is best ping-pong player in China, he is!'

Racking my brains, I desperately tried to think of the name of the UK table tennis champion.

'Ha, what about Desmond Douglas then?' I chirped a few seconds later.

The sad-faced man who, up until then, had restricted himself to nodding his head, excitedly blurted out, 'Argh, Desmun Dug-ass, errr, Dug-ass, I beat Dug-ass in Shanghai, I am...errr, I am better than Dug-ass.'

Although I wasn't entirely convinced of the old man's credentials, it did transpire that he'd won some kind of tournament in Shanghai back in the 60s. Not to be outdone, I proclaimed I too had represented my country at a sport and then spent a troublesome hour trying to convey to my fellow passengers, through a series of sketches, the tremendous skills and intricacies required to represent Wales at Subbuteo. In hindsight, I should never have bothered.

Notwithstanding this, the evening had passed quickly and pleasantly and about nine-thirty, we settled down for our second night's sleep aboard the train. Just as I pulled the bed sheets over me, though, Mike Reid let off two of the loudest and unheralded farts I'd ever heard. Up until then, in the five weeks I'd been in China, I've never heard a local person fart and when I woke up just before daybreak, I swear I was still chuckling to myself.

Now, though, peering out of the window into the drizzle, I was sitting up in my seat, for we were finally approaching the town of Guilin, much renowned for its surrounding scenery, and, in particular, the huge limestone peaks so often depicted in Chinese scroll paintings. On first sight, these strange looking pinnacles looked quite surreal, like giant tree-clad volcanoes rising through the mist. And the closer we got to these extraordinary haunting peaks, the more lifelike they became and they seemed to take on an almost paternal character. Towering down over the town, it felt like they were all standing there with their arms folded keeping a protective eye over proceedings in their little commune below. Finding yourself in such an unfamiliar landscape can often be unnerving, but accustomed to the mountains of Wales, I immediately felt at home. As soon as the train pulled into Guilin, however, I quickly jumped aboard a local bus and set off for Yangshou, a smaller and quieter town set in the heart of the countryside fifty miles further south.

Arriving early afternoon, I found myself a room in no time at all and headed back out for a wander. The cafes and bars that lined the main street all seemed to be geared towards backpackers with menus advertising burgers, chips and pancakes and the atmosphere instantly took me back to that memorable morning in Bangkok when, pulling up on Khao San Road in the just a couple of hours after I'd touched down, I'd received my first stirring insight into backpacking culture. Just as I was thinking back to those few minutes when the four of us—myself, Gibbo, Caroline and Pat—had remained sat in our stationary tuk-tuk on the busy side street, totally overwhelmed by the plethora of guesthouses, snack stalls, travel agencies, video cafes, and souvenir shops, staring incredulously at the pavements overflowing with fellow travellers, I suddenly heard my name being called. In a flash, I swung around and glanced over my shoulder. 'Jim, over here!'

Sitting around a table outside the rather ironically named 'Hard Rock Café' were Jasper and Piere, grinning away like a pair of Cheshire cats. Rushing over to join them, we greeted each other like long lost friends.

'So, how long have you been here?' I asked pulling up another chair.

'A few days,' replied Jasper.

'Look's like a nice place,' I said, as Pierre began tucking in to a truly mouth-watering banana fritter. Ravenous after my long journey, I quickly caught the owner's attention, pointed to the plate and ordered one for myself. Then we started catching up with all we'd been doing.

'So where did you go after Chengdu?' I asked. 'Did you make it to Emei Shan?'

Emei Shan was one of China's four holy mountains and the Danes had been hoping to travel there after I'd left them in Chengdu. After my trip to Huang Shan, I was desperate to find out how they'd got on.

'Ya, it was good,' said Jesper, 'although we didn't make it to de top.'

'Why not?'

'Because of de weather, dey had to close off de top part of de mountain.'

'We had to sleep in a monastery on de way up,' chipped in Piere, wiping his mouth with his hand.

'Wow, bet that was good!' I said.

'No, it was freezing,' said Piere again, 'we hardly got any sleep.'

'And what was Kunming like?'

'Good,' they replied in unison.

'But the journey dere,' added Jesper, shaking his head

'Why, what happened?'

'We had to travel in hard seat.'

'How long was the journey?'

'Eighteen hours.'

'Shit. Eighteen hours in hard seat?'

'Ya, and den we missed de connection, so we had to sleep on de station.'

'Shit.'

'Piere, tell Jim about dat night we got drunk?' said Jesper, as a bowl of muesli arrived at the table.

Piere frowned for a second. 'Oh my God, I'd forgotten about dat.'

It turned out that one night in Kunming, they'd returned to their accommodation blind drunk only to find the front door of the guesthouse had been locked. They decided that the only thing they could do in the circumstances was to break a window to get back in, and the next morning they'd been made to cough up 300 yuan to the owner of the establishment for the damage. As soon as they finished telling this story, I couldn't help thinking that, although I'd been enjoying travelling by myself again in the past couple of weeks, I really was missing out by not having anybody to share my adventures with. Stories such as this, it seemed, became that much funnier when you had somebody there with you when they happened and this was a downside of travelling alone that I simply hadn't considered before. For a few seconds, I even began to question whether I'd have been better off sticking with the Danes after all.

Anyway, we were still chatting an hour later when they introduced me to Slim. Slim was the owner of the Hard Rock. He sat down to join us and immediately started to tell us all about how he'd set up his business, and then reeled off all his ambitious plans for improving his establishment. Given that his place appeared to be one of the most popular hangouts in the town, he appeared to have done remarkably well for himself considering he still could have only been in his early thirties. And like all good entrepreneurs, he quickly saw business opportunities when they arose, for within minutes, he'd already talked me into sending him back some tapes and posters for his restaurant when I got to Hong Kong. Soon after, the Danes got up to go. They were heading back to Guilin later that afternoon before flying on to Shanghai so we all shook hands once more.

'Maybe we'll see you in Hong Kong?' said Jasper before we parted.

'Yeah, now that *would* be good,' I said, and this time I really meant it.

Upon returning to my guesthouse, I learnt from the receptionist that this had been the first dry day of the week. It therefore seemed worth trying to get as much done in what remained of the day as possible, so I decided to book a late afternoon fishing trip on the Li River. As the receptionist started filling out the appropriate forms, I asked her what the forecast was for the next few days.

'Rain,' she replied shaking her head.

'What, rain tomorrow you mean?'

She nodded her head and smiled.

'And Friday?'

'Rain Friday too,' she said, putting her hand over her mouth to contain her laughter. So much for the warmer climes of the South! She then informed me that the fishing trip would only go ahead if they could find some more guests to go on the trip, so while the staff rallied around phoning other hotels, I went back out for another walk.

As I made my way down to the river, it began to dawn on me just how lucky I'd been in encountering so few Westerners thus far. Ever since Tiananmen, the number of overseas visitors to the country had plummeted, and as a result, the Chinese seemed mightily relieved to see foreigners back on their soil, for wherever I went, I'd generally be welcomed with open arms. It felt as if I had the whole the country to myself and I was thriving on the attention. From hereon in, however, it appeared all this was about to change. There were discernibly more backpackers and tourists in Yangshou than any place I'd previously been to, and these numbers were only likely to increase the closer I got to Hong Kong. Still, for the time being I wasn't unduly bothered, for back outside, the profusion of lush vegetation—rubber plants, palms, cassias and towering clusters of bamboo—was incredibly soothing on the eye, whilst down at the river, the families of dozing water buffalo lying motionless in the reeds seemed to perfectly encapsulate the laid-back feeling of the town.

Passing the bus station on the way back up the street, I couldn't help noticing three backpackers who, by the looks of things, had just arrived. Surrounded by a large group of hawkers, one of the girls was jabbing her finger at one of the men.

'Look, we want a guest house, not a hotel!' she screamed.

Without second thought, I wandered over to see if I could help.

'I don't fuckin' believe these people,' cried the shaven headed girl again. She turned around to her colleagues—a tall

127

gangly guy with dreadlocks and another girl dressed in a long cashmere pullover and monkey boots—and then tilted her head. 'C'mon, lets get out of here.'

Finishing their cigarettes, the couple wearily got up off their rucksacks and duly followed their unrepentant leader as she barged her way through the crowd.

'There's actually three or four cheap guesthouses just down the road,' I mumbled as she stormed past. Stopping in her tracks, she turned on her heels and scowling, replied: 'Look mate, if we'd wanted your help, we would have fuckin' asked for it, right.'

With my peace of mind shattered in an instant, I turned around and carried on walking, wondering why on earth I'd bothered.

By the time I'd returned to the guesthouse, I'd fallen into a mood of deep despair. I suppose this was a result of a few things, primarily other backpackers who were plainly ignorant and rude, and also the fact that I'd found myself thinking more and more about my family and friends over the last couple of days. I'd now been away five weeks; easily the longest time I'd been out of the UK, so maybe this was also beginning to play a part. Were these, I wondered, the first signs of homesickness setting in? Perhaps it was the weather too. I had really been expecting sunshine in Yangshou and now that I'd arrived, it was still just as murky and overcast as it had been in Shanghai. When I returned to the hotel, though, I was greeted with some good news. The fishing trip was going ahead at seven, so I decided to return to Slim's. Hopefully a good meal and a couple of beers would raise my flagging spirits.

The Hard Rock was empty, save for an American family sat in a corner. From their conversations, I managed to deduce that the son had been studying in China and had recently been joined by his parents and sister who were here on holiday. They were discussing the wave of anti-smoking lobbies currently sweeping across their homeland, whose cause the father was fully behind. 'Should consign them to their own bars so they can all die in peace,' he bellowed, rubbing his hands expectantly. My instant reaction to this nearly compelled me to light up on the spot, but that would have been childish, even by my standards. Slim, as I said, was a natural entrepreneur and seizing the opportunity, quickly went over to their table with some of his merchandise and within minutes, the father had purchased 'Hard Rock Cafe' T-shirts for all his family. Thankfully, it wasn't too long before I was given some respite from his booming voice when another backpacker entered and pulled up a chair at my table. He introduced himself as Brad and proceeded to tell me in a broad Australian accent all about the wild Christmas he'd had in Yangshou, culminating in a 24-hour drinking session, which had apparently started on Christmas Eve and gone all the way through to 2pm on Christmas Day. He was now hoping to travel to Kunming but had already attempted to set off on three separate occasions without apparent success: the first time he'd missed his bus completely, the following afternoon he'd turned up at the station only to discover there was no service that day, and earlier that morning, he'd boarded the bus, but had felt so bad that he'd had to return to Yangshou after four hours. I would have been slightly more sympathetic if he'd not been wearing another one of those long olive green military coats, which looked fine on Chinese Commander-in-Chiefs but ghastly on western backpackers. He then went on to talk about the strange couple he was currently sharing a dormitory with, a sweet and unassuming couple who I'd briefly met myself back in Shanghai. 'Shit, these guys just aren't on the same wavelength,' he exclaimed. 'D'you know, earlier this morning, I asked them what the exchange rate was when they left Shanghai. The bloke stood up, nodded his head and said: "Yes, it is cold isn't it, I think I'll put an extra jumper on"!'

Returning to my guesthouse for the evening fishing trip, I met our guide in the reception who, after walking me over to another hotel, introduced me to Reilly and David, two chatty and frightfully well-spoken middle-aged Canadians booked on the same trip. Both were bearded and bespectacled and both were unashamedly camp. David, who'd been teaching in the northeast city of Shenyang, had recently been joined by Reilly,

129

who'd travelled there to give a lecture, and they'd spent the last few weeks travelling down through China together. As we followed our guide through the streets towards the river, Reilly asked me where in China I'd been.

'Well, I flew into Beijing.'

'Oh, Beijing, lovely, lovely'

'And then I travelled down to Xian'

'Yes, Xian, the walled city. That's just what we did.'

'And then I went down to Chengdu'

'Oh, Chengdu, we did that as well, lovely, lovely.

'And then I went on to Chongqing'

'Chongqing...Did yoooouuuu? Chongqing, David, he went to Chongqing!'

When we reached the river, an elderly Chinese man, dressed in a fur hat, anorak and wellies, was waiting by the shore in a long canoe-like boat. A lantern hung from a pole at the front of the vessel whilst further back six or seven cormorants were perched at regular intervals all along one side. Another American family joined us soon after, and we all jumped aboard a separate motorised vessel with our guide, following behind the old man who was stealthily manoeuvring his canoe down the river with a long paddle. After ten minutes, the motor was turned off and as we drifted towards the centre of the water into the night, all of us looked on in fascination when the birds were finally let into the freezing water one at a time. The water itself was crystal clear and, in spite of the darkness, we were still able to see each of the birds glide along underneath us, resurfacing every time a couple of minutes later with a slippery fish in their beaks. More often than not, the old man would wrest the flapping fish from the cormorants' bills and then chuck it into a large wicker basket at the end of the boat, although a few times, he'd leave the birds to help themselves to their catch.

'I'm sure they're getting more than their supper's worth,' I whispered to David.

'Oh my dear fellow, their necks are tied,' he replied.

'Their necks are what?'

'They're tied.'

130

I stared at him blankly.

'Their necks are tied to stop them swallowing the fish.'

'Aah, right,' I muttered under my breath, wishing I'd kept my big mouth shut.

Half an hour or so later back at the shore, we clambered off the boat in the dark and, rather comically aided by David's failing torchlight, fumbled our way up the path back to the main street. Passing a candlelit bar where several other backpackers and tourists were sat around chatting, we decided to stop off for a drink. After ordering some beers and a bowl of fried peanuts, we then spent a couple of delightful hours chatting about the joys of travelling in China, the friendliness of the people and the respective sights we'd seen, and it was incredibly refreshing to meet people who, by and large, had the same positive feelings towards the country we were travelling through. So many people I'd spoken to, up until now, had continually complained about China. Admittedly, travelling through this country had not been without its problems, as I could all too easily testify, but my overriding feeling was that if you persevered, then you'd eventually get your just rewards. David and Reilly went on to talk about their travels in the UK. They told me how much they'd enjoyed both Scotland and Ireland and the more they spoke, the more I began to realise, much to my embarrassment, how little of my own country I'd visited. After running through my itinerary again, I then recited the story of the old fisherman on the Grand Canal barge who'd mistaken me for a member of the Royal Family. They were suitably amused. 'Oh David, isn't that just such a funny story!' said Reilly, who'd been knocking back Tequila chasers in between beers and was keen to carry on drinking. David, however, wanted to get back for an early night, so we eventually exchanged addresses and agreed to meet up again in Hong Kong in a couple of weeks' time. Lying in bed later on, I again thought how nice it had been to chat for a few hours in the company of a couple of people who didn't have all the usual pretensions and hang-ups of other travellers and who weren't looking to constantly plague you with travel advice. After the afternoon, this tonic couldn't have come at a better time.

There was no need to get out of my bed the following morning to check the weather as I could hear the rain teeming down outside. Turning over again, I went back to sleep, hoping it was just a shower but an hour later, there was still no let up. The receptionist, it seemed, had been spot on with her forecast. I spent a few more hours confined to my room, wondering if my plans to hire a bicycle and explore the countryside would be thwarted. Early afternoon, becoming increasingly hungry and impatient, I took a short stroll around to Slim's and berated him for making the rains return. Just after I'd sat down, though, the American family sauntered back in, and because I couldn't face listening to the father droning on again for another afternoon, I politely cut short my breakfast and trudged back to my room. Then, at precisely 3pm, the drumming on the roof finally stopped and the skies lightened. Without haste, I donned my hat and gloves, rushed out to hire a bicycle and headed off along the countryside roads to Moon Hill, a renowned local beauty spot. When I got there forty minutes later, it seemed my long wait had finally been worthwhile for the views, only enhanced by the precipitation, were breathtakingly captivating: vast fields full of bright red poppies, their flimsy creped heads silently fluttering in the breeze under the shadows of the surrounding peaks; a farmer in a lampshade hat, slowly leading a lone water buffalo across a paddy field, and the craggy peaks themselves— covered in vegetation and shrouded by mist—now looking distinctly ominous and looming so close up. I spent a wondrous hour roaming the countryside, continually reaching for my camera and although I didn't get to see Moon Hill itself, a pinnacle famous for a moon-shaped hole in its peak, this no longer seemed to matter.

CHAPTER 10

GUANGZHOU

CHAMBER OF HORRORS

30th December 1989–1st January 1990

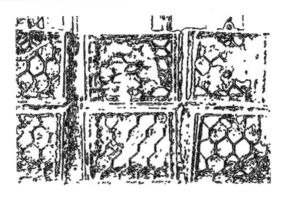

The activity in the market was frenetic: hordes of sodden locals, laden with bags of produce, scurried between the stalls in the morning drizzle; turtles of all different sizes lay dormant in buckets; snakes and gigantic eels restlessly swirled around in tanks; and goats' and sheeps' heads dangling languidly on rails, stared vacantly into space. Fish were being expertly spliced open with razor sharp knives, their innards sploshing all over the wet bloodied tables; chickens and ducks hung upside down, skewered on hooks, and tiny kittens meowed from their cages. Rabbits peered out of wicker baskets, pigeons and birds, also behind bars, chirped merrily away, and the big sad eyes of racoons caught your every glance. Two graceful young deer, concealed in a cage partially covered by blankets, paced up and down anxiously and next to them, silently lay a couple of

133

mysterious looking creatures that I could only assume were anteaters.

I'd come down to Qingping market to see for myself just how notorious a place it was. I had read about the market, I had seen pictures of it on television and I'd heard other backpackers in the youth hostel talking about it earlier in the day. I can't remember who it was exactly who'd described it as notorious, but the word 'notorious' is not one you forget in a hurry. Indeed, it's one of those few words that conversely arouse both curiosity and an uneasy sense of foreboding. If something is described as notorious, you want to see it but you don't. It's a gamble. You know it'll be bad, but how bad? Do you run the risk? More often than not, the desire to find out for yourself if this thing, whatever it is, should really be referred to as notorious, outweighs the alternative of burying your head in the sand and staying clear. Well, it does for me. The Qingping market can, without a shadow of a doubt, rightly claim to be notorious.

Crowds of people had gathered around one stall in particular, so creeping over, I stood on tiptoe craning my neck. It was then I saw the steaming marble white torso of a creature that, just seconds before, had been skinned alive. At first, I couldn't make out what it was. Its trunk was the size of a lamb, though its ears were noticeably more pointed but when I spotted the fur on its feet, I realised, to my utter horror, that the poor creature was a dog. Well, it *had* been a dog a few minutes ago. Just then, in front of my very eyes, its throat was slit and a jet of crimson blood squirted onto the pavement. Clasping my arms around my stomach, I turned around and, staggering off, desperately tried to stop myself from vomiting.

After leaving Yangshou, where it had rained for virtually two whole days, I'd arrived in a drizzly Guangzhou (formerly Canton) the previous afternoon. Having read that buses and trains often get fully booked at weekends, I was keen to arrange my onward transport to Hong Kong well in advance, so I'd called in at the CITS office at the station where I made a snap decision to book a ticket on the overnight boat on Monday night. This meant I'd be spending New Year in Guangzhou.

As a result, I decided to seek out the city's youth hostel in the hope I'd meet some other backpackers who'd be up for partying the following night. But when I arrived half an hour later, saturated and forlorn from the relentless rain, I had a tricky decision to make. Did I opt for my usual single room where I could catch up on my recordings at leisure or should I check into the dormitory where I'd have a far better chance of meeting fellow travellers? The prospect of forsaking my privacy ultimately proved too much of a sacrifice although as soon as I pushed open the door, I knew I'd made a grave mistake. A decidedly rickety looking bed, covered by a mustard coloured blanket blotched with unsightly stains, took up virtually all of the room. Beige ceramic tiles mysteriously stopping halfway up each wall convinced me on the spot it had once been a bathroom and above these tiles, hung tattered peeling layers of putrid turquoise wallpaper. But what was concerning me more than all of this tawdriness was that there was something missing. My eyes darted circumspectly around the room. I walked over to the wardrobe and yanked open the doors, but it was empty. I knelt down and looked under the bed, but there nothing on the floor except for a couple of empty beer bottles. I got back to my feet and scoured the room once more, to no avail. The sad fact of the matter was there was no television. I wouldn't have ordinarily minded, but I'd spent much of the train journey reading the schedules for the forthcoming week and one of the Hong Kong channels just happened to be broadcasting a number of live football matches from home, so I'd carefully torn out the listings and tucked them into my trouser pocket for safekeeping. In a fit of fury, I reached back into my pocket, promptly screwed up all the cuttings and hurled them into the bin. Then, after changing my clothes, I'd set off in the rain to the market where the heartbreaking sight of those poor despairing creatures quickly made me realise how petty and insignificant all my gripes had been over a room with no telly.

Encouragingly, when I returned to the youth hostel late in the afternoon, several other backpackers were sat around chatting in the bar area. Taking a seat nearby, I pretended to write a letter so that I could eavesdrop on the conversations, hoping an opportunity would present itself for me to join in with the chat, but my well-intentioned plan failed to materialise. Situated a few blocks away, however, was the luxurious and towering White Swan Hotel, so with nothing much better to do, I decided to call in there instead. Planting myself down on a sofa in the lobby, I picked up a copy of *The Hong Kong Standard* and then read of more gloom and doom: firstly the editorial column that predicted that the recent uprising in Romania would only lead to more unrest in China, and then of the previous day's earthquake in Newcastle, Australia which had left over twelve people dead and hundreds injured. One small article, though, tucked away on one of the inside pages, did bring a smile to my face. It described how Chinese students had recently resorted to dropping small glass bottles on pavements as a means of protest against their much-maligned leader. The significance of this rather odd ritual was apparently all to do with the surname of Deng Xiaoping, which roughly translated meant, 'little bottle.' Now that *did* merit a chuckle.

Noticing, on one of the leaflets, that the hotel possessed an in-house sauna, I wandered over to the reception to make some enquiries as to the price. To my surprise, it was substantially cheaper than I'd been expecting so I decided I'd indulge myself the following afternoon in preparation for the evening's festivities. But before I returned to the youth hostel, there was one more thing to do, and that was treat myself to an excessively expensive dish in the hotel restaurant. One of the rules the leadership had passed since I'd been in China was that on leaving the country, any surplus Chinese FECs could only be exchanged for half their original value. I was damned if I was going to give back a single paise of my hard earned money to the Chinese Government. Charging foreigners more for hotel rooms and train fares was one thing, but this new policy stank of blatant extortion, so I was determined to spend all of my remaining currency in the days that followed. The mouth-watering platter of Malaysian food—chicken satay, nasi goreng and prawn rolls—that followed was thus the perfect start to my little spending spree.

Situated on the Pearl River, that bisects the southern part of the city like the Thames does London, Guangzhou was renowned for being a major port and trading centre, and its history dated back over a thousand years. The Portuguese were the first Europeans to set up a trading base in the 16th century and were followed soon after by the Dutch, and then the British who brought with them vast quantities of opium from India to exchange for silks and teas. When the Chinese tried to prohibit the trade of the drug in the 19th century, the British responded by opening fire on Chinese ports. This precipitated the Opium Wars and these in turn eventually gave rise to Hong Kong being ceded to the British. In eight years' time, though, this ninety-nine year treaty was due to expire and Britain would have to hand back its control of the colony to the Chinese. Guangzhou, with a population of five million people, was just 70 miles from Hong Kong and as a result, had been heavily influenced by the massive influx of western goods arriving from the colony. As I went to bed that night, I was already getting quite excited about Hong Kong, especially because the continual rain was turning my perception of Guangzhou into another grey and dreary city like Shanghai.

Before I headed back out into the wet the following morning, I met 'Canadian Dave'. I was sitting in the foyer, quietly glancing through *The Hong Kong Standard* when another backpacker sat down next to me and commented on how informative the feature on Canada was in that morning's edition. 'I should know, you see, that's where I'm from. Dave's the name, by the way,' he said, stretching out his hand. We got chatting and he proceeded to tell me all about the four-week trip around China he was just about to embark upon. He was, however, a bit concerned. He went on to explain how he'd travelled around Thailand last year in the company of a young Thai girl who had taken care of his 'every need' during their trip. Now he was planning to set off on a similar trip, this time with a Chinese girl in tow. At first, I thought he was joking, but when I realised he wasn't, I couldn't help but to laugh out loud. For a few seconds he sat there looking rather bemused.

'Do you know,' he proclaimed, 'I've spent the last five days in Guangzhou going around the bars and discos in the big hotels trying to find a girl who'll come with me.'

'And how d'you get on?' I enquired.

'Not very well, I can tell you! They all go home at ten o'clock.'

Just for curiosity, I asked him how much he'd be prepared to pay to spend a night with a Chinese girl. He had it all worked out:

'Forty dollars for a hotel room and fifty dollars for the girl 'top whack." He paused for a few seconds and stared at me. 'You've been travelling around here a bit. Is there anywhere you could recommend?'

After thinking back to a story Slim had told me about a girl from New Zealand he'd befriended in his restaurant who'd ended up paying him to escort her for a week to Kunming, I suggested that maybe he should make his way up to Yangshou, as it was probably the closest place he'd find in China to Thailand. And with that, I got up, shook his hand and wished him luck. He was clearly going to need it.

Mid-afternoon, after a couple more hours wandering around the sodden streets, I dashed back over to the White Swan for my eagerly anticipated sauna. I started off with a shower and then sat in the steam room, I showered again and then swam in the pool, I showered again then sweated in the sauna, and then I showered a fourth time and lay in the Jacuzzi, before showering once more, just to make sure I'd scraped off every remaining speck of dirt and grime ingrained in my body. So by the time I finally emerged from changing rooms, a full hour and a half after I'd gone in, I felt totally revitalised and all set for New Year's Eve and, over another appallingly expensive dinner in the restaurant, contemplated my plan of action for the night. My best bet, I concluded, would be to check out the bar in the foyer of the youth hostel early evening where a number of backpackers had congregated the previous night. Assuming they were all going out to celebrate, they'd hopefully be reconvening there again tonight, and convinced that I wouldn't be the only lone backpacker looking for some company, I felt sure I'd be able to tag along. Failing that, then there was always the option of the disco at the White Swan to fall back on. When I returned to my room, however, I didn't feel too clever so I took a couple of Paracetemols and decided to have a lie down. If it was going to be a long night, a little nap now could just turn out to be a very prudent move and besides, it probably wasn't worth venturing down to the bar much before eight in any case. So I drew the tattered curtains, undressed and collapsed on my bed. A couple of hours later, I was woken by the sounds of exploding firecrackers. Slightly disorientated, I sat up for a few seconds momentarily forgetting where I was. Rubbing the sleep from my eyes, I could hear in the distance the faint and intermittent echoes of revellers shouting and laughing. Suddenly remembering it was New Year's Eve, I leapt up and reaching for my clothes, glanced down at my travel clock. The digits said: 2.45. Strange, I thought, must have been a power cut. Yanking my jeans up, I stared back at the clock again and frowned. If there *had* been a power cut, then the LCD should be flashing. Something wasn't right. Racing over to the window I pulled back the curtains. The streets outside were dark and deserted. I stood there for a couple of seconds scratching my head. It couldn't really be 2.45, surely? Just then, I heard the sound of giggling below. As I peered down from the window, a young western couple, decked out in party hats and streamers, were staggering up the street and although their arms were locked around each other's waists, they were veering uncontrollably from side to side, as if competing in a three-legged contest. As I stood there watching them for a few seconds, the young man blowing incessantly into a party whistle whilst the girl, with a finger over her lips, desperately tried to contain her laughter, my worst fears were all but realised.

When I awoke the next morning, I still felt aggrieved that I'd missed out on all the partying, failing to comprehend how I could have allowed myself to sleep through the whole evening. Still, this was my last day in Guangzhou, and Hong Kong now beckoned. As I packed my rucksack later on, I began to reflect on my time in China. The last six weeks had certainly flown by, that was for sure. Walking out of the terminal building at Beijing that glorious autumnal morning now seemed like months ago and overall, I couldn't have felt more pleased with all that had happened since then.

In spite of the low points—frequently finding myself lost, the frustrations I'd often experienced trying to make travel reservations or secure accommodation, the hugely disappointing trip down the Yangtze River and the gloomy weather here in the south—I couldn't really complain. With the exception of the odd cold, I had stayed healthy, I hadn't once found myself in a position where I'd felt threatened or in danger, and all of my belongings remained intact. And besides, the highlights more than made up for these: Tiananmen Square, the Great Wall and the Forbidden City in Beijing were all unforgettable in their respective ways; seeing Shanghai and imagining it in its glory days had sent blood shooting through my veins and the spectacularly haunting scenery of Yangshou only typified my idyllic perceptions of rural China.

But the real high points weren't these. No, the most fulfilling moments I'd experienced were the ones I'd shared with other people and, almost without exception, it was these individuals who'd made those experiences special. If I'd not met the old fisherman on the boat, for instance, then my trip down the Grand Canal would have been an infinitely forgettable experience. Likewise, if it hadn't have been for Bob, I'd never have been treated to a traditional Chinese banquet. Indeed, it was only by following the uncle and nephew back to the railway station in Tunxi that led to those two most memorable nights, firstly on top of Huang Shan and then, playing Mastermind with Chang and Cheng at the train station. I was even beginning to see the funny side of that infernal trip down the Yangtze River now—Yaan droning on in his lumbering voice, Robert pissing in the street, the dead dog, sitting in the barbers in Wanxian talking about the Japanese. And the more I thought about it, the more I realised this. Christmas Eve in the Peace Hotel had all the makings of such a great night, but fizzled out all too disappointingly because I'd not had anyone to share it with. And it was no coincidence that now in Guangzhou, where the only person I'd met was a guy who was running around the city like a dog on heat, I was feeling quite despondent. Well that, and I suppose last night's fiasco. So although I often hankered for my own time and space, I had much to be thankful for to these people, for without them, China would have been a very boring place. Fortunately, I already had quite a few people lined up to meet in Hong Kong.

With my packing done, I headed out for some food, managing to get rid of my remaining Chinese currency with a final lunch in the White Swan. Then, after checking out of the youth hostel late afternoon, I made my way to the quay and boarded the overnight ferry. The boat itself was surprisingly clean and comfortable and far superior to the two boats I'd travelled on in China. I was sharing a cabin with three other passengers. One of the men, dressed in a suit and open-necked shirt, promptly introduced himself as 'Chung Wong Kwoo' before adding, 'Please call me Tommy,' and as soon as the boat pulled away from the dockside, he invited me to join him in the bar. Before doing so, I needed to change some travellers' cheques into Hong Kong dollars, but as we walked down the corridor, he informed me there were no such facilities on board. Stopping in my tracks, I cursed myself for spending my remaining Chinese currency. 'Come on, don't worry,' Tommy insisted, 'I'll buy you a beer.' Hesitating for a few moments, I stood there peering out of the window. We were travelling at a fair rate of knots, for Guangzhou was almost out of sight. China, it seemed, was already behind me, and a toast sounded good. 'Yeah, why not?' I replied. 'I'll pay you back when we get to Hong Kong.' Although we were the first people in the bar, other passengers were quickly streaming in so we quickly pulled up a couple of bar stools. Once Tommy had ordered some beers, he asked me where I'd travelled and after running through all the places I'd visited, briefly describing what I'd thought of each, I paused to raise my glass. 'To China,' I said.

'To China,' he repeated with a wry smirk and we clinked glasses.

'And what about you?' I said. 'Here on business?'

He told me he'd been in China for the last month working for his brother's company in an industrial area on the outskirts of Guangzhou and was now travelling back to Hong Kong, where he lived.

'So what does the company do?' I asked

He chuckled for a few seconds. 'We import ink,' he replied rather sagely.

'Ink?' I said, looking at him quizzically.

'Export too.'

I shook my head. 'Ink? You mean...' and then made a drawing gesture with my hand.

'Ssh,' he hissed, rolling his eyes at a small party of businessmen who were now stood just a few feet away. Then, rubbing his fingers against his thumbs, he whispered: 'Good money. Very good money.'

As the bar began to fill up, he went on to tell me how much he was looking forward to getting back home. He'd recently got married to a girl from China and I presumed she was the main reason he was yearning to get back. Leaning forward on his stool, he peered longingly into his empty glass for a few seconds, ordered another couple of beers, and then disappeared off to the toilet. When he returned, I asked him what the feeling was in the colony about Hong Kong being handed back to the Chinese in 1997.

He shook his head. 'Many people won't stay. They are frightened by what China will do.'

'But where will they go?' I asked.

'Canada, Australia, England as well, wherever they can. Lots of people I know have already applied for visas. For those with money, it's okay. They can visit their relatives in these countries now and apply for residency whilst they're there, but the poor will have no choice, they'll have to stay.'

'And what do you think the Chinese will do when they come in?'

He shrugged his shoulders and sighed.

We carried on chatting for a while, predominately about his brother's business and the difficulties they were experiencing in dealing with all the Chinese bureaucracy and red tape so, before long, the conversation became quite laboured. Unfastening a couple more buttons on his shirt, he yawned deeply, pulled out a packet of cigarettes and then waved the barman back over.

'No, no more for me thanks,' I said, before he could get another round in. Tommy's yawning was becoming infectious for I suddenly felt overcome with tiredness myself, but not wanting to appear rude or inhospitable, I remained in my chair listening to him get all his gripes about the authorities off his chest. Three more beers later, Tommy was slouched in his stool, his head lolling uncontrollably up and down. He'd only nodded off momentarily, but he clearly couldn't stay here as he was, so leaning over, I gently prodded his arm. With a startled look on his face, he squinted for a few seconds, and then waving his hand, beckoned me closer. I leant over a little more, lowering my head so it was close to his. 'I hate the Chinese,' he whispered, 'I hate them.'

I slowly nodded my head for a few seconds, noticing the tears welling up in his bloodshot eyes.

'I want to get out of this country, I hate China,' he continued, slurring rather incoherently.

As I put my finger over my lips, he glared around menacingly, and for a horrible moment, I feared he was going to get up on his stool and make this proclamation to everyone in the bar, but he just sat there peering again into his empty glass.

'I think it's time to head back,' I said eventually. Much to my relief, he struggled to his feet without any remonstrations and we wearily trudged back to our cabin. Fortunately, when we got back there the lights were already off and the other two passengers were fast asleep so, whispering, I thanked him again for the beers and told him I'd see him in the morning.

143

CHAPTER 11

HONG KONG

BACK TO THE FUTURE

2nd–8th January 1990

Not long after 7am, I was standing completely mesmerised on the Kowloon side of the harbour. I had been staring inanely at the views of the skyscrapers over on Hong Kong Island for over fifteen minutes and I was still trying to get my breath back. The scene was not entirely unfamiliar; I'd seen it a hundred times on television, in books and on postcards, but the sheer magnitude of these buildings as they now stood before me, shielding the early morning sun, was difficult to take in. Nearly everything I'd seen in the last five weeks had been based on history and tradition, yet this procession of futuristic and ultra modern edifices only personified the wealth, affluence and prosperity associated with the colony. This was capitalism on a scale I'd never seen before and, arriving after six weeks in China, it was a huge shock to the system.

The very first thing I'd noticed when I'd first stepped off the ferry had been the series of familiar bright yellow plastic placards directing me towards the customs hall and departure lounges, the kind more synonymous with airport terminals back home. Comforted that these signs were now in English as well as Pinyin, I'd made my way outside the ferry terminal where I was treated to the sight of double decker buses, kiosk stands brimming with newspapers and glossy magazines, four-door Mercedes, and billboards advertising European lagers, fast food restaurants and Seiko watches. After China, it felt as if I'd just finished a long term in school and had now been let loose in a Butlins holiday camp. It was then, when I'd turned the corner, that I'd caught my first glimpse of the skyscrapers. It wasn't that I hadn't expected Hong Kong to be different to China. No, of course I knew it'd be different, but having arrived here from a country seemingly locked in a time warp, I wasn't prepared for the contrast to be so vast. This was something I definitely hadn't bargained for. I continued to look around in awe as the rest of the colony began to stir. Rush hour would soon be beckoning.

I'd decided to base myself for the next seven days at the Hong Kong youth hostel at the top of Mount Davis, and to get there, I needed to take a bus. The banks wouldn't be open for another couple of hours, which was a bit of a problem, as I still didn't have any Hong Kong dollars. However, just around the corner from the quay, I noticed a cashpoint machine. I had two credit cards with me in my money belt and seemed to recall writing down the pin numbers somewhere before I came away. Quickly, I rummaged around in my rucksack in search of my address book and sure enough, found the four-digit numbers listed on the back page. Hurrying over, I inserted the first card into the slot and typed in the code. A couple of seconds later, a message came up on the screen: 'For cash withdrawals, please contact your bank for authorisation.' I tried my other card and typed in the number again. This time there was no message, so I proceeded to the 'withdraw cash' button and bingo! Five crisp hundred dollar notes (£30-£40) wheeled out of the machine. For a few moments, I stood there in a state of incredulity. Thousands of miles from home, I'd just stuck a plastic card into a hole in the wall, typed in a number and it had churned out a wad of cash. I was beginning to warm to Hong Kong already.

Returning to the quay, I then made the ten-minute journey on the Star Ferry over to Hong Kong Island. After locating the bus station, I searched for the shelter that the no. 47 bus, the only one that scaled Mount Davis, would depart from. As if by magic, no sooner had I found the stand, a no. 47 pulled in. This was getting better and better. I jumped aboard, paid my fare and sat back in my seat, watching the view of the colony unfold beneath us as we made the long climb up the western side of the island. The higher we got, the quieter it got and twenty minutes later, with the mountainside suburbs long behind us, we were trundling along narrow hedgerow lanes bordered by endless rolling sweet-smelling meadows. Stopping at a crossroads, I spotted the signpost to the youth hostel. Leaping to my feet, I rang the bell and jumped off at the next stop. When I got back to the junction, though, I stood there, hands on hips, staring up at the sign indignantly. Two kilometres? Surely it couldn't be that far. Still, I suppose my run of good fortune had to run out sooner or later. So I set off up the steep, single-track road, muttering and grumbling to myself, toiling in the morning heat. The walk to the top took an age, and by the time I finally reached the hostel and heaved my rucksack down, my shirt was clinging to my back. It was still only 9.30 and judging by the startled look on his face, the owner seemed surprised to see me. Check-in was restricted between the hours of ten and four and I guessed that most people arrived later in the day. Nevertheless, he showed me to a dormitory room where I dumped my bags, then washed and changed. Ten minutes later, I walked back out of front door and headed back down to civilisation to explore Hong Kong.

First port of call was the main post office in Central to see if there was any mail waiting for me. I was only really expecting a couple of aerogrammes from my parents, but when I was handed a large bundle of post from the clerk, my face lit up. I quickly removed the elastic band. There were twelve letters in all: three from the folks, one from my Nan, a couple from one of my brothers and sister and no less than six from old college friends. I hurried out of the post office and spotting a McDonald's opposite, darted in, ordered a McChicken Sandwich, a Filet-o-Fish and a large carton of Fries and, stuffing my face, frantically tried to digest the contents of the mail. Although there was no earth shattering news to report, there was an abundance of gossip and trivia, interspersed with various newspaper cuttings from the sports pages, a couple of Page 3 pin-ups and half a dozen photographs of drunken mates.

Still in a state of euphoria, I proceeded to wander around Central for a while, up and down streets cast in shadow by looming offices and tower blocks, affording myself a wry smile at all the office workers rushing around in their suits. So many times when I had been working in London, I would look on in envy at the Australian and Canadian and Kiwi backpackers milling around the City. Me in a suit and them in shorts and T-shirts; me on a tube travelling to work, them unfurling tourist maps of the capital; me on my way home, counting down the months to go and them studying their guidebooks, planning which country in Europe to visit next. And now, at long last, the roles had finally been reversed and it was me wandering the streets with a rucksack on my back without a care in the world while they rushed about like headless chickens worrying about meetings, lunch appointments and office politics. It was a mighty fine feeling, I can tell you!

A few hours later as I made the climb back up Mount Davis, I couldn't have felt more pleased to be here in Hong Kong. Amongst my original plans, I *had* been hoping to make a two-day trip to the neighbouring Portuguese colony of Macau, although I was now beginning to wonder whether I'd have time to fit this in. Don't get me wrong, I hadn't exactly got a jam packed social calendar mapped out for the week, but there were a number of people that I was hoping to catch up with whilst I was here. There was Nicole, the big British nurse I'd met in Beijing. It would be nice to get in touch with her again, even if it was just to call her and say hello. I'd also located the whereabouts of the Harbour Hotel where David and Reilly, the two Canadians I'd met in Yangshou, were staying. David, if I recalled, was due to fly out in a couple of days' time although I specifically remembered Reilly talking about a party at the foreign correspondents' office on Saturday night, and having assured me he'd be able to wangle me an invite, a suitably entertaining evening seemed on the cards. Then there was Tommy, my friend on the ferry who'd so generously paid for my beers. The very least I could do was return the compliment and buy him a few drinks back. And who knows, perhaps I'd bump into the Danes again, so maybe it *was* going to be a hectic week after all.

'Right,' said the youth hostel owner early the next morning, handing me a mop. 'You can wash down the kitchen floor.' I looked at him as if he was mad and very nearly told him to do it himself. This was the first time I'd stayed at a youth hostel and I was not familiar with the protocol. I subsequently learnt that the accommodation rates were so cheap because guests were expected to volunteer and muck in with various cleaning jobs around the hostel, which was fine so long as you knew that. Thankfully, soon after, the owner had gone over to a couple of girls and told them they could wipe down all the surfaces in the kitchen, and I'd realised I hadn't being singled out. However, by the time I'd finished my designated chores, I'd already made up my mind to find another place to stay. The atmosphere in the hostel the previous night had been far from homely, with guests continually vying for the use of cooking facilities and tables throughout the evening. I'd also been amazed to discover that the front gates to the hostel were locked at 11pm each night. With notices pinned onto boards in the hall listing hostel rules and errand duties, the place felt more like a school, and was not my idea of a place that you could come back to and relax. I also couldn't face a whole week making the long climb up and down Mount Davis every day, so later that morning, I headed off back down the winding path to search for another place to stay.

After taking the Star Ferry back over to Kowloon, I managed to secure a room shortly after in Chungking

Mansions, a name synonymous for cheap accommodation in downtown Hong Kong. The ironically named Mansions were anything but; reached through a set of stinking elevators found at the end of an innocuous shopping arcade off Nathan road, the busy high street that bisects the centre of Kowloon, they were instead a labyrinth of endless squalid corridors comprising guest houses, offices, shops, factories, restaurants, private apartments, hairdressers and travel agencies. After wandering indiscriminately up and down the sixteen floors for over an hour, I was eventually persuaded by an Indian guy called Tom to take a room in his domain. The room itself was tiny, with just enough space for a bed, and was enclosed by some flimsy partitions that didn't even reach the ceiling. It did, however, have its own toilet and shower, though its crucial selling point and prized asset sat snugly on a table on the end of the bed: a portable television set. The rate for the accommodation was significantly more than the youth hostel, although it was a price I was more then happy to pay as it meant I'd now be a lot closer to the action of Hong Kong. I'd also have the freedom to come and go when I pleased and not have to worry about chores!

I was quite taken by Kowloon itself, a thriving neon-lit shopping district interspersed with fast food outlets, restaurants, curry houses and bars, and far more lively than the stuffy business area of Central I'd walked around the previous day. But before I could explore the downtown area in earnest, I needed to return to the youth hostel to check out and pick up my rucksack. On the way, I dropped in to the Harbour Hotel to try to catch up with David and Reilly. The receptionist confirmed they were indeed staying there, but when he called their room, there was no reply, so I left them a message saying I'd call again later.

After making the long climb back up the mountain, I caught up with the owner in reception. It had been bugging me all morning who it was he reminded me of. He was a dour man perhaps in his late fifties, and of medium build. Although he was balding, long brylcreemed strands of hair whipped across his pate. His dress was smart; dark slacks, a lightly chequered white shirt rolled up at the sleeves and, in spite of the humidity, he insisted on wearing a dark green woollen tank top. His disposition was rather grumpy and he treated all the guests with a certain degree of circumspection. He was sweeping the hall when I walked in, shaking his head and then I finally got it. He was the grouchy old houseowner in *Scooby Doo*, the one who the gang exposed at the end of every episode as the villain of the piece. The shaking of his head was the final clue and I was just waiting for him to mutter something like: 'Baa, what's this pesky kid doing back here this time of day?' I gulped, for I now had to tell him I was checking out. In fact, my rucksack that lay by my feet had already given it away.

'Leaving us are you?' he chirped.

Staring at the floor, I nodded.

He eyed me up and down. 'You're in the forces, aren't you?' he said, now grinning at me.

'No, funnily enough a few people have asked me that recently,' I replied.

'Doesn't surprise me, that,' he chuckled. 'Nope, that doesn't surprise me one little bit.'

I hadn't expected such joviality, and as a result, felt obliged to tell him I was only moving on because I wanted to be based somewhere more central. He nodded his head indifferently, evidently unperturbed by my sudden departure. But then what did he care? He'd probably been stuck on top of this mountain for years, watching people come and go as they please and it would only be a couple more hours before the next batch of new arrivals turned up. So, after squaring up the bill, I heaved my rucksack onto my back and—feeling rather like the Grand Old Duke of York—made my way back down the mountain again. When I got back to the Chunking Mansions, it was early evening and time to make a few phone calls. Vaguely remembering the nurses telling me back in Beijing that there was no charge for local phone calls in Hong Kong, I was still surprised when I actually found this to be the case. I tried Tommy first but there was no reply. When I looked at the crumpled up piece of paper again, I realised he'd given me his work number, so I'd have to try again in the morning. Then I called Nicole. Her flatmate answered and informed me she was away on leave until the end of the week. I then tried David and Reilly again, but after being put through to their suite there was still no reply, so returning to my room, I whiled away the evening lying on my bed watching the coverage of one of the Super Bowl play-offs.

The following morning, I took a bus to the fishing village of Stanley, apparently a popular residential area for ex-pats. When I arrived, this was all too apparent as there seemed to be significantly more western faces here than oriental ones. The harbour itself was pleasant enough, lined with souvenir shops and restaurants whilst junks, sampans and brightly painted fishing boats bobbed up and down in the water. The quay, though, was horribly congested and overrun by parties of tourists. Predominantly middle-aged and elderly, they sauntered up and down the waterside in their short-sleeved shirts, shorts and sun hats, persistently stopping abruptly in my path either to pose for photographs or to point at the boats on the water.

'Hey, Martha, gee look at that one,' cried one. 'Fancy travelling back home in that thing?'

'Hell, no,' came the reply, 'but I bet you a dollar Gerry would if he could take one of those Wanchai girls back with him.'

I tried my utmost not to let them get me down but it was no use. One man, wide as he was tall, was wearing a T-shirt that was ten times too small for his gargantuan stomach, a pair of long shorts with pale blue socks and navy plimsolls. And if this wasn't bad enough, he was carrying around a white plastic bag, emblazoned across which were the letters S-a-i-n-s-b-u-r-y-s. 'Who, for chrissakes, comes to Hong Kong and walks around with a supermarket bag?' I kept asking myself.

The more I walked around Stanley, the more riled I became. Another middle-aged man, having his palm read by an Indian fortune-teller, was dressed, I kid you not, in white trainers, white socks, white trousers and a white windbreaker. He stood

151

leaning over with one foot on a wall and his other hand teapot-like on hip, glancing around imperiously with his head in the air. He thought he ruled the world. I then spotted another tourist, with a camera over one shoulder and a holdall over another, filming the view of the bay with a video camera. Nothing, but nothing, gets on my nerves more than people walking around tourist places with video cameras, and I always make a point of purposely standing in their view whenever I see people using them. I shook my head in dismay. I'd only been here twenty minutes but it was already time to get out of Stanley. Without haste, I caught another bus to the floating town of Aberdeen. This time, the harbour was filled with yachts, catamarans and boats that had been converted to restaurants to cater for tourists. I stayed for five minutes, decided it was also far too busy and commercialised, and promptly got a third bus back to Central.

After spending the rest of the afternoon harmlessly whiling away a couple of hours on a Star Ferries cruise around the harbour, I stopped off at a telephone box on the quay.

'Hi, is Tommy there now?' I asked the receptionist after being connected.

'Hold on,' she replied and the line went silent. A few seconds later she came back on. 'You phone this morning?' she asked.

'Yeah, a couple of times. You said Tommy was out on business. Is he there now?'

'Yes.'

'Can I speak to him, then?'

There was a pause. 'He on phone.'

'Oh, okay, can I hold or shall I phone back?'

There was another pause. 'Can you say again?'

'Er, don't worry, I'll phone back.'

Five minutes later, I tried again. 'Hi, it's me again. Is it possible to speak to Tommy now?'

'No, ees no possible.'

'Is he still on the phone?'

'No, he go to Guangzhou.'

'What, you mean Tommy's gone to Guangzhou?'

'Yes, he gone.'

'When? When did he go?'

'He go this morning.'

'But you just said he was on the phone?'

'No, he not here.'

Taking the hint, I hung up, although I was still slightly perplexed as to why Tommy didn't want to come to the phone. Infuriatingly, there was very little I could do about it, and this day was seemingly going from bad to worse. When I arrived back in Kowloon around early evening, though, something momentarily brought a smile back to my face. Whilst I was waiting for the lift, a couple of cheery black guys in jogging trousers and vests were lugging a load of cases into one of the other elevators. There seemed to be a running joke in the lifts at the Chunking Mansions as whenever a certain weight was reached—normally that of six or seven people—a buzzer sounded and somebody had to jump out before the lift would operate again. I couldn't help thinking that these guys had no idea of this but just as I was about to warn them, my lift arrived. Seconds later, up on the ninth floor, I stood for a few seconds listening as the predictable commotion sounded from the bottom of the other shaft:

'Hey, man, why aren't we moving?'

'Dunno, bro, but that thing's sure making a hell of a racket.'

'Shit, now the doors won't close. Press the button again,'

'I am. I'm pressing it, I tell you. Nothing's happening. C'mon, stop looking at me like that!'

'You know what? This damn lift is fucked.'

Quickly remembering the impending party on the weekend, I stopped off on the way back to my room to make another call to the Canadians. If my memory served me correctly, David would have already left to fly back home, so I suspected Reilly would be even more pleased to receive some company. I dialled the number again.

'Good evening, Harbour Hotel,' answered the receptionist.

'Yes, good evening, can you put me through to room forty-two please,' I asked.

'One minute, sir, I'll just connect you.'

A few seconds later, the receptionist came back on. 'Sorry, sir, the guests in room forty-two have checked out.'

'Checked out? What, both of them you mean?'

'Yes, sir.'

I could have sworn that Reilly had said he would be in Hong Kong until the 7th of January. That was Sunday but it was still only Thursday.

'Are you sure?' I asked.

'Yes, sir, they both left this morning,' he replied.

'I don't suppose they left another address at reception?'

'No, sir, they didn't leave any messages. Is there anything else I can help you with?'

'Er no, no thanks,' I replied, before hanging up.

So much for my busy social calendar then! It now looked like I'd be spending the entire week by myself, and this, in one of the most sociable cities of the world. Coming so hot on the heels of the New Year's Eve debacle, this was a crushing blow.

I woke up the next morning in a more philosophical mood. Admittedly, I was still feeling rather sorry for myself, but there was no point moping about it so I decided to take a trip out to the island of Cheung Chau. Arriving at the ferry terminal just before ten, I quickly made my way to the back of the crowded boat and found a seat outside where I could sit and soak up the morning sun. As the ferry sailed out of the harbour, leaving all the hustle and bustle of Hong Kong behind, a sultry looking girl with blonde spiky hair came and sat down next to me. Dressed all in black and smoking a cigarette, she was tall, arty looking, almost punky. I guessed she was in her early thirties, perhaps over here either studying or working. After a few minutes, I could see her out of the corner of my eye brushing her fingers through her hair which, if my memory served me correctly, was quite a positive body language sign; one that could possibly indicate the attraction was mutual. I thought of asking her where she was going, but on a ferry to Cheung Chau, that seemed pretty obvious, so I tried to think of something else to

154

say to her to start a conversation. I contemplated, 'Beautiful day today,' harmless enough, yet each time I looked up, I failed to catch her eye and the longer I left it, the more difficult it became. In the end, I bottled it and buried my head into my book although I quickly found myself reading the same page over and over again, not really taking any of it in. As I sat there staring up to the sky and grimacing, some lyrics from a Prefab Sprout song—'Missed chances and the same regrets'—began to circulate in my mind. In fact, they kept coming back to haunt me for the remainder of the one-hour journey.

The bay of Cheung Chau, when we arrived, was pretty and picturesque and, if it hadn't been for the oriental appearance of the locals, I could have easily been mistaken for assuming I was in a little fishing town on a Greek Island. It was baking hot, the warm sun reflected off the white walls of tavernas, and the water in the bay shimmered in the bright light. The junks and fishing boats, moored in the harbour, slumbered, deep in siesta, and a tranquil atmosphere and slow pace pervaded. I *had* been planning to do some mountain walking and explore the island, but I was so taken with the town that I spent an hour or so idly walking up and down the quay instead. Feeling a little peckish, I eventually stopped at a restaurant and ordered some lunch. When I next looked up from my table, my heart started beating nineteen to the dozen. Walking into the restaurant straight towards me was the girl from the ferry. This was it. It had to be. She's going to come over and talk to me. She is. She's coming over to talk to me. Oh my God. She bloody well is too. Shit, what do I say? Composure. Come on now. Sort yourself out or you're gonna blow it. Stopping just a few feet away from me, she picked up a menu and studied it for a minute or so. Then, placing the black folder back on the tablecloth, she turned around abruptly and casually walked back out to another bar across the road. Bollocks. What happened? I should have got up and said something, invited her over to my table. Oh God, you moron. You bloody idiot. I sat there for a while, unable to finish my food, which in itself was a total rarity. I was smitten. It was the only explanation. I picked up my newspaper and every couple of minutes, kept looking over to see if I could catch the eye of the girl, who was now sat on a table across the street in clear view. Surely, this couldn't have been coincidental? As soon as she'd finished eating, I purposefully got up and, feigning an exaggerated yawn, stretched my arms out as wide as I could so she could clearly see I was leaving. Then, slowly walking back down the quay, I stopped at the first shop I passed, carefully positioned myself behind a postcard stand and, spinning the rack around, took a sneaky look back to see if she was following. I couldn't see her. Damn, maybe I'd blown it. I waited there for a further ten minutes, but there was still no sign of her and with the shopkeeper now throwing me suspicious glances, I quickly grabbed a handful of cards and took them to the counter, promising myself that whatever happened, I'd talk to her on the ferry on the way back.

After wandering around a few more shops, I eventually pulled up a chair at another bar on the quay, ordered a beer and sat down in the afternoon sun to write some of the postcards I'd bought, but no matter how I tried, I couldn't stop thinking about the girl. God, if I could just make that all-important first move on the way back it could be brilliant. She fancied me; that was obvious. All the tell-tale signs were there: the way she'd sat down next to me on the outward journey running her fingers through her hair, the fact she'd followed me into the restaurant and then sat on a table across the road in full view. We were bound to hit it off. All I needed to do was break the ice. I began to picture what would happen. We'd probably talk non-stop all the way back. As we approached Hong Kong, I'd suggest we go for a meal and she'd take me to a nice romantic restaurant. We'd dine in candlelight and at the end of the meal she'd invite me back to her luxurious apartment overlooking the harbour where we'd sit up until the early hours drinking whisky and flirting audaciously with each other. She'd eventually ask me if I wanted to stay the night, we'd end up making mad, passionate love until daybreak, then I'd persuade her to accompany me for the rest of my travels and we'd settle down in England together and live happily ever after.

Half an hour later, I boarded the three o'clock ferry back to Hong Kong knowing precisely what I had to do. As I entered the passenger lounge, I glanced nervously all around the room, but to my alarm, she was nowhere to be seen. Quickly, I scurried outside to see if she was sitting on one of the decks but she wasn't there either, so I stood next to the ticket collector staring back down at the quay, desperately hoping I'd see her, running towards the gangway. Five minutes later as the boat slowly pulled away from the jetty and made its way back to Hong Kong, all I wanted to do was throw myself overboard.

In order to raise my flagging spirits, I dived into a Kowloon curry house later that evening and treated myself to a huge plate of poppadums, a fiery Chicken Madras and a couple of cold lagers to wash it all down. It seemed to do the trick for I woke up in a much better frame of mind and, remembering the promises I'd made to my friends in China, quickly scribbled out a letter to Lu Xiao, picked up some tapes and posters for Slim and duly called in at the post office to despatch them. With my guilt ridden conscience somewhat eased, I then took the tram up to Victoria Peak where, on a gloriously sunny day, I was blessed with some stunning all-encompassing views of the harbour. Directly beneath me stood an urbanised concrete jungle, hundreds of towering white apartment blocks littered with sporadic specks of whites and blues from washing hung out of windows and verandas to dry in the breeze. Beyond these, and looming even larger, were the sinisterly darker tower blocks of the offices and banks that so spectacularly dominated the skyline of Hong Kong Island. And in between the processing plants and drums of oil refineries way out in the distance, was a vast expanse of shimmering blue water dotted with motionless cargo ships, cruise liners and oil tankers. As passenger ferries silently plied their way back and forth across the harbour between the flotillas, the only sounds that filled the air were the chirping of birds and the odd stop-start noises of hammering and drilling from below.

I spent an hour or so walking along the road that circled the peak, stopping every five minutes to reach for my camera although by the end, my mind was beginning to wander. On the way up, I'd seen a sign outside one of the pubs advertising televised football, and I assumed that this could only mean live coverage of one of the FA Cup games from back home. Having missed out in Guangzhou, I was now even more determined to quell the increasing withdrawal symptoms I was having for my beloved game and if I could while away a Saturday afternoon in a British pub watching a game on TV, I was sure all my disappointments of the past few days would be quickly forgotten. So buoyed on by the prospects of sitting on a bar stool quietly supping a Guinness or two as twenty-two red-nosed players frenetically chased an orange leather ball up and down a snow covered pitch for ninety minutes, I took a final photo of the harbour and returned to the tram station. When I arrived back down in Central ten minutes later, all the pavements were strangely deserted. Three or four days ago when I'd called in at the post office, they'd been packed with shoppers, commuters and office workers. But now, it was virtually silent and, except for the odd taxi or bus, the streets were empty too. A Saturday here really did feel like a Saturday whereas in China, there'd been no obvious telltale signs indicating whether a particular day was a business day or weekend.

I entered the doors of the 'Mad Dogs' pub just after 2pm. There were not many people inside the spacious, dimly lit lounge, so feeling peckish, I ordered some lunch. The food, when it arrived, was delicious—an enormous helping of chicken and ham pie, mushy peas and fat brown chips. Returning the empty plate to the bar, I asked the barmaid what time the football was coming on.

'John,' she shouted out to the kitchen. 'What times the footy on?'

'Half an hour,' came the reply.

'I don't suppose you know who's playing?' I enquired, pushing my luck a little.

'D'you know who's playing, John?' she yelled again.

This time the reply was muffled, so she disappeared off to

the kitchen and returned a couple of seconds later.

'He says it's Scottish.'

I returned to my table with a pint of Guinness somewhat disheartened, firstly as it wasn't English football and secondly, because I'd realised by now, that due to the time difference, the coverage couldn't be live. With nothing better to do, I decided to wait for the game nevertheless and was soon joined by a middle-aged man in a kilt and a couple of old guys smoking pipes and drinking scotch whom I surmised were also waiting for the football. Three o'clock arrived and the television screen finally flickered to life. 'About time too,' I muttered under my breath. Then, on the screen, appeared a crackling black and white picture of a television mast, followed by the words: 'The 101 Greatest Moments of Scottish Sport.' I stared at the television incredulously. A hundred and one greatest moments of Scottish sport? That, in itself, was a bit of a joke. Besides Archie Gemmill's brilliant solo goal against the Dutch in 1978 and a few stirring Scottish rugby union victories against the English, I was struggling to think of ten, let alone a hundred, great moments of Scottish sport. I continued to look around the room in disbelief, desperately hoping that the video was just some precursor to the highlights of a recent old firm clash, but half an hour later, we were still on no. 74, some tartan trousered golfer prancing around the green at Muirfield or St Andrews, and realising that this was the main event and there was no football, I finished my drink, slammed the empty glass down on the table and walked out of the pub in disgust.

Sunday was the big horseracing day in Hong Kong. I'd never been to a race meeting before, so the next morning I decided to travel over to Shatin in the New Territories to see for myself what all the fuss was about. Before I set off, though, I couldn't resist the temptation to nip into a branch of Marks & Spencer I'd passed the previous day. Ten minutes later, armed with a packet of Frazzles, a chicken tikka sandwich and a bottle of orange juice for an afternoon picnic, I made my way to Kowloon station and, from a spotless litter free platform, boarded a plush air-conditioned carriage already crammed full of racegoers, many busily studying the form guides in the morning papers on their cushioned seats. After passing through a dozen or so more equally exemplary brightly painted stations, all the passengers abruptly got to their feet and surged towards the doors of the train. As it pulled to a stop, these crowds spilled onto the platform, emptying the carriages in seconds. Following the great throngs of people, I arrived at the course just a few minutes before the start of the meeting and, after paying the nominal entrance fee of 14 dollars (80 pence), excitedly made my way through the turnstiles across to the terraces of a modern white roofed grandstand. The steps were packed with thousands of spectators, nearly all it seemed men with cigarettes dangling out of their mouths, some still scouring their newspapers, others shielding their eyes from the sun and squinting down towards the track where on the lush striped green turf, a line of workers in netted lampshade hats were carefully trampling down the course.

Picking up a card, I discovered the afternoon meeting comprised eight races in all, scheduled at thirty-minute intervals and although I was planning to have a small bet, I decided to make some trial selections for the first couple of races before I parted with any of my hard earned cash. As floods of people continued to make their way through the entrance gates, many making a beeline down to the front where spectators were now standing seven or eight deep, an announcement came on the tannoy to signal the start of the first race, sending a ripple of murmurs across the grandstand. Seconds later, the voice of the commentator began to boom out of the speakers. As the start line was out of view, I peered up at one of the many television screens strategically placed around the viewing enclosure, following the horses as they set off down the back straight. Before long, the commentator's voice was getting faster and louder although the horses, obscured by the advertisement hoardings on the far side of the course, were still nowhere to be seen. As soon as they emerged from the bend, though, a few seconds later, the whole grandstand en masse got to its feet. The shouting and hollering got louder and more vociferous and spectators, urging their favourites on, began to beat the air with rolled up newspapers. In a flash, the horses thundered past, surging towards the finishing post with one last straggler bringing up the rear. The results came up on the screen almost instantaneously. Quickly checking my predictions, I discovered none had figured amongst the first three finishers.

I went on to fare better in the second and third races, managing to pick both the first and second places in each and then tried to calculate how much I would have won if I'd been brave enough to put any money on. The fourth race, the San Miguel Tankard Challenge, was the big race of the day and this was the one I'd been waiting for. However, when I studied the formbook, it seemed pretty clear that the race would almost certainly be won by one of the two joint favourites. Consequently, the odds for both horses weren't great so I decided to bide my time instead and, after tucking in to my M&S picnic, meandered down to the front of the grandstand to take some photos. I spent a quarter of an hour in all, pacing up and down the concourse, looking for the best place to capture the horses as they tore along the home straight. After finally finding a viewing place I was happy with, I twiddled my thumbs for a while, patiently waiting for the start of the next race. Two or three minutes later with the commentator in full flow, I slowly followed the horses and jockeys around the far side of the course. This time they seemed to be taking an eternity to cover the distance. As they approached the far bend, I lost sight of them momentarily as they disappeared behind the hoardings again, but with the thudding sound of stampeding hooves getting louder and louder, I raised the camera to my face in preparation. And then, moments later, they came into view, eight charging mad-eyed beasts, and their frantic jockeys bouncing up and down on their saddles in their brightly coloured caps and puffy silk shirts, now hurtling towards me. Winking into my viewfinder, I desperately tried to get them into focus, waiting for the precise moment for them to pass. In a flash, the thumping sound reached a crescendo. I pressed the button on my camera but it didn't click. The horses charged by in a split second, leaving a cloud of dust rising from the grass in their wake. When I looked down at the camera, I saw that the shutter was still closed and, for a few disbelieving moments, I just stood there cursing my stupidity. Half an hour later, as I made my way back out of the main gate, the announcement confirming the result of the fifth race came over the tannoy; it had been won by a 45-1 outsider. Maybe I should have put a bet on after all.

The next day was my last in Hong Kong and I decided to spend it by returning to the lovely island of Cheung Chau. Just like the other day, as soon as the ferry left the main stretch of the harbour between Kowloon and Hong Kong Island, the clouds miraculously disappeared and were replaced by blue skies and sunshine, but sadly, this time there were no mysterious girls aboard. After walking up and down the harbour a few times, I pulled up a table on the quay, stopped for some lunch and spent an hour basking in the sun with a couple of cold bottles of San Miguel, thinking about the past week. There was no doubt that Hong Kong had been a welcome respite after the comparative hardships of travelling in China: the home comforts of McDonald's, Marks & Spencer, pubs and curry houses, the fact that English was so widely spoken, the lovely islands with their whitewashed tavernas, not to mention the hordes of tourists, made the colony feel like an oriental Majorca. My only regret was that I had no one to enjoy it with, for Hong Kong was not a place, just as a holiday resort isn't, to find yourself on your tod. The only saving grace had been moving from the youth hostel to Chunking Mansions where I'd been able to while away the evenings in front of my television watching re-runs of old movies and the climax to the American football season

Arriving back in Kowloon mid-afternoon, I stocked up on sun-tan lotion, a couple of bootleg music cassettes and some new films for my camera, and spent the remainder of the evening packing and reading about Malaysia. Then, right at the end of the night, I came across my hip flask in my rucksack.

There was a little bit of duty free whisky left at the bottom, which would duly serve as a welcome night cap and mark my last night in the colony. However, when I went to pour myself a glass, it was full of floating bits of cork and gunk, so I had to throw the contents down the sink. It seemed to perfectly sum up my fortunes in Hong Kong.

CHAPTER 12

MALAYSIA

LIFE'S A BEACH

9th–13th January 1990

The two things that hit me when I stepped out onto the tarmac at Kuala Lumpur airport were the intense heat (the temperature was a stifling thirty degrees) and the fact that at 7.30pm, it was still light. After clearing customs relatively quickly, I jumped into a taxi and asked the driver if he knew of the Lee Mun Hotel, an establishment in Chinatown that Gibbo and the others had previously stayed at. He nodded his head unconvincingly and although he succeeded in getting me to Chinatown, he couldn't find the hotel, so after paying the fare, I hopped out and stopped to ask a few more people on the street if they know where the Lee Mun Hotel was, but none of them did either. Then, after aimlessly wandering around the streets for a further fifteen minutes, a bearded man in a cheesecloth robe and skullcap appeared from a doorway and offered me a room for 17 dollars. It was far too hot to be searching for a hotel that I'd only be staying at for one night, so after he'd shown me the room and I'd haggled the rate down a little, I thought, 'what the heck.' Quickly completing all the paperwork, I then dumped my rucksack on the bed, had a quick wash and headed out to explore in what remained of the evening.

It wasn't too long before I came across a bustling evening market. In the middle of a large cobbled square, crowds of locals—giggling girls in brightly coloured saris, veiled women mysteriously holding their noses, and T-shirted moustachioed men looking cool and resplendent in their flip-flops and sarongs—were milling up and down the aisles between rows of stalls all decorated with strings of white light bulbs. The merchandise was of a wide variety: stainless steel saucepans, radio and cassette players, baskets of nuts and dried fruit, kitchenware, music tapes, replica football tops and various other knick knacks, and if I hadn't stocked up on provisions the previous evening, I'd have been more inclined to have a mooch around. My thirst, however, was getting the better of me so I took a seat at a table on the perimeter of the square and ordered a cold beer. A couple of minutes later, as I sat there contentedly watching the world go by, another backpacker came bounding over.

'Mind if I join you?' he said.

'Please, pull up a seat,' I replied, glad of the company. The resulting conversations were light and relaxed and, refreshingly, weren't exclusively about our respective travels. I told him how I'd been watching some of the coverage of the recent Super Bowl on television and, for an American, he possessed a surprisingly good knowledge of English football. It was boxing, though, that we shared common ground on and we spent a thoroughly rousing couple of hours reciting all the great bouts of years gone by:

'Okay, how about that Sugar Ray—Duran fight, then?'

'Goddamit, yeah, what did they call it? 'The Brawl in Montreal' wasn't it?'

'That's it. That was an epic. Didn't Leonard lose it on points?'

'Yeah, he did, but then he won it back.'

'That's right, just a couple of months later. That was the one when Duran's corner threw in the towel. Cor, they were some fights.'

'Weren't they just?'

'And who was that other guy around at that time?'

'Which one?'

'You know, the tall fella. What was his name now?

'Oh, you mean Hearns, Tommy Hearns.'

'Yeah, that's it, what did they call him? 'The Hit Man.' That's it, Tommy 'the Hit Man' Hearns. Do you remember his fight with Leonard? Now that was a classic.'

'Didn't the ref stop it near the end?'

'He did, in the fourteenth. They reckoned Hearns was way ahead on points, but Leonard finally knocked him down.'

'And then Hagler came along.'

'Hagler! My God, how could I have forgotten Hagler? Marvellous Marvin Hagler. Now *he* was some boxer. Did you see that fight he had with Minter?'...And so it went on.

When we eventually parted, I returned to my room with a newfound spring in my step. After all the disappointments of Hong Kong, it suddenly felt good to be travelling again. Chance encounters such as these were what backpacking was all about. Whiling away an evening over a few beers, in a bustling market square in a city I hardly knew, with a fellow traveller I'd only just met and would probably never see again in my life. This was more like it; this was how I should be spending my evenings, not holed up in a guesthouse in front of the TV every night!

With my faith in humanity all but restored, I boarded a bus the next morning and headed north. Whilst I'd been in Hong Kong, I'd called in at the Malaysian tourist office one afternoon to make some enquiries about the possibility of getting to a beach resort in the short time I'd be here. The staff had turned out to be very helpful, almost too helpful in fact. After plying me with brochures and catalogues, four or five of the girls had sat around debating amongst themselves the best place to go.

166

The eventual consensus was that I travel up to Pangkor, a small island largely inhabited by fisherfolk situated off the west coast of Malaysia in the Straights of Malacca. They'd then spent a further fifteen minutes advising me on everything I needed to know about the island: how to get there, what injections I'd need, the best places to stay, what time the sun set every day and so forth.

The lushness of the surrounding scenery on the road up from Kuala Lumpur came as a welcome surprise. Passing through a succession of rubber plantations, dense upland forests and jungle covered ravines, the abundance of vegetation was quite unexpected. Compared to the barren and arid landscapes I seemed to remember of southern Thailand, Malaysia felt much greener and alive. Notwithstanding this, the journey seemed to take an age and it was well after three by the time we arrived at a place called Lamut. After a 40-minute ferry journey over to Pangkor, I shared a taxi across the island with a fellow Japanese traveller to one of the popular beach resorts where I rented my own private hut; literally just a room on stilts with a mattress on the floor. By now, it was late afternoon and with no time to waste, I deposited my rucksack and quickly made the short walk through the palm groves down to the sea. The beach when I got there was long—perhaps thirty minutes walk from one end to the other—and although there were only a handful of people dotted along the stretch of dark sand, many were of the young blonde variety, and gallingly bronzed and tanned. Suddenly becoming conscious of how pale my skin was in comparison, I purposely left it until sunset when the beach was virtually deserted before sheepishly creeping down to the shore for a swim. The wait was finally worth it, though, for the water was surprisingly warm and with my white body safely submerged, I splashed about in the waves for a while like a little kid.

Early evening, I wandered over to the bar for some food. A small group of backpackers were sat around a couple of adjacent wooden tables chatting and telling jokes, seemingly happy in their own company. Still, this was only my first night and there was plenty of time yet to make new acquaintances. Besides, I wasn't unduly bothered, as I was quite keen to get through the remaining chapters of my book. I'd started reading *In the Land of Oz* a few weeks back and it seemed somehow imperative that I finished it before I arrived in Australia myself. Now, without any distractions, it looked like I'd finally be able to do so, so after some dinner, I happily retired back to my hut, suitably pleased with my new surroundings.

The sun the next day was blisteringly hot and, determined not to burn, I sought refuge late afternoon in the shade of my room. When I awoke a couple of hours later, I lay on the mattress for a while, staring up at the thatched roof, wishing I had more time to spend in Malaysia. I was due to arrive in Australia in just two days' time and I couldn't help thinking it would have been nice to have had a whole week here lazing on the beach before I landed in Sydney on Sunday. I suppose the realisation that the first part of my holiday was coming to an end was now finally dawning on me. Although I'd obtained a working visa for Australia before I'd left, I'd really been hoping I'd not have to use it. I now knew that I almost certainly would, as the £4000 that was to have lasted for the duration of my trip was already nearly gone. If I was going to spend a full year in Australia, which had always been my plan, then I was going to have to work somewhere along the line, which would inevitably entail looking for a job and also finding a place to live. And what work would I do? Three months ago, I'd been celebrating the fact that my banking days were finally behind me. Now I found myself contemplating the awful prospect of having to work in an office again. I could, of course, try to pick up some casual work, but the money wouldn't be good and saving would be difficult. Could I *really* face going back to office work? God, what a horrible thought. I even began to wonder whether I should just cut short the amount of time I spend in Australia so I wouldn't have to worry about office work again, but that would effectively mean missing out on India, which was the last thing I wanted to do. It looked like I'd just have to bite the bullet. Depressed by these thoughts, I quickly adjourned to the bar for a cold glass of lager.

Later in the evening, after reading the heart-warming account of Howard and Rosalind Jacobson rescuing a pet dog from a pack of dingoes at Ayers Rock, I sat on the steps of my hut for a while, savouring the balmy air, the chittering cicadas, the sound of the waves gently lapping the shore as the palm trees rustled in the breeze. Ten minutes later, staring up at the twinkling stars in the night sky, thinking how wonderful the world was and what a pleasure it was to be in a place such as Pangkor Island, I heard some strange noises. They were coming from one of the neighbouring huts and sounded like a couple cavorting. At regular intervals, the girl would make a series of bizarre high-pitched shrills that I could only liken to the sounds made by Woody Woodpecker. Each time she did, they'd both burst into fits of giggles. It was quite funny when I heard it the first time although my mind was boggling as to why it should repeatedly be so amusing. Perhaps they were stark bollock naked, lucky sods. Twenty minutes later, with the same noises still emanating, my patience was wearing a bit thin, so I went back inside, switched off the light and jumped under the sheet.

An hour or so later, I was awoken by some different sounds. At first, I thought I was just imagining it, but every few seconds, I'd pick up a faint soundbyte. I sat up for a while straining my ears. Far off in the distance, someone was singing. It sounded like an Asian voice and in the background, a guitar was being gently strummed. Moments later, I began to recognise the song. It sounded familiar but what it actually was still escaping me. I started humming the tune in my head and slowly but surely, the words followed. And then I got it. It was now unmistakable. Somewhere outside someone was singing *Puff the Magic Dragon*, a tune I'd not heard since my days at junior school. Indeed, just hearing this magical song again after so many years was quite magical in itself, but here, sometime after midnight on a tiny island in Malaysia? This was something I had to check out. Quickly pulling back the sheet, I crept to the door of my hut and slowly pushing it open, poked my head out. No more than a hundred yards away, a group of young people were sat around the bar listening to an Indian guy singing. Just as I was about to wander out to join the group, a few of them got up, high-fived with their friends and headed off back to their huts. Typical, I thought, always the bridesmaid! Much later on, I was woken again, this time by the sound of rain lashing down outside. It didn't let up and I slept fitfully for the remainder of the night.

It was still chucking it down when I woke up the next morning, which in theory should have been my cue to pack my things and jump on a bus straight back down to Kuala Lumpur a day earlier than planned. After all, what was the point in staying here if I was going to be confined to my hut? But for some reason, I was not in a particularly decisive mood, so I stayed in my room to finish the final chapters of my book. Around eleven, the rains stopped and almost immediately, clear blue skies reappeared. When I emerged a few minutes later, it was already baking hot, so I reached for my towel and trotted down to the beach, really pleased with myself that I'd decided to stay. I hadn't been lying down for long when a girl with long blonde plaits, dressed in the skimpiest of black bikinis perfectly accentuating a shapely hourglass figure, sat herself down no more than twenty yards away. Nothing particularly unusual about this on a crowded beach, but twenty yards away on this stretch of virtually empty sand was either an incredible coincidence or a flagrant come-on and suddenly, I was in a panic again. I kept looking up at her and I'm sure she kept looking at me and for some bizarre reason, I found myself humming another tune. This time it was *Summer*, the old Bobby Goldsboro classic — 'Was a hot afternoon, the last day of June, and the sun was a demon, doodle doodle doodle doo.' The eye contact went on intermittently for another half an hour before she eventually got to her feet and gathered up all her stuff. 'No, don't go, please don't go,' cried a little voice inside me, but she was already sauntering across the sand back to the huts. Shaking my head, I lay there for a while cursing to myself. What was I? A man or a mouse? I clearly hadn't learnt the lessons of Cheng Chau. And to make matters worse, as I slowly trudged back to the huts shortly after, I could already feel my skin beginning to burn. In my rush to get down to the beach, I'd completely forgotten about the strength of the midday sun and this had easily been the hottest day since I'd arrived. So when I went to bed later that evening, I really didn't hold out much hope for a good night's sleep. The gathering rainstorms had returned with a vengeance, my back and neck were stinging from sunburn and I still couldn't get that damn 'doodle doodle doodle doo' out of my head; all of which made the fact that I slept right through to eight without stirring once all that more remarkable really.

When I arrived back in Kuala Lumpur late the following afternoon, I jumped into a taxi and made a beeline straight for the airport. My flight wasn't departing until midnight, so after hours of sitting around, reading, constantly peering up at the clock and generally succumbing to mindless boredom, I eventually wandered over to the bar and got chatting to a couple of young blokes sitting on barstools. One was Australian, the other British and both were in high spirits. It appeared they'd just met at the bar and discovered they were waiting for the same flight to London. The Australian, who'd flown in from Bali, had decided on the spur of the moment to visit his brother in the capital. He didn't know how long he'd be spending there—he hadn't even told his brother he was coming—and he only had 400 Australian dollars with him. Perhaps even more alarming was the fact that he was dressed in just shorts, flip-flops and a vest and I shuddered to think what the temperatures would be when he touched down at Heathrow on a freezing cold January morning.

Unfortunately, my flight was seriously delayed. What made it worse was that we all boarded the plane on time, only to find ourselves stuck in a sweltering cabin for over four hours while the ground staff and engineers worked on a mechanical problem. The Qantas cabin crew did all they could in difficult circumstances by serving up food and drinks, whilst the captain, keeping us informed throughout, continually apologised for a problem that was clearly out of his hands. When we finally took off at 4.30am, I quickly nodded off, although many of the Australian passengers later exploded into anger when they were informed they'd have to expect lengthy delays at Sydney airport because they'd missed their connecting flights. I had worries of my own, though, as when we finally crossed over Australian soil, I began to feel strangely apprehensive and nervous, even more so than when I'd left London for China.

PART 2

AUSTRALASIA

CHAPTER 13

SYDNEY

UNDER A SOUTHERN SKY

14th–24th January 1990

Manly, a popular resort on Sydney's North Shore, is bounded by sea on three sides. At the end of its peninsula lies North Head whilst across the water a couple of miles away is South Head and it's these two famous promontories that mark the entrance to Sydney Harbour. On its eastern shore, looking out towards the Pacific, is the popular long sandy beach characterised by the magnificently tall and gracious Norfolk Island pines that line its promenade and the grand St Patrick's College which, perched on top of the hillside, dominates the southern skyline. Linking the beach to the harbour shore on the western side (where the Sydney ferries dock) is the Corso, Manly's main shopping street, and this is where most of the bars are found, as I was soon to discover.

I ended up staying in Sydney for ten wonderful months, and

175

nine of these were in Manly. But it wasn't all plain sailing. No, far from it.

It all began back on the plane. As we started to make our descent, I couldn't stop fidgeting in my seat. What was it about Australia that was making me so tetchy? I had been travelling now for two months, I'd successfully navigated my way down through China, Hong Kong and Malaysia without any hitches and had struck up many new friendships in the process, so my confidence should have been sky high. Yet here we were about to land in Sydney and I was a nervous wreck. Indeed, by the time the plane shuddered to a halt at the terminal building, I was trembling so much I felt sick. Purposely remaining in my seat until all the other passengers had disembarked, I eventually got to my feet, reluctantly gathered my bag from the overhead locker and, stepping over all the plastic beakers and crumpled-up newspapers strewn across the aisle, slowly made my way down the empty plane to face the music.

Twenty minutes later, as I tentatively waited for my rucksack to appear on the baggage carousel, I glanced around the arrivals hall. It was packed with other passengers but something was amiss. I looked around again, gazing at all these people and then it finally began to click. For the last eight weeks, I'd been continually stared at, glared at, leered at and even laughed at by local people. At first, I'd found this quite intimidating but after a few days, I'd become quite used to it and in truth, as time wore on, I began to thrive on all the attention. Being a stranger, especially in such a vastly populated land such as China, meant I was a constant source of fascination and I was only too happy to ham it all up. And without even stopping to think about it, I'd been expecting Australia to be no different. But now, all these pink, wide-eyed, big nosed faces I was staring at looked no different to me. Suddenly the boot was on the other foot. I was no longer an outsider, or a misfit, or a funny looking foreigner, I was now just one of the crowd and the game was seemingly up.

I spent my first few weeks in Sydney holed up in a Kings Cross hostel. Inhabited almost exclusively by other British backpackers, all the talk in the first two or three days was about work and the problems of getting any. One guy told me the situation was desperate. The next day, he said, was the first official day that the factories re-opened after the long Christmas break so the phones lines would be jammed all day with people phoning up for jobs on spec. Another bloke said there were six thousand backpackers staying in Kings Cross alone; half of whom he estimated would also be looking for work. In spite of all the gloom and doom, I was a little sceptical, as I've always maintained that if you really want something in life, you'll get it. The fact that nearly all the girls in the hostel had managed to pick up work was a case in point. And from what I'd seen in that first week, there seemed to be far too much sitting around and grumbling about the work situation and not enough people getting up off their backsides to try to find jobs. I was beginning to realise just why the Aussies dubbed us 'whinging poms.'

Although I did register at a number of employment agencies in the days that followed, I chose to spend most of my time finding my feet and wandering around Sydney. I visited the sights: the Harbour Bridge, The Opera House and the Rocks, I caught up with my cousins who were in the middle of their own backpacking trip and I replied to all the letters that had been waiting for me at the post office. Notwithstanding this, the apathy of the other backpackers gradually ground me down. Try as I did, I really couldn't summon up any enthusiasm about the prospect of work and, before long, the hostel was slowly driving me to despair. Then, on day twenty-two, I received some long-awaited good news.

'Jim?'

'Yeah,' I grumbled down the receiver.

'It's Tracy. Guess what? We've got ourselves a unit.'

'Brilliant!' I exclaimed. 'When can we move in?'

'Some time next week, I think.'

'That's brilliant,' I repeated, clenching my fist.

I'd managed to get in touch with Tracy—a bubbly, fun-loving friend from college—a couple of days after I'd first arrived. She had travelled to Australia via Canada and Hawaii with her brother and his mate, and they'd been staying with Tracy's cousin in Sydney for a few weeks while they tried to find some work. So a week later, the five of us moved into a bright airy three-bedroom bungalow in Fairlight, a leafy suburb right next to Manly. By the middle of February, I'd managed to pick up some work in a factory and at long last, everything was fitting into place. The job was to replace the current warehouseman, who, rather ironically, was leaving to travel around South East Asia. He trained me up in all aspects of the job: how to drive the forklift truck, how to unload the deliveries that came in two or three times every day and how to keep the warehouse in order. The money wasn't that great, but it paid the rent and food and more importantly, the drink, which was just as well really, as the first three or four weeks in the flat were simply frenetic. Every weekend, we'd go out as a group and do just what all the Australians backpackers did in Earls Court: we drank ourselves stupid and partied like there was no tomorrow. And it wasn't just Thursday, Friday and Saturday nights either, for whilst Sundays back home are generally regarded as quiet, reserved days, in Sydney, everybody came out, and pubs and bars were full all day long with people eating and drinking from lunchtime right through to midnight and beyond. 'And when,' as they say, 'in Rome...'

It wasn't long, though, before my housemates fell out and the atmosphere in the house rapidly deteriorated. It's probably fair to say that most people dislike confrontation but I go out of my way to avoid it at all costs. Consequently, I adamantly refused to take sides and, becoming increasingly fed up with all the continual bickering and squabbling, I found myself spending more and more time out of the house. Before long, I'd joined a library and many evenings, I'd go there after work, often for hours on end, submerging myself into books just to distance myself from all the shenanigans. It was on one of these nights that I picked up a Roald Dahl *Tales of the Unexpected* book. I'd been a huge fan of the 70s cult TV series, having spent many a Saturday evening sat in front of the television desperately trying to fathom out the macabre twist at the end of every episode before the silhouetted dancing lady appeared on the screen. Three of the stories I read that evening stood head and shoulders above the rest and all were written by the same author: a certain W Somerset Maugham. The following evening I returned to the library and took out a collection of his short stories. His writings immediately captured my imagination. Invariably set in exotic locations in Asia and the Pacific Islands in the 1920s and 1930s, the recurring theme in the majority of the stories was that of travellers and settlers struggling to come to terms with the strange customs of native lands. And although I didn't know it at the time, I was to go on to read many more of his works over the months to come. Indeed, so enthralled did I become with his writings that his books rarely left my sides for the remainder of my travels. But back in the house, the rows continued unabated. The weather also took a turn for the worse when Cyclone Nancy arrived. For days and days, torrential rains and storms battered the city and it went on to be declared the wettest February in Sydney's history.

Thankfully, at the beginning of April, the tensions in the house were eased somewhat. Ricky, a terrifically sociable and much-loved mutual friend, who'd often joined us in the watering holes of Manly in those first few weeks, was due to fly back to the UK at the end of the month. We had a big farewell weekend planned for him, but before then, he needed a place to stay as the lease on his bedsit had expired. So for the duration of the time he stayed with us, a self-imposed truce was enforced and all other matters were put to the side. And then, after my first week in sole charge of the warehouse, an advert for a tax specialist appeared in *The Sydney Morning Herald*. It was the same advert I'd phoned up about just weeks before, only to discover that the vacancy had to be filled by an Australian national. As soon as I saw it again, however, I just knew I'd have to go for it. The salary was 30,000 Australian dollars (£15,000) and although I was enjoying my job at the warehouse, the money in comparison was nowhere near as good. The most I could feasibly save a week from my factory earnings was a paltry £25. If I could somehow get this job, I'd then be able to accumulate a decent sum of money. If not, then my plans to travel back through India remained in serious jeopardy. I read the advert again. The position was for somebody with exactly the same experience as myself, so that was all well and good, but the problem I had, of course, was that I wasn't an Australian resident. There was only one thing for it.

A week later, I received a letter asking me to go along for an interview. Wearing a pair of trousers, shirt and tie (all borrowed from one of my housemates) and a brand new pair of shoes, I jumped on the bus to North Sydney clutching onto a makeshift file containing my new CV. The interview was with the personnel officer and it didn't get off to a particularly good start. My background did not come into question; instead, she began to air concerns over my supposed lack of experience in this highly specialised field. But the knowledge I'd gained over three years working for two rival American banks and liasing with tax offices all around the world was priceless. I knew this because of the elevated status I was quickly afforded just a month into my second job in London, when I set about saving the bank's customers millions of pounds by claiming back taxes nobody there knew they were entitled to. Yet it was no use. As hard as I tried to convey this to the personnel officer, it all went straight over her head. Maybe she'd been expecting somebody older to turn up, I don't know, but for whatever reason, she was convinced I was under qualified. The one thing I was not lacking in for this position, however, was experience. Fail me on dress, tell me my face doesn't fit, question my commitment, whatever, but please, please, please, don't have the audacity to tell me I'm lacking in experience. Realising that I was banging my head against a brick wall, I then even surprised myself by getting up and promptly cutting the interview short. I was simply not prepared to sit for a minute longer being interrogated by a woman who clearly didn't know the difference between a tax reclaim and a tax refund, so I told her that I was obviously not the person they were looking for, thanked her for her time and marched straight out of the room.

A couple of days later, I received a call from the bank asking me to go back for a second interview with one of the senior managers. Luckily, I had resisted the initial temptation I'd had to throw away my shoes in the fit of rage that had followed the first interview. Now I was quietly confident. So the following week, I got back from work late afternoon, put on the same borrowed clothes again and made another thirty-minute bus journey back to North Sydney. The manager, or Vice President as the American banks like to call them, came down to greet me in reception, then took me up to his office. It directly overlooked the Sydney Harbour Bridge and Opera House, and the views over the twinkling waters of Port Jackson as the sun was beginning to set were breathtakingly mesmerising. In fact, for a few moments, I just stood there transfixed, staring down at the twinkling headlights of the silent cars as they crossed the bridge below us. Lucky buggers, I thought, they'd all be heading home to enjoy another barbecue in their gardens on a gorgeous warm summer's evening. Spotting me staring, he commented, 'Bit different to England this time of year.'

I quickly tried to regain my composure. 'Yep, you could say that,' I replied.

He seemed a friendly enough chap and his warm, gentle demeanour and closely cropped beard reminded me of a young Richard Branson. He looked down at my CV again.

'So let's get this right, then,' he said in a softly spoken voice. 'You moved back to the UK with your mother when your parents divorced and you've now come back to spend some time with your father.'

'Yeah, that's it.'

'And is he very ill?'

'No, no, they found a shadow on his lung. At first, they thought it was a cancerous growth but they now reckon it's pleurisy.'

'Oh, I'm sorry to hear that.'

'Aw, I'm sure he'll be all right soon.'

He looked me up and down for a couple of seconds.

'And how long did you say you've been back in Sydney?'

'Aw, just a few weeks,' I replied, tugging at my shirt. 'Yeah, sorry about that, I'm still waiting for the rest of my clothes to arrive.'

He smiled for a moment.

'And it says here you...'

Oh God, here it comes, I thought, the dreaded question. Don't tell me: 'It says here you were born in Sydney, so does this mean you are in fact a bona fide Australian resident and if so, can you solemnly declare this to be the case.' Come on now, get a grip, all you've got to say is you possess dual nationality and the job is yours.

He paused for a moment, looked back down at my CV and this time, finishing the question, said, 'It says here you've previously worked for an American bank?'

'Yes,' I squeaked, 'I did. Sorry, I mean I have,' I added, wiping my sweat soaked brow. 'Two in fact.'

After firing off a string of technical questions, all of which I answered coherently and concisely, he then pulled out his trump card by asking how much I knew about *Avoir Fiscal*, the complicated and much misunderstood French tax system. It was so complicated, in fact, that it had taken me a full six months to finally grasp all of the complexities and odd little nuances so intrinsic to the procedures of recovering taxes in France, but once I had, the information had been safely stored in my mind for good. So after I'd explained the convoluted tax reclaim process in great detail, he seemed suitably impressed, so much so that he offered me the job on the spot. I told him I'd be thrilled to take up the position and, subject to references and formalities, he informed me that I should receive a formal offer in the post the following week. Shaking my hand, he showed me out of the office back to the lift and as I skipped down the stairs out of the building, I couldn't help wondering to myself whether he knew a little more than he was letting on. I was sure he knew about my nationality but I suspected he was prepared to ignore the fact in exchange for the invaluable information I could impart on European tax regulations. It seemed like a fair deal to me. There was still something I needed to do, though. Dashing across the road, I pulled open the door to a phone box and quickly dialled my old boss's number in Bournemouth to forewarn him he might be getting a call.

Now I was faced with the embarrassing task of telling the factory I'd be leaving, after they'd invested both time and money in training me up for the position. And unsurprisingly, when I did a couple of weeks later, the news went down like a lead balloon. I finished work there on the Friday of Ricky's final weekend and was due to start my new job at the bank the following Monday. The big planned farewell for our departing housemate, however, turned into a 48-hour drinking session and, in spite of the six or seven large glasses of water I'd thrown down my neck late Sunday night, I still felt terrible the next morning. Sweltering in my brand new woollen suit, I waited at the bus stop promising myself I'd never drink again. The bus duly arrived on time, but twenty minutes into the half-hour journey, I looked down at my crisp white shirt and saw that four or five patches of damp perspiration had appeared down my front. Indeed, by the time I got off the bus, the whole of my shirt was soaked with excess alcohol and when I went to wipe my forehead, that too was soaking wet. Although it was still only 8.30, the streets were bathed in bright early morning sunshine and the searing heat was already unbearable. Taking a few tentative steps down the hill towards the office, I started to feel faint. This was not good. All I wanted to do was crawl back into bed. So with seemingly no other alternative, I just about made it to the phone box on the other side of the street and, blaming it all on a dodgy pizza I'd eaten the previous night, told the office I wouldn't be coming in. Brilliant! My first day of my new office job and I'd thrown a sickie.

Thankfully, it didn't take me too long to settle in. Within weeks, everything was going reasonably well, or at least as well as could be expected. Because I didn't have any long-term career aspirations, I had little in common with most of my work colleagues. By this, I mean I wasn't prepared to grovel and pander to my superiors in order to get on, although quite frankly, given that I was largely left to work on my own devices, I wouldn't have had to do much of this in any case. But

I was getting paid good money and that was all that counted. That said, I still had to be careful in case somebody twigged. 'Doing much over the weekend, Jim?' a colleague would often ask. 'Aw, you know,' I'd reply, 'I'll probably go and visit dad for a couple of days. They reckon he could be out by the end of May.' In fact, I felt a bit like a spy, someone who was leading a double life. I adamantly refused to go along to any of the bank's social functions, fearing that a fatal slip of the tongue would more likely occur after a few after-work beers, I distanced myself from my colleagues and avoided all office small talk like the plague, and I generally just kept my head down and immersed myself in my work. The only person I did chat to in the office was Basir, a friendly faced clean-shaven Afghani who also lived in Manly. Basir, or 'Basir the Bold' as I affectionately nicknamed him, had been in Sydney for just seven months, having spent the previous four years living as a refugee in India after being forced to flee his home in war torn Afghanistan. We took the same bus to work and often bumped into each other in one of the many bars in Manly over the weekends. He was a tremendously calm, sensitive and laid-back character and he, like me, loathed his job at the bank. What we shared in common was the secret knowledge that we'd only be working there for a matter of months, for he was planning to return to India in January, and spent much of his time at work just dreaming he was back there. I knew this because on a number of occasions, I'd catch him at his desk idly drawing pictures of the palm-fringed Goa beach he was yearning to return to.

I'd sometimes go to his tiny bedsit at the weekend, where over time, he taught me the proper way to cook Indian food. He told me not to fry onions before they go into a curry as it imparts their flavour, he showed me the method of rinsing basmati rice five or six times and soaking it for hours in cold water before it's boiled, and explained how much better food tastes when it's slowly cooked in a pressure cooker. His curries were, without doubt, the best I'd ever tasted and I immediately took on board his culinary secrets. He also introduced me to Rob, a Dutch guy who also took the same bus to work. Rob was a warm and pragmatic person, also of similar age, who worked for his father's company and spent much of his time travelling around Asia and the Pacific supervising the installation of cash registers in many of the world's biggest hotels. (It was years later before I discovered that his family business was worth millions but, such was his character, he never felt the need to divulge this to me.) He too often frequented the Manly Pacific bar on a Friday or Saturday night, and a close friendship between the three of us slowly developed, especially when the World Cup began in June.

Back in the house, meanwhile, the atmosphere was almost back to normal, largely due to the arrival of a new housemate. Sue was another English traveller that Tracy had met in one of the bars in Manly and within days, they'd become inseparable soulmates. I christened them the 'terrible twosome', as they quickly became adept at using their undoubted good looks and charms to maximum effect. Quite often, they'd wander down to the bars of Manly in the evening and somehow conspire to return a few hours later completely legless without having paid for a single drink between them. And as I was quickly settling into a routine of going to bed straight after dinner in order to get up at midnight to watch the coverage of the football, we'd often pass like ships in the night. So whilst they were sitting in the lounge in bathrobes at 7pm with their hair in towelled turbans, powdering their cheeks and painting their toenails, I'd be supping down my nightly cup of Horlicks in my dressing gown and slippers. And when I was sat on the same sofa hours later, patiently waiting for the start of Costa Rica versus Scotland, or Brazil against Sweden, they'd be staggering back in, giggling hysterically, eager to divulge all the accounts of their various dalliances.

The first big weekend of the tournament saw England play Holland. Rob and Basir came around at midnight, I cooked a big curry and we spent the night drinking, smoking and chatting, waiting for the game to kick off at 5am. When it did, we were hardly in a fit state to watch it, let alone even care which country won. As it happened, the game petered out into a drab goalless draw. Basir continued to come around for a lot of the games, and we spent many a night watching the tournament unfold and following England's progress to the semi-finals after memorable and nail-biting victories over Belgium and Cameroon. Indeed, such was the mounting excitement that by the time the long awaited semi-final against Germany finally arrived, Sue, Tracy and her brother insisted I wake them at 4am so they could join Basir and myself to watch the match.

Now everyone who watched that epic game still probably remembers exactly where they were that night and everybody, I'm sure, has their own story to tell of that momentous evening, so I won't bore you with the details as we all, sadly, know only too well what happened. Instead, I'll cut to the chase. Chris Waddle had just ballooned his kick over the bar and we, like millions of others back home, were sat around in stunned disbelief still unable to take our eyes off the screen; the German players, the management and all their coaching staff deliriously running around the pitch in raptures as the devastated England players sat on the grass in tears forlornly looking on.

'Anyone for a cup of tea?' somebody asked. I glanced up at the window and noticed it was now light outside. Basir got up and, shaking his head, patted me on the shoulder as he left, and then the rest of us shuffled silently back to our rooms to get ready for work. And yet in spite of the huge disappointment, I remained somewhat philosophical about the outcome. The one thing I could take comfort from was that I was not back home, for I knew that all the hype and media attention there leading up to the game would have made this cruel defeat infinitely more difficult to take. But when I got into work an hour or so later, the reaction of my boss knocked me sideways. He was a harmless and endearing old fellow with the friendly face of a kindly uncle, and if he hadn't told me a few weeks before that he was German, I'd never have suspected it for he spoke without the slightest trace of a Teutonic accent. He also had no interest in football whatsoever, or for that matter, sport in general. So when I arrived in the office, what was the very first thing he did? He poked his head around my desk and tauntingly waved a mini German flag in my face. I knew he only saw it as a bit of good fun, but I was still incensed at his insensitivity, so much so that I marched straight down the stairs, out through the front doors and stomped around the block three times in succession to try to calm myself down. Satisfied that all my homicidal inclinations had finally been laid to rest, I returned to my desk twenty minutes later and it was, perhaps, not without coincidence that he didn't come near me again until the following day.

With the lease on the bungalow due to run out at the end of July, Tracy and Sue left to start travelling, although I still needed to save considerably more money before I could even think about travelling again myself. Rob had once mentioned in passing that I'd be welcome to stay at his apartment if I was ever short for accommodation, so one Friday evening, I tested the water.

'Er Rob, um, you know you said the other week if I was stuck for a place to stay?'

'Yeah, sure, you want to stay at my place?'

'Well, I dunno. I mean, well, what d'you think?'

'Yeah, no problem. Hey, dat's what friends are for, you know.'

'So you don't mind.'

'Hey, it'll be good, man. When were you tinking?'

'Well, er, next weekend actually.'

'Next weekend? Shit.'

'Well, if it's a problem...'

'Hey no, it's no problem.'

'But you'll have to let me know how much you want.'

'Forget it,' he said waving a hand in front of his face. 'I don't want anything. I'll tell you what. Just pay for the food and drinks.'

'What, are you sure?'

'Look, as I said, dat's what friends are for.'

'Okay, in that case, it's my round then. What you having?'

'How about a gin.'

187

'A gin it is then.' And with that, I signalled to the barman. 'Two of your best double gins please, mate.'

I ended up staying in the apartment for nearly three months and it worked out really well. Rob's company paid for the apartment and he was overseas pretty much every other week. Whenever he came back, I think he was glad of the company, and we spent much of the time sat in front of the television watching the extensive sports coverage on Australian television over a few beers. It was also a huge relief to be in a place where there was no bickering. During the weeks that Rob was away on business, I made use of the time catching up on my letter writing, not just to friends and family at home, but also to people I'd met so far on my travels. Ever since I'd set off, I'd devoted hours and hours to writing letters and the more I wrote, the more letters I received. Within a few weeks, I was again rewarded with replies. Firstly, David and Reilly, the two Canadians I'd met in Yangshou wrote back apologising for missing me in Hong Kong. The first day I'd called their hotel, they'd been in Macau, and Reilly had then brought forward his flight back to London by a couple of days, so this explained why he'd checked out prematurely.

The second letter I received was from Lu Xiao. Like all the others that had preceded it, it was beautifully written. Again, he was overjoyed to hear from me—'I was very happy to get your letter and every students in our class were very happy too.' His anecdotes were both touching and amusing. He went on to write: 'I find you are the kindest foreign man that I've met. I think we can become good friends. If we become old men (for example, 80 years or so) in the future, and we meet again, we will be very, very, very exciting, isn't it?'

A week or so later, I received a third letter from Arizona. It was from Bob, the guy I'd met on the Yangtze River trip who had so kindly arranged to put me up at Nanjing University. He wrote about what he'd been doing since he'd arrived back in the States and mentioned that he'd received my postcard from Huang Shan: 'and I was real glad to hear that everything worked out for you.' I was definitely not, however, prepared for the next paragraph of his letter, which left me chilled to the marrow.

'After leaving you in China, we continued onto Shanghai. On route to Shanghai, my friend Chong Lee and I had some problems. In a town called Wuxi, we stayed over for the night, in preparation for a morning boat down the Grand Canal. Unfortunately, the hotel we stayed in disapproved of our cross-cultural situation and decided to turn us in. At midnight, five undercover cops came barging into our hotel room and left with Chong Lee. That was the last time I saw her. Just another day in the Middle Kingdom. I'm still waiting for her to respond to my letters.'

August arrived and the weather took a turn for the better although world events were suddenly thrown into turmoil when Saddam Hussein decided to invade Kuwait. Days later, Operation Desert Shield began. US Troops were quickly deployed to the region to protect Saudi Arabia and tensions mounted as a huge military force was assembled to prepare for a possible offensive action.

Around this time, I was also receiving regular letters from Tracy and Sue filling me in with all the details of their travels up the Queensland coast and constantly reminding me what a brilliant time they were having. These only served to make me more restless and, keen to start travelling again myself, I decided to set myself a target to leave Sydney by mid-October. Having finally arrived at this decision, I handed in my notice at work the very next day. By the end of September, I'd booked a round trip to New Zealand and Fiji, departing early January. This, after a brief visit to relatives, would leave me with three whole months to travel around Australia at my leisure so I booked a Circle Greyhound bus ticket, giving me the freedom to hop on and off whenever I wanted within a prescribed itinerary. I finished work a fortnight later and then set about embarking on a final week of preparation and planning before I set off.

My biggest headache was trying to find Rob a suitable leaving present. I'd been indebted by his hospitality in putting me up over the last few months and I desperately wanted to get him something special to show my gratitude for his generosity.

Rob had, for many months, sworn blind that you couldn't purchase original Dutch Gin anywhere in Sydney, but I eventually managed to find a specialised shop that stocked it, so I purchased a large one-litre bottle to present to him together with a copy of the Twelfth Man *Wired World of Sports* tape. *The Wide World of Sports* was Channel Nine's equivalent to *Grandstand*, but the *Wired World of Sports* was a spoof take-off. It featured hilarious impersonations of all the comment-ators, including a brilliant sounding impression of Riche Benaud opening his report on a test match in India with the immortal lines: 'Typical fuckin' stinking hot day here in Bombay.' Rob loved his sport and when I'd first played him the tape in the flat, he'd been in stitches. When I finally presented these to him, he seemed suitably impressed and typically insisted that we open the bottle on the spot so that I could sample a glass of 'real gin.'

Then, in my last week, something quite unexpected happened: I got lucky. In fact, my love life exploded into action and in the space of six hedonistic days, I troubled the proverbial scoreboard no less than four times. I daren't go into the details for fear of incrimination and embarrassing the people in question and, besides, this is ostensibly meant to be a book about my travels. However, after already alluding to a few previous bungled encounters in this department, it would be grossly unfair of me not to elaborate just a little.

I suppose, in some ways, I shouldn't have been that surprised, not because I profess to be a prolific lover, no, far from it, but more in view of the fact that historically, my love life had always been a very stop start affair. Indeed, many years later, Gibbo and I spent the entire duration of a flight back from Mexico City, charting on a couple of graphs the respective conquests of our youth and although our final totals weren't that dissimilar, the line on his graph was practically horizontal, whilst mine in contrast was wildly sporadic; weeks, months, years even, with virtually no activity at all, interspersed with five or six purple patches which repeatedly sent my line careering off the paper.

I often wonder how much of this was solely down to my body language betraying my under confidence and low self-esteem. I have a feeling that whenever I was in one of these long barren spells, I must have had a crazed look in my eyes, a look of total desperation that not only frightened members of the opposite sex away, but sent them scuttling off in different directions by the dozen. Yet as soon as I did finally manage to sleep with someone, I'd always seem to find myself quickly inundated with offers of rumpy-pumpy, with girls almost queuing up to avail their services. It was like the London bus syndrome. You stood at a bus stop waiting for half an hour in the pouring rain then suddenly the sun came out and three double deckers turned up all at once. It was as if my guard had finally been let down and subconsciously, I suddenly became more calm and relaxed and, consequently, a more attractive proposition altogether.

So up until that last week, I was in the middle of another one of these long periods of inactivity. It was, in fact, a particularly lean patch even by my standards. The truth of the matter was, I'd not slept with anyone for virtually the whole of the preceding year leading up to my departure and, much to the increasing delight of my housemates, I'd only hit the mark just once in Sydney when a 40-year-old divorcee had picked me up in a local bar one night, driven me back to her apartment in a bright red Ferrari and plied me with dope and beers. And even then, I'd nearly blown it by falling asleep on her sofa. But she meant business and as soon as the sun came up the next morning, I was cajoled into action. And whilst the stirring sight of her jumping off the bed, peeling off her T-shirt and standing there audaciously with her hands on her hips still lives long in the mind, my abiding memory of the whole affair actually came a few hours later when she gave me a lift back to our bungalow. I knew that when I got back, I'd be subjected to a severe grilling from my housemates as to my whereabouts the previous night. What I certainly wasn't anticipating, though, was that they'd all be gathered in the kitchen patiently awaiting my return, so when we pulled up outside our bungalow that Saturday morning and I saw half a dozen grinning faces peering out of the window, frantically waving their hands in the air and furiously tapping the pane, I didn't know where to look and by the time I eventually climbed out onto the pavement after a final peck on the cheek, I felt like 'little Johnny' being dropped off outside the school gates.

But perhaps what was arguably even stranger about this sudden flurry of activity was that, even after months and months of wondering whether I was ever going to sleep with anybody again, when these opportunities did finally present themselves, I invariably failed to pick up the signals. Significantly, they were all with girls who, up until then, I'd assumed were just good friends and when, one by one, these friendships suddenly crossed that line of no return, I was left reeling. Yet whilst all of this was great for my ego and confidence, especially as I was just about to start travelling again, they were in reality nothing more than lustful end of night flings fuelled by alcohol. So as I say, it was quite a frenzied week and although I didn't know it at the time, when it came to romance that—with one notable exception—would virtually be it for the remainder of the trip. You see what I mean now by fits and starts?

When my last day in Sydney finally arrived, Rob, who'd taken the day off work especially, insisted we spend it drinking in one of our local bars and unbeknownst to me, a procession of friends (and, I hasten to add, lovers) arrived throughout the course of the day to wish me farewell. Late afternoon, after they'd all departed, just the two of us remained. My bus for Melbourne was leaving at 7pm and I told Rob that it was time for me to call a cab. With that, he reached into his pocket and handed me a few coins. 'Before you go,' he said, tilting his head to the other side of the bar, 'put a couple of tunes on the jukebox for old times' sake.' I walked over to the machine at the corner of the virtually empty bar and glassy-eyed, stared at the selection of songs, searching for two that would remind me most of my time in Sydney. After much deliberation, I opted for Paul Norton's *Under A Southern Sky* and Cold Chisel's *Khe*

Sanh. The first was a melancholy tune whose lyrics perfectly encapsulated the mood of someone feeling homesick in London, reminiscing about their beloved homeland. For Australians, the second hardly needs introduction. Cold Chisel are one of the country's best-loved groups and *Khe Sanh*, first released in 1978, still remains one of the most requested songs on Australian airwaves. In spite of its controversial lyrics—the song is about a Vietnam veteran struggling to settle down after his return—the track is upbeat, though the genre is difficult to describe. I'd guess you could call it a cross between folk, rock and roughhouse soul and, featuring the unmistakably gravely voice of Jimmy Barnes, its sound somehow personified the Australia I'd come to love: raw, rugged and unpretentious. Its huge popularity amongst Sydneysiders was finally brought home when I realised that it was virtually always the last record played in bars to signify the end of an evening when all who remained staggered to their feet for one final singalong.

So when these tracks finally came on some ten or fifteen minutes later, I was compelled to order another final round of drinks. This delay already meant that I'd be cutting it fine to get over to Sydney in time to get my bus and, to make matters worse, when my cab arrived, the inept driver proceeded to drive straight into the rush hour traffic. As I sat helplessly in the back of the taxi for forty minutes, humming along to *Khe Sanh* as we inched our way across the Harbour Bridge, I afforded myself a wry smile when I realised the irony of the lyrics—'And the last train out of Sydney's almost gone.' Indeed, by the time we finally crossed the water, I knew that my bus had long since departed so I didn't even bother to go along to the station. Instead, I hopped out at a phone box, rang Rob to tell him that I'd be needing his sofa again for another night and then called my Auntie Bunty in Melbourne to let her know that, due to entirely unforeseen circumstances, I'd be arriving a day late.

CHAPTER 14

MELBOURNE

VISITING THE RELO'S

25th–29th October 1990

Bunty Busby and her mother, Aunty Ive, lived in a pretty little suburb called Mornington some twenty-five miles south of Melbourne. Arriving in the Victoria capital early morning, I called them from the station. It was Bunty who answered the phone.

'James? Where are you?...Right, you'll need to get a train to Frankston. Phone us back when you know what time you'll be arriving and we'll be there to pick you up,'

Because I hadn't seen them for years, I was slightly apprehensive on the train down. The Bunty I remembered, like so many of my aunts (all of my mother's friends were called aunts) was a rotund and larger than life character. Whenever we went round to visit, she'd sit curled up in her chair with a packet of cigarettes by her side, chatting incessantly with my mother for hours on end, cackling with laughter as she repeatedly wafted away the clouds of blue smoke rising from her ashtray. As soon as I got off the train an hour later, I recognised Bunty straight away. She hadn't changed a bit, indeed, if anything, she somehow looked younger than I recalled. Aunty Ive too looked remarkably sprightly for her eighty years; moving to Australia ten years ago had obviously done them both the world of good.

Later in the afternoon, as we sat in the garden chatting about our families and my travels, Bunty happened to mention in passing how tatty their outdoor furniture was looking so, without second thought, I gladly offered to whitewash their chairs and tables. It was a job I thought would only take a few hours, but by 6pm the following afternoon, I realised I'd totally underestimated the task in hand. In fact, it was going to take another full day to finish the job completely. I wasn't complaining too much, though, as it was quite a therapeutic task as they go and because I could do it sitting on the lawn, it meant I was able to bask in the sun at the same time. So early the next evening, after I'd scrubbed all the paint off my arms and legs in the bathroom, Bunty dished me up another hearty dinner, a succulent thick cut steak served up on a plate piled high with chips and peas, but just as I was about to pick up my knife and fork, Sarah, Bunty's second daughter dropped in. Now twenty-eight years old, she was still exactly as I remembered: fresh faced with sparkling white teeth, huge brown eyes and luxuriant Palmolive skin, the epitome of good health. Sadly for me, she was now happily married with a couple of children. She was taking her two young boys, Rhys and Lucas, to watch her husband, Jamie, play in a netball game later that evening and wanted to know if I'd wanted to go along. Chewing on a mouthful of particularly chewy beef, I nodded my head, assuming she'd meant basketball, yet sitting in the car twenty minutes later, she reiterated that it was, indeed, a netball match we were going to see. Slightly perplexed, I really wanted to say something but feared whatever I did would be perceived as a slur on Jamie's manhood, so I prudently bit my lip instead. So of course, by the time we got to the sports centre half an hour later, I was fully expecting to see a dozen fully grown men running around in frilly skirts with gay abandon but it turned out to be nothing of the sort. The game was incredibly fast without so much of the physical contact of basketball, and as a result, seemed much more technical. It was also fiercely competitive, and any preconceptions I'd had that the players would be lacking in male chromosome department were well and truly dispelled.

After I'd spent another morning whitewashing, Jamie and Sarah came around again the following lunchtime and invited me along to a barbecue at Jamie's parents' house. When we arrived mid-afternoon, preparations were well underway. In the kitchen, half a dozen clucking women busily preparing food, were cheerily gossiping away, whilst outside in the garden, their partners stood idly around the barbecue like bees to a honey pot, swigging back beers and discussing last night's big Aussie Rules game. Keen to help, I asked Jamie if there was anything I could do.

'You can get the chooks and snags from the fridge if you want,' he replied.

I smiled, remembering my bewilderment upon receiving exactly the same command at my very first barbecue back in Sydney a month after I'd first arrived. On that occasion, I'd trotted off to the kitchen, wondering just what in heaven's name it was I was supposed to be looking for.

'What are you after, Jim?' somebody had asked after I'd been staring blankly into the fridge for over an hour.

'Um, chicks and snoogs,' I'd muttered in reply.

'There, right in front of you,' said the voice again as I peered at a bowl of pink chicken breasts. 'And the snags are on the shelf below.'

I fumbled around until my hand reached a huge plate of sausages.

'Yeah, that's it, you've got 'em.'

Balancing the food in my hands, I hastily made my way back outside.

'Jim! What happened to you?' cried one of the hosts. 'We were just going to send out the search party.'

196

I suppose the ideal riposte to this would have been something along the lines of: 'Sorry mate, went for a 'tommy' then sat on the 'apples' having a 'chinwag' with the 'trouble,' but instead, I stood there rather pathetically and muttered, 'Don't ask.'

So this time, I returned from the kitchen just a couple of minutes later and hung around listening in to all of the big game chat. Then, after surviving a couple of hours being introduced to all the family and friends, I enjoyed a thoroughly rousing discussion with a couple of Jamie's mates in which we went through every sport we could think of, debating which of our two countries held the respective ascendancy. Now, I liked the Aussies, I liked the Aussies a lot. I liked their self-belief, their cheery nature, their embracing hospitality, I liked their camaraderie, their abounding spirit, their zest for life, I especially liked their drollness, their sarcasm and dry humour, but nowhere did I like them more than on the sportsfield. One thing I'd learnt above anything else during my time in Sydney was the extraordinary passion they have to win every game, race or contest they compete in. If we in this country had half of their confidence, determination and steely grit, I was sure we would no longer be the nation of sporting losers that we'd undoubtedly become. Much has been said about Australian sport and why, in particular, the Aussies are so damn good at it, for when it comes to sport, they unquestionably have the 'Midas touch.' Unlike many others, though, I was not a subscriber to the popular theories that their success was solely down to academies, training techniques or even the favourable climate. No, it seemed pretty clear to me that a lot of it was purely down to mindset. Australia is still a relatively new country located in a far corner of the globe. So far, in fact, they almost have to shout to be heard on the world stage, a bit like a kid does from the back of a classroom. Consequently, its people seem infinitely more disposed to put down their mark in the field of sports. The determination to succeed has almost been inbred in their culture whereas we in Britain come from a far older society where such a resolute passion and untold desire no longer exists. Whilst our governments rely on sending our troops into battle to galvanise the country, Down Under, they despatch their athletes and sportspeople to all parts of the world and then sit in wait for their heroes to return armed with medals, trophies and awards. And good luck to them too, that's what I say. Anyway, back in the garden, with the score standing at 73-2, we'd reached another bone of contention. This time, though, I stood my ground and argued my case vociferously.

'Yes, I know they're only plastic men, but we still have a Subbuteo World Cup every four years for God's sake. Surely, even you must know that.'

'All right,' they conceded, shrugging their shoulders, 'we'll give you that one,' and with the drop of a hat, I'd somehow pulled the score back to 73-3.

'Okay, what about conkers?' I quipped, now on a roll.

Back in Sydney, I'd booked an open Greyhound bus ticket on a prescribed route that—with the exception of Western Australia—would take me to nearly all the main tourist places in Australia and bring me full circle back to Sydney in January. Up until now, my plans had been to visit Bunty and Ive in Melbourne, then double back to Sydney and head straight up to the Queensland Coast, no doubt spurred on by the letters I'd been receiving from Tracy and Sue. The next morning, after another day toiling in the garden, I decided on a complete about turn and reversed my entire itinerary so that I continued in a clockwise direction. This new route would take me across to Adelaide, then northwards through Port Augusta, Coober Pedy and Ayers Rock right up to Darwin at the top end of the country before cutting across to Cairns and the Great Barrier Reef from where I could follow the east coast back down to Sydney.

I'd come to this decision for two reasons: the first being I simply hate doubling back on myself, and the second, because I wanted to spend Christmas somewhere on the Barrier Reef. My first Christmas in Shanghai had been a huge anti-climax, so I was determined to make sure that this year, I'd be somewhere

where I could really let my hair down. If I'd persisted with my original plans, then there was every chance I'd end up stuck in the middle of nowhere for Christmas, somewhere deep in the heart of the Outback. A beach resort on the Queensland coast, however, was far more likely to offer the party atmosphere I was looking for, so the decision was made.

So after calling the Greyhound office at 9am and confirming a seat on the bus to Adelaide later that afternoon, I presented Bunty and Ive with a couple of boxes of cigarettes, and left some beers and wine for Sarah and Jamie along with a few packets sweets for the boys as a token of thanks for their hospitality. Everyone here over the last few days had gone out of their way to make me feel welcome and at home and it really was quite humbling. After that, Bunty dropped me off at Frankston station and I eagerly boarded the train back into Melbourne. It was time to start my Aussie walkabout.

CHAPTER 15

ADELAIDE

PETROLHEADS

30th October–7th November 1990

Arriving in Adelaide at daybreak, I jumped on a tram and heading straight for the beach resort of Glenelg some twenty minutes away, quickly managed to find a place to stay. The hostel was a big 'Scooby Doo' house right on the seafront, complete with shutters, towers and creaking doors. The owners had set aside an annexe for backpackers and were charging just $10 a night, so I booked in for two. Staying in the dormitory were Tom and Fidelma, and when I returned to the room after some breakfast, Tom started chatting in the friendly and amiable manner that all the Irish do. He told me they'd arrived here the previous night and that they'd only been in Australia for just over a week. He and his sister were taking a wander into the city later on and he asked if I wanted to join them, so a few hours later, the three of us boarded the tram back into Adelaide.

After familiarising ourselves with the city centre, we spent a

200

couple of hours in the baking hot sunshine wandering around the circuit for the Grand Prix, where all the final preparations were being made for Sunday's big race. Now, as anyone that knows me will attest, I'm definitely not a Formula One fan or, for that matter, a 'petrolhead' (the term affectionately used by nearly all Australians to describe members of the motor racing fraternity). Indeed, I just fail to grasp why people get so worked up by cars going round and around a track for hours on end, but that said, you could really sense the anticipation and excitement lingering in the air.

Either side of the scalding tarmac, clipboard wielding safety inspectors in suits and hard hats wandered up and down, religiously checking the huge wire fences and safety barriers; in the team garages of Ligier, Osella and AGS, crews of boiler-suited mechanics lay beneath their race cars with spanners and wrenches, frantically making final adjustments to their vehicles; all along the trackside, countless blue 'Foster's' hoardings were carefully being slotted into place by stewards in luminous bibs; up in the grandstands, teams of workers regimentally scoured the aisles, wiping down the bright yellow and green seats and unfurling matching coloured parasols, whilst back on the tarmac, pairs of forklift trucks working in tandem relentlessly ferried concrete slabs and safety tyres up and down the track. Glasses clinked from hospitality tents, hammers banged on the scaffolding, walkie-talkies crackled as sunglassed officials bellowed instructions back to their subordinates and, every so often, the roar of a furious engine would erupt from one of the pits causing the spectators milling up and down the home straight to literally jump in the air in fright. And I have to admit, as soon as we walked by Nigel Mansell's enclosure, all three of us impulsively reached for our cameras and unashamedly snapped away.

'What d'you reckon?' said Tom later that evening. I'd been sitting on my bed back in the dormitory when he rushed over with a copy of the local newspaper and, thrusting it under my eyes, pointed to a small advert for strawberry picking work on a farm in the Barossa Valley.

'So, what d'you think?' he said again.

'Looks good,' I fibbed, for fruit picking was, by all accounts, backbreaking work.

'We were hoping to get your advice.'

'Go on.'

'Well, we've only been here a few days, so we don't really know much about getting work.'

I proceeded to tell them all about tax file numbers, working visas and what to say and what not to say when phoning up for jobs, but even then, Tom was still looking a bit hesitant.

'Would you mind phoning up for us?' he asked, handing me the newspaper, so a few minutes later, I happily called the number and arranged for them to go up to the farm the next day so they could find out a bit more about it.

Waking up to another cloudless day, I headed straight for beach the next morning to soak up some sun and as the hours passed, I gradually felt myself beginning to unwind. Even though I'd finished work three weeks ago, my final fortnight in Sydney had been hectic, as I tried to balance meticulous planning for my onward travels with farewell parties, packing and, well, the confounding rush of jiggery pokery, which had taken me so by surprise. Melbourne had been nice, although staying with relatives, no matter how warm and hospitable, means you're always on your best behaviour. But now in Adelaide, the atmosphere in the hostel was relaxed and informal and the city itself felt far more genteel and calm after the bustling suburbs of Sydney and Melbourne, so I started thinking about staying here a bit longer.

The next morning, I decided to do just that and after calling in at the Greyhound office to reschedule my next onward journey to Monday, the day after the Grand Prix, I stopped off at a supermarket in the city centre. As I was whistling my way along one of the aisles, merrily topping up my basket with packets of noodles and tins of sardines, I happened to bump into a girl who'd been in my class at college. Standing there both with our hands over our mouths, it took us a few seconds to get over the shock.

'Oh my God,' she finally blurted. 'What are *you* doing here?'

'Travelling,' I replied. 'What are *you* doing here?'

'Travelling too.'

'Bloody Hell.'

'This is incredible'

'Isn't it?'

Sarah was with an Irish friend, Cathy, and they'd been backpacking together around Australia for the last three months. She told me that they'd both managed to pick up a couple of weeks' work here in Adelaide in the run-up to the Grand Prix and we quickly made arrangements to meet up the night before the race. When I walked off twenty minutes later, however, I was still in a state of shock and started to wonder what the odds would be of bumping into someone you knew on a particular day at precisely the same time in the aisle of an Adelaide supermarket some 10,000 miles from home. Racking my brains, I tried to think of how many people in the world I knew, or to be more accurate, how many people I could claim would recognise me if they saw me walking down the aisle of an Adelaide supermarket. At first, I thought about five hundred but then I stretched it to a thousand which, in retrospect, might have been slightly on the generous side. I then tried to balance this figure with the total number of people in the world, though I didn't know what the population of the world was—infinitely more than a thousand—but however many there were, it was still nonetheless an incredible coincidence. When I got back to Glenelg, I rushed into the dormitory to tell Tom and Fidelma that something extraordinary had just happened, but they'd already checked out.

Early Saturday evening, I met up with Sarah and Cathy as planned at a pub on Rundle Mall, Adelaide's busy pedestrianised shopping street. Unexpectedly, they had two blokes with them, who turned out to be unbelievably dull and boring—obviously petrolheads just here for the Grand Prix.

The girls, I discovered, were just as bewildered by the two, who it emerged had befriended them from a previous pub and followed them here. So while one of them was at the bar and the other decided to nip off to the toilets, we legged it out of the pub as fast as we could. Back outside, the mall was now hopelessly congested. In between the buskers, clowns, jugglers, mime artists and musicians, the streets were thronged with hundreds of people who'd descended on the city for the race, all seemingly intent on drinking and partying through the night. Maybe these petrolheads weren't such a dull lot after all. We carried on moving from pub to pub, savouring the carnival atmosphere and joining in with all the revelry but as the night wore on, the alcohol kicked in and took its toll, and I ended up losing Sarah and Cathy somewhere in the crowds. Eventually managing to flag down a passing taxi, I arrived back in Glenelg sometime after midnight and staggered back up the esplanade to the hostel, half expecting in my drunken stupor to be greeted on the steps by Wilma, Shaggy and the gang. Then, after ten minutes fumbling around for my keys, and another ten trying to find the keyhole, I somehow prised open the front door lock, crept through reception and, glancing bleary-eyed up at the large clock hanging in the hall, stood there for a few seconds scratching my head. The big hand was on the ten, the small on the four.

I ended up watching the Grand Prix on the television in the hostel, firstly because I'd got a raging hangover, secondly because I thought the $35 admission was exorbitant and thirdly because I just couldn't see the logic of watching cars flashing past my eyes and screaming in my ears for two and a half hours non-stop. Besides, the race was the last of the season and the championship had already been decided a couple of weeks before when Ayrton Senna had clinched the title in Japan, which, for all intents and purposes, made this Grand Prix a 'dead rubber'. Nevertheless, it turned out to be quite an eventful contest with Senna sliding into a tyre barrier on the 62nd lap leaving Nelson Piquet fighting to stave off Nigel Mansell into second place.

I checked out of 'Scooby Doo Mansions' the following morning with a slight tinge of sadness and then took the tram back into Adelaide for the final time. The headlines on the front of the morning's *Adelaide Advertiser* read: 'Piquet Sizzles, Cher Frizzles'—a reference to the Brazilian's Grand Prix victory and the supposed flop of the American pop star's live outdoor concert in a nearby park immediately following the race.

All the talk on the bus to Port Augusta was about the Grand Prix.

'Did you see the race?' said a voice a few rows up.

'Yeah,' came the reply, 'but next year I'm gonna save up the two hundred dollars for one of those gold seats.'

'Were you out on Saturday night?'

'Yeah, too right mate, didn't get back in until seven-thirty... some night, eh?'

'Yeah, some night.'

I was sitting halfway along the bus by the window. Next to me was a girl in her twenties and across the aisle, dressed in boots, shorts and vest, was a strapping hulk of a man with a thick black beard and tattoos of skulls and crossbones up each arm. It had only just gone eleven, but he'd already knocked back three cans of beer. Crunching another can in his hand, he leant over to the girl and said, 'Go to the race?'

'Yeah,' she nodded.' I went to the race,'

'Go to the Cher Concert?'

'Yeah, I stayed. She was fantastic. I was just two rows from the front.'

'So where you heading?'

'Aw, Port Augusta.'

'Mmm... Me too. Surprised we haven't seen each other before. You living with your folks?'

'Aw, no, with a fella.'

And with that, 'Giant Haystacks' leant back in his chair, cracked open another beer and, turning his shoulder, just gazed out of the window.

The bus arrived in a sweltering Port Augusta mid-afternoon and it made a nice change to get off and not be hounded by people urging you to stay at their particular hostel. On Saturday night, Cathy had questioned me as to why I was bothering to stop in Port Augusta and after wandering the around the town for fifteen minutes, I wondered just why I had. I'd read that Port Augusta was the town where the Stuart Highway—the 1800-mile road that pierces the centre of Australia right down the middle—began and that the town had become a strategic stepping off point for the pioneers of the outback at the turn of the last century. And whilst the languid dusty streets of wooden houses vaguely resembled the set of a spaghetti Western, every slatted window shutter was closed, the paint flaking balconies and verandas were desolated, and a pervading smell of creosote hung in the air. Indeed, there seemed to be nothing here of note except a few shops and a couple of empty pubs, one of which I stopped in at to enquire about backpackers' accommodation. The girl behind the bar casually mentioned there were beds in the dormitory room upstairs for $10 a night, so without second thought, I quickly nodded my head. She showed me to the room where I found Terry from Korea and Carol from Switzerland. They were both lying lethargically on their beds at opposite ends of the small room, seemingly uninterested in their respective books that lay open in front of them, as if they were just here biding their time. Clearly relieved to see a new face, they quickly sat up and we chatted briefly about our respective travels, then, one by one, we reached for our pillows, turned over and dozed off. Later in the evening, I took another wander around the town just to make sure I hadn't missed anything. Except for a couple of stray dogs scavenging for food, the deserted streets were still spookily quiet and the rocking chairs still weren't rocking, so I returned to the still empty pub, trudged back up to the dormitory and passed the rest of the night yawning in front of the telly with my listless roommates.

The next day was Melbourne Cup Day, the big horserace that, for a couple of hours on the first Tuesday of every November, traditionally brings the whole of the country to a standstill. The race wasn't due to start until 2.30, so after spending the morning aimlessly wandering around the town again, I called in to the tourist office and discovered there were two sightseeing excursions departing early afternoon: one to a power station, the other to the Flinders Ranges, an area of mountains, gorges, valleys and plains some fifty miles north east of Port Augusta. Not feeling particularly inspired by either, I returned to the pub just in time to watch a horse called 'Kingston Rule' storm through the field to win the big race by a length. Then, I started to twiddle my thumbs. My bus wasn't leaving until later that evening and I'd already checked out of the dormitory, so I finished my beer and with nothing better to do, headed out again. Just as I was contemplating how I was going to pass the next six or seven hours, I stumbled across a library. As soon I entered, I realised that this was not just any old library. On the contrary, for there were computers, magazines, newspapers, maps, compact discs, audiocassettes, videos and photocopiers and, quite possibly, more books stacked on the shelves than in any other library I'd been in, not just in Australia, but anywhere and a large proportion of the publications happened to be spanking new latest editions. And what's more, it was fully air-conditioned, which provided welcome relief from the oppressive afternoon heat. Just why Port Augusta, of all places, should have had such a fine public reading establishment was beyond me, but it did and needless to say, I took full advantage. I ended up spending the remainder of the afternoon there, checking out all the references and information pertaining to the remaining countries on my itinerary, and so content was I in this oasis of riches, I could have quite happily stayed there all night. The staff, however, judging by the way they kept glancing at their watches and coughing, were keen to get home and when they unsubtly switched off all the lights just before six, I felt like the last drunk propping up the bar.

The Greyhound bus eventually arrived at 10.30. As soon as we set off, I quickly curled up in my seat, hoping to sleep, but it was no use, especially after all those who *had* managed to nod off were abruptly awoken by a loud thud from the front, causing the bus to violently swerve, first one way, then the other. For a few terrifying seconds, I held my breath as the driver fought to keep control of the vehicle but miraculously, he somehow managed to stop it veering off the dusty track. As soon as the bus rolled to a stop, he leapt up from his seat and dashed down the steps, presumably to see what had happened. As others on board began to mutter amongst themselves, I peered out of the window into the darkness. Seconds later, the driver climbed back aboard and calmly announced, 'Sorry about that folks...kangaroo,' and with that, everyone settled back into their seats as if this kind of thing was just a regular occurrence. Definitely no sleep for me then for the rest of the journey.

Coober Pedy, famous for its opals, was said to have one of the most extreme climates in Australia. I'd read that because the daytime temperatures here often soar to 50°C (122°F) and above, much of the accommodation was built underground.

'If you have an opportunity to visit these homes, you'll be surprised how cool it is below the surface...' my Insight guidebook said.

Not so at Tom and Pat's, the hostel I booked into just after 9am. With its wooden panelled interior and disturbingly low ceiling, my windowless room was stiflingly hot and airless. I certainly didn't remember asking them for a sauna when I checked in, but that clearly appeared to be what they'd given me. The owners, though, were extremely friendly, and within the hour, I found myself aboard their minibus with a group of seven others on a guided tour of the opal mines. Tom talked enthusiastically all the way there, telling us how opals had been first discovered here in 1915 by a fourteen year old boy out prospecting for gold with his father somewhere south of Coober Pedy, how the mining had developed into a multimillion dollar industry when the European migrants arrived in the 1960s to seek their fortunes and how the name Coober Pedy, taken from the Aboriginal kupa piti, roughly translates to 'white man in a hole.' By the time we'd resurfaced after a short descent into one of the mineshafts, however, I'd decided to rename it, 'white man's hole,' for the landscape was so utterly desolate and barren it felt as if we'd been transported to another planet. All around us were huge mounds of earth that looked like giant molehills, the remnants from old mine shafts that had simply been abandoned over the years. The whole area was devoid of trees, dust swirled around into our faces, there was an eerie lack of sound whilst up in the sky, a pair of huge crows ominously circled.

Tom warned us not to stray too far, as there were many sunken shafts (some as deep as 80 feet) all over the opal fields just waiting to swallow up unsuspecting fossickers. Quite frankly, the whole area was so bleak and sinister, I wasn't going anywhere, holes in the ground or not. Informing us that opals of a decent size, that the miners had failed to exhume, still lay in the ground waiting to be dug up, he encouraged us to start rummaging through the piles of earth.

'There's always someone,' he said, 'who'll find a good 'un and make themselves a nice little fortune.'

'How much?' cried eight voices all at once.

'Aw, a good few hundred dollars if you're lucky.'

And with that, we all started frantically digging with our hands, tossing earth between our legs like rabid dogs burrowing the ground for bones. The heat, though, was stifling, the air listless and before long, the sweat was pouring into my eyes but I soldiered on relentlessly, hoping amongst hopes I'd come across that elusive stone that would pay for my passage back through India. Twenty minutes later, I still hadn't found a sausage. In fact, all I'd seemingly managed to do was replace one big mound with another. Yet just as I was about to give it up for Lent, I struck lucky and unearthed a jagged piece of milky-coloured stone the size of a large grape. Admittedly, it wasn't quite in the same league as the 'Olympic Australis,' the fabled 143-ounce opal discovered in 1956 by Frank Tethridge and Bert Wilson, but a cursory call to Sotheby's still wasn't entirely out of the question. Putting it securely in my pocket for safekeeping, I wandered back to the bus wondering whether I should show my prized discovery to Tom. Of course, when we arrived back at the jewellery workshop shortly after, there were two dozen pieces twice the size of mine sitting on the cutting table waiting to be faceted, and I realised there'd be no need to divulge my secret find after all.

I whiled away the remainder of the day back in my furnace. I say, while away, although that's not strictly true because I was so overcome with lethargy, I couldn't do a single thing. I tried to take a nap, but an hour later, I was still staring at the ceiling eyes wide open. Pulling out my Walkman, I tried listening to some music instead but each time I inserted a tape, I found myself pulling it out again a few minutes later and replacing it with another. Becoming increasingly restless, I turned to my latest Maugham book but thirty minutes later, I was still hadn't progressed past the first chapter, so reaching into my rucksack again, I pulled out an aerogramme and started to drop a line to the lads back home, but even this was difficult and I couldn't manage more than a couple of lines. By now, it was late afternoon, virtually the entire contents of my rucksack were strewn across the bed and the temperature had dropped considerably. Reaching for a blanket, I peered up at the ceiling and shouted, 'More coals on the fire, please.' Minutes later, I finally nodded off.

Early evening, whilst I was out getting some food, I happened to bump into four of the girls who'd been on the opal tour that morning. I'd sort of recognised one of them earlier on in the day and it had been bugging me ever since why she looked so familiar. As soon as I saw them wandering up the street, it finally dawned on me. She and her friends had just arrived at the hostel in Glenelg on the morning I'd left. After introducing themselves—Wendy, Micky, and two others whose names I failed to get—I asked them how they'd got on in 'Scooby Doo Mansions', which, to my delight, they all found most amusing. They told me that they were out on a recce, trying to find out if there was any nightlife in Coober Pedy and asked me if I want to join them on their quest. It took me precisely a single nanosecond to accept the invite and off we went, just me alone with four girls out to paint the town red and suddenly, I was in dreamland. Skipping down the road, I discovered three of the girls were Swedish—unfortunately, not quite the luscious blonde stereotypes that immediately spring to mind (although I suspected the boys back home wouldn't necessarily have to know this when the story was eventually recounted)—whilst Wendy, the fourth, was Australian. Starting off at the aptly named Desert Cave, an underground warren full of dimly lit dinky little alcoves, I asked the girls what they wanted to drink and, while they were conferring, wandered over to the bar and ordered myself a schooner of lager, desperately trying to clear my mind of all thoughts of champagne baths, baby oil massages and five-in-a-bed romps that were swimming around my head. A couple of minutes later, Wendy came over with their order—a lager shandy, two Cokes and an orange juice—not exactly the kind of drinks that were going to set the night on fire, but still. Planting ourselves down on a sofa, we chatted enthusiastically for a while about all the places we'd visited and all the ones we were planning to, but by the time we got to the second bar, I sensed they'd become a bit wary of me, especially once they'd discovered how long I'd been travelling alone. It turned out they were only nineteen, which probably explained why they were travelling as foursome, and I quickly realised that any fantasies I had about the way the night could pan out were, in reality, just that: pure fantasy. They were, nevertheless, good fun and seemingly enjoying travelling together and although we visited a couple more watering holes, my tiredness from the overnight journey began to get the better of me and I eventually decided to call it a day. In fact, by the time I got back to my room, I was so dead on my feet, I could barely keep my eyes open, though this still didn't stop me scribbling out another page to the lads, describing exactly what happened to me the night three naked Swedish girls accosted me in a Coober Pedy sauna.

CHAPTER 16

THE RED CENTRE

THE HUSTLER

7th–12th November 1990

The kangaroo population of Australia at this time was estimated to be just under eighteen million, marginally more than that of the country's general population. I mention this purely because I'd been gazing morosely out of the window for five interminable hours and had still yet to spot a single 'Skippy', or 'Joey' for that matter, bounding across the outback. (Indeed, I never did get to see a kangaroo in the wild or, come to think of it, a koala, which after twelve whole months in Australia must have been some kind of record in itself.) When, a further three hours later, we finally approached Yulara, the base camp for Ayers Rock, I stared out of the window again, this time in dismay, for running all around the perimeter of the large circular road were a procession of shops, supermarkets, hostels, bars, motels and hotels. I hadn't been expecting to find a modern purpose built resort here, well certainly not one on such a scale.

After procuring a room, I jumped aboard another coach for an afternoon trip out to Ayers Rock and the Olgas, the mass of huge boulders some twenty miles to the west of Yulara. Stopping at various gorges, caves and rock formations for photo opportunities, all we seemed to do for the first few hours was hop off the bus and then hop back on again and by late afternoon, I was getting a strange feeling of déjà vu. With the lowering sun now blazing directly into our eyes, Ayers Rock was still nowhere in sight and I was seriously beginning to wonder if I was sitting on the wrong bus. It seemed I wasn't the only restless one either, for the expectant chatter circulating around the bus at the start of the trip had now been replaced by fretful whispers and murmurings of discontent as people all around me repeatedly glanced at their watches. So when our driver finally informed us that we'd soon be arriving at Ayers Rock, just in time for the sunset, a predictable barrage of ironic whistles and cheers resonated from the back.

When we pulled up at the viewing area a couple of minutes later, the car park was packed with empty coaches, camper vans, four-wheel drives and pick-up trucks, whilst out on the brick red sand, hundreds of tourists with cameras in hand were already lining the perimeter fence two or three deep. To make matters worse, a significant proportion of these spectators just happened to be wielding the dreaded video cameras and were recklessly spinning on their heels like marines with bazookas. But when I caught my first momentary glimpse of the rock from the coach window, all of this counted for little for I was overcome with a such a feeling of breathtaking exhilaration, it suddenly made all the long waiting finally seem worthwhile. When Howard Jacobson had visited the 'immense mauve pebble' he'd likened the surface to 'the skin of an animal; creased, and enfolded and a little weary, but also soft to the touch,' and I could see exactly what he meant. But whilst it was indeed mammoth-like in appearance, the thing that struck me most about the rock was its overpowering size. It was far more imposing than I could ever have imagined and it was only on seeing this colossal monolith of sandstone that I could even begin to appreciate just why it holds so much cultural significance for the Aborigines. According to our guide, who was now stood at the front of the bus giving us a brief resume, the people native to this area, the *Anangu*, had lived in the region for over 20,000 years and certain archaeological evidence, such as the numerous aboriginal paintings found in caves around the base, clearly seemed to substantiate this fact.

'It was only in 1987,' he continued, 'when the rock and surrounding area were finally handed back to the Aborigines that the sacred monument reverted to its traditional name, *Uluru* (great pebble),' which rather begged the question just why on earth it had been taken away from them in the first place. With the impending sunset looming, however, I feared now was not the time to be delving too deeply into the history of Australian politics, so as soon as he finished speaking, we hurriedly piled off the coach to try to find our own vantage points. Not being the tallest person in the world can sometimes have its advantages so, drawing on the sympathy card, I hopped around on tiptoe for a while at the back of the crowds, craning my neck as I desperately tried to peer over their shoulders and, sure enough, within a few minutes, I found myself being ushered to the front. Squatting down, I knelt there for a while gazing in a kind of semi-trance watching, as the sun slowly lowered, the rock gradually changing in colour from a glowing bright rust to a dark shade of mahogany, just as everybody had said it would. Twenty minutes later, after the sun had finally disappeared, everyone in the crowd started to clap, cheer and whistle and then, gathering their belongings, quickly began to disperse. Slowly following them back to their cars and coaches, I climbed aboard our bus still on an emotional high. It was exactly the same feeling I'd had after climbing the Great Wall.

'If you're wondering why we're setting off so early, it's so all those who want to climb the rock can do so while it's still relatively cool.' He had a point. It was, after all, only just gone

214

7am. Hans, our driver and guide for the second trip I'd booked to Ayers Rock, was an enterprising character and one who clearly relished his job, for he spoke for over an hour non-stop on the way to *Uluru* and so enthusiastic was he in delivering his commentary that by the time we got there, he still had the full and undivided attention of every single passenger on board.

When we reached the foot of the rock itself, though, I was in for a nasty surprise. I *had* been expecting the climb to the top to be nothing more of an amble, a steady stroll up a gentle slope, but when I peered up, I had second thoughts altogether. The ascent looked perilously steep and the top of the rock lay high above us somewhere far up in the gods. Quite a few of our party took one look at it and decided to remain firmly rooted at the bottom and I didn't blame them one little bit. Now I was here though, I knew I'd have to make the climb. The first two hundred metres up a gradual incline were fine, nothing more harmless than a walk in the park, but then I came to the particularly precipitous section. It was so steep, in fact, that a long chain had been cemented into the ground to help climbers haul themselves up. All of a sudden my blood was running cold. Amazingly, there were some foolhardy souls in front of me climbing up this part on their hands and knees, but not me. Call me a chicken, a mouse, a big girl's blouse, whatever you want, I don't mind, because without any qualms, I wandered over to the side and quickly took my place at the back of the wussies' queue. Ten minutes later, grabbing onto chain with my sweaty hands, I slowly began to yank myself up, not daring to look back at the harrowing drop below. Even though it was still only just gone eight, the heat was already unbearable and before long, drops of perspiration were tantalisingly trickling down the side of my nose. With my hands still glued to the chain, all I could do was shake my head as if I had some kind of uncontrollable twitch. God only knows what the person behind was thinking. Indeed, when I finally got to the end of the chain, I noticed I'd left in my wake an embarrassingly large traffic jam. Much to my relief, this turned out to be the most difficult part of the climb to negotiate and the rest of the ascent, made over gentle plateaux and more friendly gradients, was far less taxing. It took just over an hour in all to reach the top and as soon as I had, I joined another long queue, duly scribbled my name in the visitors' book, and then wandered off in search of the Coca-Cola dispenser. It was only ten minutes later, however, that I realised Hans had been pulling our leg. I mean, a Coca-Cola machine on the top of Ayers Rock—yeah right! Still, he'd managed to reel me in hook, line and sinker and I couldn't believe how gullible I'd been in falling for it. The descent back down took only half the time although I was still mightily relieved just to get my feet back on the ground, especially when Hans casually informed us that five people had actually died falling from the rock and many more had suffered fatal heart attacks. Why on earth had there been no mention this in my guidebook? And why, for that matter, had Hans not mentioned it before we left the bus? But then, maybe by now, I should have known better.

Alice Springs is pretty much right in the centre of Australia. If you had a blank map of the country, and were asked to stick a pin into where you thought the centre was, the chances are that you'd make a hole very near to Alice Springs. It's a town steeped in history, much of it charted in the city's numerous museums. When I took a wander into the city centre the next morning, I wasn't particularly in museum mood, so I called in to the Greyhound office instead to confirm my next travel arrangements. All the people I'd spoken to in the last few days seemed agog that I was spending more than 24 hours in Alice Springs, but I just saw it as another chance to recharge my batteries. It was also an opportunity to let some of the same faces I'd been seeing on a recurring basis ever since I'd left Adelaide get a day ahead of me. The Milanka Lodge also had the added bonus of a swimming pool which, when I got back later on, I found I had all to myself, so I happily whiled away the afternoon lazing in the sun.

Loads of backpackers arrived overnight, so the pool was much busier the next day, most of which I spent reading my latest Maugham book and monitoring the various groups around me. There were a group of tattooed young lads dressed in cut-off denims and football shorts, boisterously cracking open cans of VB and amateurly trying their hands at a barbecue. They shouted, joked, laughed and jeered amongst themselves and then threw each other in the pool where they shouted, joked, laughed and jeered a little louder. But as rowdy as they were, they still found themselves competing for the limelight with a large stockily built guy in a Yankees cap and mirrored sunglasses who, sitting on a deckchair in just his Speedos, was ranting on endlessly to the people sitting either side of him.

'Hey have you been to the rock yet?' he bellowed. 'Gee, that's a funny ol' place. Kind'a spooked me out you know. All that thing about that girl with the dingo. They've made a film of it too, I hear. So where are you guys heading?... Darwin, no shit? I'm going there myself next week.'

Over in the corner, two of the Swedish girls from Coober Pedy who'd arrived overnight, lay motionless on their towels in bikinis, seemingly happy just to be soaking up some sun whilst another girl in a cheesecloth top, German I think, sat under a parasol with her head in a book, totally unperturbed by all of the din. The person I was most intrigued by, however, was a lone and enterprising Japanese girl who, I'd discovered, had been travelling extensively around Australia all by herself. I knew this as when she'd been sat by the pool earlier on, she'd found herself being grilled by the all-embracing American and as I tuned in with interest to the subsequent conversations, I couldn't help feeling it must have taken an awful lot of guts to do what she was doing. Later on, she was reading a travel guide in the kitchen and I managed to get chatting to her, though after a few minutes our conversation was abruptly interrupted.

'D'you mind?' came the voice. I looked up to see a long-haired guy in a denim jacket eyeing my packet of Bensons on the table, but before I had chance to nod my head, he was already helping himself. And with that, he promptly pulled up a chair.

'Shit, what a place tis is!' he exclaimed in a deep Belfast brogue. 'Had my car stolen last week, you know. Police reckon it was Abo's. Got it back a few days later d'ough. Problem was, I had all my stuff in tare. Dey say I'll be lucky to get any of it back, tieving bastards.' Clearly liking the sound of his own voice, he carried on in full flow. 'Yeah, I'll sell te motor now, and hitch up to coast, t'en get a boat to Indonesia.'

I sat there in silence wondering where all this was leading. The Japanese girl glanced at me wide-eyed, clearly a bit taken aback though this might have had something to do with the fact she couldn't understand a single word he was saying.

'Yeah, t'en I'll get a flight to Tokyo,' he continued. 'Gonna pick up some work tare teaching English. Should be a doddle. You can earn tirty dollars an hour you know. Ain't t'at right?' he said, now looking at the girl.

She quickly lowered her eyes

'Teaching English?' I said to her, speaking very slowly. 'He says you can get thirty dollars an hour teaching English in Japan?'

'Yes, yes,' she said, nodding excitedly. 'Maybe forty.'

'Jesus,' said the Irishman, helping himself to another cigarette. 'Is t'at where you're from t'en, Tokyo?'

Sinking deeper into her seat, she threw me a fear-stricken glance.

'He wants to know if you live in Tokyo?'

'Er no, no,' she said. 'I live in...' and then imparted a place I hadn't heard of.

'Well, that's no good t'en,' said the Irishman, waving away a cloud of smoke from his eyes. 'I was hoping she'd be able to tell me where to stay.'

I could probably tell you where to go, I thought, but it wouldn't be remotely close to Japan.

And with that, he got to his feet. 'Right, let's go and get rid of t'at pile of scrap. Mind if I take another for te road?

'Dig in,' I replied. Well at least he'd asked this time.

I glanced at the Japanese girl when the coast was clear and, shrugging my shoulders, ruefully shook my head. She smiled back endearingly, then quickly reached for her travel guide again.

Early evening, boarding the bus for Darwin, I met Fergal and Helen. Fergal, unsurprisingly, was also Irish but this time full of joviality, and Helen, his girlfriend from the north of England, was just as bubbly. After chatting for an hour or so, I curled up into a ball over a couple of seats and clocked up a few hours' sleep before being abruptly awoken at some ungodly hour by the sound of another tremendous thud from the front of the bus. This time, it wasn't a kangaroo we'd hit, but a bull, and it had left its mark with a huge dent to the front corner of the bus.

Late the next morning, stopping for lunch at the town of Katherine, I encountered for the first time a group of Australia's much-maligned indigenous inhabitants. Whilst I'd seen quite a few Aborigines in Sydney, I'd never actually conversed with any myself, predominantly because the general consensus from many colleagues I spoke to in the office was that they were all drunken, troublemaking layabouts who shouldn't be afforded the time of day. Admittedly, the few I *had* seen were invariably slumped around the gangways of Circular Quay or staggering incoherently (and on one particular occasion, rather menacingly) around O'Connell Street's pedestrian mall with cans of grog in their hands, so I'd never had cause to condone or even refute these sentiments. Consequently, I'd left Sydney not really knowing any better, assuming when it came to Aborigines, this kind of behaviour was just par for the course. So you can imagine my sense of unease when following Fergal and Helen into a spit and sawdust pub just down the road, I spotted, sitting under a cloud of cigarette smoke behind the pool table in the corner, a couple of red-eyed Aborigines surrounded by a table of empty beer glasses. In fact, they happened to be the only other clientele in the bar and whilst the others didn't bat an eyelid, their mere presence stopped me in my tracks.

'Hey, c'mon Jim,' said Fergal, tilting his head towards the table. 'D'you fancy a game?'

Walking closely behind, I set up the balls, whilst reaching into his pocket, Fergal flicked a coin high into the air.

'So what you calling?'

'Tails,' I replied, remembering the old expression that used to be shouted around the playground in my schooldays—'Tails for Wales never fails.'

'Right,' he grinned a few minutes later after I'd dispatched the remaining black into the middle pocket, 'I'll get you back dis time.'

As he bent down to put some more coins into the slot, one of the Aborigine guys came over to the table and pointed to the blackboard where he'd chalked up his name.

'Oh well,' said Fergal, after he'd popped his head up. 'I'll go and get another beer in then.'

'Good idea,' I bleated, 'I think I'm gonna need one.'

Picking up my glass, he smiled at me wryly. 'Same again?'

'Yeah, please,' I muttered as he made his way back to the bar, 'you can make it a double if you want.'

Nervously, I set up the balls again, and then flicking a coin onto my wrist, waited for my opponent to call. Dressed in ragged oil stained jeans, trainers and a long pale orange T-shirt, he was vigorously chalking the end of his cue and had a look of concentration on his face that suggested he meant business. As far as I was concerned, however, winning the game wasn't that important; I just didn't want to find myself overawed by the situation. This in itself, though, wasn't going to be easy because by now, several more Aborigine guys who'd ambled in from outside had gathered around the table and were looking on intently. The coin had come up tails again so opting to break, I tentatively reached for my cue. Placing my quivering hand flat on the baize, desperately trying to settle myself down before splitting the pack, I glanced up to notice that Fergal and Helen had already wandered back over, presumably to lend some moral support. Somehow, I broke quite well, scattering the balls all over the table although none had actually disappeared down any of the pockets. My opponent, cigarette dangling from his mouth, languidly walked around the table carefully surveying the lie of the balls and then casually pocketed three yellows in quick succession.

After he missed on the next, I picked up my cue again. Fortunately, quite a few of the reds were in good potable positions and I quickly got to work. Five shots later, I was still at the table and many of the Aborigines, who'd been avidly watching every shot, were now muttering disconcertedly. When I missed my next pot, they all heaped advice on to my opponent as to which shot he should play, not that he really needed it, for in spite of his lethargic demeanour, he confidently despatched another couple of yellows in no time at all. Not including the black, there were now just two reds and two yellows left on the table and it was clearly going to be another close game. He potted one of the remaining yellows, then missed. I potted one of the reds, then missed. Returning to the table, he then doubled the last remaining yellow into the middle pocket, but at the same time, cannoned into the red leaving it perilously close to a corner pocket tucked behind the black. Seemingly unperturbed, he took aim with the intent of deflecting the black out of the corner but in the process unwittingly pocketed my final red, leaving me with a relatively easy chance to win the game with two shots on the black. Or so I thought. The two shot carry-over rule on the black ball has always been a very grey area in pool. In some quarters it applies, in others, the penalty privilege is rescinded and you're only allowed one shot. I glanced over to my opponent to seek clarification.

'Two shots?' I asked, sticking up my fingers. Grinning across the table, he shook his head. So it was all down to my next pot. Stooping down again, I leant over the table, desperately trying to keep my composure.

'Come on, Jim-lad,' shouted Fergal from somewhere behind. I tried to concentrate but it wasn't easy with twenty pairs of lucid white eyes bearing down on me. Slowly, I pushed my cue forward and sent the white ball rolling down the baize towards the black. Although I thought I hadn't hit it hard enough, the contact between the white and the black was just enough to nudge the ball into the corner pocket. Breathing a deep sigh of relief, I looked up to see a beaming smile on my opponent's face. Shaking hands across the table, I nodded my thanks, handed the cue over to one of the grinning group and wandered back over to the bar for a well-earned beer, realising that Aborigines perhaps weren't all the drunken layabouts I'd previously taken them to be.

CHAPTER 17

DARWIN

CROCS AND ROCKS

13th–16th November1990

Just after 6am, I sleepily made the short walk with Fergal and
Helen to the bus station. We'd booked into a Darwin hostel late
the previous night and were now just about to embark on a day
trip to Kakadu National Park. Upon boarding the coach, we
were somewhat surprised to learn that we were the only three
passengers booked on the outing, so with nobody else to wait
for, we set off straight away. If Tony, our guide and driver for
the day was disappointed by the small turn out, though, he
certainly didn't show it, for he chatted enthusiastically to us all
the way, recounting, amongst other things, the full history
behind the fierce controversy surrounding the mining of
uranium at Jabiluka.

Jabiluka stood in the middle of the Kakadu National Park,
which back in the early 1980s had been declared a World

Heritage site. It was one of the country's most sensitive wilderness areas, covering an area of nearly 20,000 square kilometres and was home to nearly 300 varieties of birds, around 100 species of animals, over 1500 types of plants and a quarter of all Australian freshwater fish. It also had significant cultural values. The Aboriginal people had continuously lived in the area for over 25,000 years and there were as many as a thousand recorded sites in the park tracing their legacy in the form of Aboriginal rock paintings. Indeed, the park itself took its name from the Aboriginal language *Gagudju*. In 1970, when four uranium deposits were discovered in the Alligator Rivers region, concerns were immediately voiced by environmentalists over plans to develop them and, in particular, the Jabiluka site, located in an area of exceptional natural beauty on Aboriginal land. The Commonwealth Government set up an environmental inquiry in 1975 to look into one of the four sites at a place called Ranger, and reported two years later that this mine could go ahead provided certain measures were taken to safeguard the surrounding environment. Ranger opened in 1980 under intense scrutiny, though the rows over the proposed mine at Jabiluka and the other two sites had carried on unabated.

Tony remained somewhat philosophical over the issue. He'd resigned himself to the inevitability that uranium would eventually be mined at Jabiluka, but still remained concerned, firstly over the environmental dangers to Kakadu and secondly, as to whether the Aborigine people would receive adequate compensation for ceding their land rights. He then went on to speak passionately about the plight and discrimination of the Aborigine people, informing us how nearly all the problems he came across were invariably with the Aborigines in the 25 to 40 year old age group.

'If,' he said, 'the youngsters could be kept occupied and interested with a particular interest or activity—a sport or a hobby, perhaps—then they wouldn't see the need to resort to alcohol. It's just that they've got nothing to do; they're all good kids, but they're basically bored out of their minds.'

He made no secret of his plans to quit his job in order to set up a local community centre, thus enabling him to devote more of his time in helping the young Aborigines. And this wasn't just a pie in the sky ideal either; an old schoolmate of his had just been appointed head of the Commonwealth Employment Service in the Northern Territory and Tony had already been in touch with him to discuss the feasibility of setting up just such a project.

The journey to Kakadu took nearly three hours, but as we'd all been listening so intently, it felt more like thirty minutes. When we'd first boarded the bus, I have to admit I'd feared the worst but Tony appeared to be thoroughly enjoying escorting just the three of us. It must have made a pleasant change for him to be able to stray from the regulatory commentary he was required to deliver, day in day out, to coachloads of ageing tourists. Today, though, it seemed the shackles were off and he could talk openly and candidly to some impressionable young people, knowing that what he was telling us could actually make a difference. And it was too, for I was beginning to see the whole Aboriginal issue in a totally different light. Perhaps now, if I saw one staggering towards me at Circular Quay, I'd at least try to nod my head in acknowledgement instead of just turning my shoulder and walking the other way.

Mid-morning, after we'd stopped off at Nourlangie Rock to see the famous Aboriginal paintings—etchings of skeletal fish, birds and animals that had been carved into the rocks thousands of years ago—we sat ourselves down on a circle of boulders nearby. Tony, grinning to himself as he twiddled with his moustache, pointed to a eucalyptus tree some fifty yards away and calmly informed us that it happened to be the home of for a pair of deadly spiders. 'I can tell you a funny little story about that tree if you want,' he said. Not needing to be asked twice, we quickly gathered around. One day not so long ago, it transpired, his tour party had stopped here for some lunch. After ten minutes, he'd glanced up and noticed that the female spider was gradually lowering itself down on its web. Sitting on the rock directly beneath was a rather large Japanese tourist

225

who was just about to tuck in to a long crusty baguette. As the spider continued to inch its way down, Tony, not wanting to cause undue alarm or panic, shouted to his party, 'Okay folks, can you all move over here please, time to move on.'

They all got to their feet except for the unsuspecting Japanese character who refused to budge until he'd devoured his roll. By now the spider was hovering literally just inches above his head. When he'd finally finished stuffing his face a couple of minutes later, he casually gathered his belongings, slowly got up and strolled over to the rest of the group, still completely oblivious to the impending danger. As we sat there shaking our heads, a wicked smile appeared on Tony's face. 'Should have kept quiet and left the bugger there,' he mused. 'Certainly would have livened up the day a bit.'

Glancing down at his watch, he then asked if we were hungry. We all quickly nodded our heads. 'Okay,' he chirped, 'time for some bush tucker.' Right on cue, my tummy began to rumble and drooling at the prospect of succulent kangaroo steaks and crispy fat chips, I leapt to my feet. Tony, his eyes twinkling, still had an ominous look of mischievousness etched across his face, however, and instead of returning to the bus, beckoned us over to another nearby tree. Exchanging rather perplexed looks, we picked up our daypacks and skirting well clear of the spider's abode, followed him over to the tree.

'Okay,' he said, tilting his head towards a long spindly branch. 'Now keep an eye on this.' Then, with the back of his hand, he began to gently tap the piece of bark. Almost immediately, an army of brown ants trooped to the surface. Deftly picking one up between his fingers, he raised his hand to his face, squeezed the green case of liquid on the ant's back into his mouth and then gestured to us to dig in. For a couple of seconds, the three of us looked at each other open-mouthed. Then, completely surprising myself, I promptly leant over, timidly picked up one of the ants and, copying Tony's actions, pinched its sac to release an acidy, vinegary-like liquid onto my tongue. Fergal and Helen knew they now had no option but to follow suit. It took them a while, though, but after finally entering into the spirit of things and discovering ant juice was actually quite tasty, we all gratefully helped ourselves to a few more. Mind you, it still came as a huge relief to find ourselves sitting under a tented canopy outside the Cooinda Hotel shortly after, each with a mountainous bowl of Spaghetti Bolognaise under our noses. A rather strange choice of food given the location but I wasn't complaining: a plateful of worms still beat the hell out of a handful of ants.

The leisurely boat trip we took down the Yellow Water Billabong after lunch turned out to be the highlight of the day. We'd been told that the scenery we'd passed through that morning had been used as the backdrop to the film *Crocodile Dundee*. If this was the case, then the afternoon's landscape was straight *Out Of Africa*. The river itself was deathly still with an abundance of lilies gently floating on the surface like giant green crepes. Black and white jabirus and spoon-billed ducks lazily patrolled the shores for fish, long necked darters, balancing precariously on spindly branches, carefully monitored the banks of the river where baby crocodiles lay motionless, sheltering from the scorching afternoon sun, whilst out on the barren horizon, an occasional jagged tree stump rose from the flat marshland. Siesta time. And yet even though the landscape echoed of Africa, the river had its own kind of spirituality that still somehow felt uniquely Australian.

We were indebted to Tony for making the day such an interesting and enjoyable one, and when he finally dropped us off back in Darwin late afternoon, we strolled back to our hostel discussing how lucky we'd been in having such an enthusiastic and informative guide. Before we got back, Fergal and Helen decided to stop off for some food, so I returned to our dormitory and met Jim. Jim was American, not the archetypal brash loud American, but an American who fully understood that a proper conversation generally requires both subjects to listen and speak in equal measures. (After meeting Bob and Dave in China, I was beginning to wonder if I'd been a bit too harsh in tarring all Americans with the same brush, but there again, two swallows didn't make a summer.) Jim had been working in an accountant's office in Melbourne for getting on two years and had packed in his job to go travelling. He was another of a growing band of people I'd spoken to who had nothing but wonderful things to say about New Zealand, where he'd just spent the previous month.

For the time being, though, I was more interested in finding out first hand if Darwin was actually what it had been reputed to be: the beer drinking capital of the world, so later in the evening the two of us headed out into town. Stopping at the first pub we came across, a large and dimly lit saloon type establishment on the side of the main street, we sidled up to the bar and duly ordered a couple of beers. It was hardly jammed packed with drinkers, and even though it was only Tuesday night, I'd still been expecting to see a few more punters inside. I wouldn't even say that the patrons that were here were drinking staggering amounts of beer either; everyone seemed quite civilised and comparatively sober. Maybe there was just a prolifery of bars in the town. Ferrying our schooners of Kakadu Beer across the dusty wooden tiled floor, we sat ourselves down at a small round table, but just as I was beginning to recount the details of my day trip, a passer-by promptly put his fist through the window only three or four feet away from where we were sitting, sending shards of shattered glass all over the pub floor. Nobody else in the bar bat an eyelid: all the punters quickly returned to their conversations, the old guy behind the bar just nonchalantly shrugged his shoulders and ten minutes later, the shattered glass still lay in smithereens all across the floor. Rather unnerved, we quickly knocked back our beers and returned to the hostel a little sooner than planned.

CHAPTER 18

CAIRNS

HULA HULA TIME

17th–27th November1990

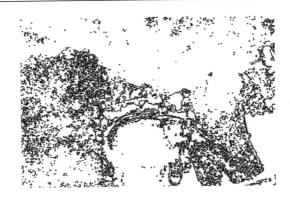

I arrived in Townsville dog-tired. By the time I boarded another bus half an hour later for the final leg to Cairns, I'd had it. Bring on another forty-eight hour journey for all I cared. Yet in spite of my tiredness, I was brimming with excitement. It was Saturday morning and I'd arranged to meet Tracy and Sue at a hostel called 'Caravella 149'. (Bit of a stupid bloody name if you ask me, but there you go.) Discovering the hostel had a complimentary pick-up bus, I jumped aboard and sat in my seat for twenty frustrating minutes whilst the driver, idly chatting outside to one of his mates, waited for another bus to arrive at the station. When it eventually did, there were no more passengers to pick up. Typical!

As I was checking in to the hostel, I scoured the visitors' book in reception. There was no mention of Tracy or Sue. I checked the noticeboard in the hall. No messages from the girls there either. The fact they were obviously not here didn't come as a great surprise—not that they were necessarily unreliable, but sometimes you just get that feeling and I'd already run this scenario through my mind as we'd approached Cairns on the coach.

Late afternoon, with nothing much better to do, I took a wander into the town centre and it didn't take long to realise I'd finally reached the Club 18-30 coast, for so much in Cairns was geared to young people. There were countless booking offices advertising a multitude of trips—snorkelling trips, fishing trips, diving trips, island trips, rainforest trips, bushwalking trips, balloon trips, barbecue trips, white-water rafting trips, helicopter trips, even bungy jumping trips. There were bars and nightclubs. There were restaurants and takeaways catering for every palate—Asian food, European food, Middle Eastern food, vegetarian food, Australian food, Far Eastern food, seafood, fast food, junk food, takeaway food. There were more bars, and there were shops—bookshops, clothes shops, sports shops, shoe shops, diving shops and souvenir shops. Oh, and there were also a few more bars.

Now, if I had been here by myself, I'd be cynically slagging the place off as a cheap and tawdry beach resort full of screaming drunken girls and beer swilling louts. As it happened, though, I wasn't, I was going to be here with friends (assuming of course that Tracy and Sue finally managed to prise themselves away from Magnetic Island) so I quite liked what I'd seen of Cairns so far and returned to Caravellas in much better spirits. I hadn't been back long when there came a knock on the door. Jumping up from my bed, I opened it tentatively. One of the hostel staff stood there and informed me there was a telephone call for me down in reception. It must be the girls, I thought. As I quickly followed her down the stairs, I suddenly feared the worst. They weren't coming. They were calling me to tell me they weren't coming. Oh girls, you can't let me down now...Please don't tell me you're not coming...Pleeeaaaase. Nervously picking up the receiver, I heard Tracy's voice on the other end.

'Jim? Jim?'

'Yeah, Trace, it's me.'

'Listen, I haven't got many coins so I'll have to be quick. We're going to spend the weekend here. It's a long story but we'll be coming over on Monday, so we'll see you then.'

And with that, the line went dead. I put the receiver down and breathed a huge sigh of relief. I could live with that. A couple more days to kill, but yep, I could live with that.

The *Insight* guidebook I had on Australia provided nothing like the priceless information and advice for backpackers that the *Lonely Planet* guide did, although it did have some wonderfully bright coloured photographs of Australian people and places, as well a series of useful maps. As I was reading up about Cairns in my room the following morning, I came across an intriguing passage entitled *Beware The Boulders.** It read:

*'Another warning: about 45 minutes south of Cairns, in some of the most ruggedly beautiful terrain along the route, you'll come across a little town called **Babinda**. If it's hot, and it usually is, the traveller may be tempted to detour from the highway through Babinda to the much-signposted mountain picnic and swimming area called **The Boulders**. After a short walk through rainforest, he may be tempted to plunge into the gurgling stream for a refreshing dip.*

Good advice is to do no such thing. The Boulders has claimed at least 25 lives this century. It's breathtakingly lovely, but it's also one of the most naturally dangerous spots in the country— and that's saying something. Unfortunately, tourism being such a competitive business, The Boulders' grim toll has not led to the closure of these drowning pools but to the hatching of a so-called Aboriginal legend, wherein the spirit of a beautiful Aboriginal princess is said to lure young male travellers to their destruction. Sadly, the legend seems to be self-perpetuating. This is one tourist trap that plays for keeps, as its list of young victims attests.'

*From *Insight Guide to Australia*, ISBN: 0245-54184-5; 3rd edn, 1988, reproduced by permission Apa Publications and Insight Guides.

After reading this, I prudently decided to spend the rest of the day safely lounging by the guesthouse pool.

A couple of nights later, I was back in Magnums, a very lively bar full of backpackers and tourists and seemingly *the* place to be. I'd wandered down to the bar the previous afternoon. It had been packed then—as I said, Sunday was the big drinking day in Australia—but now it was six o'clock Monday evening and far more civilised, so I sat down for a bite to eat. Not long after I'd finished my food, I looked up and spotted Tracy and Sue coming through the door. As soon as they saw me, their bronzed faces lit up. After we'd embraced, I returned from the bar with a round of drinks and for the next hour or so, sat there unable to get a word in as the 'terrible twosome', plying me with countless photos of their new friends, raved non-stop about Magnetic Island.

'And that's Dave. I liked Dave'

'Yeah, I liked Dave too.'

'Aw, Sue, do you remember that day he took us all out on the boat?'

'Yeah, that was such a good day, remember diving off that rock?'

'Oh God, yeah. I'd forgotten about that, you should have seen it, Jim.'

'Yeah, we stopped off and everyone climbed this rock and jumped into the water.

'Jim, it was so high that I never thought we could do it. You went first didn't you, Sue.'

'Mmm, I really didn't think you were going to do it, Trace.'

'Oh God, I know.'

'I don't think the Danish girls jumped.'

'No, they didn't. And then you jumped again, Sue. Aw, Jim, it was brilliant. And here's Geoff and Paul'

'Hey, d'you remember that night when they pushed everyone in the pool.'

'Aw, that was so funny, Sue.'

'Wasn't it Geoff's birthday?'

'Yeah, that's right.'

'Trace, that reminds me, what was the name of that Finnish guy who had the hots for Simone?'

'Oh, you mean the one who stayed in his hut all day? I dunno, but he was a bit odd.'

'Yeah, I thought that too. He gave me the creeps.'

A hundred and fifty stories later, my ear was so bent it was in danger of falling off, so I was mightily relieved when the girls eventually suggested we head back to Caravellas. As I lay in bed later that night, however, I couldn't help thinking how great Magnetic Island sounded. It seemed like the obvious place to spend Christmas, but worryingly my money was quickly running out; of the 1000 dollars I'd set aside for my travels around Australia, I only had 160 left and I was beginning to wonder if I was destined for another anti-climactic Christmas.

Mid-afternoon a few days later, we were sat on the steps of our self contained cabin, one of eight or nine that surrounded the communal Jungle Lodge, staring in wonder at a couple of majestic peacocks strutting about only two or three feet in front of us as they repeatedly unfurled their stunning array of emerald and azure feathers. We'd booked ourselves on an inclusive two-night trip to Cape Tribulation, some 150 kms north of Cairns, and had arrived here just after lunchtime. Bordering a lush green tropical rainforest, the area was another that had been designated a World Heritage site and it seemed like a perfect place to spend a few days de-toxing before we returned to Cairns at the weekend. When, a couple of hours later, I made the startling discovery that I'd now been away exactly a year, though, these well-intentioned plans went out of the window. The girls insisted we should celebrate this anniversary accordingly and even though the shop had just closed for the day, Tracy decided she'd try to use her charms by asking the German travellers in the cabin next to us if they had any booze we could 'borrow' until the next day. She returned a couple of minutes later with an unopened five-litre cask of wine to be greeted by huge cheers and the celebrations dutifully commenced.

So the next morning, nursing our heads, we set off on a $4^1/_2$-hour guided walking tour of the rainforest. Jim, our guide leading the party of twelve was another terrifically enthusiastic and informative chaperon. Twenty minutes into the trip, stopped in a clearing in the forest, he gathered us around, pointed to a tree a foot or so behind him and said, 'This, my friends, is the *Gympie-Gympie*.' Not entirely sure exactly what it was we were supposed to be looking at, I peered up half expecting to see another hairy spider inching its way down from a branch. Jim then calmly informed us that this seemingly harmless looking tree actually happened to be one of the most deadly plants in the world. 'Even the slightest graze against one of these leaves' he said, 'can leave a grown man paralysed. Just brush one of these nettles and you will be in agony.'

He went on to explain that the toxins it releases cause intense pain to any part of the skin that comes into contact with the plant nettle, especially in the first thirty minutes.

'The discomfort,' he continued, 'can last for weeks, months and years, returning in particular when the skin is prone to fluctuations in temperature. There are many stories of humans and animals going mad after exposure to the plant. Oh, and one final thing,' he added. 'There is no known antidote.'

By now, we'd all sheepishly retreated a few paces. Jim, beckoning us over to the tree, instructed us to look carefully at the leaves, and to memorise exactly what they looked like. One at a time, we crept to within a few feet of the plant, carefully checking our footing for any unsuspecting vines that could trip us up and send us careering towards a life of intolerable anguish. Close up, the leaves were large, green and heart-shaped with tiny purple dots at the top and certainly looked harmless enough although you could probably say the same about our own little stinging nettles back home. A little further on, he pointed to another plant, this time one whose tendrils could reach out and grab you as you walked past. I was now beginning to feel really uncomfortable. Indeed, the longer I spent in Australia, the more I seemed to find out just what a dangerous country it was: sunken mine shafts in Coober Pedy, perilous sandstone rocks in the desert, poisonous spiders in Kakadu, drowning pools in Cairns, and now deadly stinging plants and trees that attacked you for no apparent reason. As we continued deeper and deeper into the rainforest, my eyes peeled for heart-shaped leaves and wiry palms, Jim, pointing out various stick insects and luminous green lizards along the way, informed us that much more wildlife—dingoes, wild pigs, bats and snakes—could be seen on the night treks into the rainforest. Not for me they wouldn't. We ended the trek at a particularly scenic spot where situated under a mosaic of lime green, were a series of cascading waterfalls, gurgling streams and steaming rock pools. Jim, resting a foot on a boulder, said we were free to jump in for a swim. Some of the group did, though I abstained, convinced that the waters would be infested with blood sucking leeches and man-eating piranhas. Still, in spite of all the dangerous wildlife and treacherous terrains, something infinitely more terrifying just happened to be lying in store for me the very next day.

It started innocuously enough when, just after nine, we boarded one of the two mini-buses for the drive back to Cairns. Tracy was excited as she was meeting her boyfriend later on and we were all looking forward to a big Friday night in Magnums. Around lunchtime, half an hour or so outside of Cairns, we stopped off at a picnic site on a grassy verge overlooking the sea, and as we piled out of the vehicle, the second bus pulled up behind us. Our guide, Dave, quickly gathered the two groups into a circle and enthusiastically told us all about the competition he'd been harping on about all morning.

'Whoever wins,' he implored, 'must do the jump this afternoon. The jump is free, but it can't be exchanged, it can't be sold, and it can't be transferred to another person. The person who wins the competition *has* to jump this afternoon.'

'All right mate,' I muttered to myself. 'Keep your bloody hair on.'

'So, if you don't want to bungy jump or you're unable to bungy jump, for whatever reason, move aside now.'

Immediately, about a quarter of the group stepped to the

side. I was just about to join them when Tracy asked me what I was doing. Shaking my head, I told her I wasn't bothered about bungy jumping, especially here.

'Nope,' I said, defiantly.' If I'm going to do one, I'll wait 'til I get down to New Zealand.'

'Oh, go on Jim, you have to, it's only a bit of fun and besides, you're never going to win.'

I supposed she was right, and not wanting to be thought of as a wimp, I returned to where I'd been standing.

'Okay folks,' shouted Dave. 'Right, I'm now going to toss a coin in the air. All of you who think it's going to be heads, stand on this side,' he said, throwing out his left arm, 'and all those who think its gonna be tails, stand on this side,' he continued, tilting his head to the right. 'All those who call it correct, stay in and all those who don't are out, it's as simple as that and we'll keep going until we have a winner.'

Opting, as I always do, for tails, I joined the group on the right. With the two groups assembled, Dave flicked the coin up into the air and watched it fall onto the grass. As he went to pick it up, he grinned and glancing to his right, calmly announced it had landed on tails.

The 'heads' group of about fifteen, including Tracy, walked back to the abstainers.

'Okay, same thing folks, all those who think this one will be heads, move to the left and all of you who are calling tails, to my right.'

Staying put, I remained in the tails camp. A few seconds later, flicking the coin higher in the air, he bent down to retrieve it. Looking this time to his left, he grinned again. I breathed a momentary sigh of relief. Then abruptly he turned on his heels. 'Ah, had you going there didn't I? Guess what? It's tails again.'

The heads group, all looking relieved, except for a lanky Scandinavian guy (no doubt Finnish) who was seemingly desperate to win, scurried back to the increasingly larger group of spectators. Reassuringly for me, Sue was still in the remaining group of seven or eight, but on the third flick of the coin, she called heads, and for the third time, it came up tails. I was now concerned. In fact, I was beginning to crap myself. On the fourth toss, I called tails again on the assumption that a heads would surely come up this time. Amazingly, it came up tails again. Not totally convinced, I went over to check that the coin, still lying on the grass, had definitely landed on tails. It had. Still not convinced, I turned the coin over just to make sure it wasn't double-sided, but the head of the Queen was plainly peering off to the right.

There were now just three of us left in and I was trembling. Physically and mentally trembling. Glancing up, I saw Tracy and Sue waving and laughing from the crowd. I looked back down to the ground, shaking my head and, clasping the bridge of my nose between my thumb and forefinger, screwed up my eyes. This was serious shit now. Someone please tell me this can't be happening. This time it *had* to be heads. It can't come up tails for a fifth time. It can't.

I looked at the two other girls trying to work out what they were going to call. It had to be heads.

'Okay then folks, what's it going to be then?'

Gazing up to the skies, I quickly made the sign of the cross on my chest. When I looked across, I saw that both the girls had moved to the left. They were calling heads. Both of them. They were both calling heads. I froze on the spot. If I joined them, then it would be stalemate and we'd all have to call again.

Fuck it, I thought. I'll go tails. We'll see. I'll show them. Remember, tails for Wales never...

And then, metaphorically, the penny finally dropped. If it's tails for Wales then...Fuck, what had I done? If tails for Wales never fails and I *didn't* want to win, then I should be calling heads! Fuck, fuck, fuck, that's it!

But just then I heard, 'Okay, good luck folks, here we go.' It was too late, I'd already moved to the right. In slow motion, I watched the coin swirl in the air, slowly following it reach the apex of its trajectory before it slowly began to fall. And then, it landed silently on the grass. In a flash, the three of us rushed over to Dave's feet. FUCK...ING...HELL. Fuck.

Fuck. Fuck.

'Okay ladies and gents, I can now confirm we have ourselves a winner.'

I peered over to the large group. It was like one of those scenes in the movies where you see people shouting and cheering, but their sound is muted. A few seconds later, Tracy and Sue came racing over.

'Jim! Jim! You've won! You've won!' they screamed, patting me on the arm as I walked around in circles with my hands cupped over my nose.

'It is Tim isn't it?' asked Dave

I shook my head, eyes still closed.

'And the winner, folks, is Tim. Come on now, give him a round of applause.'

Winner? Winner? It's not winner, it's loser you fuckin' idiot. You don't win a bungy jump, you fuckin' lose one. And you can't even get my fuckin' name right, you absolute wanking, cunting, fuckin' tosser. Fuckin' hell. Fuckin' fuck, fuck, fuck. Please, please, please, tell me that this isn't happening, please. My only crime was calling wrong. Now I was about to walk the plank.

It took us thirty minutes to reach the bungy site, although it felt more like thirty seconds. When I got off the minibus, I was so terrified, the proverbial tortoise was already poking its head out of the shell. Everyone was patting me on the arm and back and wishing me good luck and it was then that I looked upwards and saw the tower for the first time. Set in a clearing amongst some dense woodland, it was high, ominously high, shitscaringly high. My only words of comfort came from Dave. 'Look, don't worry about it,' he said as he escorted me up the long zigzag metal staircase to the top of the 144-foot gantry, 'I've done it five times and it's still just as scary now. It's only natural. There'd be something wrong with you if you weren't nervous.'

Yeah, but you're not jumping now, are you, you fuckwit.

When we finally reached the top, I was asked to sign a disclaimer of liability which, to be quite frank, was a bit of a joke in itself, but I could barely pick up the pen, let alone make a signature as my hand was shaking so much. I glanced over to the platform. There was a young guy perched on the edge of the tower ready to jump. I recognised him from Caravellas, although as he prepared to launch himself off the tower, I had to look away simply because I knew my eyes would follow him down and that was one direction I definitely didn't want to look. Dave introduced me to the gum chewing AJ Hackett crew. Tanned, fit, and decked out in caps and Ray-Bans, they were coolness personified. To their credit and my surprise, they were also very reassuring. As they set about binding my feet together and attaching the rope, they talked to me the whole time.

'Okay Tim, don't be nervous, there's absolutely nothing to worry about.'

Well, not for you maybe, 'cause you're not bloody jumping, are you?

'It's perfectly safe. Hundreds of people jump every day. We've been doing this for years. No worries mate, you'll be fine.'

I really wanted to say something, just an 'okay,' or a 'cheers,' or even an 'actually it's Jim, not Tim,' but my brain was so paralysed with fright that all links to my voicebox had already been severed, so I just dumbly nodded my head.

'Okay, what'll we do is count you in: five, four, three, two, one and then you jump. Whatever you do, make sure you go first time. If you don't and you hesitate, it'll be ten times worse second time around.'

As they helped me to my feet, I peered out towards the azure waters of the Coral Sea shimmering in the distance. What I was supposed to do now was let go of both the crew and the rails, shuffle out to the edge of the tower, stand motionless while they counted me in and then leap out to the horizon with my arms outstretched. But try as I did, I just couldn't let go and each time I tried to stand up straight, my body fell backwards with my arms flapping to grab back onto the rails.

'Okay Tim, Tim, okay, right, stand up there Tim... okay... now let go Tim, okay, let go, that's it Tim... okay... no... just try and stand up Tim... okay... that's it... okay... now stand up

Tim...you've got it, that's it Tim... that's it... you're fine... okay...
that's it... okay...

As I stood there quaking in my boots, one of the crewmembers
instructed me to wave at the photographer on the gantry to the left,
but I still didn't dare look, as if I did, I'd make the fatal mistake of
looking down. Instead, I limply flapped my hand.

Okay, here we go then...Five'

Now? Hold on a second, just wait...

'Four'

Oh fuck!

'Three'

No, slow down!

'Two'

Oh fuck!

'One'

For a single, gut-wrenching moment, I glanced down and
saw a tiny pool of muddy grey water beneath me, and then,
arms glued to my side, made a tiny hop

A

N

D

S

U

D

D

E

N

L

Y

I

W

A

S

F
A
L
L
I
N
G

S
I
L
E
N
T
L
Y

I
N
T
O

S
P
A
C
E

Seconds later, I was catapulted back up into the air. My head was shuddering, my arms were flailing and my body was spinning horribly out of control. I'd survived the drop, but now my worries had shifted. Were my feet still attached to the bungy? If not, then I'd be thrust into the air like a human torpedo. Then, all of a sudden, I was falling again and it was at this point I realised my chances of survival had been significantly enhanced. Indeed, so overjoyed was I still to be alive that when I bounced up a second time, I desperately wanted to shout something like, 'Wey hey, look at me flying through the air,' but all I could manage was a whimper. A few more springs up and down later, I was hanging upside down, spinning around like a coiled flex. The man on the dinghy beneath me held up a pole, which my clammy hands eagerly grasped, and then the bungy was lowered down gently until I was lying face down in the rubber boat. 'Enjoy it then?' grinned the boatman as he began to unclasp my feet. Staring right through him, I gravely shook my head. After he'd paddled the boat the two or three yards to the side of the pool, I struggled to my feet and, still unable to speak, went to shake his outstretched hand. And with that, I unceremoniously pushed myself over the side of the dinghy, collapsed into a heap on the wooden gangway and lay there staring up to the skies. A few moments later, Tracy and Sue came running down the steps.

'Jim, Jim, What was it like?'

Hard as I tried, though, the words still wouldn't come out and the girls, eventually leaving me to my own devices, took a wander up to the top of gantry. As I sat in silence by the side of the pool for a while, just trying to gather my thoughts, I craned my neck towards the top of the tower and made out the figure of a plucky Japanese girl teetering on the edge of the precipice. I'd seen her pacing up and down minutes earlier—one of the crew had whispered to me as he was binding my feet that she'd been up there for over an hour—and I now found myself shouting words of encouragement up to her. She stood there hovering on the edge for getting on a minute, but just when I thought she was going to turn back again, she jumped. For a split second, I saw her terrified screwed up face as she approached the ground and then she was gone again, hurtling back towards the top of the tower like a catapult. When she was lowered down into the dinghy a minute or so later, I clapped and whistled, then rushing down the steps to greet her, patted her on the shoulder as she clambered out of the boat. She was clearly still in shock, though, constantly peering back up to the tower and shaking her head as if trying to comprehend the magnitude of what she'd just done. But with the life beginning to return to her ashen face, she finally muttered something to herself in Japanese, then afforded me a broad and exuberant grin, and I realised that a sense of camaraderie had just been established between two fellow jumpers.

For the next twenty minutes, I sat and watched a succession of other people make the $85 jump from the tower. Some looked confident, a couple looked nonchalant, one or two even looked arrogant, but most, like me and my Japanese friend, were frozen with fear. When we were eventually summoned back to our minibus, I was still being congratulated by all on board. I felt like a hero. The remainder of the short journey back to Cairns was spent going over the jump again and again in my mind and trying to come to terms with the reality that a bungy jump was such an unnatural thing to do. I mean, to jump off a 144-foot tower and effectively cheat and deprive the force of gravity, just when it thinks it has you in its clutches, is a fundamental defiance of logic. I remained in a state of euphoria all afternoon and even when we went out later that evening, was still on a huge emotional high, overdosed with adrenaline, so much so that the first few schooners of beer at Magnums were drained in record time. Within minutes, the bungy jump story had been recounted for the first time and if I'd had my way, I would have quite happily spoke of nothing else all night. All the talk in the bar, however, was of Margaret Thatcher and the shock news from back home that she'd resigned as Prime Minister the previous day. Unlike my doughty Japanese colleague, though, it appeared the indomitable lady of British politics had been pushed before she jumped.

CHAPTER 19

MAGNETIC ISLAND

AN AUSTRALIAN CHRISTMAS

28th November 1990–3rd January 1991

After a few more days in Cairns, I split from the girls and, following my instincts, headed straight for Geoff's Place, the backpackers' resort on Magnetic Island where Tracy and Sue had spent the last two months, in the hope that I'd be able to pick up some work there too. To my relief, I was offered a job on the spot that paid for my room—well, a cabin shared with seven other backpackers—as well as breakfast and evening meal. But the work I was given, cleaning showers and toilets, was not at all pleasant and I set about trying to get it done as quickly as possible each day. It was a job that was supposed to take four hours but within a week, I'd got it down to two. Most of the other backpackers staying at Geoff's Place were British and virtually all of them were working there too—gardening, cooking or cleaning—and I got the feeling that most of the group that had been here with Tracy and Sue had finally moved on and now another bunch of backpackers were establishing themselves as the new kids on the block. Encouraged by the management to do so, we participated in nearly all of the trips they organised every week. There were sunrise walks with complimentary chicken and champagne breakfasts, picnics on the beach, boat trips out to the Great Barrier Reef, horse riding sessions at a nearby ranch, diving courses, evening spit roasts as well as the daily barbecues. Within a few weeks, a healthy relationship had been formed between the full time staff and the backpackers with everybody looking forward to the traditional end-of-day game of water polo in the pool and the banter that invariably followed long into the evenings. By mid-December, I'd decided to stay on for Christmas for I'd made many new friends during the first month and furthermore, I hadn't broken into any of my dwindling funds set aside for my Aussie Walkabout. I was still, however, unable to change my cleaning job for another and resigned myself to the fact I was destined to be a toilet cleaner for the rest of my life.

Christmas Eve finally arrived with everyone in high spirits, but so too did Cyclone Joy, bringing with it torrential rains and gale force winds, forcing us to spend the evening and all of Christmas Day in an adjacent building, sheltering from palm trees and coconuts that were brought crashing to the ground. Mercifully, just after midday, the eye of the storm bypassed the island and we set about getting through the ready supplies of booze laid on by the management. At some point in the afternoon, I phoned home to wish my family Happy Christmas, although my recollections of the evening remain few and far between. But even though the Cyclone had passed, the rains continued all through Boxing Day and the day after, and I was, by now, keen to move on. So, after somehow managing to board one of the few remaining ferries back to Townsville that hadn't been cancelled, I made my way by bus 300 kilometres south to Airlie Beach.

A couple of days later, a group of friends followed me down from Magnetic Island to celebrate New Year's Eve. Aside from a rather comical and almost abortive journey to one of the packed local pubs, resulting in us paddling knee-deep through the waterlogged streets of the nearby town, it wasn't a particularly memorable night, but I was at least able to spend it with a group of friends and this time I actually managed to see the New Year in, which, in itself, was a big improvement on last year in Guangzhou. Well let's be honest, anything would have been an improvement on Guangzhou! The deluge, though, didn't let up, confining us to our cabins for days on end. Indeed, if anything, the rains seemed to be getting heavier and we woke one morning to reports that twelve inches had fallen through the night. Rooms were flooded, roads closed and travellers stranded and by the end of the week, I was desperate to get out. Friendships that had taken so long to establish were now hanging by a thread and being holed up so long together was clearly taking its toll. People were fractious, relationships were strained and jokes that had been funny a couple of weeks ago had now lost their humour. But overnight, my prayers were answered. The pattering on the roof had finally ceased and I woke up to see the sun for the first time in a fortnight. Again, I was lucky enough to board one of the few remaining bus services still operating and set off on a hazardous eighteen-hour journey south, through flooded roads and across swollen rivers, down to Brisbane.

I'm still not sure to this day quite how I actually did make it down to Brisbane—three weeks later, many of my friends were still stranded in Queensland as many of the roads remained impassable—but after a four hour wait at the Transit Centre, I wearily boarded another bus to take me further south and exhausted from a sleepless overnight trip, my tiredness finally caught up with me. When I awoke late afternoon, I sat up in my seat, gaping out of the window. Plunging the narrow streets into a gloomy blanket of shade were a succession of international hotels, nightclubs, casinos, cinemas, bars, fast food joints and towering beachside apartment blocks. We were passing through Surfers Paradise, though infuriatingly, its gloriously renowned white sandy beaches were completely obscured by this garish mass of concrete. 'Cocktail Dreams', 'Hard Rock Café', 'Crowne Plaza', 'Jupiter Casino' flashed the blinking pink and blue neon signs. Surfers Paradise? It felt more like Vegas-By-The-Sea. By way of contrast, the rather more sedate and laid-back town of Byron Bay, just fifty miles down the Gold Coast Highway, sounded like the ideal place to while away a few days so, an hour later, jumping off the bus, I booked into a hostel there and spent two wonderfully relaxing days lying on the beach, lapping up the warm sunshine and quietly reflecting on the past twelve months.

With only ten days left in the country, my Aussie walkabout was by now nearing its end and if truth were told, I was feeling a little disappointed with myself. I'd been in 'Oz' for nearly a year but I couldn't help feeling that I'd only scratched the surface of the 'real Australia.' What's more, it began to dawn on me that I'd hardly established any genuine friendships with Australians to speak of during this time and, consequently, it seemed I'd be leaving as the same anonymous stranger to the country that I'd been when I'd first arrived. Looking back, I wondered if I'd have been better off getting a job on a ranch in the Outback or trying my hand at fruit picking. Instead, I'd spent nine months working in Sydney and then visited all the places that nearly every other Briton flocked to see, but it was too late to turn the clocks back now. One thing I did know, though, was my travels around Australia would have been almost forgettable if it hadn't been for the likes of Tom, Hans, Tony and Jim. The fact that my visits to Coober Pedy, Ayers Rock, Kakadu, and Cape Tribulation had all been such enriching experiences was solely down to these four characters. Down to earth and bounding in enthusiasm and humour, they were, without exception, a credit to their profession.

So I started thinking ahead again and found myself increasingly looking forward to re-commencing 'meaningful travel.' Although the last few months had been fun, they hadn't thrown up nearly enough of the same kind of challenges and tribulations that China had and I needed be put on my mettle again. I hankered for places that would really test me. I longed to be hassled, inconvenienced and tormented once more, to be thinking on my feet, not just some of the time, but all of the time. I yearned to be that strange looking foreigner I'd been in China. Above all, I *had* to get back to travelling alone.

First up was New Zealand. Over the last few months, virtually everyone I'd spoken to who'd visited the 'Land of the Long White Cloud' had told me just what a quiet, beautiful and unspoilt place it was, and although it wouldn't necessarily subject me to the hardships I was looking for, I was hoping my first attempt at hitchhiking would at least provide some of the stimulus I was craving. After that it was Fiji for a couple of weeks, and then the big one, India, surely the ultimate test and one I was already working myself up into a frenzy about.

But before all that, there was loads of running about to do in Sydney. There'd be mail to pick up, flights to be booked, injections to be arranged, boxes to be sent home, films to be developed, clothes to be bought, friends to catch up with, as well as the small matter of an Ashes Test match at the Sydney Cricket Ground. I couldn't wait.

CHAPTER 20

SYDNEY

THE OLD STOMPING GROUND

4th–11th January 1991

Whilst I'd been going through my belongings in Byron Bay, I'd come across a spare key to Rob's flat. Vaguely recalling that he was planning to visit his family in Holland for a couple of weeks over Christmas, I figured that if the cat was away, then the mouse could stay, so as soon as I arrived back in Sydney, I jumped on the ferry to Manly and made a beeline for his apartment. Standing outside the tenement block early afternoon, I rang the buzzer to his room two or three times. To my relief, there was no reply so, hopping into the lift, I made my way up to the seventh floor, hurried down the corridor and banging on the door, waited for a few seconds. There was still no reply, so I tentatively put the key into the lock, turned it gently, slowly pushed open the door and crept in. Even then, I was still half expecting to see him crashed out on his bed for

Rob loved his sleep, and would often not surface until late in the day, but thankfully, the apartment was empty. Dropping my rucksack onto the carpet, I scoured the room to see if there was any information lying around that would tell me when he was due back. At first, I'd thought that if he wasn't around, I could feasibly spend one or two nights here without him knowing on the pretence that I was just picking up one or two of my belongings I may have left behind. But if he wasn't back for a while, then providing I kept a very low profile around Manly and successfully avoided his friends, I'd effectively be able to crash here for the whole week and save myself a load of money in the process. Just then, I heard a key turning in the lock. The front door swung open and in marched Madeline, Rob's small but formidable Armenian girlfriend. With my heart pumping, I stood there frozen to the spot. I'd been caught red-handed, virtually breaking into Rob's flat, and this after he'd put me up free of charge for nearly three months.

'Jim!' she cried. 'What are you doing here?'

Good question, Jim, just what, precisely, are you doing here?

'Err... Hi Mad... How's things... I've just stopped off to... er, pick up my coat... Haven't seen it have you?'

'No, don't think so. Are you sure you left it here? Rob's back in the Netherlands, you know, he's spending Christmas and New Year with his family.'

'Aw, really?'

'How long are you back for?'

'Aw... just a week, I fly to New Zealand on Saturday.'

'Aw, Rob will be so disappointed; he gets back on Sunday. Are you coming back to Sydney again?'

'Umm, not too sure, I've got to book my flights this week. You keeping well?'

'Yeah, fine, had a nice Christmas. I've just come around to tidy the flat and pick up some of Rob's washing. So how was Australia, Jim?'

'Aw, brilliant thanks, went down to Melbourne and then Adelaide for the Grand Prix.'

'Wow, did you see the race?'

'Well, sort of. I actually ended up watching it on television.'

'What, you were in Adelaide but didn't go to the race?'

'Aw, it's a long story.'

'Did you go to Ayers Rock?'

'Yeah, it's massive, the climb up was terrifying.'

'And after that?'

'Aw, up to Darwin, then met up with Tracy and Sue in Cairns.'

'Aw, how are they?'

'Yeah, they're fine, although Tracy got deported.'

'Deported?'

'Yeah, that's another long story. Strange about that coat though, could have sworn I left it here. I've still got this spare key, Mad, so maybe you better take it.'

'Aw, thanks. Are you gonna catch up with any of the others?'

'Err, I'll probably go round and see Basir.'

'Aw, he'll be really pleased to see you. He's been acting really kind of strange the last few months, Rob doesn't see too much of him now.'

'Yeah, maybe I'll go around now. Yeah, I'll do that. Anyway Mad, good to see you, maybe catch up with you later. If I don't get back, say hello to Rob from me.'

'Okay. Well, if we don't see you, have fun in New Zealand.'

'Aw, cheers, better dash.'

And with that, I picked up my rucksack, hastily retreated out of the door, walked quickly as I could towards the lift and pressed the buzzer three or four times. Seconds later, jumping into the elevator, I stood for a few agonising moments waiting for the doors to close and, as soon as it started to descend, let out a massive sigh of relief.

After that, I called in at Basir's. He was excited, really excited, for he'd finally packed in his job and was setting off for Goa in just a couple of days' time. He told me he'd seen less and less of Rob over the last few months because he'd been spending more time with Mad, and then proceeded to fill me in with all the rest of the local gossip. Late afternoon, after he'd conjured up another one of his delicious curries, he returned from the kitchen with a small black tin, and sitting down cross-legged on his mattress, pulled out a packet of Rizlas. 'I was gonna save this for my final night,' he said, squinting down at a small gripper bag protruding from the money box, 'but now you're here, I think it's time for some 'boomshanka.' '

Basir loved his 'boomshanka'. Coming from Afghanistan, one of the world's largest producers of hashish, it seemed almost to be in his nature. I think it also enabled him to rid his mind of the increasing anxieties he was having over his adopted homeland. Admittedly, he could have done a lot worse as a refugee than to end up in such a wonderful country as Australia, but this still didn't detract from the fact he'd been thrust straight into an entirely different culture and he seemed to be finding the pace and values of a Western society often difficult to comprehend. I'm sure working for an American bank didn't exactly help in this regard either for the heady business of high powered office politics must have been so far removed from all he was used to. And so troubled was he by the unyielding wheels of capitalism that when he couldn't get his hands on any 'boomshanka' (for some unknown reason he always insisted on referring to it as this) he'd turn to drink instead, which is why I'd frequently find myself stood in the local bar on a Friday night, listening to him getting all his gripes about work off his chest. 'Dese people,' he'd say, referring to our office colleagues, 'I tink dey are all crazy. All dey do is run about all day, in and out of meetings. All day long, I tell you. Ees really facking crazy. I don't understand it.'

But now all of this torment was nearly behind him, for in just a matter of days he'd be returning to his beloved Goa, and it was truly heart warming to see him so excited. We spent the remainder of a suitably introspective evening smoking, snacking and chatting long into the night. I recounted various exploits of my walkabout, he told me stories about his family and his homeland, we made plans to meet in India in a few months' time but the conversation invariably kept returning to his love for

Goa. I've already mentioned how possessive I felt about Thailand after my memorable first visit to the East, and Maugham, in the latest book I was reading, had touched on this very subject: the affinity a person can develop for a particular place.

'Sometimes,' he writes in *The Moon and Sixpence*, 'a man hits upon a place to which he mysteriously feels that he belongs. Here is the home he sought, and he will settle amid scenes that he has never seen before, among men he has never known, as though they were familiar to him from his birth. Here at last he finds rest.'

Listening to Basir talking so fervently that evening, these sentiments could just as easily have applied to him.

Back in October, after I'd booked my flight to New Zealand, I'd purchased a ticket for the third day of the third Ashes Test at the SCG (Sydney Cricket Ground.) Ever since then, I'd been looking forward to January 5th with increasing anticipation and now that this long awaited day had finally arrived, I could hardly contain my excitement. I'd already watched Australia win the first Test in Brisbane on television when I was up in Cairns, and in spite of taking another first innings lead in the second Boxing Day Test in Melbourne, England had again capitulated in their second innings and lost the game by eight wickets, so found themselves 2-0 down in the five-match series.

I'd been keeping a close eye on the action over the last two days in a game England *had* to win if they were to reclaim the Ashes. They'd gone into the match hampered by the loss (through injury) of Angus Fraser, England's most successful bowler in the first two matches. Alan Border had won the toss for Australia and elected to bat on a good wicket, and at the end of the first day, which had seen David Boon fall just three runs short of another hundred, Australia had finished on 259-4. By the time they'd finished their innings, though, late Saturday afternoon on the second day, this lead had been increased to 518. Gooch and Atherton had survived a few nervous overs in the final session before bad light had stopped play, so when I arrived at the ground on a blazing hot Sunday morning, England had it all to do.

My main concern on entering the ground, however, was not so much how long the openers would survive, but whether I'd able to take any booze in or not. I couldn't imagine for one minute that the fun lovin' Aussies would prohibit alcohol in the ground, although much had been made in *The Sydney Morning Herald* in the last couple of days of the plans to clamp down on rowdy crowd behaviour after the particularly disorderly Boxing Day Test at the MCG. Erring on the side of caution, I'd decided to top up a bottle of Coca-Cola with a healthy measure of whisky, but it turned out I'd been worrying about nothing for I made it through the turnstiles without even so much as a search.

The ground, when I entered, looked resplendent. The bright green roofs of the Noble and Bradman Stands glowed under the sun, the flags above the clock-towered Members' Pavilion gently fluttered in the breeze, and the terraces, bisected by four strategically placed towering floodlights, were packed with expectant spectators in floppy hats, short sleeves and sunglasses. And out on the hallowed turf, play was already under way; fifteen men in their pristine white flannels, two with contrasting black ties and trousers, stood in the distance, congregated around the middle of a sumptuous vast flat carpet of tightly cropped grass.

I'd tentatively arranged to meet one of the guys from Magnetic Island at a particular part of the ground at eleven o'clock. After waiting for half an hour, I concluded he wasn't going to show up, so made my way instead to a large open section of terracing where a number of Union Jacks were flying. Forty or fifty loyal England fans had accumulated by the boundary fence and, wandering down the steps to join them, I listened on with interest to their accounts of the previous two Test matches.

'Didn't see you in Melbourne, Trev?' shouted one guy to another bloke a few rows back.

'No, mate, I was still in the doghouse after Brisbane.'

'Cor, yeah, that was some night! Going down to Adelaide?'

'Yeah, should be all right for that. And you?'

'I'm gonna see how we get on here first.'

'Don't hold your breath, then.'

Nearly all the people around me appeared to know one another and although all were resigned to the fact that our boys were simply not in the same class as the Aussies, they remained remarkably buoyant. Out on the pitch, meanwhile, Gooch and Atherton were bravely surviving some hostile Australian bowling and eventually made it to lunch with their wickets still intact, Gooch on 50 and Atherton, 33.

By the time play restarted, the ground had filled up even more and before long, both the Australian bowlers and the home crowd were becoming increasingly frustrated by the dogged determination shown by the England openers. And as the afternoon session progressed, I found my views of the titanic struggle taking place in the middle being constantly hampered by my fellow countrymen as they took it in turns to bring back plastic cups of lager to their mates. Each time they deposited the beers, they'd be greeted with a huge cheer. The amount of beer spilt on each of these trips visibly increased the longer the afternoon wore on and the ironic cheers got steadily louder. Just after 3pm, though, when Gooch was finally caught by Ian Healy, the Australian wicket keeper, the whole atmosphere in the ground changed. The noise levels rose all around the stands and as the alcohol began to take its toll, some of the England contingent around me got to their feet and shouted back defiantly, exchanging good-humoured banter and insults, not just with the home crowd, but also with some of the fielders. And back out in the middle, the pressure was building too. The Australians now had their tails up and could scent more wickets and sure enough, a couple of minutes later, Larkins was run out for 11. The England batsmen somehow survived the next few overs and made it to the tea break on 150-2, with Atherton now on 58, and Robin Smith, 17. In the very first over after the interval, however, Healy took his second catch, this time from the bat of Smith. By now, my plastic bottle was all but empty and as I struggled to my feet, I looked up to see a beaming David Gower making his way to the crease, being greeted with equal shouts of encouragement and derision from those around me. Without further ado, I quickly made my way over to the bar to grab myself a lager, stumbling all the way and grinning idiotically. This was the first ever Test match I'd been to and I couldn't believe what a great occasion it was turning out to be. All the people here were intent on enjoying themselves and having a great day out. Win, lose or draw, who cared? It was a glorious hot day, the beer was flowing and at times, the cricket going on out in the middle felt almost incidental.

When I returned, David Boon, the small, chubby and pugnacious Australian batsman with the bushy walrus moustache was fielding just twenty feet or so away from us. A long haired bloke in his thirties, who'd been playfully taunting people all afternoon, got up and staggered down to the boundary fence. He was also moustachioed and looked more like an Australian than a Brit, dressed in cut-off jeans, flip-flops and vest. For a few minutes, I kept a watchful eye on him, wondering whom his next insult would be directed at. He was staring at Boon, but he surely wasn't going to start ridiculing the feisty Tasmanian? Or was he? No, he couldn't be that stupid. I mean, this was the man who, just eighteen months ago, had allegedly set the record for most beer consumed by an Australian sporting representative by getting through fifty-two cans of beer on the flight to England for the last Ashes Series. With a reputation like that, I suspected he was not a person to be trifled with.

Just then, back out in the middle, Gower made one of his strokes that had become his trademark, an effortless and graceful pull shot to the off side. The burgundy leather ball flew past Boon, who turned to give chase. Seconds later, it crashed against the advertising hoardings just a few feet in front of us. Boon trudged over towards us with a rueful smile on his face and was greeted with the predictable jeers and barracking. Picking up the ball, he hurled it back to the middle but as he scampered off, our friend at the front cupped his hands over his mouth and shouted at the top of his voice, 'Hey fatty boon boon.' Boon immediately turned around scowling to see who the culprit was. Instead of hiding, Vestman, proudly waved his hands above his head, and yelled, 'Over here, fatty boon-boon.' For a split second, I thought Boon was going to come racing over to Vestman, yank him over the barrier and start laying into him, but this was not at a football game, this was a cricket match and cricket matches — as I was quickly discovering — are civilised affairs. Seconds later, though, Boon, a natural showman, exacted his revenge. As the fielders got ready for the next delivery, he retreated three or four steps back towards the boundary fence and with his hands clasped behind his back, subtly gave Vestman the finger. It was a gesture that only those in the crowd standing directly behind him could see, but all who could spontaneously burst into hoots of laughter. Vestman was suitably enraged and although he tried to hurl back a few more insults, it was, by now, all too late.

The singing and chanting in the final session got even louder. Atherton, who had occupied the crease from the start of the day, stood back and let Gower take centre stage. He tamed the tired Australian attack with a few more majestic shots to the boundary and each one was greeted with huge cheers. The close of play arrived all too soon, but England had done remarkably well finishing on 227-3, with Atherton on 94 and Gower, 33.

I closely monitored the progress of the game on television the following day. Mike Atherton, after seven hours at the crease, went on to complete his ton, which became the slowest hundred in the history of Ashes Tests. Gower also notched up a memorable century in what is now regarded as one of his best ever innings and with Stewart contributing another valuable of knock of 91, Gooch threw down the gauntlet. He declared 48 runs behind Australia's total of 518 just after tea and was immediately rewarded when Malcolm and Hemmings took the wickets of both the Australian openers, Taylor and Marsh, before the close of play.

Australia started the fifth day on 38-2, but by lunch, they'd fallen to 152-5. A fresh-faced Phillip Tufnell, playing in just his second Test, had picked up all three wickets and only narrowly missed out on a hat-trick when Gower failed to hold on to a difficult catch at silly point from the bat of Steve Waugh. Suddenly, it seemed, England were in with a chance of snatching an unlikely victory so, as soon as the lunch break arrived, I jumped on the ferry over to Sydney from Manly seriously contemplating returning to the ground to watch the final two sessions. By the time I'd reached a downtown bar, though, the Australian middle order had dug in. Healy, the Australian wicket keeper was now on 69 and Steve Waugh, 20, but when Hemmings and Tufnell sent them back to the pavilion in successive overs, the pendulum had swung back in England's favour.

I still couldn't make my mind up as to whether I should stay where I was or make a mad dash to the ground. If I stayed in the pub, I could watch the remainder of the game uninterrupted. If, on the other hand, I left for the ground, I'd miss at least an hour of this absorbing contest but then I could end up watching possible history in the making. Biding my time, I ordered myself another beer and staring up at the screen, urged the England bowlers on. Frustratingly, though, Matthews and Rackemann, batting at eight and nine respectively, resolutely defended their wickets and whilst they didn't add many more runs to the scorecard, they used up much of the valuable time England were going to need if they were going to overcome their target in the few hours that remained. By the time they were both finally dismissed and Tufnell bagged the final wicket of Alderman, the Australians were all out for 205, leaving England a target of 255 from a maximum of 28 overs. Now we were really talking miracles.

After the tea interval, Gooch emerged from the pavilion, not with Atherton, but Gower, which meant they were actually going to go for it. Incredibly, they put on 81 runs in the first eleven overs before Gower was caught in the slips. Alan Border, the Australian captain, then trapped Larkins for a duck a couple of overs later and when Stewart was run out with the score on

100-2 and Gooch was caught by Border soon after, the run chase was effectively over. Although Smith and Atherton batted defensively for another half an hour, the match was eventually declared a draw, and the Australians had successfully retained the Ashes, heralding the start of an unrivalled period of dominance over their arch rivals that would slowly drive fans of the English game to near despair.

I spent the next few days running around doing all the things I needed to do before I left for New Zealand and Fiji, and after weighing up all the options, comparing fares and routes, finally booked a flight to Bombay for the 26th February. This would give me three days back in Sydney after Fiji, a brief overnight stopover in Singapore and a provisional date of 26th June for my onward flight back to London from Bombay. I also received some unexpected good news. A letter from Gibbo waiting for me at the post office stated he and Caroline were hoping to travel over to Nepal at Easter to meet me for a two-week holiday.

Back in the Gulf, meanwhile, tensions were rising. The UN Security Council deadline of 15th January for Iraq to unconditionally withdraw from Kuwait was fast approaching and all the signs indicated that they wouldn't pull out. A huge US led coalition force had now been assembled in the Persian Gulf and all the news bulletins were speculating about the likelihood of air strikes on Iraq. As a token of reassurance to my parents, I sent home a copy of a Singapore Airlines advertisement placed in *The Sydney Morning Herald*, confirming the re-routing of their flights to avoid the Gulf.

CHAPTER 21

NEW ZEALAND

A HITCHHIKER'S GUIDE

12th January–9th February 1991

I remembered the Mackenzies well. They were a charming and sprightly elderly couple who'd stayed at our farm the preceding year when my parents were running a small scale bed and breakfast. After travelling around Europe, Dawn had arrived in serious discomfort after spraining her ankle, so my father spent the week mollycoddling her as they waited for her injury to mend. I had been introduced to them one evening after my mother had told them all about my impending trip and Bruce insisted I look them up, if and when I made it to New Zealand. So before I'd left Sydney, I'd dropped them a quick line to let them know that I was planning to visit their country in January. My flight to Auckland had touched down on Saturday afternoon, and after a leisurely day exploring the city, I'd called in to the post office first thing Monday morning where I discovered a letter waiting for me from Dawn. She said they'd be delighted to see me again, that I'd be more than welcome to stay and instructed me to contact them as soon as I arrived, so before heading south, I called her to let them know that if all went to plan, I'd be with them by the end of the week.

Many people had told me how easy it was to hitchhike around New Zealand, though not having ever done it before, I was a bit apprehensive. I needn't have been, as by the time I arrived in Wellington two weeks later, not only was I a fully-fledged convert, I was a fanatical hitchhiking nut. Aside from the obvious merit of being a totally economical way of travelling, it enabled me to meet a diverse cross section of people. My lifts to Rotorua later that day, for instance, comprised:

1. Three young Samoan boys driving (without a licence) a big transit van full of melons and peaches to a local market.
2. A Maori couple on their way to court to lend support to a friend up on a charge of GBH.
3. An elderly sheep farmer and his nephew.
4. A Kiwi and a Swede backpacker also heading to Rotorua.

When I arrived at my destination mid-afternoon, I couldn't believe just how easy it had all been. My longest wait between lifts had been ten minutes and it had taken just five hours to make the 150-mile journey south. I was now beginning to wonder whether I should have hitched around Australia too.

The city of Rotorua was one of the North Island's leading tourist resorts, primarily because of its renowned abundance of geothermal activity. Situated some 300 metres above sea level on a volcanic plateau that runs through much of the central North Island, the area has, for twenty thousand years, literally been a simmering thermal hotbed. I called in at the visitor centre late in the afternoon and, overwhelmed by all the fliers for sprouting geysers, bubbling mudpools, hot springs, volcanic lakes, thermal pools, green pools, brown pools and blue pools, decided to book myself on an escorted full day mini-bus trip that took in all the main thermal activity sights, which is why at nine o'clock the following morning, I found myself sheepishly retreating three or four steps from a 100-foot fountain of gushing water that had just inexplicably burst to the surface of the silica terrace a few feet in front of me. The Rohutu Geyser was one of the liveliest in the region, erupting around twenty times a day, although its smaller faithful companion, the Prince of Wales Feather Geyser, held the dubious honour of always managing to spray its stuff first. The Whakarewarewa Thermal Reserve (*Whaka* for short), in which the geysers were contained, was a large steam-filled park full of meandering pathways, wooden boardwalks and ornate bridges, and for the next hour we proceeded to make our way around the forested grounds stopping, a bit like golfers do, at each of the numbered mudpools, lakes and geysers before moving on to the next. It also housed a Maori Arts and Crafts centre, a sort of self-contained village full of straw and mud huts, various workshops, museums and souvenir shops as well as a large wooden ancestral meetinghouse. I took a seat at the back of this hall shortly after and sat there in silence with the rest of our group as a group of grass skirted spear-waving locals trooped in from the side door. As we nervously shifted around in our seats, they stood there for a nearly a full minute staring at us menacingly, rolling their eyes and wagging their tongues before spontaneously bursting into a rousing rendition of the *haka*. Now whenever I've watched an All Blacks' game, I've never been able to fathom out what the best riposte to the *haka* can be from the opposition. Some teams stand in a line and try to face it head on, other teams huddle in a circle with their arms locked around each other's shoulders, a few have even had the temerity to turn their backs on it. But so fearsome is this tribal war dance I think if I were a player, I'd have to cite my 'dodgy' cruciate knee ligament and call for a stretcher to cart me back to the dressing room. And after this stirring performance, I was beginning to wonder if I'd ever make it out of the changing room in the first place.

We spent the next few hours wandering around a host of other places in the region with wonderful sounding names such as 'Hell's Gate', 'Champagne Pool', 'Inferno Crater' and

'Frying Pan Lake', and breathing in the recurrent nauseating smell of sulphur that followed us around wherever we went. Late afternoon, after circumnavigating a large, bubbling and particularly sinister looking fern clad cauldron of mud, we pulled up at the Te Wairoa Buried Village. Sometimes, when you're subjected to too much of one thing in a given space of time, it can be almost overwhelming. I'd already experienced this sort of feeling at the Forbidden City in Beijing and by now, I was fully expecting this last stop of the day to be the one that broke the camel's back. In fact, the Buried Village turned out to be a little gem.

Situated on the banks of Lake Tarawera, the Maori village of Te Wairoa had once been a thriving staging post for tourists. In the mid-19th century, Victorians were flocking here in their droves to bathe in the fabled Pink and White Terraces. Cascading into the nearby Lake Rotomahana, the fanned steps of these terraces were filled with boiling hot silica rich waters, warmed by the magma below. As word quickly spread of the inherent bathing and healing qualities of the waters, the terraces were widely being touted as the eighth wonder of the world. Travelling by steamer to Tauranga, tourists would stopover on the shores of nearby Lake Rotorua before checking-in to the Rotomahana Hotel, and then, under the escort of local guides, they'd be taken across the waters on rowing boats to the terraces. The influx of visitors to the area saw this tiny little village and other neighbouring settlements flourish and before long, the population of Te Wairoa had increased to a heady couple of hundred. But the sudden increase in wealth to the local community did not please all. Tuhoto Ariki, an old *Tohunga* (priest) of great power, told the villagers that their reliance on the cash economy was not in keeping with local tradition and warned them their greed would eventually be punished, and when a phantom canoe was sighted on the lake on the morning of the 31st May 1886, the old *Tohunga* proclaimed disaster would quickly follow. Ten days later, in the early hours of the 10th June, nearby Tarawera Mountain erupted, lighting up the night sky for miles around. So loud were the roars of the explosion, they were said to be heard as far away as Auckland. As basalt magma poured into Lake Rotomahana, the terraces were obliterated, literally blown out of the water, whilst the village of Te Wairoa and two smaller villages were engulfed for over four hours by a rain of falling rocks, lava, ash and boiling hot mud, burying the settlements with debris. Over 150 people lost their lives that night and although the old *Tohunga* survived, the locals refused to dig him out of his *whare* (house) claiming that he'd used his magical powers to spark the disaster. Poignantly, after being pulled out still alive four days later by a party of Europeans, he died the following week.

After passing through the museum, I spent another fascinating hour wandering around the grounds. Many of the dwellings such as the Tohunga's whare and the Baker's Oven had miraculously remained undisturbed, whilst others, like the Rotomahana Hotel, had been painstakingly reconstructed. As so often on a trip of this sort, it seemed that the best had been saved to last, although in this case, I wasn't entirely sure if this was quite the intention.

The following morning, I travelled north west back up to the city of Hamilton and then back down the west coast road to New Plymouth. My angels of virtue this time came in the form of a vicar, two New Zealand students studying Chinese medicine, a car dealer, a rather hoity-toity Englishman who'd recently emigrated here, and a truly fearsome looking Maori whose breakneck driving had me constantly reaching for the door handle.

Just minutes after I'd called them from the high street in New Plymouth, Bruce and Dawn came down in their car to pick me up and as soon as we got back to their house, they quickly set about repaying my parents' hospitality. In fact, Dawn began to treat me like a long lost grandson. She dished me up a great plate of pie and chips, she plied me with cups of tea, she washed my clothes, she even ran me a bath. In between all this, we spent much of the afternoon chatting about the countries they'd travelled to in Europe after they'd left Wales, discussing how my family were keeping and talking about my travels.

Early the next morning, they took me for a full day tour of the area and, almost inevitably, our first stop was the vast looming dormant volcano that dominated the skyline of New Plymouth and much of the surrounding area. The locals referred to it as Mount Taranaki although James Cook had decided in 1770 to christen it Mount Egmont instead. Either way, it spectacularly rose 2500 metres up from the coastal plain and the fact that it hadn't erupted for over three hundred years was of little consolation. All this said to me was that if it had been dormant for so long, then it was long overdue in exacting its vengeance on Cook for giving it such a poncey name in the first place. How could you give such a fearsome looking mountain a name like Egmont? It was tantamount to calling a Rottweiller Ethel. As far as I was concerned, this loveable beast had every right to feel embittered, but having recently discovered just what volcanoes are capable of, I didn't want to be the one on the receiving end of its scorn. And that's exactly why I spent two hours creeping up lower slopes of the snow-capped peak on tiptoe. While Bruce and Dawn were huffing and puffing, oohing and aahing and repeatedly stopping to admire the views, I was struggling on in silence, wishing inside they'd just be quiet. 'Aren't you going to take a photo?' they'd ask. A photo? Were they insane? Just a click from my camera could stir this magnificent creature and this was a slumbering giant that was not to be disturbed. When we eventually turned around, I got on my knees and whispered, 'Good volcano, we'll leave you in peace now,' but all the way back down, my ear was kept firmly to the ground for the impending rumble. Back in the car park, Bruce, the indomitable host, was unrepentant. 'She's usually covered in mist, you know. I think you've been lucky to see her in all her glory. Right, come on, I think we'll go for a relaxing drive through the countryside.' It was only twenty minutes later, however, when we were safely out of distance of cascading streams of molten hot lava that I could even begin to think about relaxing.

But true to his word, we were soon ambling along quiet single-track lanes lined with thick bushy hedges and rolling green fields and I did, indeed, slowly unwind. Quite often, we'd emerge from a bend and lurch to sudden stop as a short-sleeved farmer, whistling and bellowing instructions to his dogs, tried to herd his flock across the road. And these weren't the standard sized flocks I was used to either, these were vast armies of sheep, sometimes four or five hundred in number, and we'd often end up sitting there with the engine off for ten, fifteen, sometimes twenty minutes, patiently waiting for them all to disappear. Back home, if I was stuck for this long at a level crossing, I'd be sat in my car effing and blinding, but here, in the tranquil New Zealand countryside, it didn't seem to matter one little bit.

I took a wander into New Plymouth the following morning and in a surprisingly decisive mood, bought the sleeping bag I'd need for a planned trek in the South Island. I also booked an internal flight from Christchurch back to Auckland in a few weeks' time. Air New Zealand had a special offer on—the normal economy fare of $532 had been slashed to $130 (£40-45), which represented a huge saving and one I'd have been stupid not to take advantage of. More importantly, this would save me a great deal of time travelling back to the North Island overland, leaving me with two full weeks to travel around the South Island at my leisure.

I spent my final evening in New Plymouth in the Mackenzie's conservatory, listening to Bruce and an old friend of his reciting tales of their hunting and fishing trips. Seeing them nattering away in their rocking chairs reminded me of Jack Lemmon and Walter Matthau in *Grumpy Old Men*. Not that they were crotchety, but just the way they sat there reminiscing:

'Mmm, do you remember that day you caught a twenty-pound salmon on Blue Yonder Creek.'

'Yes, I do. Oh, I remember that day all right, that was the same day we got chased home by the bear.'

'My God, so it was.'

'You should have seen it, Jim, it was a fearsome looking beast.'

'Mmm, I thought our numbers were up that day.'

'Ten foot high it was.'

'No more, twelve at least.'

'I think that salmon was the only thing that saved us.'

'Mmm, I didn't want to let it go, did I?'

'You certainly didn't! I had to grab it from your bag.'

'Still, he seemed to enjoy it.'

'I'm sure he did. My God, those were the days.'

'Mmm, they certainly were.'

At the end of the evening, Bruce brought out his sizeable and vastly impressive collection of war medals and we all eventually retired to bed rather misty-eyed after a few too many whiskies.

By a stroke of luck, some friends of the Mackenzies happened to be travelling south the next day and kindly offered to take me as far as they were going. So after thanking Bruce and Dawn for their hospitality, the couple dropped me off just outside the small town of Palmerston North the following lunchtime and within minutes, I'd managed to hitch a single lift all the way down to the Wellington. The driver this time was a middle-aged academic quite high up in New Zealand education who'd evidently had a big hand in establishing the Open University in these parts. He'd travelled extensively all over Asia and the Pacific, so the resulting conversations on each of the countries he'd visited made the long journey pass all too quickly.

As soon as I arrived in the capital late afternoon, I made my way straight to the Indian embassy, where I received my first taste of the confounding bureaucracy so synonymous with the sub-continent:

'So, what you're saying is that you won't be able to issue me with a visa for India today?' I said to the man behind the counter again.

'No sir, as I said, for your application to be processed, we need both a letter from the British Consulate and a telex from the embassy in London.'

I looked at the man indignantly.

'So how am I supposed to do that, then?'

'If you leave us your passport, we will do that.'

'You can do that?'

'Yes, sir.'

'And how long will that take?'

'About ten days.'

'Ten days?'

'Yes, sir, maybe two weeks.'

'But I'm flying out in two weeks.'

'I'm sorry sir.'

'So I have to come back here in two weeks.'

'Yes, sir.'

'But I wasn't planning to come back to Wellington.'

'We can post it, then, sir.'

'Post it? Where to?'

'Where are you flying from?'

'Well, I'm flying from Christchurch back to Auckland in a couple of weeks and then on to Fiji.'

'We can send it to Christchurch.'

'Can you send it to Auckland?'

'No, sir'

'But you can send it to Christchurch.'

'Yes, sir.'

'What, so you have an office in Christchurch, then?'

'Yes, sir.'

'And what happens if it doesn't turn up in time?'

'When do you arrive in Christchurch?'

'In about ten days' time.'

'Then this should be no problem.'

'But you said it could take two weeks.'

'No sir, I think ten days will be sufficient.'

So after filling in about seventy forms, I reluctantly left my passport with him and, a full hour and a half after I'd entered, stomped out of the building.

I ended up staying a couple of days in a depressingly wet, windy, and consequently, largely forgettable Wellington before making the 3$^1/_2$-hour ferry crossing across the Cook Straight.

Although heavy low clouds obscured much of the scenery, I was still tremendously excited by my first sight of the South Island. It was the rugged mountainous scenery I'd been expecting of New Zealand that, with the exception of Mount Egmont, had been somewhat lacking in what I'd seen of the North.

My plans on arrival at the old gold mining town of St Arnaud were to spend a few days trekking in the surrounding Nelson Lakes National Park so, calling in at the National Park Office down by the lake, I promptly booked a four-day pass, which allowed me to follow the extensive track system and stay overnight in any of the twenty or thirty Department of Conservation huts dotted around the park. Although there were lockers in the office, I was reluctant to part from my beloved rucksack, so I set off lugging all of my belongings on my back, not that I'd particularly minded because the scenery was simply breathtaking. The calm still waters of Lake Rotoiti lay in front of me, ten miles long, four miles wide, bordered on three sides by mountains and forests. In the distance towards the south, the direction I was heading, was the Travers Valley whilst above the vast purple snow-capped Mount Robert to its right were the deepest and most brilliant blue skies I'd ever seen. I set off whistling and humming tunes like *I Can See Clearly Now*, now beginning to understand for the first time in my life just why this trekking lark was so popular. The joy, though, was short-lived. The first part of the track along the eastern side of the lake passed through a long stretch of dense woodland and before long, the paths had disappeared into a treacherously slippery quagmire from the heavy rains that had fallen over the previous few days. My trainers immediately seeped in water from the wet soil beneath my feet and I continually had to grab onto branches of trees to stop myself from falling flat on my arse. I stopped three times in the first hour to change my socks, yet each time I set off again, I could feel the excruciating pain of blisters already forming around my ankles, and the fact that—all because of a sudden rush of blood to the head back in China—my prized walking boots were now languishing somewhere at the bottom of the Yangtze River only added to these woes.

By mid-afternoon, I'd already got through the two cans of Coke I'd brought with me and I was sweating so profusely through walking with such a heavy load that my clothes were now clinging uncomfortably to all parts of my body. Finally emerging from the woods, I consulted my map to consider turning back. Estimating that the distance to the first hut was two to three miles, marginally less than the distance back to the lake, I eventually decided to soldier on. An hour later, though, I was beginning to think I'd made the wrong choice. I'd only seen a handful of people since I'd been here, and all of these were back at the head of the lake. I was getting the same tired, worried and emotional feeling I'd had when I'd been turned away from the hostel on Huang Shan. All I kept wondering about was what the facilities would be like in the hut. My imagination started to run riot—log fires, spit roasts, bevies of Swedish hikers—who knows, maybe these trekkers had it all worked out. But when I finally reached the hut forty minutes later, I was in for a big disappointment. Not only was there nobody else there to greet me, there were also no cooking facilities. Well, there were if you'd happened to bring your own portable gas cooker. I stared at the sign on the wall in astonishment. Portable gas cooker? Damn, I knew I'd forgotten something. Silly old me. How could I have forgotten my portable gas cooker? Rummaging around in my rucksack, I pulled out my last soggy cheese roll, devoured it in about twenty seconds and then sitting on the bed, peeled off my damp clothes, wincing as my blisters were exposed to the air for the first time. With nothing else to do but wait to see if anybody else turned up, I pulled out my sleeping bag, unfurled it onto one of the bunks, and jumping under the cover, reached for *The Moon and Sixpence*. Let's see if Maugham could get me out of this one. I woke up the following morning still alone and braced myself for my return journey. It made little difference, though, for the agonising walk back to the head of the lake was every bit as painful as expected.

Because the South Island was much less populated than the North, I decided to put my hitchhiking on hold for the time being and on a damp drizzly morning, headed southwards on New Zealand's famous 'Magic Bus' service towards the Franz Josef Glacier, halfway down the South Island. Just thirty minutes into the journey, however, our now not-so-magic bus broke down. With the weather deteriorating by the minute, our driver informed us that a new coach was on its way out, but an hour and a half later, I was still sat in my seat glumly staring out of the window at the rain, which was now coming down in torrents. By the time the new bus turned up twenty minutes later, all hopes I had of seeing the glacier that afternoon had effectively been dashed for the resulting delay meant we wouldn't now be arriving until well after nightfall, although in truth, the high winds and atrocious conditions would have probably put paid to this in any case. Indeed, by the time we finally approached the mountainside village late that evening, many of the surrounding roads were already rendered impassable as a result of flash flooding, so counting my blessings, I booked into a hostel for the night, just hoping I'd be able to set off again in the morning. We'd been told to re-assemble at 8.30am, but it was nearly 2pm by the time we eventually got away and even then, we were incredibly lucky. Bypassing landslides, flooded rivers, uprooted trees and taking diversions around bridges that had been completely washed away, we later discovered that one of the roads we had earlier travelled on had collapsed only hours after, making travel out of the area impossible for the following three days. It brought back all the memories of Cyclone Joy.

By the time we arrived in Queenstown early evening, the rains had thankfully long since departed. Queenstown was *the* big ski resort in the winter and a large international outdoor activity centre in the summer and was, therefore, not very cheap. The so-called 'alpine village' was surrounded by mountains and based on the side of a lake fifty-two miles long. I'll say that last bit again if you want. The 'alpine village' was surrounded by mountains and based on the side of a lake fifty-two miles long. Fifty-two miles long? That was a freakishly long length for a lake. I'd been brought up very near to a lake myself but I still couldn't imagine for one minute what it would be like being brought up here:

'Hi mom, me and Danny are just going for a ride around the lake.'

'Okay darling, you take care now. If you're not back by next month, you know dad and I'll get worried.'

However, all I'd been thinking about on the bus journey down was booking a bungy jump at Skipper's Canyon the following day. Skipper's was the ultimate AJ Hackett site—a jump of 71 metres (some 88 feet higher than Cairns) from a terrifically scenic suspension bridge spanning a narrow gorge over the Shotover River. Now, before you start scratching your head wondering if I'd completely lost my marbles, let me try to explain. Cairns, Friday 23rd November, 1990 is a date that is indelibly etched in my mind. It remains (and probably always will) the most terrifying day of my life. It's right up there with losing my virginity, getting drunk for the first time and attending my first football match in my ten most memorable days of all time. So why a person who suffers from acrophobia should even be contemplating—let alone looking forward to—another death-defying leap from a bridge of a prodigiously greater height just two months after surviving such a petrifying and gut-wrenching ordeal is, indeed, perplexing.

Let's then examine the possible scenarios:

Had Cairns successfully exorcised my fear of heights once and for all?

No, I don't think so.

Did I possess one of those mad streaks that perhaps made me some kind of closet masochist?

Not that I was aware of.

Had I met a beautiful Maori girl on the bus who I was hoping to impress?

Oh, if only.

Was it just bravado?

Not exactly, although I think we're getting slightly warmer.

So could it have just been that the actual jump itself had been banished to a dormant part of my brain so that all that remained in my memory was the surging dose of adrenaline that had followed my previous bungy?

Yeah, now we're probably talking.

I had bungy jumped once and had dreaded every single second of the experience but the prize, the reward, the end result of being able to proudly walk around with an AJ Hackett shirt on my back (only those who jump are actually given the commemorative T-shirt) and proclaim to all who knew me—and even those who didn't—that I'd now bungy jumped twice, was the only thought occupying my mind. Girls, as we spoke, would be shedding their clothes all around the world in adulation, lying down before me in homage to King Jim, bungy jump extraordinaire. However, as the bus got closer and closer to Queenstown, the part of my brain that had safely locked away all those terrifying moments of fear suddenly began to stir. For days, weeks even, I had been convinced that nothing in the world was going to stop me jumping again but now I was beginning to have second thoughts. Indeed, by the time we pulled into Queenstown and I stood at the bottom of the steps of the AJ Hackett office, not only had this filing cabinet been prised open but it had also leaked all the memories of the palpitations, the trembling, the inability to speak or move, to every single other area of my brain and a fierce battle was now raging between good and evil.

'Go on. Do it, jump again, you know you want to.'

'Don't listen to him, you'll kill yourself.'

'Pants. Think about all those girls. They'll be flocking to your feet.'

'Oh, come on, you know what you're like with heights. If you don't hit the ground, your heart'll pack up.'

Doing my utmost to ignore these voices swimming around my head, I sidled up to the girl sitting behind the counter.

'I think I want to do a bungy jump,' I squeaked.

'Okay, we have two sites, Wairiku and...'

'Shotover,' I snapped, before she had chance to finish. 'I want to jump from Shotover.'

'Okay then, let's have a look. Mmm, looks like tomorrow's

fully booked.'

Tomorrow? Fully booked? This definitely wasn't what I'd wanted to hear. It was going to take every single ounce of courage to psyche myself up before I put myself through the whole thing again and I had just assumed that I'd be able to do the jump first thing the next morning and then spend a couple of days wallowing in glory. The thought of not being able to jump in the morning hadn't once entered my head.

'We could probably fit you in late afternoon the day after, though,' she added.

Late afternoon the day after? That would mean two nights and two days getting myself in a right state fretting about it all.

'Would you like me to book you in, then?'

'Er, let me have a minute to think about it,' I gulped.

Wandering back to a seat, I stared up at the panels of television screens on the wall. They were all playing videos of people leaping from each of the AJ Hackett sites and Skipper's Canyon now looked infinitely more daunting than Cairns.

Just then, another couple who'd followed me in wandered up to the counter and started chatting to the girl. Quietly getting up from my seat, I crept towards the door.

'Excuse me, sir,' came a voice from behind. 'Did you want me to confirm that for Tuesday, then? ...Sir?...Sir?

There were loads of things to do in Queenstown—jet boating, white-water rafting, helicopter trips, steamboat cruises, fishing trips—but unfortunately they all cost money and with another six months to go, money was already tight. So the next day, I forked out a couple of dollars for a ticket on the Skyline Gondola and after being whisked to the top of the 450 metre Bob's Peak in a glass egg, spent an hour or so staring out at the views from the lookout platform. Across on the horizon stood the indigo coloured Remarkables Mountains, tapering off to the north and south as far as the eye could see. At the foot of mountains lay the still, dazzling blue waters of the mother of all lakes, Wakatipu, and bordering its shore directly below was Queenstown, which from these lofty heights now took on the appearance of

Toytown. Every so often, a tiny car would slowly make its way along one of the grid lined streets, disappearing for a minute as it passed through an avenue lined with dot-sized fir trees. I'd follow its progress waiting for it to come back into view and inevitably, it would pull up, stop on a drive of a matchbox house and a little stick man would emerge, no doubt carrying a copy of the morning paper under his arm. Even though it was an extremely popular international resort, it still felt a calm and tranquil place and was surprisingly uncrowded, so much so that every day here had that lazy feeling of a Sunday.

Just after the crack of dawn the following morning, I jumped aboard another coach for an excursion to Milford Sound, widely regarded to be one of the country's most spectacular sights. On paper, the most famous of New Zealand's fjords didn't look that far away. Indeed, a cursory glance at the map in my guidebook the previous evening had revealed a distance of no more then fifty miles, so I was somewhat startled to discover, just minutes after we'd set off, that our estimated journey time was a whopping three and a half hours. Unbeknownst to me was the fact that stood between Queenstown and Milford Sound were the imposing Richardson and Humboldt Ranges of the Southern Alps, wave after wave of folding glacial mountains rising up to 3000 feet in height, separated only by a certain aforementioned lake, which in itself happened to be over three miles wide. Given such unforgiving terrain it was, therefore, hardly surprising to learn there were no sealed roads as such connecting the two to the north of the lake. Our driver, cheerily informing us of all this, then proceeded to read out our prescribed route: 'Initially, we'll be heading sixty miles south where we'll pick up State Highway 94, travel another forty-five miles west to the pretty lakeside town of Te Anau before doubling back up another sixty or so miles on the famous Milford Road. Weather permitting, we should arrive in good time for your midday cruise. Until then, I suggest you just sit back in your seats and enjoy the wonderful scenery.' And what wonderful scenery it was. It started off sedately enough, meandering along tranquil lakeside roads, in and out of countless tunnels hewn deep into the heart of the surrounding mountains, emerging time and time again to the sight of early morning windsurfers silently skimming across Wakatipu like teams of ice dancers. Yet still drowsy from the early morning start, all I could do for the first hour as I gazed down at the bobbing waves gently lapping against the shore was battle to keep my eyes open. Before long, the sun happily came to my rescue. Rising above the mountains, the glare of its reflection on the dazzling waters was blinding and, copying all those around me, I gratefully pulled back the curtain and settled back into my seat.

When I awoke a couple of hours later, spots of rain were flecking the windows and we were passing through a tunnel of green, a dense beech forest overrun with primeval ferns glistening with beads of water from the early morning dew. We were, by now, deep in the heart of Fjordland, an area of exceptional beauty and also one prone to earthquakes, avalanches and landslides and for the remainder of the journey the ever-darkening surrounding mountains became increasingly rugged and precipitous. Descending into the dank, water-dripping Homer Tunnel—1270 metres in length and hollowed out of a seemingly impenetrable slate-coloured rock face—we emerged ten minutes later into Cleddau Canyon, a narrow U-shaped valley steeped in pockets of swirling mist. Unable to resist the offer of a quick photo stop, four or five doughty passengers jumped out to snap a few shots of the tunnel entrance, then we continued to wind our way down the narrow road for a further ten miles, over numerous one-way bridges spanning gushing muddy rivers and gurgling streams. When we turned the final bend into Milford Sound Valley, however, fully expecting to get our first sight of the glaciated 1600-metre Mitre Peak spectacularly rising from the waters, my heart sank, as heavy grey clouds and fog had reduced visibility to a few feet and we could only wonder what lay beyond. This area was renowned for being one of the wettest places in the world and the rain, that had been steadily pouring down ever since I'd woken up, now looked all set to ruin another sightseeing trip. In this instance, though, it proved to be the saviour for as soon as we filed off the bus moments later, I realised that this whole place had been brought to life simply *because* of the rains. It was the sound of torrents of water noisily gushing down the steep mountainsides all around us that first stirred the imagination. It was as if the rain gods had been disturbed from their slumber and were exacting their revenge at being woken by launching the furious tides of frothing water that were crashing down into the valley. And with the clouds so low, the scenery was diluted to greyscale, just adding to the eerie atmosphere, and you realised that here, the forces of nature were not to be taken lightly.

Boarding the large white passenger boat that was waiting at the side of the wharf, we then embarked on a two-hour cruise up and down the 12-mile long fjord. Amazingly, some of our party defiantly remained on deck as the boat set off, though one by one, they slowly filed back into the shelter of the cabin with their heads between their tails, unable to cope with the twin attacks of lashing rain and the swirling spray of water tumbling down from the ledges of the surrounding cliffs. It was quite unsettling not knowing just how high the mountains around us actually were and the poor visibility effectively dashed any chances we had of catching sight of the dolphins, penguins and seals that could normally be seen on the trip. Still, the overriding feeling that nature held the upper hand here was immensely satisfying and, as far as I was concerned, more than made up for the apparent lack of wildlife.

I left Queenstown the following day and travelled further south, again by bus, to Invercargill, New Zealand's southern-most city. As soon as I arrived, I was resigned to ditch what tentative plans I'd had to travel over to nearby Stewart Island. With a population of just over 450, the island was a haven for natural wildlife and I'd got this romantic notion in my head that it would be wonderful to spend a couple of days in such an unspoilt and quiet place, staring out towards the ice caps of Antarctica. But when I arrived in Invercargill, it was incredibly blustery, frighteningly cold and ominously bleak and Stewart

Island suddenly didn't look such an attractive proposition after all. However, seventeen miles south of Invercargill was Bluff, a fishing port famous for its oysters, and having travelled this far south, it seemed imperative that I at least cast my eyes on the sea so, depositing my rucksack in a local hostel, I quickly made my way there instead by local bus. Down in the bay, the howling wind coming in off the Pacific was blowing a gale: scraps of paper and cellophane were being gusted into mid-air, telegraph poles were rocking back and forth and so inflated was my bomber jacket, I was in serious danger of being swept up to the skies like a helium balloon. Nevertheless, with my hands deep in my pockets and my head bowed, I staggered up and down the virtually deserted quay for a while, looking up only once or twice to stare out at the choppy black waters. In truth, besides a couple of seafood factories and a large aluminium smelter on the other side of the harbour, there wasn't that much to see in any case, but there was still something incredibly gratifying in looking out to the sea knowing that the next substantial mass of land was a mere 3500 miles away.

Fifteen minutes later, after scrambling across the headland to Stirling Point, the New Zealand equivalent of Land's End, I was staring up at the yellow criss-cross signpost indicating the respective distances to the Equator, London, the South Pole and the like when I was greatly heartened to spot another intrepid soul braving the elements. The man, dressed in an orange cagoule, shorts and hiking boots, was stumbling towards me with a walking stick in one hand and a folded map that was flapping about wildly in the other.

'Why-aye, man!' he bellowed in a broad Geordie accent as he stopped to catch his breath. 'Not really the day for this.'

'Yeah, it's a bit windy,' I shouted back.

'Bit windy?' he yelled, carefully wiping the condensation from his glasses with a handkerchief. 'Ay, lad, ye can say that again!'

We didn't stand around chatting for long, it was far too cold and squally for that, but before we departed, we hastily agreed to swap cameras and quickly took it in turns to stand beneath the sign posing for the photographs with clenched teethed smiles. Mission duly accomplished, I then returned to Invercargill late afternoon where my spirits were revived by one of the best fish and chips meals I'd ever tasted.

Simply to get a break from coaches, I travelled the next morning to Dunedin by train. Dubbed 'the Edinburgh of the South,' the city, steeped in culture, was home to the country's oldest university as well as numerous museums, stately houses and art galleries. Also paying a visit to Dunedin the very same day was the Rainbow Warrior #2, so later in the afternoon, I took a wander down to the harbour to have a look at the new vessel. It was four and a half years before (just before midnight on the 10th July 1985 to be precise), when the original Greenpeace boat was ripped apart and sunk by two bombs in Auckland Harbour, killing in the process one of the twelve crew members. The boat had been preparing to lead a flotilla of ships from New Zealand to the Moruroa atoll in the Pacific Ocean to peacefully protest against French nuclear testing when, acting on orders from the their government, members of the French secret service planted the incendiary devices in the boat's engine room. It was an act of terrorism against an organisation founded on the principle of non-violence that outraged the world and, in particular, New Zealand, a country with a strong anti-nuclear policy. The two secret agents were subsequently, and somewhat bizarrely, caught and arrested a few days later when they tried to return their van to an Auckland hire company, and each were later sentenced to ten years in jail. On Greenpeace wishes, the boat was later sunk with full Maori ceremony in clear blue waters just off the North Island coast. Meanwhile, after a two year enquiry, a panel of international arbitrators ordered the French Government to pay Greenpeace just over $8 million in damages and part of this settlement was used to finance the construction of the Rainbow Warrior #2, which had just been completed in Germany.

The new boat, docked on the side of the harbour, looked immaculate, its hull gleaming from a fresh coat of dark green gloss, emblazoned with the trademark rainbow and a couple of leaping dolphins. It was much larger than I'd expected too, and the hundreds of people scouring its decks and milling around the quay only seemed to confirm the country's full support and continued backing for the Greenpeace causes. After a short mooch around the vessel, I then finally learnt how the Rainbow Warrior had got its name. It had been inspired by a North American Indian legend, which had prophesised that when man had destroyed the world through his greed, the Warriors of the Rainbow would rise to save it again. With the greatest army the world has ever seen now assembling in the Gulf, I suspected this might not actually be too far off.

If Dunedin had strong Scottish connections, then Christchurch had quintessential links to a certain English University city whose college it was named after. I arrived there the following lunchtime and so taken was I with the place, I ended up staying for four days. The contents of the following letter written to my parents perhaps best describe my feelings for the place:

I'm more impressed with this city than any other I've come across in New Zealand and Australia, and I reckon that if I ever get sufficiently brassed off with the UK, then Christchurch would, without doubt, be the place I'd move to.
- It's very English, full of parks, cathedrals and lovely architecture. A river runs through the city likening it to Oxford.
- It has a good climate—very warm and clear in the summer, cold and fresh in the winter.
- It's only 1½ hours away from some of the best ski resorts in the country.
- It's on the coast, with lovely beaches just out of town.
- The shopping is good, there are plenty of amenities, it is uncrowded and the people are friendly.
- It's one of the very few cities I know without a McDonald's in town.
The good things about Christchurch!

It also possessed a superbly welcoming medical centre where I managed to get all my injections done for India. Much to my relief, I was also able to pick up my passport and visa for India, which had arrived from Wellington just 24 hours before I was due to leave. Talk about cutting it fine! The good news, though, was that I'd been granted a six-month double entry visa, which was exactly what I'd requested in order that I could temporarily leave the country to meet Gibbo and Caroline in Nepal and then return to India afterwards.

Although the flight back to Auckland from Christchurch was hugely disappointing—largely due to a permanent blanket of clouds that obscured all the scenery below—it was nice to be back in 'The City of Sails' again. It didn't have the frenetic hustle and bustle of most of the big cities I'd visited and, as a result, felt far more homely and welcoming. Indeed, looking back on the past few weeks, I wondered whether I should have set more time aside to spend in New Zealand and less in Australia, but hindsight is such a wonderful thing. One of the things I *had* been hoping to establish at the outset of the trip was the viability of one day emigrating to Australia, but New Zealand had effectively pulled the rug from under its feet, for as a place to visit, it had lived up to all the high expectations: the people had been extraordinarily friendly, the scenery was often breathtaking, and the country in general was wonderfully clean and unspoilt. There were many uncanny similarities to the UK too—the size of the country, the temperature, the climate and the plain fact it was an English speaking nation. The big difference, though, was in population. Here, it was only just over three million compared to fifty-six million back home and this unquestionably made it a country I'd consider moving to if I ever got sufficiently brassed off with the UK. The people overall seemed less bullish than the Australians too, although remained fiercely proud of their identity. I also got the impression that an intense competitiveness existed between the two countries, and I suspected that the Australians invariably got the final word purely because their country was so much larger, thus enabling them to throw their weight around a bit more and bully their little neighbour into submission. All in all, then, not that different to England and Wales, really.

CHAPTER 22

FIJI

CULTURE SHOCK

10th–22nd February 1991

To say I'm not a relaxed flyer would be something of an understatement although, oddly enough, I find airports themselves strangely comforting places. I suppose it was Venice, some fifteen years beforehand, that sparked my fear of flying. Up until then, sitting on an aircraft high above the clouds had always been great fun. Okay, there were still plane crashes but, more often than not, they always seemed to happen in some far-flung place I barely knew about, and since most of our family holidays were taken in Europe, I never had cause for concern. So, after two weeks frying in the sun of Lido De Jesolo during that scorching summer of 1976, I was, as usual, looking forward to the adventure and excitement of our return flight home. With the temperatures approaching 30°C, we arrived at the airport in good time for our lunchtime departure only to discover that our flight had been seriously delayed so, with nothing much else to do, we sat and waited in the sweltering departure lounge. It was three hours later, however, before an announcement finally came over the tannoy informing us that our plane was ready to board, and by the time we climbed up the steps of the waiting aircraft, positioned on a far corner of the airfield, the heat of the fiery Italian was so stifling I genuinely thought I was going to pass out. The crew, though, were keen to catch up on lost time, and as soon as we got on board, they quickly ushered us into our seats and just minutes later, the doors were closed and the plane made its way to the end of the runway where it waited for what seemed like an eternity.

'Why aren't we moving?' I asked my parents, over and over again.

'Just be patient,' came the same reply. 'We'll be going soon.'

And then, at last, we did. The engines screamed to life, the overhead lights went out, the plane jolted forward and then slowly but surely began to accelerate down the runway.

'Hey, we're going,' cried my little brother across the aisle, but he'd spoken too soon for twenty seconds later, approaching the terminal building with the whole fuselage shaking like a tumble dryer, the pilot aborted the take-off and as the aircraft screeched to a stop at the very end of the runway, the Italians on board were screaming in fear. Sitting in my seat quietly tugging at my T-shirt, I looked up at my mother for comfort and saw a look of terror in her eyes that I'd never seen before. Seconds later, the co-pilot calmly announced that there was nothing unduly to worry about—the delay of the plane waiting on the tarmac had simply caused one of the engines to overheat—and assured us that by the time we reached the other end of the runway, we'd be able to take-off again. However, two more aborted take-offs followed, both equally as terrifying as the first, before the captain finally came on and reluctantly informed us that we'd just have to wait for the engine in question to cool down. But by the time he attempted our fourth, and thankfully faultless, take-off after an agonisingly long wait back at the end of the runway, the tension on board was unbearable. My mother was clutching onto my father's hand for dear life, the Italians were all crossing their hearts, even the flight attendants looked decidedly ashen-faced and the cabin was so silent you could hear a pin drop. For the remainder of the flight, I never once took my eyes off the suspect engine from my window seat, convinced that it was about to explode into a ball of flames and by the time we finally touched down at Gatwick, the seeds of doubt over the safety of flying had been sown in my mind once and for all. So ever since then, I have not been a comfortable flyer although I do find airports to be reassuring places. In fact, I'd go so far to say I'm quite fascinated by them because, more often than not, an airport is the very first thing you judge a country (or region) by. Whether it be the layout, its facilities, the staff or just the ambience, the airport seems to be somewhat indicative of just what can or may lie in store for you in that particular country or region. An airport does say an awful lot about a place. Well, I think they do in any case.

Perhaps under the heady influence of Maugham, I arrived in Fiji fully expecting to be greeted at the bottom of the plane's steps by scantily clad Pacific girls who'd drape garlands of fresh flowers around my neck the moment I set foot on the tarmac. Sadly, I was in for a bit rude awakening. Unlike the other countries I'd visited, I'd done very little reading up on Fiji as, rather ironically, I'd been intending to use the fortnight here to exclusively read up on India. So when I picked up the in-flight magazine and made the discovery that nearly half of the Island's population were Indian, I was somewhat put out. Not that I'd got anything against the Indians, of course, but I had assumed that I was travelling to a Pacific Island where most of the people would be Polynesian and Melanesian, and whenever a place is significantly different to how you expect, it's rather an unsettling experience. When I walked into the arrivals hall at Nadi (pronounced *Nandi*) International Airport, I got another shock. It was an antiquated dimly lit building that felt rather like a large tin shed and as airports go, it was not a very reassuring place at all. Judging *this* country by its airport made me wonder just what I'd let myself in for in coming to Fiji.

What I did know was that Fiji itself was made up of hundreds of islands, and that the largest of these was Vitu Levu. Although I had no guidebooks as such to refer to during my two weeks here, I did have a rough plan of what I wanted to do mapped out in my mind because, back in Auckland, I'd spent a very productive afternoon in the main library carefully scribbling down notes from the various travel guides on Fiji. The all-inclusive resort of Beachcomber Island, off the west coast of Vitu Levu, sounded like a great place to party, although this fortnight would have to serve as an exercise in spending as little money as possible. (It's funny now to think of how I'd berated that traveller back in Beijing at the outset of my travels for being so obsessed with conserving money. Now, a year or so on, I found myself doing exactly the same.) So for this reason alone, I decided to give it a miss and took a bus instead to a cheaper place called Nananu-I-Ra, an 870-acre island located off the north coast, where I booked into a beachside cottage occupied by a Japanese traveller and two Danish girls.

I spent the first few days relaxing in the gardens, content to while away most of my time sitting in the sun and reading my latest Maugham book, *The Magician*, a wickedly dark thriller set in Paris at the turn of the century. Based on the life of Aleister Crowley, a renowned London necromancer, it wasn't one of the author's most enjoyable works, largely because of the subject matter, but it was still Maugham all the same and his vivid descriptions of characters and their surrounding environments continued to stir my imagination.

Although I didn't see too much of my roommates during the day, we had a whale of a time in the evenings, continually sitting up in our beds and laughing hysterically for, in spite of the nets above our beds, we found ourselves being bitten alive night after night by the squadrons of mosquitoes that had taken up residence in our hut. Every evening, the four of us would lie in our bunks tossing and turning for hours on end, repeatedly slapping our cheeks, foreheads and arms, desperately trying to ignore the maddening little creatures as they hovered around above us, but it was to little avail. Time and time again they launched kamikaze attack after attack on our exposed flesh and all we could do was leap from our beds at regular intervals throughout the night, turn on the lights and hunt the perpetrators down. And each time, after we'd finally settled back under our sheets, satisfied that we'd now killed them all off, the incessant high-pitched buzzing would return five minutes later around our ears and the inevitable giggles would start up again.

With more blotches on my body than a Dalmatian, I eventually decided it was time to escape and, overdosed on quinine, made a five-hour journey down the south east coast to Suva. Cedric Belfrage, the renowned writer and socialist said in his 1936 book, *Away From it All; An Escapologist's Notebook*: 'It was a hell of a way to have come to find anything so little like Fiji,' and when I arrived in the capital, I knew just what he meant. Instead of the metropolis full of international shops and neon lights I'd come to expect of a major city, Suva was a bustling port with a rather ramshackle town centre where the Indians seemed to greatly outnumber the Fijians. Indeed, seeing these two rival communities side by side for the first time reminded me of the two clans depicted in a favourite childhood book, *Fattypuffs and Thinifers*. I can't remember much about the story itself but the imaginative illustrations were incredibly vivid and the resemblance, it has to be said, was quite uncanny: the Fijian men (and quite often, women, for that matter), big boned, flat nosed and rubber necked, sauntering around without a care in the world whilst their spindly moustachioed counterparts hurriedly dashed up and down the pavements with bags of shopping in their hands like there was no tomorrow.

After securing a room, I wandered back into town, staring out at the rusty hulls of black and turquoise cargo boats moored on the dockside for a while, as the gulls squawked high above, and then called in at the terrifically colourful municipal market further along the waterfront. The large open-fronted building, set under a corrugated tin roof, was lined with rows of long tables all stacked high with vegetables—great bundles of artichokes, sticks of radishes, piles of carrots, tubs of tomatoes and boxes brimming with corncobs—whilst Indian women in bright coloured saris and light flowery frocks out doing their Saturday shopping thronged the aisles. Every now and then, they'd stop at one of the tables, pick up a handful of produce and enquire on the price. The white-shirted seller would quickly plonk the vegetables on the scales and shout out a figure, which would always be met with a shake of the head. Yet unlike China, there was very rarely any animosity or bitter wrangling, this cursory rejection was all part of the process and, amidst twinkling eyes and gleaming smiles, a suitable price would then be brokered. By late afternoon, I was dead on my feet and as I trudged back along Victoria Parade—lined with colonial style hotels, government buildings, botanical gardens and municipal parks—for an early night, the shadows grew long and the sun dropped behind the mountains, leaving in its wake a majestic early evening indigo sky flecked with dazzling strokes of ambers, salmons and tangerines. Sometimes, when you're presented with such a scene of overwhelming beauty, everything else pales into insignificance and for a few brief moments, Fiji didn't seem such a bad place after all. And then, just a couple more paces on, a ten-ton seagull that had been hovering above promptly shat all over my shoulder.

The next morning, I took a ferry over to the old capital of Levuka, on the island of Ovalau. The town, like the country, had a rather turbulent and chequered past. Established in the 1830s as a whaling settlement, Levuka had attracted hordes of traders, sailors, plantation owners and convicts to its shores and quickly developed a reputation for being a wild and virtually lawless port. Trade boomed on the quayside where, at it's height of popularity in the 1860s, more than fifty pubs and hotels lined the rowdy waterfront catering to all kinds of these unscrupulous characters. But when the self-proclaimed Fijian king offered to cede to the United Kingdom in 1874, four years after the United States had turned down his initial offer, the Fijian Islands became a crown colony and all of this changed. Colonial administrators duly arrived bringing with them tens of thousands of Indian labourers to work on the sugar plantations, and the British, slowly but surely, set about exerting their influence on both the town and country, finally restoring order to the island. Eight years later, restricted by the lack of space in Levuka with its steep mountainous backdrop, they moved the capital to Suva, which effectively signalled the beginning of the end of, what was once, one of the major South Pacific trading posts. Fiji itself, meanwhile, went on to gain its independence in 1970, though fierce racial tensions still existed between the indigenous Fijians and the Indians who, even now, were still prevented from owning land on the Islands.

I arrived in Levuka early afternoon and was immediately charmed by the town. It conjured up in my mind the exact mental picture I had of a typical Pacific port depicted by Maugham in one of his novels and this was exactly what I'd been expecting of Fiji. Big white colonial homes nestled on the hillside set amidst lush green vegetation—trailing bougainvillea, hibiscus vines and towering coconut palms—and overlooking a waterfront steeped in history. Somewhat hesitantly, I made my way along to the Royal Hotel, a past relic of the bygone era that was claimed to be the oldest continuously run hotel in the South Pacific. I was sceptical because I was hoping to stay here and had read that there were some affordable rooms available for backpackers but I'd read the same kind of thing about the Renmin Hotel in Chongqing (Dalek Central) only to be told that no such rates existed. However, this time my luck changed. There were, indeed, budget rooms available in a large cottage situated in the gardens for just $6 (£2) a night. I booked in straight away, blissfully unaware that I'd just stumbled across my very own Utopia, and so idyllic were the surroundings, I ended up staying for four days although I could have quite happily remained for another forty. I spent nearly all of my time basking in the solitude of the hotel lounge, reading up on India from my newly acquired guidebooks. Each morning after breakfast, I'd walk barefoot across the polished hardwood floor, sink myself down on one of the wicker chairs and sit there for a while listening to the antique clock on the wall quietly ticking away and the overhead fans whirring high above as the arecas and rubber plants gently swayed in the early morning breeze. Then I'd pick up one of my guidebooks and read for a few hours, taking the odd wander over to look at one of the sepia pictures of the old Levuka waterside hanging on the wall and, after breaking for a bite to eat, return to my seat in the afternoon to start another chapter, monitoring the sun inch its way across one shuttered window to another until it finally plopped into the sea. It was heaven and Fiji, after all the initial disappointments, had finally come up trumps.

Upon my return to Suva, I called into a bank one afternoon to exchange some money and as I was doing so, got chatting to one of the staff behind the counter. He asked me about my travels and was greatly interested to learn of my banking experience in the UK. With a long queue forming behind me, he beckoned me over to the glass and hastily invited me back to his house for dinner, so I returned at the end of the day and met him outside the building. Prakesh was an Indian Fijian who, it emerged as we sat in the back of a taxi, had had the dubious honour of being one of the staff on duty when his branch of Westpac Bank had been set upon by assailants in Fiji's first ever armed robbery just before Christmas.

His house, located in a quiet, run down suburb of predominantly paint-flaking wooden bungalows some fifteen minutes out of the city, was tiny; the downstairs comprising a box of a kitchen and a sparse and dingy candle-lit lounge with just a couple of armchairs, a small table and a 50s style radio set that stood on the mantelpiece. He introduced me to his wife, Raeuna, and their three-month-old baby boy and as soon as she went upstairs to put the infant to bed, Prakesh duly poured out a couple of beers. We sat in the lounge chatting for a while, whilst Raeuna returned to the kitchen, and the more Prakesh talked about himself, his job and his family, the more I realised just how poor they were as a family. Their struggle to survive on so little money seemed indicative of life in Fiji and not for the first time, I found myself acknowledging just how fortunate

I was in being able to travel. The traditional Indian meal that Raeuna had been busily preparing (ever since Prakesh had phoned her earlier in the afternoon) was eventually served up and the food—dhals, chapattis, and dishes of curried meat, potatoes, vegetables and rice—was delicious. The customs, however, took a bit of getting used to. Eating the meal with our right hand was the first shock and then discovering that Raeuna, because she was female, couldn't eat until Prakesh and I had finished was another. I desperately wanted to ask Prakesh to allow her to join us, it seemed so unfair, especially as she'd been toiling away for so long behind the beaded curtains but on the other hand, I was a guest in somebody else's home and I didn't want to offend. So I sat there doing all I could to avert my gaze away from Raeuna as we greedily stuffed our faces.

Towards the end of the evening, after she'd finished clearing up the dishes in the kitchen, Raeuna was promptly ushered up to bed, and the beers and whiskies we'd been drinking all evening finally took a hold on Prakesh. His eyes were bloodshot, he was slurring his words and I was becoming increasingly unnerved by his emotional outbursts against his employers, the politicians and the Fijians. As he proceeded to tell me how difficult it was trying to support a family on such a paltry income, he constantly grabbed onto my arm, and the tears began welling up in his eyes. I'd already seen this kind of outburst on the boat to Hong Kong when Tommy, in a very similar state, had stood up and berated China and its people, and just as I did then, I sat there in sympathetic silence not really knowing what to say. Well, what could I say? There was nothing I could do to help his plight (save give him a load of money I didn't have) but at least he was getting it all off his chest. Eventually, well into the early hours of the morning, I struggled to my feet and told Prakesh I thought it was time for me to leave. He called a taxi and with a certain amount of relief, I jumped into the cab ten minutes later. In spite of this, their kindness and hospitality throughout the night had left me quite humbled and a few days later, I made a point of sending them a card of thanks for the evening.

When I arrived back in Nadi, with a couple of days still left before my flight back to Sydney, it felt as if my time in Fiji was already over as all my thoughts and attentions were now concentrated exclusively on India. Fiji, in the middle of the Pacific Ocean, was the place furthest away from home that I'd visit on my travels and it marked the point where I'd effectively turn around and start heading back towards London. Remarkably, it had now been over a year since I'd left China and whilst I'd enjoyed my time in Australia and New Zealand and, for that matter, Fiji, India now beckoned. China and India had always been the two places that I really yearned to visit at the outset of my travels and just a few weeks back, I'd discovered that my fascination with these two countries was shared with a very unlikely character. I'm not sure what it was that actually led me to pick up a biography on the Kray Twins in the first place, but I did. The book, entitled *Our Story*, had been compiled from a series of interviews with London's two most notorious gangsters from Gartree Prison, where they were both still serving their life sentences and it was a fascinating, chilling and often moving account into their turbulent lives. It was probably this passage in the introduction, narrated from Reggie Kray in December 1987, that actually persuaded me to buy it:

...For years now we've talked about going to India and China, two of the most beautiful countries in the world. Every time I see Ron, that's all he really wants to talk about—how we'll go to India and China and what it'll be like.

Then I got this letter from him—and it bloody nearly broke me up. Me, the man who was called the hard man of Parkhurst, the toughest con in the place. What it said was this:

Dear Reg,
I have reason to believe that I will never get out.
I feel a bit sad tonight, as much as I have resigned myself to the fact that I won't be getting out. I would have loved to have come to India, China and all the other beautiful countries.

But I hope you will visit all these places, as that will compensate me, if you go instead. It will make me happy that one of us has been to all these places. Apart from this, I am very happy.

God bless
Ron

Those, to me, are the words of a man who has lost hope. After twenty years of trying, the system has finally crushed the spirit of my brother. That's why I now want to tell my side of the story, and why I want Ron to tell his...*

When I first read this, my eyes nearly popped out of my head. It felt as if someone up there was watching over me, delivering constant reminders throughout the course of my trip about just how fortunate I was to be travelling to these places. And if they were, then they were doing a bloody good job, as I certainly didn't underestimate just how lucky I really was. How could I when a man who'd set his heart on visiting the very same two countries that I'd longed to see would probably never get his chance to do so?

*From *Our Story:* Reg and Ron Kray with Fred Dinenage, Pan Books/Didgwick & Jackso, 1989, ISBN: 0-330-30818-1, reproduced by permission Macmillan Ltd.

PART 3

INDIA

CHAPTER 23

BOMBAY

WELCOME TO INDIA

27th–28th February 1991

I had a good friend at college called Blair. We shared a room in our first term and after Christmas, the two of us, along with a couple of other guys, moved out of the bed and breakfast accommodation we'd been allocated into a spacious Victorian flat overlooking the sea. As well as being a fit and extremely active individual, Blair was an upstanding, very matter-of-fact kind of person, almost regimental in his ways, which was not that surprising as both of his parents had served at length in the Royal Air Force. Rather fittingly, he also spoke very well and was tremendously enthusiastic in whatever he did.

After the Easter break, Blair returned to the flat with the news that he was going to spend the summer vacation travelling around India, and for months and months all I heard about were his plans for the trip—where he was going to go, how long he was going to spend in each place and how magnificent the whole venture was going to be. Indeed, by the time the term finished, Blair had spoken so much about his trip that I almost felt as if I was going there myself.

A few months later, I returned to Bournemouth for the start of our second year to share a new flat with Kay and Denise, two girls I'd met on a previous course. Travelling with all my boxes, bags and earthly belongings on the train back down to the South Coast, I wondered how soon it would be before my old roommate called around to tell me about his amazing trip. In fact, I didn't have long to wait at all, because by the time I arrived at my new lodgings, he'd already phoned to say he'd be dropping in after tea. When I answered the door later that evening, I had the shock of my life. Blair stood there, almost unrecognisable by the weight he'd lost. He looked a shadow of the person I remembered from just a couple of months ago. He also had a pained look of anguish etched across his face.

'Jim,' he blurted. 'Do you have a toilet?'

'Yeah, of course, but don't we get a hello?'

'Shit, sorry Jim. Where is it?'

'Err... down the corridor and through the living room.'

And with that, he rushed past me, down the corridor and through the living room. When I followed him back inside, Kay and Denise, sitting curled up in front of the television, looked understandably startled.

'What's wrong with Blair?' asked Kay. 'Is he all right?'

I shrugged my shoulders.

'He doesn't look very well,' added Denise, shaking her head.

'No, that's what I thought,' I replied.

Minutes later, Blair emerged. 'Shitty death, that was close!'

'Dodgy stomach?'

'Yeah, you could say.'

'So, how was it then?'

'What?'

'Well, India of course.'

'Jim... you would not believe it!'

'Good time, then?'

'Err...let's just say it's good to be back home, back in Blighty.'

'Well come on, tell us all about it.'

He glanced at his watch. 'Do you want to go up to the Richmond?'

'Yeah, sure, could do with a beer.'

Blair winced. 'Beers are out for me. Err, look Jim, this sounds a bit of strange thing to ask but do you have a toilet roll I can borrow?'

The girls, I think to Blair's relief, decided to stay in front of the television and so the two of us headed off and, minutes later, sitting in the pub, he told me his extraordinary story, starting with his arrival in India.

'Jim, you wouldn't believe it. Streuth, it still makes me shudder just thinking about it.'

'What does?'

'Well, where shall I start?'

'Err, at the beginning maybe?'

'Okay, okay. I arrived at Delhi Airport and, Jim, do you know what? I was too frightened to leave. You should have seen the place. I came through customs and sat in the arrivals hall for three hours, three bloody hours! Can you believe it? Jim, I can tell you now, if there had been any seats available on that flight back to England, I would have turned around and gone home immediately. Shitty death, you should have seen it—I have never in my life seen so much poverty. It was frightening. I sat there just trembling, thinking: 'Blair, what have you done? Just what *have* you done?"

'Was it really that bad, then?'

'Streuth, yes. If you saw those beggars on the streets of Delhi, Jim, you would weep. Some were just stumps, with no arms and legs, others were horribly disfigured by leprosy. And the poverty? I have never in my life seen anything like it. Many were so poor they lived in gutters on the streets, literally.'

He went on to tell me the rest of his story and I sat there spellbound, reliving the nightmare with him. He told me how he eventually summoned up the courage to finally leave the airport, of how he struggled to come to terms with the abject squalor on the Delhi streets over the days that followed and, after somehow overcoming the destitution all around him, how he managed, albeit rather belatedly, to then embark on his planned route around India.

However, worse was to follow. A couple of weeks into his trip, he picked up a bout of the dreaded 'Delhi belly', which went on to plague him for the duration of his travels, and this ultimately made the remainder of his time in India an even more unpleasant, uncomfortable and harrowing experience. It was shocking to see the profound effect that India had on him, especially after all his meticulous preparation. The first thing he did when he returned home was visit his doctor's who confirmed that he had, in fact, contracted amoebic dysentery, and the poor soul was still suffering with the effects of this excruciating disorder months into the new term. After college, Blair went on to join the RAF whilst I started work in Bournemouth and over time, we gradually lost touch, but his story only confirmed just what an enigmatic country India was.

But it wasn't only Blair I was thinking about as the Singapore Airlines 747 circled the Western Ghats preparing to make its final descent into Bombay: everyone I'd spoken to who'd been to India had their own fascinating story to tell, and invariably, they all seemed to involve becoming crook. Gibbo, Pat and Caroline had all gone down with chronic diarrhoea when they'd stopped there on their way back from Thailand, which I'm sure tarnished their impression of the country; Gary, a friend from the bank I worked at in Bournemouth, had suffered the same fate on his recent visit to the subcontinent whilst Tim, my cousin's husband, had lost so much weight during their nine weeks in India that by the time I'd met up with them in Sydney a full four months later, he was still barely recognisable.

And now I found myself sitting on the plane trying to psyche myself up for what lay ahead. Although I was tremendously excited by India, I was, at the same time, equally apprehensive. I knew that if I could somehow manage to stay healthy, the chances were that I'd really be able to enjoy the country to the full, but if I didn't, then...well, I really didn't want to dwell on that too much. Hopefully though, my time in China had stood me in good stead. Certainly, both countries were vast in size and both were incredibly populated, so that must have given me some kind of head start as far as preparation goes.

A couple of other pressing issues, though, were giving me much more cause for concern. The first was the small matter of the Gulf War. I'd spent the previous night in the departure lounge at Singapore Airport watching all the rolling coverage coming in on the television monitors. Just five days before, the ultimatum made by President Bush for Iraq to withdraw its troops from Kuwait had passed. A Soviet-led peace plan had also been rejected, so Allied forces had been sent in and the long awaited ground war had finally begun. I'd been closely following the situation for days, and the news breaking from the airport was that the US and coalition forces had already successfully liberated the city of Kuwait after only four days of combat, and that the Iraqi troops were now on the retreat. Although this came as something of a relief, I wasn't at all certain how the news would be greeted in India, especially amongst its Muslim population, and I was beginning to brace myself for some kind of backlash

Then there was my financial situation, which was becoming more precarious by the day. I'd already resigned myself to the fact that I would be returning home in debt, which had always been my worst fear, and in a matter of weeks, virtually all my remaining money would be gone, so the last few months of my travels would have to be financed almost exclusively by Messrs Access and Visa. The only thing in my favour was that India and Nepal would be significantly cheaper countries to travel around than Australia and New Zealand.

I had a rough itinerary mapped out in my mind of the places I wanted to visit. Gibbo and Caroline were flying in to Nepal on the 28th March, exactly four weeks from now, so my plans were to spend a couple of days in Bombay finding my feet, before heading down to Goa where I'd hopefully meet up with my old mate, Basir the Bold. Thereafter, I'd cut across to Madras, travel north to Calcutta and then cross into Kathmandu via the hill resort of Darjeeling. After Nepal, I wasn't too sure. My flight home was not until the 26th June, so I'd still have over two months to explore the rest of India. But there was plenty of time to think about that yet. In the meantime, I just had to focus on my arrival.

The plane landed at Sahar International Airport not long after midday, and whilst the state of the airport itself was nowhere near as bad as I'd expected, the tiny and unkempt Duty Free kiosk, especially after the plush and luxurious shops at Singapore, was almost laughable. I couldn't believe for one minute they'd ever make a sale there. As I joined the queue for passport control, I was greatly encouraged by the reaction of one of the officers on duty as he inspected my little black book. The photograph on the inside cover showed the picture of a rather fresh-faced, bushy haired teenager. The officer studied it hard, repeatedly glancing up at me and then back at the picture, searching for the comparison to my now weather beaten face and severely cropped hair. Pointing to my chest, I nodded my head vigorously and then, at last, a broad smile appeared on his face. I grinned back and as he ushered me through, he tapped me on the back of the head and with a knowing look, said, 'Okay, friend.' Just this simple gesture gave me a tremendous surge in confidence. It was as if he was telling me: 'You'll be all right here with that kind of attitude, you'll be okay in India,' and I strode into the baggage hall feeling that all my fears about India had finally been allayed.

After picking up my rucksack, I joined another long queue for customs. Quite a few Indians behind me started to push in, which visibly irritated a middle-aged German lady standing a couple of places ahead. Waving her arms, she began to remonstrate with them but the Indians simply stared back at her with looks of such incredulity that only a person with three heads would expect to receive. If this poor lady, bless her soul, was getting into such a state over something as trivial as this, then she was clearly going to have her work cut out during the rest of her time in India.

After changing some money, I then called in at the tourist information centre in the arrivals hall. I *had* been under the impression there was a ferry service operating from Bombay to Goa but was informed there wasn't. I'd also thought that the following day was the *Holi* festival (the day where people indiscriminately throw water over each other with much fervour from dawn to dusk to commemorate the end of winter), but I was told that this was the day after. Suddenly, I had no real reason to stay in Bombay overnight, so I toyed with the idea of heading to Goa straight away. Before that, though, I needed to get a bus into Bombay so, bracing myself for the rush of hawkers, I tentatively made my way out of the terminal building. To both my surprise and relief, only three or four kids came bounding up asking, 'What is your country?' and the like, but before I had chance to answer, I quickly found myself surrounded by touts.

'You need hotel?' they cried, brandishing hotel cards in my face.

'I have cheapest room in Bombay.'

'Eighty rupees for guesthouse in Colaba.'

'No, I have cheaper, seventy for room with bathroom.'

By a stroke of luck, the bus pulled in a few seconds later so, heaving my rucksack onto my back, I barged through the crowd and made my escape.

As soon as we set off, the moustachioed man seated next to me started chatting. He was a meteorologist from the southern city of Hyderabad and had just returned from a 'workshop' in Sydney where he 'd been studying the weather patterns of the wetlands of Australia with a number of other Asian and Australasian delegates. Another man, more swarthy looking, then joined in on our own little conference from the seat behind. The meteorologist asked him what he was doing in Bombay. He replied by saying he was currently trying to return to the oil company he worked for in Iran, but had been experiencing a lot of difficulties in getting a seat on a flight back there. His visa had all but expired, so he was now off to visit the offices of another airline. He seemed completely oblivious to the fact that a full-scale war was currently taking place in the region, which would have surely explained why he had been encountering so many problems, although I refrained from bringing this point into the conversation.

By now, we were passing through the slums on the outskirts of the city—vast intermingling townships of shacks, huts and hovels built on surrounding mudflats strewn with litter, crumpled tin cans, discarded rubber tyres and rusty oil drums. As I stared out of the window, watching half naked kids ankle deep in waste running amuck with scrawny chickens, goats and cows, the meteorologist started talking about the Mardi Gras in Sydney, which had taken place whilst he was there. He didn't agree that homosexuality should be allowed, and certainly couldn't take on board how it was so flagrantly displayed in such a prominent public festival, especially in Australia. I informed him that, contrary to the national stereotype, Australian males weren't all beer swilling sexists, and there actually existed in Sydney a large and thriving gay community and what's more, that prohibition wouldn't necessarily stop homosexuality as people would still practise same sex whether it was legal or not. He asked me if it was illegal in any of the countries in Europe. 'Not as far as I know,' I replied, before adding that there were subtle differences in the laws of other countries over things like the age of consent. He shook his head, still clearly uncomfortable with the whole thing.

A few minutes later, he started to talk about some kind of magical place he'd heard about in Sydney.

I frowned. 'What kind of magical place?'

'It's called Bundeye. It's a beach and everybody who goes there aren't allowed to wear any clothes.'

'Ah, you mean Bondi.'

'Yes, yes, Bundeye.'

'Well, it's not actually a nudist beach as such.'

'It's not?' he replied, looking somewhat crestfallen.

302

'No, not really, but there are other nudist beaches in Sydney.'

His eyes lit up in an instant. 'What, no clothes at all you mean?'

I nodded, and with that, he waved his palm towards his face, indicating that he was going to tell me something secretive. Playing along, I tilted my head towards him.

'When I get back to Hyderabad,' he whispered, 'there'll be a girl from Canada waiting for me.'

'Oh, right,' I said, raising an eyebrow, assuming he was inferring she'd been sent over as part of an arranged marriage. I asked him if this was the case. He frowned a little, wobbled his head and then said rather defiantly, 'If I don't like her, then I won't marry her.'

'Have you seen a photograph of her?' I asked.

He nodded.

'Well, what was she like?'

'I think she's a bit fat,' he said, cupping a hand over his mouth. 'She might have to go on a diet.'

As the bus passed Chowpatty Beach and made its way down the long and tree-lined Marine Drive, a welcome breeze blew in from the bay. Minutes later, the last remaining passengers alighted and as I followed them off the bus and took my first tentative steps onto Indian streets, it felt as if I'd been transported back in time by a hundred years. Heaving crowds of people trudged up and down the roads and pavements, almost in slow motion; black and yellow Ambassador taxis beeped their horns incessantly; spindly men in dhotis pushed huge wooden carts and trailers; and cows, some in the middle of the streets and others lying across the pavements, sat there idly seemingly unperturbed by all this frenetic activity. Although the streets of Shanghai and Hong Kong were crowded, there was not the same mass of vibrant humanity (or, for that matter, cattle) as there was here. Bombay, as a city, felt so much more alive.

All of the street signs were in Sanskrit and, therefore, completely indecipherable so I reached down for my guidebook to try to get my bearings. A traveller with a rucksack on his back and a map in his hand is always an easy target for touts and this time there was no escape as, for the next ten minutes, I was approached by a string of peddlers.

'Cheap room, sir? I have cheapest rooms in Bombay. Not far. Only five minutes.'

'Shansh maanee? Good rate. Twenty-two rupees for dollar.'

'Something to smoke? Hashish? Something stronger?'

'You want girls? Come, I take you now, give you best price.'

Each time, I smiled, politely shook my head and moved on, carefully stepping over the cows as I did and, in the heat of a steaming hot afternoon, battled my way to the tourist information office. Upon my arrival, they confirmed that there definitely wasn't a ferry going to Goa. They also told me that their overnight tourist bus to Goa had already left, but informed me that there were many private bus services going there that departed virtually every hour so, stepping outside, I hailed a taxi. The driver asked me where I was going and soon after, stopped alongside a long rectangular dusty park bounded by gothic buildings and towering palms. Pointing to a long line of parked coaches, he said, 'Goa buses.' Shoving my rucksack out of the door, I jumped out, paid him his fare and twenty minutes later, after just three hours in Bombay, I was on my way again.

The bus arrived in Panjim, the capital of the former Portuguese colony, just before lunchtime the next day. To get to the city itself, I had to take a short crossing by open top ferry across the silty shallow waters of the Mandovi River. As soon as we reached the shore on the other side, I quickly made my way through a series of narrow winding streets to the post office where, much to my relief, a letter was waiting from Basir. In it, he told me that he was staying at a place called Baga. He said I needed to get a bus north to Calangute from where I could make a short walk to Baga and gave me the name of a beachside bar where I'd be able to find him. After stopping for some lunch, I wearily trudged back down to the river, stepped onto the ferry again and traipsed back to the bus station. I'd now been travelling solidly for three consecutive days, starting with a bus trip to Sydney Airport and followed by an eight-hour flight to Singapore, two more shuttles in and out of Singapore, a five-hour flight to Bombay, another transfer into the city, an eighteen-hour bus journey to Panjim and two short ferry crossings made under an unrelenting sun. Consequently, by the time I boarded the bus for the final hour-long journey, I was totally shattered.

It was late afternoon and still blisteringly hot when we pulled into Calangute, a lively and colourful market town set deep in the heart of a jungle-like forest. Following Basir's instructions, I hurriedly made my way down towards the beach, continually stepping out of the way of the streams of young men on mopeds who were whizzing up and down the sandy track like angry bees. As the lowering sun blazed down over the palm groves, I struggled along a long dusty back road running parallel to the sea, towards a large hill at the far end of the beach. For a further thirty minutes, I continued to stagger along this seemingly endless lane, past numerous other guest houses and bars, toiling under the weight of my rucksack, the constant growls of the high-pitched bike engines only adding to my woes. Yet just when I thought I'd missed it, for the hill that lay ahead was looming ever larger and the bars, by now, were few and far between, I came across a wooden sign on the side of the track which, pointing to the sea, said: 'Britto's Bar and Restaurant—This Way.' Rubbing my soaked brow, I excitedly stumbled along a path through the coconut palms and emerged onto a virtually deserted long sandy beach. With the sounds of crashing waves filling my ears, I kicked off my trainers and, for a few invigorating moments, stood there staring back along the coast at the dozens of brightly coloured fishing boats moored along the shore, now finally realising what Basir had been trying to convey in his drawings. But with the soles of my feet seemingly on fire, I quickly turned around and hopping across the scalding sand, made my way towards the open-sided beachside bar. Except for a middle-aged couple sat in a corner playing cards, the place was empty, so I wandered up to the bar where, behind the counter, a young Indian man was stood cleaning glasses.

'Hi, I don't suppose you know where I could find Basir?' I asked.

'Basir?' he said, flashing me a broad, white-teethed smile. 'He be coming here later.'

'Later?' I said, somewhat disconsolately.

'Don't worry,' he said, checking his watch, 'every night he come here, he come soon. You want drink?'

Ordering a beer, I dropped my rucksack on the floor, flopped down into a wicker seat and sat there for a while, resting my aching feet on my pack, lapping up the cool breeze and staring contentedly out at the sea. Despite my tiredness, my first twenty-four hours in India had been nowhere near as traumatic as I'd envisaged and I was just blissfully happy to have finally reached my destination. And then Basir turned up.

CHAPTER 24

GOA

ORANGE, PINEAPPLE, WATERMELON...YOU LIKE?

28th February–10th March 1991

Basir knew I was coming. Well, I'd told him I was. Whether he actually believed me or not, I wasn't too sure, as his first reaction at seeing me supping a beer in his local bar was one of great surprise. Rooted to the spot, he stood there for a couple of seconds, staring at me wide-eyed then, throwing open his arms in embrace, cried: 'Bloody hell, Jim the Bugger, you made it!' Shaking his head, he pulled up a seat and, peering back towards the bar, pointed to the empty bottle on the table. 'So, when did you arrive?' he asked, as the young man came over with a couple more beers. For the next few minutes, I tried to fill him in with the details of my episodic journey but he just continued to shake his head, repeating time and time again, 'I can't believe you're here.' Then, with a twinkle in his eyes, he grabbed onto my knee and whispered, 'Hey, guess what? Tonight, full moon.'

Now it was my turn to shake my head. 'Full moon?' I said, puckering my lips and glancing up to the sky.

'Full moon, big party, big boomshanka!' he beamed, throwing back his head and laughing manically. 'Fuck, I can't believe you arrive on full moon, dis is crazy.'

'So what time does this, um, party start?' I asked a few seconds later, for the light on the beach was now fading rapidly.

He waved his hand. 'Relax, we're in Goa. Nothing happens until after midnight.'

'Midnight?' I said, screwing up my face.

'Hey, don't worry, you can stay at my mine, I'll get you a place of your own tomorrow,' and with that, he nonchalantly reached across the table for the menu.

As we started catching up on all we'd been doing since we last saw each other in Sydney, I could see, even in these first few minutes, how much more at home Basir was here. He smiled more, he laughed more, he talked more animatedly and he seemed so much more relaxed, almost like a caged animal that had now finally been released back into its natural surroundings. He knew all the people in the bar too, and even got the meal put on tab.

Every hour, I kept asking him if we should be making a move to the party, but it was well after midnight when we finally got to our feet. Jumping on the back of his moped, he took me back to his accommodation, an unfurnished whitewashed hut located under a clump of palms in a sparse area of scrubland well back from the beach. There was no electricity in the room, so as he fumbled around in the dark for a candle, I fished out a pair of jeans from the bottom of my rucksack and began to unfurl my sleeping bag next to his mattress on the floor, only to hear Basir chuckling in the shadows.

'What, what's wrong?' I asked, bemusedly.

'I wouldn't worry about that,' he chortled, 'the party'll be going on all night.'

All night? This was getting curiouser and curiouser. Just

what kind of party was this going to be? I needed to find out. 'So, is it far, this party?' I asked.

'It's in Anjuna.'

'Where's that, then?'

'Oh, it's one of the neighbouring beaches, just over the hill.'

Whilst I'd been getting changed, Basir had been carefully rolling a joint, which he now handed me and as I took my first deep drag, I got the feeling that this was just going to be one of those nights. Twenty minutes later, I jumped on the back of his moped again and we headed off back into the warm night air.

I was fully expecting that we'd arrive at the beach and find twenty or thirty people sitting around a fire. Someone would have a guitar and we'd spend a couple of hours chatting over a few more joints, having a bit of a singsong and probably end up skinny-dipping in the early hours of the morning. But as we approached Anjuna, scores of people, some walking, some marching quickly, and many more on mopeds and motorcycles, were all heading towards the increasingly loud pulsating sound of dance music. With my heart beginning to race, we eventually reached the top of the hill and as I peered down to the beach, I stopped in my tracks. Beneath us, I could make out hundreds and hundreds of people—Europeans, Indians and Asians—many dressed in elaborately bright and vivid colours: luminous oranges, yellows, pinks, turquoises and lime greens. After Basir parked his moped, we hurriedly made our way along a path that ran down through the trees and when we arrived at the beach ten minutes later, another incredible sight awaited. All across the sand, Indian ladies had laid out row after row of wicker mats and blankets, upon which were great spreads of snacks—fresh fruit, canned drinks and pots of tea—all magically illuminated by kerosene lamps. Vast numbers of revellers were sat around these mats chatting, drinking, eating and smoking, whilst others were already lying flat out on the sand seemingly dead to the world. Nearby was a large square of sand, surrounded by a cluster of towering palm trees all decorated with strings of bright lights, and on this makeshift dance-floor, a mass of bodies were gyrating to the steady thud of trance music blaring out from four huge black speakers strapped to the trunks of the trees. The sheer scale of the party was mesmerising.

Still trying to get my breath back, we sat ourselves down on one of these mats and no sooner than we had, Basir, completely out of the blue, asked me if I wanted to take a pill.

'A pill?' I said, somewhat startled, 'What, you mean a tab?'

'Full moon,' he grinned, nodding his head mischievously.

I stared at him for a couple of seconds, unable to contain my shock, not so much that he was asking me, but more because he was thinking of taking one himself. I knew Basir loved his joints, but ecstasy? I'd never have guessed. Scratching my head, I thought about what he'd said for a few more seconds. Although I'd been partial to the odd joint in my time, I'd never felt the urge or temptation to experiment with anything else. Up until now, that was, and if there was ever a time and a place to try something else, then this surely had to be it. Without further thought, I told him I was game on if he was. With that, he leapt to his feet, made his way over to a group of Europeans sitting on another mat a couple of feet away from us and returning a few minutes later, handed me a small white pill. I asked him what I do. 'Just swallow it,' he replied which, after he'd taken his, I did. As I sat there still a little flummoxed, he proceeded to tell me the reason that so many people were dressed in these dazzling colours was to commemorate the *Holi* festival, which was being celebrated the next day. As he was speaking, though, I was busily trying to concentrate on feeling for the first effects of the drug kicking in. A few more minutes later, I told him nothing seemed to be happening but just as I started thinking we'd been duped with a couple of Paracetemols, the two cows lying at the end of the mat started to give me suspicious looks. 'Oh fuck, here we go,' said a little voice inside my head, 'strap yourselves in, we're going for a ride!' Still squinting at the chomping creatures in front of me, I started shuffling about on my backside, trying to move away from them, although I didn't feel very in tune with my body. Holding up my palms, I stretched open my fingers, but could no longer feel my hands. My head felt heavy, like a cannonball, and the thudding of the drumbeat was getting progressively louder and faster. Before long, I saw Basir staring at me. Still grinning, he mouthed a few words, though I couldn't hear what it was he was saying. He pointed his thumb up in the air, but my legs felt like jelly. Reaching for my arm, he hoisted me up and for a few seconds, I just stood there like a newborn doe trying to find its feet, still watching out for the two dodgy-looking cows.

Stumbling along a narrow path of sand running between the mats, I followed Basir for a hundred yards or so until the music was so loud it was almost deafening. Clutching onto my arm, he pointed towards the palm trees. Now, it doesn't pain me at all to say this but I've never been a comfortable dancer. Every party or wedding I go to, I always make a point of basing myself as far away from the dance-floor as is humanly possible and I'll only shuffle about in a totally uncoordinated manner to music if I'm totally paralytic or someone physically drags me onto the floor at the end of the evening. All this, however, was about to change for bold as brass, I dashed onto the square of sand and danced like I'd never danced before. I was, without doubt, shit hot. I was in the groove, I was hot to trot, I was rock steady, I was John Travolta, I was Michael Jackson, I was Michael Hutchence, I was Tom Jones, I was James Brown, I was Rod Stewart. Forget *Stars In Their Eyes*, I had stars coming out of my ears, because for the next two hours I was all of these people all at the same time. In fact, I was all of these people on speed. I was, quite simply, 'Lord of the Dance.' And all the while, as I swung my arms in perfect synchronisation to the ceaseless melody of hypnotic riffs blaring out of the speakers, blissfully lost in my own little world, it felt as if all the shackles had been removed, all the obstacles—the red tape, the bureaucracy, the things that constantly hamper you back home—had suddenly disappeared and all that mattered now was moving my body in time with the music.

Gazing up periodically to look at the people around me, I was sure some were staring at me, but I didn't care, the music was all that counted and deep down, I knew it could only be because my dancing was taking everyone by storm. And my

God, there were some particularly provocative girls on the dance-floor too, whom I knew I couldn't fail to be entrancing. Yet just as I thought I had total control of the floor and that all the people around me were in awe of me, marvelling at my movements, my gyrations and my audacious pelvic thrusts, I finally met my match. Dressed in just a flapping suede loincloth and brown furry boots, a heavily bearded man with thickset long hair appeared in front of me, taking on for all the world the appearance of 'Captain Caveman.' Shaking his head rhythmically to the beat of the music, he pumped his clenched fists up and down by his side and stomped his feet on the sand as if he was walking a treadmill. Seconds later, I found myself copying his actions, performing the same drill which I kept up non-stop for well over an hour and if it hadn't been for my sweat-drenched body crying out for rehydration, I would have probably remained on the dance floor all night. Eventually wiping my soaking brow, I staggered across the sand, purchased a bottle of Bisleri from one of the Indian ladies sitting nearby, greedily gulped the contents down in one and then set off in search of Basir.

Wandering haphazardly along the shore, I spotted him a few minutes later sitting around a mat with a small group of travellers. With his hands clasped together by his mouth, he was inhaling from a small brown pipe full of ganja, which was being passed around from person to person. As I went over to join him, the acrid smell of the smoke was overpowering. Kneeling down next to him, he handed the pipe to me and said, '*chillum*'. I looked at him dumbly, not knowing what to do, so he showed me how to lock my hands together around the pipe and then inhale. As soon as I did, I nearly choked to death. The intoxicating smoke burnt my throat and lungs and when I exhaled, I spluttered and coughed so much that my eyes filled up with tears. Hastily passing the pipe on to the person the other side of me, I sat there desperately trying to compose myself while Basir introduced me to the rest of the group.

'So, how long have you been in India, then, Jim?' said a dreadlocked guy sitting opposite. Through squinting eyes, I glanced up and replied: 'Not long.' It was all I could muster for the time being.

An hour or so later, the sun came up and the bright fluorescent colours adorned by the partygoers became a sight to behold. Almost in recognition of this, I leapt to my feet and returned to the dance-floor. With the effects of the drugs wearing off, though, my tiredness finally caught up with me and after collapsing in a heap on the sand, I rejoined Basir and we eventually headed back to Calangute to catch up on some much-needed sleep.

The following day, Basir got me my own hut next door to his and we spent the rest of the week lying on the beach and lazily whiling away afternoons in various beachside bars, sitting around eating, chatting and playing backgammon with various people Basir had met. On some of these days, I'd wander down to the beach on my own and spend a few hours lying on the sand, leafing through my guidebooks, and it wasn't long before I'd struck up a cosy little friendship with two of the Indian women who spent their days walking up and down the sand selling fresh fruit to tourists. Every time they came along, they'd always greet me with the same line: 'Orange, pineapple, water melon...you like?' (The upward inflection on the 'you like?' always rising to a pitch so high, it was almost a squeal.) Invariably, I'd ask them for a watermelon, which they'd chop up in front of me, and we'd happily sit there and slowly devour it between us under the shade of a moored fishing boat. Quite often, they'd stay around for over an hour chatting about England, asking about my family, my job and, more pertinently, why I didn't have a girlfriend. It was a good question and one I was repeatedly unable to answer.

Basir was very wary about the Indian Police who we regularly saw wandering around the sandy paths close to the tourist haunts. He'd told me that they had recently been clamping down on people with drugs. Somebody he knew had been caught with a tiny amount of grass just a few weeks ago and only managed to escape serving a long time in an Indian jail by paying the officer a hefty sum of a thousand dollars in *baksheesh*. Apparently, the guy had had to phone his parents who'd eventually bailed him out by wiring the money over. 'You have to be very, very careful,' he told me. 'Many of the police here are corrupt and sometimes they'll plant drugs on you just for *baksheesh*.' Just a day later, our own huts were raided.

It was late afternoon and I'd been sitting outside under one of the trees for over an hour diligently reading up on India when I heard a whistle. Glancing up, I noticed Basir was looking somewhat startled. Leaping to his feet, he sprinted into his hut, darted back out again over to the nearby well and dropped something down into the chasm. I knew in an instant that something was up, because Basir was probably the most laid-back person I'd ever come across. Even getting Basir to walk briskly to work back in Sydney whenever we missed our bus was difficult enough, so to see him suddenly bolting around like a demented rabbit meant that something was definitely afoot. Seconds later, a couple of police officers silently emerged from behind our huts. Pointing to the doors, they asked Basir if they could go in and have a look around. He nodded his head submissively and the two men duly disappeared. As Basir started pacing up and down, I sat there for a while with my head in my hands, fearing the worst and wondering how my parents would react on learning I'd been banged up in an Indian jail.

'Hi, Mum, it's me'

'Oh, it's you! Where are you?'

'I'm in Goa.'

'Everything all right? How's the Delhi belly?'

'Yeah, the tummy's holding up fine.'

'And you're having a good time? '

'Yeah, India's great. In fact, I could end up here a little longer than planned.'

'Why? You're not in trouble are you?'

'Well...'

'You are! What's happened? William! William! It's James! He's in trouble!'

'Er, Mum, I might need to ask you a big favour.'

'What kind of favour?'

Exactly. Just what kind of favour? How was I going to get out of this one? Such a scenario didn't bear thinking about.

Basir, wandering over, stood there for a few minutes, rubbing his hand up and down the back of his neck.

'They won't find anything in there,' he said eventually.

'Yeah, but you said the other day...'

'I know, I know,' he nodded, 'that's the worry.'

For a few seconds, we both looked back at the huts. They each only had one room, so small in size you could barely swing a cat. What was taking them so long? They'd been rummaging around inside for getting on ten minutes. What could they be doing in there? Whatever happened, that was it with drugs and me. From now on, I'd stick to beer. Moments later, the two men finally reappeared and, marching over, proceeded to rattle off a series of questions: When had we arrived in Baga? How long were we planning to stay here? What countries were we from? Could they see our visas? Then, after inspecting our passports and muttering a few words to each other, they somewhat reluctantly sauntered off. For the next twenty or thirty seconds, I lay on the ground looking up to the sky gulping in huge intakes of breath. As soon as they were out of earshot, Basir informed me that the whistle had been a signal from one of the guys in the other huts who, fifteen minutes later, when the coast was finally clear, came out to join us to discuss the raid. Both were mightily relieved. I was still trembling.

We spent a couple more days hanging out and although the season here was coming to an end, the whole 'scene' that Basir, perhaps unwittingly, was part of started to get me down. Well, it didn't actually get me down, but I just couldn't be doing with it. Quite often, we'd stop in a bar for some lunch, where there'd inevitably be a group of people sat around a table chatting and pontificating. Always, within the group, a kind of unspoken hierarchy seemed to exist, determined by the number of times you'd been to Goa or how long you'd been there this year. And at the top of this hierarchy there'd always be one person holding court that everybody else was seen to look up to. One afternoon, it was a French man with a beautiful girlfriend (who Basir would play backgammon with whenever he could), another day it was a strangely familiar long haired Irish guy with a guitar. Now, I've always been under the impression that every person you meet, whatever their colour, caste, religion, sex or age, should, at the very least, be afforded the right to be greeted on equal terms and my aforementioned ignorance over the plight of Aborigines in Sydney had only reinforced these beliefs. The terms on offer here, though, were based entirely on how familiar a face you were.

The French, it has to be said, lorded it the most. Invariably commandeering the largest tables, they'd sit around en masse for hours on end in their sarongs and skimpy thongs, playing draughts and backgammon, eating, smoking, drinking and, chatting incessantly, wildly gesticulating with their hands. They barely acknowledged the local staff: each time they came over to clear their plates, they'd lean back recumbently in their chairs blowing cigarette smoke in their faces; they repeatedly switched between English and French whenever it suited them and when other nationalities were sat at the table, they reverted to their mother tongue even more; and each time a fellow compatriot arrived, they'd be welcomed with a kiss on both cheeks and a greeting such as, 'Bonjour Mimi, where 'ave 'ou been? We 'aven't seen you for days.' And Backgammon, how pretentious a game was that? It might have had something to do with the fact I didn't know how to play it, it could have been just because it was French, but either way, I found it bloody irritating all the same.

After a week in Goa, I was ready to move on. Basir was heading off himself in a few days' time and I think he was hoping I'd travel with him. He, like me, was heading up to Nepal (via Bombay and Delhi), but I already had my own route to Nepal planned and I was really keen to start seeing the 'real India,' so early one evening I told him I was going to head off to Mysore the following day.

That night, there was another big party, this time on Bagator beach. We turned up around midnight but due to some kind of technical hitch, the music didn't start until 2am. Knowing that I'd be heading off later that morning, I decided to take it easy and stuck to a few beers. Sometime around dawn, I was sitting down on one of the rugs chatting with some people from England I'd met earlier in the week, keeping a beady eye on a young fat Japanese guy sat on the sand some twenty feet away from us on the other side of a path. The Buddha-like character had been sitting there cross-legged for the past ten minutes screwing his eyes up and reaching out his hands, palms open and fingers curling inwards and outwards as if they were trying to grab onto a couple of imaginary squidgy balls. Then, without warning, he suddenly began to beat his chest furiously with his fists and roar at the top of his voice like a crazy wild bear. Two or three people quickly leapt up and went over to see if he was okay but screwing up his eyes even more, he just waved them away dismissively. A couple of minutes later, he started to roll about in the sand, still growling and by now, people all around us, some laughing, others shaking their heads, were looking on open-mouthed. Even a few of the Indian chai ladies who'd gathered around were staring on incredulously. What on earth they were making of these antics was anybody's guess. Just as we were contemplating how much this poor guy would remember when he eventually came around, he somehow got to his feet, promptly ripped off all his clothes and charged off towards the dance floor. This sight, especially that of his big fat white bum wobbling off into the distance, had many people reaching for their sides. Thankfully, to save him any further embarrassment, a couple of girls rushed over, wrapped him in a blanket and escorted him off to get him something to drink. Sat there shaking my head, I now felt even more relieved; my decision not to indulge again had been fully vindicated, and if ever I needed proof of the adverse effects of hallucinogens, then this poor guy tripping was surely it.

I caught up with Basir a short while later. Sat amongst a group of his friends on the sand, he was chatting to the French girl again, smiling inanely through bloodshot eyes.

'I'm gonna head back,' I said, squatting down beside him.

He nodded his head indifferently, so leaving him to it, I traipsed back to Baga alone. When I finally got back to the hut, my body was crying out for sleep. I dozed for a while, though when I woke an hour or so later, I couldn't make up my mind as to whether I should head off. I knew that if I didn't, that later in the day, I'd probably regret not leaving, but if I was to make what was potentially a prolonged and arduous journey to Mysore, I really needed a few more hours' sleep. Umming and aahing, I sat with my head in my hands for twenty minutes before finally jumping to my feet. Hastily gathering all my belongings together, I scribbled out a short note for Basir and, heaving my rucksack onto my back, staggered out into the blinding afternoon sunshine to start the long slow walk back to Calangute.

As soon as I boarded the bus later that afternoon, I knew I'd made the right decision. I'd now reclaimed my own own space and was back to being 100% accountable for my own actions. Sitting back in my seat, I peered out of the window. The lush green swaying palm trees had already disappeared and the scenery was becoming increasingly squalid, dusty and barren. As the bus careered along, jolting jerkily over the bumpy roads, I thought back to the party the previous night and no matter how I tried, just couldn't get the unforgettable image of the poor Japanese guy out of my head. There'd been several other Japanese there that particular night and I wondered just what they had made of it all—this whole party scene there must have seemed so alien to them. And the Indian chai ladies too, sat around their paraffin lamps, fighting to stay awake through the course of the night—goodness only knows what must have been going through their minds? Hippies, Indians, Europeans, many drugged up to their eyeballs, continually invading their mats, demanding tea and snacks. And the whole planning of the parties, what actually went on behind the scenes? Who were the organisers, the people behind the parties? And how much did they have to pay to the Indian Police in *baksheesh* for them to turn a blind eye? Basir had told me that the beach parties had been banned for the last three years, so maybe I'd been lucky to arrive in Goa when I did. In some respects, I wondered if I would have appreciated it more if I'd arrived at the end of my travels around India, though that would be in May or June, and the season then would have been well and truly over. Maybe it was because I'd spent much of the previous month twiddling my thumbs in Fiji, I don't know, but certainly after ten days in Goa, with the whole of the Indian subcontinent at my beck and call, I was definitely ready to move on.

CHAPTER 25

THE DECCAN PLATEAU

SADDAM HUSSEIN & THE DALAI LAMA'S SISTER

11th–13th March 1991

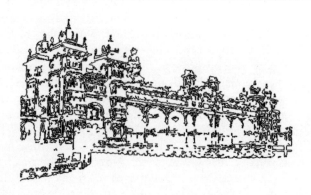

'Saddam Hussein? What do you think?'

I frowned.

'Saddam Hussein? What do you think?' he repeated.

For a couple of seconds, I was lost for words. Scratching my head, I looked at the boy circumspectly. It had just turned midnight and I was stood outside a roadside eating-house somewhere deep in the state of Karnataka. As I'd been stretching my legs at the side of the bus, a young boy selling water coconuts had come bounding up to me and after frenetically firing off a barrage of all the usual questions—What is your country? How long have you been here? Where are you travelling to?—he then completely caught me off guard by throwing in this little blinder. After a few more seconds deliberating, I pointed my index finger against my temple and started twisting it in semi-circles. He recognised the gesture straight away and, to my relief, started chuckling. I asked him what he thought.

'I think he is a crazy, bad man, too.'

The reaction from a number of other passengers on the bus when they discovered where I was from was also positive: 'From England? That is good, very good.' This came as quite a relief, as I hadn't been too sure if the events in the Gulf would affect the attitude of Indians towards me. The initial signs were that they wouldn't.

The bus itself was almost identical to the first I'd taken down to Goa. The front window, rear view mirror and cluttered dashboard were elaborately adorned with clay models of various Hindu effigies, burning sticks of incense, garlands of bright yellow and purple orchids and strings of rosary beads; alternating sounds of Hindi pop music and Bollywood videos blared out incessantly from the overhead speakers and television screens, whilst the passengers on the roof and others hanging to the rails outside only added more pressure to the sagging suspension of the hopelessly overcrowded vehicle. After eventually managing to close my ears to the din, the sixteen-hour overnight journey passed relatively peacefully and we arrived at our destination early morning. Mysore, with a population of just over 500,000 was, by Indian standards, a moderately sized city. Situated in central South India, some 750 metres above sea level, it was renowned for being one of the country's major incense manufacturers. Upon arrival, still shattered from the beach party, I took a room in the first cheap hotel I came across and promptly crashing out on the bed, caught up with some more sleep.

Later in the afternoon, batteries fully recharged, I took a taxi to the Maharaja's Palace and as soon as the driver dropped me off outside, I could see why he had been extolling its virtues for the entire duration of the twenty-minute journey. Whilst I'm not a great lover of palaces and temples, it was, it has to be said, a mightily impressive building. Completed in 1911 at a cost of 4.2 million rupees after the former palace had burned down, the 245-foot long, three-storeyed cream coloured building was designed by a well-known architect of the time named Henry Irwin. Its facade was a harmonious combination of crimson domes, elaborate arches, minarets, balconies and verandas, whilst towering over the rest of the building at its centre was a large gleaming gold-plated dome. This sumptuous exterior alone still looked fit enough to grace any Maharaja; indeed, the back of the Palace continued to be the official residence of the son of the Mysore Royal Family. And once inside, the extravagance continued—there was an art gallery, a museum and a series of lavishly decorated rooms with chandeliers, mahogany and stained glass ceilings, solid silver doors and sculptured pillars, there was even a sacred Hindu temple housed inside its walls. If every palace and temple in India was going to be as impressive as this, then I was clearly going to have to change my tune.

On the way back to my room, I stopped off at the highly acclaimed rooftop restaurant of the Dubar Hotel. Many other travellers were sitting around and the atmosphere was suitably relaxed and informal. Perusing the pages of *The Times Of India*, I spent a leisurely hour or so catching up on all that had been happening in the world. An article on the front page reported on a series of failed assassination attempts on Saddam Hussein. Although the war in the Gulf had finished, the Iraqi leader still hadn't been captured and all the speculation indicated that tracking him down was going to be far from straightforward. One American officer was quoted as saying: 'Finding Saddam Hussein will be like looking for a needle in a haystack.' The fact he was reputed to have over a dozen look-alikes clearly wasn't going to make it any easier and for the next few minutes, I sat there trying to imagine how utterly demoralising it would feel to finally find that needle only to be told you'd got the wrong one. More locally, the news was depressingly familiar: continued unrest in the neighbouring states of Kashmir and Sri Lanka had accounted for the loss of over fifty lives in total in the last two days, while back home, the Conservatives, now under

322

the leadership of John Major, had suffered a surprisingly resounding by-election defeat to the Liberal Democrats in the Ribble Valley. Removing the 'Iron Lady' from office was clearly not going to solve their problems overnight.

Folding up the newspaper, I picked up my tea and wandered over to a vacated table near the balcony. Although I'd been in the country for over a fortnight, I realised, as I looked down on all of the hustle and bustle in the square below, I'd finally reached the real India I'd been so longing to see. Bicycle bells rang, car horns blared, dirty half-dressed kids chased each other up lanes screaming and shouting, remonstrating shopkeepers shook their heads at haggling shoppers, an arm waving policemen in khaki uniform and beret stood in the middle of the roundabout blowing his whistle incessantly and there wasn't a palm tree in sight.

Bangalore—capital of the state of Karnataka (meaning 'Lofty Land')—is situated on the Deccan Plateau a thousand metres above sea level, 250 more than Mysore. As well as being one of India's largest cities, it was also one of the most affluent. Early the next morning, I made the $3^1/_2$-hour journey there on super deluxe coach which, apart from the fact it was fully air-conditioned, was no different to either of the buses I'd previously taken.

My first port of call in Bangalore was the City railway station where I was hoping to make my first train reservation in India. Many people had told me just what an infuriating experience this could be and, indeed, just before I had left the UK, I'd read a classic account of one person's desperate attempts to purchase a train ticket from Calcutta to Patna in a *Sunday Times* anthology of travel writing. Written by A.H. Cooper, the story, entitled 'Please To Make A Reservation', is four pages of fraught and fractured dialogue in which the reader is made to suffer all of the author's acute frustrations in his futile attempts to try to overcome Indian bureaucracy at its confounding worst and it remains, to this day, one of my favourite pieces of writing.

Arriving at the ticket hall mid-morning, I was pleasantly surprised at how organised and civilised the booking office looked. It was certainly not the monstrous Victorian-style hall I'd been expecting, but instead, a compact and relatively modern looking well-lit room, complete with a fully computerised reservations system. Taking my place at the back of a long queue, I looked up at the clock. It was 11am. The office closed for lunch at 1pm, which gave me two full hours to make my reservation. Surely, this couldn't be asking too much? After ten minutes, I reached the booking window.

'Good morning,' I said to the elderly man behind the counter. 'I need to get a train to Madras. I understand there is an express train.'

'Yes,' he replied, 'the Madras Mail.'

'And does that go every day?'

He nodded his head unconvincingly.

'So does that mean it goes tomorrow, then?'

Raising an eyebrow, he cocked his head a little, then pointing behind him, said rather irritably: 'This train will be leaving from that platform tomorrow morning at seven o'clock precisely.'

'Well,' I said, recovering from a sudden coughing fit, 'I'd like to make a reservation, then, please.'

He handed me a lengthy form to fill out, asking for information such as my name, my address, my telephone number, my age, my passport number, my visa number, my destination, my date of travel, my train name, my train number and a hundred and twenty other largely irrelevant questions. After completing all the details I could, he then directed me to another counter in the corner of the room, where I joined a smaller queue reserved for 'Foreign Tourists, Orthopaedically Handicapped, Concession Holders, Senior Citizens and Freedom Fighters'. Reaching the window a few minutes later, I handed the woman the form. She looked at it for a couple of seconds and then said, 'There is a waiting list for second class.'

'A waiting list?' I exclaimed, somewhat taken aback. 'Does that mean it's fully booked?'

'Yes.'

And how many people are on the waiting list?'

She looked down at her screen. 'Fifteen. There are seats available in first class, though.'

'How much is first class?'

'A hundred and eighty-five rupees.'

Quickly calculating the fare to be just over £5, I nodded my head. It was a bit more than I wanted to pay but what the heck. She wrote out the ticket on the spot and I handed over the money. Then, after one final question to check what time the train arrived in Madras, I walked out with ticket in hand. The whole process had taken just under fifteen minutes.

I spent the rest of the morning exploring the city. Like Mysore, Bangalore boasted a spectacular edifice, the majestic Vidhana Soudha, a 46-metre high government building housing over 300 rooms overlooking a pleasantly spacious park in the centre of the city. The entrance lobby, though, was only open to the public for a couple of hours in the afternoon. Undeterred, I made my way down to the shopping area of Mahatma Gandhi Road, but as I was walking around in the stifling heat, my nose started to run and my head began to ache. Realising I still hadn't had any lunch, I pulled out my guidebook to look for a recommended place to eat. The first place listed seemed good enough and, by a stroke of luck, looked like it was close by, so I made my way towards the Rice Bowl, an establishment reputedly owned by the Dalai Lama's sister. Sitting myself down in the crowded open-fronted restaurant a few minutes later, I quickly surveyed the menu and, tongue hanging out, duly ordered a chicken chow mein. The dish arrived at my table in remarkably quick time and without second thought, I gratefully wolfed down the food.

Still not feeling too clever, I hailed an auto rickshaw shortly afterwards to take me back to my guesthouse and, for the second time in less than seventy-two hours, found myself being asked, this time by the rickshaw driver, what I thought of Saddam Hussein. This still potentially remained a very sensitive subject. Just the previous night, I'd finished reading Pranay

Gupte's enlightening book, *The Challenge of Change,* which discusses India's relationship with the rest of the world after Indira Gandhi's assassination in 1984. In it, it seemed to imply that India was far closer to Russia and Pakistan than it was to the US, which both surprised and alarmed me a little, for I'd assumed India was a staunch ally of America. And, more pertinently, it seemed from the coverage of the Gulf War in the newspapers that India's position on the conflict remained far from clear. Because they hadn't come out and categorically stated their support for the US led coalition, I got the impression that India had a certain sympathy for Iraq in the conflict. Significantly, there were over eighty million Muslims in India, accounting for around 10% of the country's population, nearly all of whom, I imagined, would have come out on Iraq's side, so perhaps it was no wonder India found itself in a very precarious position. I'd only seen a handful of Muslims since I'd been here, and this rickshaw driver, judging by his stickers of the elephant-headed god, Ganesh, on his dashboard, was a devout Hindu, so I told him that I thought Saddam Hussein was crazy. Again, I got the same chuckling response.

By the time I got back to my room, I felt truly awful. My legs were aching, my head was pounding and my nose was streaming like a dripping tap. It looked like I'd picked up a cold, probably from the air-conditioning on the morning coach. Pulling back the covers, I collapsed onto my bed. I awoke again around midnight and, with my head still thumping, got up and rummaged around in my rucksack for a couple of Panadols, which I only normally take as a last resort. Two hours later, I was squatting in the bathroom with two fingers down my throat, forcing myself to retch. On top of a cold, it now looked like I'd picked up a bout of 'Bangalore belly', which I was convinced I'd contracted from the chow mein dish, as there was no way it could have been freshly cooked in the time it was served up. The Dalai Lama happened to be residing in the northern hill station of Dharamsala, a place I'd pencilled in to visit, and it was, by all accounts, possible for travellers to the town to request an audience with his Holiness. As I lay in my bed that night tossing, turning and sweating profusely, I vowed to bring up the subject of his sister's eating establishment if I managed to speak to his Reverence whilst I was there.

CHAPTER 26

MADRAS

OH, PRETTY WOMAN

14th–17th March 1991

The 7½-hour journey to Madras passed slowly. Still suffering from the debilitating symptoms of flu, I didn't move from my seat for the duration of the trip: I paid little notice to the scenery that was passing me out of the window, I made no effort to communicate to any of the other passengers around me and I just sat in silence in my compartment feeling increasingly sorry for myself. Being ill in India was the one thing I had dreaded, and now, only a fortnight after arriving, I'd been struck down with a bug; at least, that's what I hoped it was. All kinds of negative thoughts passed through my mind, not least, how this illness could seriously jeopardise the remainder of my trip. It was now only two weeks before I was due to meet up with Gibbo and Caroline in Nepal, but what was going to happen if

I still felt like this in a few days' time? I could only hope and pray that it didn't come to that. For the first time since I'd been away, I found myself wishing that I could be back at home, lying in my bed on crisp white sheets and big fluffy pillows. I was sure I had an option written into my insurance policy that would enable me to be flown back home in the case of a medical emergency. But emergency or not, I decided if I was still feeling like this next week, then I'd just have to get myself on the first flight home regardless. Although this would be a massive disappointment, there were only a few more months to go and I'd still have some wonderful memories from my travels in China and Oz.

As the day progressed, the temperature in the compartment got progressively hotter, and I could feel all my remaining energy being drained, almost sucked, from my body. After forcing myself to pick at the satsumas and grapes I'd brought that morning, I managed to sleep, albeit rather fitfully, for the remainder of the journey. Arriving in Madras early afternoon, I then made the mistake of trying to book a ticket for an onward journey to Calcutta in a few days' time. It had seemed the sensible thing to do at the time, as it would have effectively saved me returning to the station again the following day, but the queues in the ticketing hall were torturously long and by the time I reached the front forty minutes later, I was feeling so weak I was close to fainting. When I finally did get to the booking window, I discovered the fare for a seat in first class was a massive 600 rupees (roughly £15). Feeling as terrible as I did, I had absolutely no qualms about paying this. The duration of the journey from Madras to Calcutta was thirty-six hours and the state of my health was paramount, so I duly handed over a wad of notes and, struggling through the crowds, made my way outside.

Crawling into one of the waiting auto rickshaws, I asked the driver to take me to the Broadlands, one of the most popular hotels amongst backpackers. Because it was so late in the day, I thought I'd be trying in vain to secure a room here but when I arrived, my luck was in—there *were* some rooms available—

and again, I didn't hesitate in coughing up a little bit more for a single. The hotel was noted for its tranquil atmosphere and it didn't take long to see why. At the back of the building, a number of travellers were sat around chatting in a couple of airy courtyards lined with potted palms and rubber plants, and the whitewashed walls and predominance of wicker furniture gave the establishment a rather colonial feeling. Dumping my rucksack on my bed, I headed straight out to get some food. Although I didn't particularly feel like eating, I knew I'd have to try to force some food down in order to keep up what strength I had left, so I pulled up a chair in a small roadside eating establishment and sat there for half an hour slowly picking at a plate of samosas.

By the time I eventually wandered back to the hotel to catch up on some rest, it was early evening and as I passed along Mount Road, the heart of the city's busy shopping district, it felt good to be back out walking the streets again, listening to the incessant beeping of car horns, stepping over the cows lying on the pavements and watching all the shopkeepers and stall holders packing up for the night.

One of the discoveries I'd made quite early on in my travels was how I could combat feelings of despondency and weariness by submerging myself in a good book. Reading, providing the material was engrossing enough, seemed to detach me from adversity. That night was a classic example. I'd picked up *Ashenden*, my latest Maugham book—based on the author's experiences serving in the Intelligence Department during the Second World War—and within minutes, all thoughts about the state of my health that had been preoccupying my mind were banished and I was seemingly transported to another land. And when I woke up, it felt as if all the energy that had been drained from my body on the train journey had miraculously been pumped back into my veins overnight. My stomach, however, was still giving cause for concern. After spending a couple of hours dashing back and forth to the toilet, I pulled out a couple of Imodium tablets in salvation, hoping and praying they'd be able to clog up my loose bowels.

Later in the morning, feeling a little better, I made my way back to Mount Road and, calling in at the tourist office, booked a full day's sightseeing tour around Madras departing the next morning. By now, it was already approaching midday and I was beginning to feel hungry so, unable to face the thought of any more spicy food, I marched straight into the reception of the five-star Connemara Hotel, asked for a table in the restaurant and, caring little for the stares my trainers and shorts attracted from other diners, followed the waiter across the wooden dining room floor towards an empty white-clothed table in the corner.

'This one okay, sir?'

'Yes, it's perfect,' I replied.

The waiter pulled out a chair and as he unfurled my napkin, I glanced up at the lavish chandelier in the centre of the hall and then opened the shiny black leather menu.

'And would you be wanting to look at the wine list, sir?'

'No, no, water is fine,' I said, waving my hand.

The waiter smiled knowingly, then took my order.

Ten minutes later, dinner was duly served, a plate of fat freshly cooked chips alongside a succulent battered fillet of cod. If I was serious about getting better, I was going to have to pull out all the stops and if this entailed dining in the elegant surrounds of the Connemara every day, it was fine by me.

Further along Mount Road, dozens of excitable Indians were congregated outside a local cinema. Set back behind a neatly trimmed hedge on the other side of the busy two-lane street, it was an old style building with fading white walls decorated with art deco curving stripes. On a rectangular placard strapped above the portico was a large hand-painted caricature depicting the head and shoulders of smartly dressed man with a bouffant hairstyle. Looking on behind him stood a figure of a young woman with a leather bag slung over her shoulder, tilting her head as she fastened an earring under a mop of long curly brown hair. At the top of the sign in big red letters were the words *Pretty Woman*. As soon as I spotted this writing, I was overcome with a feeling of exuberance, for this was *the* film that everybody had been talking about before I'd come away and since I'd been so preoccupied with my last-minute preparations, I'd never actually got around to seeing it. Indeed, I must have been one of the few remaining people in the UK who hadn't, so given that I had nothing better to do for the afternoon, I hastily crossed over and, much to the bewilderment of the other patrons, boldly took my place at the back of the queue. Unlike home, the fact it was both a weekday and a matinee performance seemingly counted for little, because when I made my way into the auditorium twenty minutes later, it was packed to the rafters. But Indian cinema or not, there was still no escape from the lengthy preamble of movie trailers, and the very second a bare-chested Sylvester Stallone appeared on the screen wielding a M-60 machine gun, the whole audience erupted into a spontaneous frenzy of cheers and whistles. Thankfully, by the time the main picture began, relative calmness had been restored and it wasn't long before the captivating on-screen chemistry between the two leads was having its desired effect; Gere playing Edward, a ruthless millionaire and Julia Roberts as Vivian, the funny and vulnerable local hooker he meets on a Hollywood boulevard, who slowly begins to reveal his sensitive side. In fact, so enchanting was the love story that unfolded, I soon found myself cheering and whistling along with the excitable galleries every time a romantic scene, a kiss, or a moment of tenderness greeted the screen. It was, from start to finish, thoroughly engaging, a light-hearted and uplifting modern day fairy tale if ever there was one, and by the time the closing credits had come up, I was stood on my seat applauding like everybody else, thinking to myself there couldn't have been a better way to spend an afternoon, especially with an admission price of just seven rupees (20 pence). Now that's what I call value for money!

Emerging from the cinema into the late afternoon rush hour, I felt I owed it to myself to take a wander along to the beach. In truth, I think I just wanted to convince myself that

Madras was actually on the coast, as I'd been in the city for twenty-four hours and had yet to see the sea. When I got there, the long sandy beach was surprisingly clean and pleasant and, with the sun preparing to set, it was that lovely time of day when the shadows are long and colours are brilliant, and the beach was bathed in a golden suffusion of fading sunlight. As gulls squawked high above, a cool breeze was blowing in from the Bay of Bengal and, savouring the salty air, I stood there for a while gazing in wonder at the crowds relaxing in the early evening sunshine—giggling children playfully chasing each other across the sand; be-seated infants contentedly waving buckets and spades in the air as parents looked on with beaming smiles; a group of women clutching onto their saris as they paddled knee-deep in the water, and pairs of young lovers walking hand in hand along the promenade gazing into each other's eyes. Everyone, it seemed, was just happy to be here by the sea, and after Bangalore, I couldn't have felt much better myself.

Early the next morning, as I made my way along the darkened streets to the Tamil Nadu tourist office, lights flickered to life in shop windows, shadowy figures armed with boxes and bags darted between the rush of oncoming cars and cyclists, whilst in murky alcoves and doorways, huddles of blanket covered bodies began to stir, all completely oblivious to the huge grey rats scurrying up and down the gutters. Even at 6am, the streets of Madras were buzzing with activity.

Many travellers I'd met turned their noses up at these all-inclusive sightseeing trips, fearing, no doubt, they'd find themselves outnumbered by the backpackers deadly enemy, the tourist. I'm sure this was why so many preferred to travel independently to local attractions, even though this usually entailed a lot more legwork. I had no such qualms. Indeed, with the possible exception of that first outing to the Great Wall, my experience of these excursions so far had been good and, travelling solo, they were an assured way of meeting new people. This trip was no exception. Sitting next to me on the bus was a tall balding bearded man in his fifties.

'So, where you from?' he asked, in a broad Brummie accent, seconds after we'd set off. 'I'm an engineer,' he said, before I had chance to reply. 'Been working here for the last two years as it happens,' he added, and for the next twenty minutes, I could barely get a word in edgeways.

After telling me all about his work and the various places he'd been posted, I asked him what his overall impressions were of the subcontinent. He clearly wasn't enamoured. 'What do I think of India?' he snapped. 'I'll tell you what I think of India — it's a stinkin' fuckin' hell-hole.'

It wasn't so much his response but the ferocity of the reply that took me aback and I was already likening him to one of those civil servants depicted by Maugham who'd been despatched against their will to some remote tropical outpost. This was only substantiated later in the morning by his somewhat startling reaction to the locals. As we re-boarded the bus after our first stop at the temples of Kanchipuram, a group of Indians who'd congregated outside the bus were busily plying their wares. This type of thing was pretty much par for the course, and was something I'd already become accustomed in the short time I'd been in India. Yet the man's reaction to a few sandals being harmlessly poked through the window was to grab hold of one and hurl it as far as he could back out of the window. A young lad, looking understandably startled, ran off to retrieve the cork sandal only to hear the man yell, 'Go on, now piss off!' And it didn't stop there. Twenty minutes later after we'd set off again, we were sat in our seats listening to our guide talking over the microphone. When he happened to mention that Hindi had recently been declared the country's most widely spoken language, the man leapt to his feet and, at the top of his voice, shouted down the aisle: 'No, I have to disagree. English will always be India's mother tongue.'

By the time we'd reached the second temples at Mahabalipuram, I tried to distance myself from the man who I'd now concluded was utterly deranged. Fortunately, I soon managed to get chatting to a middle-aged Australian couple who'd been travelling around India for a couple of months on an Enfield. The guy, a bus driver from Perth, told me that he'd found the people they'd met here in the south far more friendly and amenable than their counterparts in the north and as he imparted some useful advice about respective places to stay in Calcutta, he came out with the classic Australian expletive, 'Fuckin' Oath.' It was an expression I hadn't heard for months and was one that still had me chuckling to myself minutes later.

Later in the day, I met another character, this time a gangly Yugoslav with raven spiky hair and earring. After stopping for some lunch, I was stood outside the bus listening to his account of some fantastic temple he'd visited in Kerala. Indeed, he raved about it with such enthusiasm that I was beginning to wonder whether it was a place I should be making an effort to travel to myself, even though it was a few hundred miles to the south. However, when he went on to describe another half a dozen places with equal verve, I realised that all the sights he'd go on to see in India would be just as magnificent. Mid-afternoon, we stopped at a boating lake running parallel to the sea. All too predictably, the Yugoslav was the first to jump onto a boat and row out across the water. He set off so fast, in fact, that before long, he was even overtaking the cars driving along the adjoining road. Twenty minutes later, panting like a bloodhound, he staggered back across the car park.

'How was it?' I enquired, as he stood with his hands on his knees, still trying to get his breath back.

'Amazing,' he gasped, shaking his head. 'You don't know what you missed.'

Around 5pm, we pulled up at our final port of call for the day, the VGP Golden Beach Resort. Here, amongst the towering palm trees on a soft scalding carpet of powdery sand, all kinds of performances were taking place. There were magicians, trapeze artists, clowns, men on stilts, acrobats and jugglers and, behind the trees, a dazzling array of snack stalls and fun fair rides. Just like the previous day at the beach, the sun was setting, the shadows were long and the bright early evening colours of pink and orange saris and indigo dhotis radiated

335

ambience. The act attracting the largest crowd was a young female tightrope walker who, clutching onto a long red and white hooped pole, was slowly and precariously making her way across a taut piece of wire, some eight feet from the ground, that had been fastened between two palms. In amongst the barefooted onlookers of white trousered youths, giggling young girls and shaven-headed priests, stood a party of schoolchildren immaculately dressed in crisp royal blue and white uniforms. Shielding their eyes from the sun, they squinted up at the woman open-mouthed, watching on in fascination as she carefully tiptoed her way to the end of the wire, and the second she finally made it to safety, they excitedly jumped up and down clapping their hands in adulation. After seeing so much abject poverty on the streets of Madras, the sheer joy and pleasure these children were deriding from the performance was a truly heart-warming sight.

On my way back to the hotel, I stopped off at a highly acclaimed restaurant, although my meal was slightly spoiled by an argument taking place on another table between a young Canadian couple.

'I thought travelling together would be different than this,' the guy remonstrated. 'I agreed to come to Madras and now you tell me you want to stay here for three days!' They continued to bicker about their travels throughout their meal and as I wandered back to the Broadlands, I knew that, even after the low points of Bangalore, I'd definitely done the right thing in leaving Goa when I did. Travelling up to Nepal with Basir, in hindsight, would have been a disaster.

I woke up the next morning constipated. I had taken the Imodium tablets some 48 hours ago and while it was encouraging to know they did exactly what they said on the box, I knew the acid test would be when my body eventually forced me to go to the toilet. Would my stools still be runny or would they be solid? Only then would I know for sure if I were finally over this bug. I'd set the day aside for R&R. I would be leaving Madras the following day on the Coromandel Express to travel nearly a thousand miles north to Calcutta and after the exertions of a full day trip, I felt I needed to rest.

For both of the previous nights, I'd been woken at 5am by the cries of incessant wailing, originating from somewhere behind the hotel. This wailing continued all day long so, late afternoon, after catching up with some letter writing in my room, I took a walk around the back of the Broadlands and after scaling a small wall, came across a large patch of scrubland where, a few hundred yards away, a line of battered cars were parked. Beyond the vehicles, hundreds of skull-capped worshippers were knelt down on mats bowing their heads in unison in the direction of a large rectangular mosque. Under its two large minarets and five open-fronted arches was a tented canopy, and beneath this were hundreds more, many in long white robes, also deep in prayer. The single wailing voice continuing unabated, although now, of course, much louder, and I found myself temporarily rooted to the spot, almost transfixed by the solemnity. Indeed, such was the sombreness that, before long, I began to feel I was encroaching, so I turned around and crept back to the hotel as inconspicuously as I could.

Sitting on my bed back in my room, I quickly pulled out my guidebook and turned to the section on religion. Stumbling across the Mosque had simply reinforced how ignorant I was on this subject and I felt that if I was to even begin to understand India, then I was going to need to educate myself a bit more in this field. Although Pranay Gupte's book had chronicled the history behind the current tensions that existed between the country's respective religions, I wanted to discover more about what each religion stood for. The *Lonely Planet* had individual sections on all of India's main religions so, not for the first time, I systematically began to read through each one, this time trying to take in more of what was written. I started with Hinduism, the religion practised by over 80% of India's people.

Hindus, I discovered, believed in one eternal god, Brahman, and although they worshipped a whole multitude of other gods and goddesses, these were widely recognised as simply manifestations of Brahman. The three most significant gods, it was proclaimed, were the four-headed Brahma, the creator;

Vishnu, the preserver; and Shiva, the destroyer and producer, although the particular god a Hindu chose to worship often came down to personal choice. Vishnu, for example, had appeared on his eighth visit to earth in the flute playing form of Krishna and because he'd been brought up with peasants, he remained a particular favourite amongst the working classes. The most recognisable and popular god of all, however, was Ganesh, the elephant headed son of Shiva and the god of prosperity and wisdom. I then read all about the social and discriminatory caste system that Hindus were born into, trying to get my head around the notion of what it must be like to discover that you've ended up as a Sudra (a worker or servant) or even worse, a Harijan (the lowest of the low) knowing that for the rest of your life you'd virtually be shunned by the rest of society. And then I came across a paragraph on Sadhus. Sadhus, it said, were the people who invariably turned their back on everything to set off on some kind of spiritual search. They were described as 'an easily recognised group, usually wandering around half naked, smeared in dust with their hair and beard matted...performing various feats of self mortification.' I had seen quite a few Sadhus loitering around the beach parties in Goa, but I was not so sure it was eternal spiritualism they'd been searching for.

I moved on to Islam. Muslims, the followers of Islam, I discovered, believed there was only one god and his name was Allah. The founder of the religion was the prophet Muhammad who, back in the 5th century, received revelations from Allah, which he'd compiled in the Muslim holy book, the Qur'an. Because Muhammad had been born in Mecca, now in Saudi Arabia, it was, I learnt, the aim of every Muslim to make a pilgrimage (or Haji) to Mecca sometime in his lifetime. I then read about Ramadan, the ninth month of the Islam calendar, when Muslims were expected to refrain from eating, drinking, smoking and sexual activity during the hours of daylight as a way of giving thanks to Allah. All this was now finally beginning to make sense. It was like the pieces of a jigsaw slotting into place. Allah, the Qur'an, Mecca and Ramadan were all familiar words to me, but I'd never really known what they'd actually meant. I carried on reading with increasing fervour, discovering how the respective murders of third and fourth Caliphs, the successors to Muhammad, had ultimately been accountable for the fundamental split in the religion that remains to this day. The descendants of the third Caliph, Uthman, had eventually became known as Sunni's whilst the descendants of Ali, the fourth Caliph, had gone on to be known as Shi'as. I also learnt that even though the official Muslim holy day was Friday, when readings from the Qur'an were recited in Mosques all over the world, that Muslims were still required to pray to Allah five times every day.

This was fascinating. What had I been doing during my RE lessons? No, that's a stupid question, I'd been behind the bike sheds smoking tabs with Trigger and Jock, of course.

I moved on to Sikhism, and the more I read, the more interesting it became. Compared to Hinduism and Islam, Sikhism, I discovered, was a comparatively new religion founded as recently as the 15th century. Sikhs, I learnt, believed in God and similarly to Hindus, thought there was life after death and that the quality of the next life depended entirely on how a person had behaved in their previous life. I then found out why all Sikh men had beards and turbans. It had all been down to one of the ten Sikh gurus, Guru Gobind Singh who, in the 16th century, had introduced five symbols so that persecuted Sikh men could easily recognise one another. These symbols—namely uncut hair, an ivory comb, shorts, a steel bracelet and a sword—were collectively known as kakkars. He had also decreed that all Sikhs, from thereon, adopted the surname Singh (meaning Lion), which effectively meant if you knew somebody with that surname, then you'd know they're Sikh. Sikhism, I read, was also a very tolerant religion, reflected in their gurdwaras (temples) that offered shelter to anyone who came to their place of worship. And intriguingly, Sikhs were particularly well-renowned for their aptitude in fields of engineering and mechanics.

I then went on to read about Buddhism, having been

completely unaware that it had been founded in neighbouring Nepal, about the Jains and their reverence for life and avoidance of injury to all living things (so much so that many even resorted to covering their mouths with cloth in order to avoid the risk of accidentally swallowing insects) and finally, the Parsis, who because they believed in the purity of elements, refrained from cremating or burying their dead and instead, left them to decompose in towers. And who said religion wasn't interesting?

The sheer diversity of all these beliefs left me dumbfounded but one fact, in particular, still remained: no matter how much I tried to deny it, there was something about the religion of Islam that made me feel decidedly uncomfortable. I was not sure exactly why this was. It could have just been my memories of being hassled by men in markets of Islamic countries such as Turkey and Morocco on family holidays, or maybe my ill-conceived notions that if Muslim women had to shroud themselves in veils, it must be down to their Muslim husbands who were forcing them to do so against their will. Perhaps it was the numerous television news reports I'd seen, covering the shockingly barbaric penalties served out to wrongdoers in Islam countries such as beheading and the chopping off of hands and so forth. But there again, it could have just been the fact that the West had just gone to war with an Islamic country, although deep down, I suspected I'd developed some kind of innate prejudice, a prejudice that perhaps had unwittingly been ingrained in my upbringing.

What I certainly did know was that my abiding memory of Madras would be the incessant and haunting wailing of the muezzin calling Muslims to prayer and, as I prepared to leave for Calcutta, I vowed to make a concerted effort to try to rid myself of this prejudice.

CHAPTER 27

CALCUTTA

CITY OF JOY

18th–22nd March 1991

I don't know if I'm alone in this, but whenever I go to get my haircut, I tend to turn into Mr Mouse. I can sit in the chair chatting happily for the entire duration of the cut but whenever the hairdresser or barber brings out their mirror, I always somehow conspire to lose my voice. They may have cut it too short, they might not have taken enough off, they could have feasibly dyed my hair purple, but as soon as that blessed mirror comes out, I just sit there in silence, nodding my head in grateful acknowledgement. I mention this because, on my first afternoon in Calcutta, I found myself doing this very same thing. The mirror duly came out and although the barber hadn't cut off nearly as much as I'd wanted, I still sat there nodding my head vigorously. To add insult to injury, I even got up from the seat and tipped the man as well. Now, normally in these

341

instances, I'll step outside, berate myself for a few minutes and then, quickly banishing it to the back of my mind, toddle off into the sunset. However, on this occasion when I got outside, I really wanted to bang my head against the wall, for this time I had even more cause to be aggrieved.

It had all begun the previous morning back in Madras. The day had got off to a worryingly bad start. I was woken at dawn, not by my beeping alarm clock, but by the loud rumbling of my stomach. As I lay awake on my bed waiting for the gurgling to stop, I sensed an acute urge to go to the toilet. When I did, I made the sobering discovery that my Imodium capsules had run their course as my bottom spectacularly collapsed on me. It was, without doubt, one of the worst cases of diarrhoea I'd ever suffered and this did not bode well at all for my long journey to Calcutta. Even more alarmingly, it effectively meant I still hadn't managed to shake off the bug I'd picked up in Bangalore.

Nevertheless, I gathered my belongings together, stuffed them into my rucksack and trudged off to the train station. Sitting in my designated compartment as the Coromandel Express departed Madras Central just after 8am was a middle-aged bespectacled lady. Dressed in an ankle length tweed skirt and matching brown jacket, she had the authoritative look of a learned schoolteacher and, seemingly unfazed by the repeated slamming of carriage doors and other passengers constantly charging up and down the corridors, I suspected this was not her first time in India. And so it turned out. Dutch by origin, she was one of those intrepid female travellers who'd fallen in love with the country on her very first visit twenty years ago and had consequently returned many times since, but although we chatted cordially for a while about the respective places we'd visited, she soon reached into her bag and pulled out a pile of newspapers. I'd also armed myself with plentiful supplies of reading material to get me through the long journey, so I spent much of the morning leafing through pages of sports magazines, swotting up on Calcutta and listening to music on my Walkman. But although my bowels were holding up, my tummy continued to churn throughout the morning, and the constant stop-start journey did little to ease this discomfort. All too often, with the screeching of brakes, the train would lurch to an abrupt halt, seemingly in the middle of nowhere and, for a few seconds, we'd look around disconcertingly in the silence, exchanging nervous glances. Then, the inevitable commotion would start out in the corridor and we'd sit there listening to the cries of excitable passengers as they peered out of the windows trying to ascertain what had brought us to this latest standstill. And each time the train eventually shuddered forward, they'd all shuffle back to their compartments until the exact same process was repeated five or ten minutes later. The only respite came some time around midday when a waiter came around to take our lunch order and returned ten minutes later with a couple of *thalis*—a selection of neatly portioned dishes served up in individual tin trays. Anything pureed was out of the question, so giving the curry, dhal and yoghurt a wide berth, I wolfed down a chapatti, crunched a couple of poppadums and then the two of us settled down again in solitude for the afternoon.

Around 3pm, I woke from a nap with the train yet again inexplicably stopped between stations, this time at a junction where eleven or twelve railway lines converged. 3.30pm arrived and we still hadn't moved an inch when a young boy came into the compartment to sweep around under the seats. Up until then, I'd adamantly refrained from giving money to beggars or gratuities to any people other than taxi drivers, restaurant staff and—funnily enough—barbers, but when my travelling companion handed the boy some rupees, I felt obliged to do the same, so reluctantly dug around for some coins in my money-belt. A few seconds later, clutching onto his tip, he nodded his head in acknowledgement and then bolted out of the compartment. He vanished so quickly, in fact, that I instinctively looked down at my feet and noticed, to my horror, my trainers had disappeared. Jumping to my feet, I heaved back the compartment door and as I did, spotted the boy leaping from the train at the end of the carriage with my beloved white Reeboks in his hand. 'Oi, you!' I bellowed and charging down

343

the corridor, hurled myself off the train and gave chase, tearing across the tracks barefoot. Seconds later, the boy glanced back over his shoulder and seeing me in pursuit, almost double took. Overcome with panic, he promptly hurled the running shoes high up into the air and scarpered off down an embankment. After hopping across half a dozen more railway lines like a firewalker crossing a bed of coals, I bent down to pick my trainers up and as I squatted there for a few seconds, trying to get my breath back, noticed a pair of shiny black leather boots a few feet away from me. Raising my eyes past a pair of neatly creased beige trousers, a thick belt encasing a truncheon and revolver, followed by a crisp white shirt with a badge on the lapel, I squinted up further to the man's face. With his arms tightly folded, he was staring at me from under his rigid cap and twiddling his moustache.

'Did you see what happened?' I cried, as soon as he ambled over. 'The little shit ran off with my trainers!'

The policeman, now with his hands behind his back, nodded his head reverently.

'He came into our compartment, you know!'

Just then there was a loud whistle. Raising his eyebrows, the officer glanced across to the train. 'Please, I think you'd better get back on. The train is about to go. But please, tell me, you are coming from which country?'

'England,' I replied.

'Ah, England,' he said, nodding his head again as if this explained everything.

Maybe it did, for as I hurried back across the tracks, a mass of blank faces were now staring at me from the opened windows and only then did it dawn on me how stupid I must have looked leaping across the tracks like a man possessed.

When we finally arrived in Calcutta's Howrah station the following lunchtime, I agreed to share a taxi with the Dutch lady to Chowringhee. She was heading for the YMCA, close to Sudder Street where many of the city's cheap hotels were to be found. To get there, however, we had to cross the Hooghly River, and to cross the Hooghly River, we had to cross the colossal Howrah Bridge, certainly impressive in size, though not in beauty. I'd read that its dimensions were similar to those of the Sydney Harbour Bridge, but whereas its Australian counterpart was aesthetically designed to look pleasing to the eye, the Howrah was a monstrous iron-clad 'Meccanoesque' structure seemingly devoid of architectural style. Not that this appeared to bother the Bengalis—and why for one minute should it?—because this 450 metre cantilevered bridge was built purely for functionality. Notwithstanding this, the sheer volume of traffic trying to cross it was astounding. Before long, our taxi had crawled to an inevitable standstill and, as I stared out into the smog at the horribly congested pavements, it felt like I was in a furnace. Outside, masses of pedestrians continually hurried by in opposite directions, frequently making way for processions of toiling coolies carrying, pulling and pushing carts and trailers stacked high with insurmountable loads of fruit and vegetables—water melons, mangoes, gourds and aubergines. Twenty-five minutes later, my shirt dripping, I climbed out of the sweltering cab and, wishing the Dutch lady well, checked into the Paragon Hotel.

Calcutta, with twelve million inhabitants was India's most populated city, and after dropping my rucksack on the bed, I headed straight back out onto the infinitely crowded streets to the West Bengal tourist bureau in order to book another day tour. Taking a shortcut down a series of filthy littered side streets, the squalor of the city soon became all too apparent. As snorting pigs snuffled up the remains of human faeces, and scavenging frothy-mouthed dogs stared at me menacingly, huge squawking crows danced on the cobblestones. Stepping over a stream of bubbling milky-grey coloured effluence pouring on to the pavement from the drain of a derelict tenement block, two large rats scurried across my path and crawled under a rusty yellow fly-infested rubbish skip on the other side of the street. A few feet away, a couple of men in lunghis squatted around a portable gas stove, spluttering from the smoke billowing out of an adjacent factory. As I quickened my pace, a barefooted man in a vest and shorts approached pulling a large wheeled cart and as I peered into the trailer as he passed, the stench of the rotten carcasses had me clasping for my stomach. Further on, a sleeping rickshaw wallah, hands behind head, was stretched out across the seat of his vehicle, dead to the world. Then, from the recesses of a murky doorway, a young boy came running up to me holding out an upturned palm. His hair was caked, his feet were black and his grubby naked body was lacerated with countless bites and scabs. He couldn't have been more than five years old. Without hesitation, I quickly reached into my pocket.

Even before I arrived in Calcutta, I'd been promising to get my head shaved for days; my scalp had been becoming increasingly itchy in the last few weeks and the pre-monsoon heat was steadily building up—the temperatures in the city were already in the high thirties and the air was suffocatingly hot. To alleviate this discomfort, an extremely short haircut was therefore now a priority, so when I passed a barber's shop on the corner of a narrow sidestreet, I dived straight in and this is when I somehow conspired to lose my voice again. But this time, in light of recent circumstances, I was not prepared to accept second best and, as chance would have it, I soon spotted another red and white striped spiralling cone further along the street. Consigning Mr Mouse to the gallows for once, I strode up the pavement, threw open the door and, jumping into the empty chair, boldly pointed towards the clippers on the shelf. Then, as soon as I got back to the hotel twenty minutes later, I rushed up to my room to look at myself in the mirror again and the second barber clearly hadn't messed about; my scalp was well and truly shaved and I'd finally got the intimidating look I was hoping for. Maybe kids on trains would think twice now before running off with my trainers.

At precisely two minutes past six the next morning, I flicked the light switch in my room. Nothing happened. I clicked it up and down a couple more times and then sighing, fumbled around in the dark for my wash bag. Pushing open the door, I staggered across the rooftop with my towel on my shoulder, sleepily rubbing my eyes. Once inside the concrete cubicle, I removed my shorts, hastily stepped into the shower and pulled the chain. The big metal hose above my head made a horrible clanking noise and then spluttered out two or three drops of water. For a few seconds, I stood there shivering, waiting to be revived by a sudden torrent of hot water but it didn't come. Muttering a string of expletives, I went over to the sink and tried the taps, but again, there was nothing. Brilliant! Firstly a power cut and now no water. Trudging back to my room, I cursed myself for not having taken a shower the day before when I'd arrived dirty and smelling after the long journey up from Madras. Shaking my head, I then set off for the tourist office.

Half an hour later, I was stood outside the coach with my fellow passengers, the lone foreigner in a group of twenty. After we clambered aboard, our guide for the day gaily informed us that the morning would be spent visiting four of the city's temples. This did not come as good news. Although I'd only been in India a matter of weeks, I was already developing the early signs of 'templeitis.' From hereon in, when it came to places of worship, it was going to take something very special to capture my imagination. But a couple of hours later we pulled up outside the Victoria Memorial and, as buildings went, this truly *was* impressive. Completed in 1921 at a cost of 10.5 million rupees, the grand white marbled museum radiated all the decadence of its era. Located at the southern end of the Maidan, a vast expanse of green in the heart of the city providing welcome relief to the congested streets, it was a curious mixture of Islamic and Classical architecture, epitomised by four Moghul styled minarets in each corner and a large pillared dome in the centre, giving it the unlikely appearance of a cross between St Paul's Cathedral and the Taj Mahal. The idea to first construct the museum was conceived by the then Viceroy of India, Lord Curzon, after the death of Queen Victoria in 1901. He suggested the most fitting memorial would be a 'stately, spacious, monumental and grand building surrounded by an exquisite garden,' though rather ironically — given that it would ultimately become one of the country's most poignant reminders of the British Raj—the costs were borne almost entirely from funds generously donated by the princes and good people of India themselves.

Filing off the bus, we proceeded to make our way through the 64-acre gardens, past the numerous bronze statues, the ornamental lakes and fountains, the sculptured trees and closely trimmed lawns, towards the huge arched entrance. With our guide leaving us to explore the museum at will, I wandered into an adjoining hall, a large gallery full of paintings depicting the city's long and chequered history and the inherent power struggle between the Bengalis and the British Raj. Now, to say affairs between the two had often been turbulent would be something of an understatement. The British had first settled in the region at the end of the 17th century when Calcutta, with its easy access to the Bay of Bengal, was flourishing as a trading port. Keen to exploit the country's vast potential, the pioneering English based East India Company had quickly established factories and trading posts in all the major cities although its plans to expand trade and secure a stranglehold over India were met with constant opposition in Calcutta, initially with the rulers of the declining Moghul Empire and then, in the mid-18th century, with their successors, the Nawabs of Bengal. In 1756, with relations between the Company and the Nawabs becoming increasingly strained, the death of the Nawab Alivardi Khan of Bengal sparked a fierce battle within the ruling family to decide who would succeed him. The East India Company came out in support of his widow, although it was her grandson, Siraj, who ultimately took over. The Company's support for his grandmother, however, earned it the wrath of Siraj and when they proceeded to start work on the reinforcement of Fort William, the newly installed Nawab saw red. On the 20th June 1856, Siraj attacked the town, capturing the fort and imprisoning the remaining British prisoners who'd failed to escape into a tiny underground cellar, where 123 of the 146 captured suffocated overnight. The incident infamously became known as 'the Black Hole of Calcutta,' and when news of the atrocity reached home shores, the British were outraged. The following year, under the leadership of Clive of India, relief troops were despatched from Madras and once the city was recaptured, a treaty was duly signed between the Company and the Nawab. A few months later, though, Siraj, betrayed by his own men, was defeated in the Battle of Plassey and assassinated soon after. With the construction of a much stronger fort complete, Calcutta went on to become the new capital of British India, a position it held until 1911 and the reason that the country's balance of power eventually had to be transferred to New Delhi was largely down to the Bengalis, who remained vociferous throughout in their pursuit to achieve independence for India.

After lunch, we moved on to the Indian Museum where we were again left to wander around the building at our leisure. No sooner had I entered, I found myself befriended by a young Indian lad. After the all too familiar repertoire of questioning— What is your country? What is your occupation? How long do you stay in India?—he decided to tag along. As I passed through a large hall housing various exotic displays of stuffed animals and birds, his questioning became more persistent.

'Where you go after museum?' he asked.

'The zoo, I think. Why d'you ask?' I replied, rather curtly.

'I come with you.'

I shook my head. 'I'm on part of a tour, so I don't think you'll be allowed.'

He shrugged nonchalantly. 'Which hotel you stay?'

'Why do you want to know?' I asked.

'Is it the Fairlawn?'

'Yes, it is actually,' I said. 'I'm staying at the Fairlawn.'

'This is biggest hotel in Calcutta,' he said excitedly.

'Mmm, I know.'

'Can we go there?'

'No, I don't think so.'

'Then I follow you.'

'Okay, fine,' I harped. 'Follow me, then.'

Walking past a huge whale skeleton into another hall, I quickened up my pace.

'Where you go now?'

'I'm going into this hall,' I said, pointing to a gallery containing an impressive selection of Tibetan and Nepalese *Thankas* (embroidered scroll paintings).

Fifteen minutes later, he was still on my tail and although I was wishing he'd just piss off, telling him to do so was not that easy. However, not long after, my patience finally ran out.

'Look,' I snapped, 'haven't you got anything better to do?'

He stood there scratching his head, seemingly unperturbed.

By the time our allotted hour was up, I still hadn't managed to shake him off and I was fuming that my enjoyment of the museum had been severely impaired. Back down in the entrance hall, I told my 'friend' that it was time for me to rejoin my fellow passengers. Waving my hand in the air, I marched off towards the bus but, to my utter horror, found him following me onto the vehicle.

'Please, you are enjoying the museum?' asked the middle-aged man in the safari suit sitting next to me.

'It was very interesting,' I replied 'but it was somewhat spoiled.'

'Spoiled? What do you mean?'

'Well, you see that boy at the front,' I whispered, 'I couldn't get shot of him. He followed me around the museum for the entire duration.'

He frowned. 'But why didn't you say anything?'

'I tried, it was no use, though, and besides, I didn't really want to get him into trouble.'

The man, craning his neck for a few seconds, bellowed something down the front of the bus. The kid stood up and defiantly shouted something back. With that, the man promptly leapt to his feet, charged down the aisle and yanking the boy up by his shirt, whispered something into his ear. Slowly getting up and muttering to himself, the kid reluctantly made his way down the steps of the bus but when he got outside, audaciously stuck up a finger to the man before dashing across the busy street. Desperately trying to keep a straight face, I thanked the man for his help. He shook his head in embarrassment and apologised, visibly annoyed that my visit to the museum had been so blighted. Shrugging my shoulders, I told him it wasn't his fault, and with that, the bus pulled off. So much then for my intimidating haircut!

The Nehru Children's Museum, our next port of call, was a wonderful concept. Its success and popularity (nearly six million people had already passed through its doors since its inauguration in 1972) was largely down to its founder, Jugal Srimal, who had the foresight to realise that children were more likely to respond to education if it were imparted through less traditional means. His dream to do something for children had clearly been fulfilled, for the museum, inundated with groups of arriving school parties, was truly delightful. The ground floor was packed with dolls and toys of all different shapes, colours and sizes, each donated from a separate nation and no country, it seemed, was precluded: China, Russia, Iran, Lebanon, Libya, Korea, Israel and Pakistan, amongst others, had all contributed which just goes to show that when children are the subjects, the political barriers that exist between countries can all too quickly be forgotten. The second and third floors were equally impressive, featuring graphically depicted scenes from the *Mahabharata* and the *Ramayana*, two of the most famous Hindu legends. There were models of demons, trolls, snakes and all kinds of other mythical creatures cast against beautifully imaginative hand painted backgrounds of temples and battlefields and, underneath each display, a written commentary described each scene in the context of the respective stories.

Last stop of the day was the zoo. I can't say I'm a great lover of zoos but I was quite hopeful about this one after reading that many of the animals were displayed in near natural conditions. The first cage I saw was that of the monkeys, however, and the look of total despair in their eyes was so heartbreaking that I didn't even bother to go any further. Instead, I planted myself down beneath the shade of a large tree and, reaching into my pack, pulled out the Dictaphone so that I could catch up with my recordings. Although I realised this would probably attract a few curious stares, I certainly wasn't prepared for the reaction that followed. Within minutes, a group of around twenty Bengalis had gathered in a semi-circle in front of the tree and, completely obstructing the path, were staring at me intently. Some were pointing, a few were chuckling, and others were muttering expectantly amongst themselves. One even had the bare-faced audacity to reach for his camera. For all intents and purposes I might as well have had a sign in front of me saying: Species—Homo Sapiens, Variety—Caucasian, Origin—United Kingdom. Failing to comprehend why somebody sitting on the grass talking into a tape recorder should be attracting quite this much attention, I began to empathise even more with the animals. Indeed, before long, I'd pulled in a larger crowd than the monkeys themselves and not wishing to steal their thunder, I abruptly clambered to my feet and, hurling the recorder back into the bag, stomped my way through the gasping crowds.

When I got back to my room early evening, there was still no running water. Unlike earlier, though, I wasn't unduly concerned. In fact, I even berated myself for having got into such a state that morning. Calcutta had been described as 'a city with soul.' Well, the people here certainly had spirit, that was for sure. In spite of all the abject poverty, the pollution, the constant power cuts and water shortages, the Bengalis seemed to take the squalor, the filth and all the other countless problems the city suffered completely in their stride. Nearly all the people I'd come across in the short time I'd been here had been courteous, welcoming and quick to smile—even the staring brigades at the zoo hadn't really meant any harm—and the city was rapidly winning a place in my heart. The fact that there'd been no running water for twelve hours had now been put firmly in perspective. In comparison to the tremendous hardships faced by so many here in Calcutta, the tiny inconvenience that I'd had to suffer by not being able to take a shower now seemed totally trivial and insignificant, and I went to bed that night totally at ease with the knowledge that both my hair and skin remained caked in the city's dirt and dust.

Perusing the various shops and indoor markets for gifts and

souvenirs, I spent most of the next day wandering up and down Chowringhee Road, picking up, amongst other things, a couple of pairs of particularly hideous chocolate coloured Y-fronts that I'd present to my friends on their arrival. When I eventually arrived back at the Paragon late afternoon, I discovered a most unfortunate accident had occurred. At first, I wasn't too sure what it was exactly that was causing so much of a stir, but from the animated gestures and startled looks on the faces of the other backpackers sat around the wooden tables in the first floor courtyard, I could tell straight away something was up. One of the many Japanese travellers staying in the hotel noticed me passing through and, recognising my face, quickly got to his feet and beckoned me over.

'What's happened?' I enquired, somewhat bemusedly, sitting myself down amongst the group. As they exchanged nervous glances, the guy who'd waved me over cleared his throat and as he proceeded to fill me in with the dramatic events, I sat there open-mouthed. Apparently, earlier that afternoon, the young man who'd been occupying the room opposite mine on the rooftop had hastily stood up on his bed and, in the process, seemingly forgot that above him, suspended from the ceiling, was a revolving fan. The resulting impact had left him with, by all accounts, a particularly severe gash to his forehead. Just as some of the group were recounting the story of the casualty being whisked off in an ambulance to the local hospital, the victim himself returned, much to everyone's surprise. As we quickly made space for him to sit down, he stood there for a few seconds smiling a little embarrassingly. His head was swathed in bandages, concealing, he went on to inform us, a large number of stitches. Considering his injuries he looked remarkably well—still a bit shocked, understandably—but relatively coherent and thankfully still in one piece. With his compatriots gathering around to comfort him, I reached down for my bag but it was only when I made my way up to my room a couple of minutes later that the full extent of his injury was really brought home. Wincing at the long trail of blood spots daubed into the concrete staircase, I staggered up the steps with my eyes watering, the crimson drops disturbingly increasing in size and frequency the higher I got. Up on the rooftop, I followed the dried stream of red across to his concrete hut. The door to his room was flapping open, making the smeared dark streaks on the bed sheets all too visible. Shuddering, I quickly turned around and, fishing out my key, counted my blessings I hadn't been back at the hotel at the time—to hear that harrowing cry or scream emanating from his room when the excruciating moment of impact happened would have been sickening.

I've always found it difficult to point my camera indiscriminately at people I don't know, so I left the hotel rather nervously at the crack of dawn to take some black and white photographs of the early morning life on the streets of Calcutta. In my pocket, I had a small wad of five and ten rupee notes to offer to the subjects I was hoping to photograph as a token of goodwill. Notwithstanding this, I quickly realised that this gesture was futile. If people don't want to be photographed, then they don't want to be photographed as I soon found out to my cost. A number of locals, seeing me walking around at this early hour with my camera, stared at me disdainfully and just as I was about to take a picture of two Indian children asleep on a bench, their mother came running over screaming, 'No! No!' As I walked on, others continued to nonchalantly wave me away, and close to the market, I found my legs being pelted by small stones. Quickly taking on board the message I was clearly not welcome, I hurriedly moved on, thinking to myself that maybe this whole thing had been a bad idea. In spite of their poverty, the people here still had their dignity and me walking around with a camera could only be depriving them of this. Only the previous afternoon, I'd found myself wondering just how it must feel for the animals in the zoo to be stared at all day long, and here I was now strolling around with my camera trying to photograph people as if *they* were animals. One thing I'd learnt over the last few days was how proud the Bengalis were as a people, so it was perfectly understandable that they should be so irate. Yet just as I was about to abandon my foray, I turned a street corner and saw a group of eight or nine young men, dressed in lunghis and flip-flops, standing around a large iron vat of water on the pavement opposite, enthusiastically throwing buckets of soapy suds over their heads as they lathered themselves down. As soon as they saw me, I timidly pointed to my camera. This time, I was greeted with beaming smiles, so I quickly clicked away.

After this, with my confidence restored a little, I made my way up to the immense Howrah Bridge to try my luck there. This time, my perseverance was rewarded; resembling a scene from the 1930s, the area around Cotton Street just to the east of the river was quite simply a photographer's dream. Against the backdrop of the vast steel cantilevered girders, clouds of smoke billowed out from brick houses and factories, wooden carts and rickshaws plied the congested cobbled streets, soot-faced children stared out of doorways, and every so often, a battered black Ambassador emerged from a dark alleyway, hopelessly trying to make its way through the mass of people laden with consignments destined for a thousand and one unbeknown destinations across the city.

Ever since I'd arrived in Calcutta, all I'd been hearing about, from street traders, from waiters in restaurants and from other travellers, was a book, currently enjoying cult status in the city, called *City of Joy*. I'd picked up a copy of Dominique Lapierre's paperback the previous day, and with my train to Darjeeling not leaving until early evening, I started to leaf through the first pages back in my room. It didn't take long to see what all the fuss as about. Indeed, it was so riveting that I barely moved from my bed for the remainder of the day. The story evolved around three characters, a struggling rickshaw wallah, a Polish priest working with the poor and an American medical graduate who'd joined the priest to help him with his mission. Based on the author's three years in Calcutta and his own first hand experiences of finding out what it was like to live in a slum, it was an utterly compelling account and a must-read book for anyone planning to visit the city.

I left the Paragon for the final time early evening with memories of a city that would remain lodged in my mind for a long, long time. It was, without doubt, the most stunning city that I had—and was probably ever likely to—come across and I was *still* finding it difficult to even comprehend just how, in spite of their appalling living conditions, its inhabitants remained so full of spirit. As the Darjeeling mail train departed Sealdah station at 7pm, I thought again about Reggie Kray and, such was the effect that Calcutta had had on me, I almost felt compelled to write to him. In the letter, I'd suggest that if he ever managed to fulfil his dream of travelling to China and India, that he should make the point of making Calcutta his first stop where—if it hadn't been already—his faith in humanity would surely be restored.

CHAPTER 28

DARJEELING

THE STRANGE CASE OF A MAN CALLED MACGREGOR

23rd–26th March 1991

Arriving at New Jalpaiguri mid-morning, I decided to ditch my plans to take the eight-hour scenic ride on the 'Toy Train' up to Darjeeling and opted instead for the quicker alternative of travelling up to the old British hill station by bus. Although I booked a ticket for the journey at the train station, the bus station itself was located some 5kms away in the adjoining town of Siliguri. To get there, I needed to get a taxi, not the traditional four-wheel type, but a cycle rickshaw, and already scores of these bike drawn carriages were setting off from one town to the other. Everyone, it seemed, who'd disembarked from the train at New Jalpaiguri was heading to Siliguri. The abundance of bikes meant that finding a rider wasn't difficult; negotiating a cheap fare with the resolute locals, though, was a little less straightforward. Commanding a virtual monopoly on the transport between the towns, the rickshaw cyclists knew they could pull the strings and, consequently, didn't need to drop their fares. So realising, after some prolonged and particularly vociferous haggling in the stifling morning sunshine, I was banging my head against the wall and, furthermore, that I'd been quibbling over what amounted to nothing more than a couple of pennies, I dispensed with the needless squabbling, agreed a fare of five rupees with a rider and finally set off to join the chaotic mass exodus. Sitting on the canopy at the back of the bike, however, was far from comfortable. It wasn't that the journey was bumpy, but more the fact I felt so uneasy sitting like a lording prince as my rider toiled and struggled in front of me in the searing heat. Twenty discomfiting minutes later, reaching a bottleneck outside Siliguri town centre where hundreds of rickshaws had drawn to a standstill, I jumped off and, paying the man double the agreed fare for his troubles, made the last few hundred yards of the journey by foot.

The bus depot itself was nothing more than a large square of dusty scrubland where all the local buses converged. I located mine easily enough, though unlike all the other buses I'd been on in India, there was no luggage hold beneath the vehicle so, much to the bemusement of the baggage handlers, I boldly clambered up the ladder at the rear of the bus and set about fastening my rucksack to the luggage rack on top with my newly acquired padlock and chain. (After the 'Reebok Incident', I was taking no more chances). Indeed, fifteen minutes later my pack was secured so tightly that Houdini himself would have had a job of dislodging it. Feeling pleased as punch, I climbed back down only to be told that this bus had now been cancelled. Glaring at the unfortunate young man who'd had to break this news to me with a look of utter disdain, I stood there with my hands on my hips watching as he scampered off to fetch the ticket inspector. The officer arrived minutes later clutching a clipboard and after confirming that I would, indeed, have to transfer my rucksack to the bus standing alongside, I stormed back up the ladder and, shouting a string of expletives to myself like an enraged 'Captain Haddock' in an episode of *Tintin*, began the arduous task of unfastening my rucksack.

Unfortunately, my troubles didn't stop here, as the new bus neither had a hold for luggage, or rails on the roof to secure my rucksack to.

'So, where am I supposed to put my rucksack now?' I huffed.

The officer pointed up at six or seven kids who were sitting on a pile of bags on top of the bus.

'Bugger that,' I muttered. 'I'm not leaving it with them.'

'Please, it is very safe,' said the officer.

'No way,' I remonstrated, peering up at the roof. 'In that case, I'll just have to take it on the bus.'

'This is not possible,' he replied, wobbling his head.

By now, the driver had started up the engine and shouting something down to the officer, pointed at his watch. Closing my eyes in despair, I squatted on the ground for a few seconds hoping the officer would at the last moment wave me on board. Looking up to the skies in salvation, I suddenly spotted two German girls sitting on the bus who'd been sat in my compartment on the train. Leaving my rucksack by the officer's feet, I quickly clambered aboard and asked them if they'd put their luggage on top of the bus. They nodded their heads but even then, I still wasn't convinced. By now, though, the driver was revving the engine furiously and I realised I had no choice but to comply. Reluctantly, I climbed back off the bus and heaved my rucksack up to four pairs of grubby hands, convinced that within minutes, the same grubby hands would be freely rummaging through my belongings. Needless to say, I spent the entire journey working myself up into a terrible state, fretting about my rucksack, fearing I'd never set eyes on it again and wondering which items in particular I should have made a point of removing before I'd left it up there.

The slow climb up the mountains was made even more unbearable by passengers jumping on and off the bus every ten minutes and it didn't take too long to realise that there were no scheduled stops as such; if somebody wanted to get off, they'd yell to the driver and if somebody wanted to get on, they indicate to the driver from the roadside with an outstretched hand. We were already packed aboard the bus like sardines, so whenever this happened, the bus seemed to stop for an eternity whilst passengers battled their way up and down the crowded aisle. And then, halfway up the mountain, when I thought this journey couldn't possibly get any worse, the front wheel of the bus suffered a puncture, and for forty tortuous minutes, I sat in my seat staring out of the window at all the other passengers stood around the driver watching as he changed the wheel, wondering to myself whether it would have been quicker to take the 'Toy Train' after all.

Darjeeling, established in the mid-1800s as a rest centre for British troops, was now more renowned for its production of tea. It stood some two thousand metres above sea level at the foot of the Himalayas and was inhabited by a cosmopolitan mixture of Indian, Chinese, Nepalese, Tibetan and various ethnic minorities prevalent in the region. The first thing I noticed as I made my way up the steep road to the town was that Darjeeling was positively cold, which after the heat of Calcutta and the south, came as a welcome relief. The second most noticeable thing after the chill was the striking absence of beggars and touts on the streets, which made just meandering up and down the winding roads a relatively pleasant experience. I called in at three or four guesthouses in all before deciding on the Dilkhusa, who were offering a single room for just 40 rupees a night. Although the dark, dingy and somewhat antiquated establishment looked very basic, it did come with an added bonus. Because I was the only foreigner currently staying here—and, for all I knew, possibly the only one who ever had—the personal service I received after I'd checked in was quite humbling. As I was pulling out my jumpers, socks and coat that had been festering at the bottom of my rucksack for the last six months, there came a knock on the door. When I opened it, a young boy was standing there with two buckets of steaming water at his feet. 'For evening shower,' he said before turning around and disappearing back down the stairs. Then, later in the evening, literally just seconds after the light in the room had suddenly gone off, there was another knock on the door. This time it was the middle-aged lady who'd welcomed me in down at reception, bringing up a supply of candles.

A couple of times during the night, I was awoken by loud claps of thunder and heavy rainfall. At 8am, it was still chucking it down remorselessly. Sat in my bed watching the splattering raindrops torpidly slide down the window, it felt like one of those cold dark January mornings back in England and, sighing heavily, I eventually turned over and buried my head under the pillow. It was another thirty minutes before I finally managed to prise myself out of my snuggly sleeping bag and even then, I could have quite happily lain there all day. But the fact of the matter was, I was ravenously hungry, and I couldn't stop thinking about one of the guest-houses I'd called in the previous afternoon that'd been advertising a breakfast menu so mouth watering, I'd been very tempted to stay there for this reason alone. So as soon as I was dressed, I wandered up the winding mountain road in the drizzle to find it and when I did, treated myself to a lavish plate of sausages and baked beans on toast, followed by a hearty bowl of banana porridge. As I sat there waiting for the complimentary pot of tea to cool down, two young trekkers on an adjacent table were discussing their recent trek to Gangtok.

'I know it was a long way,' said one, 'but I think we did the right thing, you know, those views of Kanchenjunga were unbelievable.'

'Yeah,' said the other, 'guess it was worth it in the end.'

Reaching for my guidebook, I quickly leafed through the pages and discovered that Gangtok was over seven hours away by minibus. Their interesting account, though, was quickly drowned out by the rantings of a young American woman sitting nearby. I couldn't quite work out if she'd got out of bed the wrong side or was just one of life's grumblers, because for quarter of an hour, she complained non-stop to the people sitting on the table next to her about Darjeeling: the place, the people, the hotel, the food, the cold, the mist, you name it; nothing seemed to escape her wrath.

'Oh, and did I mention the Rhododendrons?' she exclaimed. 'I didn't? Ah, well that's another thing I'll be bringing up with the agency when I get back. My guidebook said they were supposed to be wonderful but, hey, wouldn't you know it, they haven't even flowered yet!'

When her long tedious moaning was replaced by the voice of an English guy on another table extolling to his yuppie friends the virtues of Margaret Thatcher, I decided it was time to leave. It wasn't that I'd particularly got anything against Maggie as such. In fact, any lady who could storm into British politics, rouse the old fuddy-duddies from their slumbering ways and shake up the prehistoric establishment in the emphatic manner that she had, deserved a lot of credit in my book. No, it was just the way this guy was harping on in his Home Counties accent.

'Look chaps, you should be counting your blessings. I tell you, if it weren't for her, we wouldn't be sitting here right now. Anyway, I think it's time for another tea. Charles, you having one? Yes please, three more teas over here and, oh, can you bring some biscuits too?'

By now I was even rueing the fact that 'Rhododendron Woman' had already left, as I could have introduced them. Now that would have been some conversation!

Almost as soon as I stepped outside, the sun came out and the clouds lifted, momentarily revealing in the distance the snow capped peaks of the Himalayas. Without further ado, I excitedly scurried up to Observatory Hill, a renowned lookout post at the top of the town, in order to get a better view. By the time I'd arrived a couple of minutes later, though, a new wave of clouds had rolled up from the valley below and a thick veil of mist had reduced visibility to just a few feet. Trying to get my breath back, I stood on the mountain path for a while, fully expecting it to clear again, but twenty minutes later, I was still standing there staring indignantly into the fog. It felt as if somebody up there was saying: 'Right, I gave you a chance but you blew   it. This isn't just any ol' view, you know. Those mountains   you glimpsed were the Himalayas... Yeah, that's right, THE HIMALAYAS... OK, well, I'll see. Maybe if you're good, then we'll do the same tomorrow. I'm not promising now, but I'll see what I can do. Remember, we're talking about the Himalayas here. Come back tomorrow, and I'll see.'

The 29th of May is one of the most notable days of the year in the world of mountaineering. It was just before midday on this day in 1953 when an unlikely pair of climbers became the first men to reach the summit of Mount Everest. Unbeknownst to me before I'd arrived was the fact that Edmund Hillary's companion on that famous ascent was a Nepalese sherpa called Tenzing Norgay, who had actually lived and died here in Darjeeling.

After catching my first breathtaking glimpse of the mountains, I remembered one of the more useful pieces of information imparted by the highly-strung Brummie engineer I'd sat next to on the day trip around Madras. 'If you manage to get to Darjeeling,' he'd enthused 'then you must call in at the Himalayan Mountaineering Institute.' So later that morning, I did. I spent a couple of hours in all, wandering around the extensive museum, reading and learning all about the famous 1953 ascent, and it was fascinating stuff. I never knew, for instance, that so many previous attempts (six alone by Tenzing) had been made to reach the 29,035-foot mountain, and how hell-bent the British had been on becoming the first to conquer Everest. I certainly hadn't been aware that a couple of British climbers by the name of George Mallory and Andrew Irvine might have even reached the summit some thirty years before Hillary and Tenzing. (Whether they actually did or not was one of those stories that would probably always remain shrouded in mystery, as the two had never returned from the mountain to tell their tale.) And there were loads of other interesting little facts. How, for example, Tenzing could speak seven different languages, yet was unable to write; that Hillary by profession,

363

was a beekeeper, and that in his childhood, Tenzing's name was changed from Namgyal Wangdi by a lama—'Norgay' roughly translates to 'fortunate'. Another surprising discovery I made was that that Everest had got its name from a renowned Welsh surveyor working in Central Asia in the 19th century. There were loads more of these quirky kind of tales about the ascent, though it was the mystery surrounding which of the two men had actually reached the summit first that I found most intriguing. I, it has to be said, had naturally assumed it to be Hillary, as his name alone was always so synonymous with that of Everest in history lessons at school, but not necessarily so. It seemed that neither had ever revealed who'd made it first to the summit. This pact seemed to speak volumes for the strength of their relationship and also the dignified manner in which they had both conducted themselves after their feat. Both, it seemed, were very simple men who, instead of basking in their new found glory, devoted much of their remaining lives in highlighting the continuing struggles of the Sherpas, the natives of the Everest region, and helping them in their cause.

Early evening, back in the Dilkhusa, I asked the owner if she had any information about the sunrise trips to Tiger Hill. Tiger Hill was one of the highest spots in the area some 11 kms south west of Darjeeling and the early morning views there of the Himalayas were supposed to be magnificent. Apparently, on a clear day, it was even possible to Everest itself. She called the boy down, gave him a load of verbal instructions after which he promptly disappeared. Ten minutes later, he returned with the news that he'd found a driver who was willing to take me there in the morning by jeep. As I thanked them both for their help, the woman, flashing me a broad smile, pointed up to the window at the twinkling stars in the calm night sky. I took this to be an indication that the following morning would be clear and, with the driver arriving at 4am, headed up for an early night.

At 4.30, I was beginning to fear the worst. I'd been stood outside the Dilkhusa in the freezing cold for forty minutes. Each time I'd heard a car engine start in the distance or saw the lights from the headlamps of a vehicle approaching, I'd waited for the jeep to pull up, sure in the knowledge that this would be the one but after an hour of false hopes, I finally realised my driver wasn't going to turn up at all. This was a massive disappointment. Deciding to cut my losses, I made my way instead along the dark deserted streets back up to Observatory Hill to try to watch the sunrise from there. For over an hour, I stamped my feet on the icy ground and marched back and forth with my fists buried under my armpits, but just as I was about to give up the ghost, the first telltale signs of daybreak began to appear. The skies ahead ever so gradually changed from black to inky blue and then, to the right, the top of a satsuma-like ball peeped over the horizon. Almost in a flash, natures own wonderful peep show revealed a line of magnificent beige snow-capped peaks standing to attention in the distance. Up above trailing ice clouds wafted in the bright skies, whilst beneath me, waves of rolling mountains and river-bedded valleys, which up until then had been cast in darkness, were now bathed in converging hues of purples and greens. Gazing in utter rapture, the complete beauty and serenity of the scene was enthralling and even though I impulsively reached for my camera, I suspected it was a view that simply could not be properly conveyed on film. Nevertheless, I still took a couple of pictures all the same and just moments later, was glad I had for another wave of clouds rolled into the valley again obscuring the mountains within seconds. With the performance evidently over for another day, I slowly made my way back down the winding roads, wondering whether the views from Tiger Hill that morning might not have been so magnificent after all. Back at the hotel, however, the owner was distraught when she learnt that the driver hadn't shown up and although I tried to reassure her by informing her that the views of the mountains had quickly disappeared seconds after the sun had come up, it seemed to make little difference, for she was still shaking her head ten minutes later.

The next morning, I decided to change tack by breakfasting at another eating establishment. For the past two days, I'd had to put up with 'Rhododendron Woman' ranting on endlessly about her perceived shortcomings of Darjeeling, India and the world in general, so I decided to try another place to breakfast where I'd be able to eat in peace. Pulling up a seat in the crowded dining room, I ordered a cooked breakfast in preparation for the long journey to Kathmandu, and then, reaching into my bag, pulled out a pile of postcards. A couple of minutes later, a pot of tea arrived at my table but just as I'd poured myself a cup, I heard: 'You haven't been to Go-wa? My gad, you've been in India for three months and you haven't been to Go-wa? I can't believe that! Gee! Now they've got some cheap hotels, believe me. You still have to knock them down, though, but as I said, you've gotta be firm with these people.'

The voice was unmistakable. Leaning back in my seat, I couldn't quite see who she was talking to, but a wildly gesticulating arm gave her away. She was sitting in an alcove just a couple of tables down.

'If they don't come down to your price,' she continued, 'you just walk away. I tell you, it always does the trick. That happened to me here as well. You know that hotel down the road? Well, they were asking for fifty rupees a night. "Fifty rupees?" I said, "how about twenty?" Five minutes later, the man was chasing me down the road, begging me to come back. Mind you, I only stayed there one night but, hey, that's another story.'

With all hopes for a quiet and relaxed breakfast dashed, I wolfed down my porridge as quickly as I could and hastily returned to the Dilkhusa. Picking up my rucksack, I thanked the owner for her kindness and then made my way to the bus stand for the first leg of the journey back down the mountain to Siliguri.

It was at this bus stand that I first saw him. He was standing outside the Siliguri bus with his hands deeply entrenched in his pockets. Perhaps in his forties, he was tall—six feet one or two—with a long gaunt face, sallow sunken cheeks and a slightly hooked nose. A flat, rather unshapen suede cap, which had doubtlessly seen better days, partially covered his mop of curly unkempt hair whilst a bright ginger 'goatee' hung from his chin. Dressed in a grubby, dark brown woollen suit and waistcoat, with the trousers curiously stopping just below his knees (revealing a shockingly pallid pair of bony shins), his open-tongued walking boots were conspicuous only by their lack of laces. With a small canvas rucksack hanging languidly from his shoulder, he carried a flimsy leather holdall, bursting at the seams with battered textbooks, ageing manuals and a wad of loose papers that looked at any second as if they were about to fall through the gaping wide hole in the bottom of the satchel.

Continually glancing down at his wrist, he began pacing up and down and kicking the ground, sending small stones scuttling across the dusty soil. Sitting cross-legged by the door of the bus, a posse of half a dozen backpackers were happily passing around guidebooks, sharing cigarettes and exchanging various travel stories, completely oblivious to the man's attire but given that his face was totally out of their line of vision, they had no undue cause for concern, for it was the huge bulging whites of his eyes that were by far the most disturbing aspect of his appearance. I'd never seen eyes so bulbous as his, certainly never ones so harrowing. Easily the size of ping-pong balls, they possessed the same kind of maddening crazed look a startled Tom Baker would often exude in an episode of *Doctor Who*, except that the deranged stare on this man's face was permanent. They were, without question, the eyes of a madman. They were eyes that portrayed terror, torment and torture. They were eyes that with a single glance could pierce your very soul. So you can imagine my horror when, filing onto the infinitely crowded vehicle a couple of minutes later, I spotted this very same man sitting in my allocated seat.

For a few gut-wrenching seconds, I stood by the driver's seat rooted to the spot, wondering precisely what to do next. If the bus hadn't been so crowded, I would have gladly jumped into another seat and not thought any more of it but, as passengers continued to pile aboard the vehicle, virtually all of the seats were already taken. Peering up as inconspicuously as I could in order not to catch his eye, I tried to count the seats again just to make sure I hadn't made a mistake, but there was no question about it; he was definitely sitting in my seat. Showing the driver's assistant my ticket, I timidly pointed down the bus, for there was no way in the world I was going to confront him myself. Evidently unfazed by the man's dishevelled appearance, the assistant promptly marched down the aisle and ushering him into a seat in front of me without any of the acrimony I'd been expecting, held out his hand and asked him for his ticket. The man, staring manically into space, sombrely shook his head.

'Please, if you have no ticket then you must buy one,' cried the assistant. 'Which place are you going?'

'Kathmandu,' replied the man after an uncomfortably long pause.

'Very well,' said the assistant, and with that, he pulled out a pen from his shirt pocket and began to scribble something out on a small sized pad. Just as he ripped off the docket, though, the man whispered in a well-spoken English accent: 'But I may need to go to Calcutta.'

The assistant frowned. 'So please, tell me where you want to go, Kathmandu or Calcutta?'

The man, still staring blankly at the seat in front of him, sighed whilst the assistant, peering around, scratched the side of his head. He wasn't the only one perturbed, though, for the man's odd behaviour was already attracting the attention of many of the other passengers on board, Indians and Westerners alike. Some were muttering amongst themselves and exchanging knowing glances, others, clearly concerned for his welfare, were looking on at the man with worried expressions whilst a couple of young Indian boys a few rows ahead were having a whale of a time, pointing at the troubled character and giggling uncontrollably in their seats. Eventually, after a prolonged discussion between the two, the assistant issued the man a fresh ticket to Siliguri, leaving him to make up his mind where he travelled on to when he reached the bottom of the mountain, after which, we finally set off.

No sooner had the bus made the first of its meandering turns down the twisting mountain road, the man mysteriously handed a small ball of crumpled paper to two young Scandinavian girls sitting across the aisle.

'Please, guard it with your life,' he murmured to them, 'it's very important.'

Shaking their heads, they glanced back at me nervously.

'Don't worry,' I whispered although I knew this would be easier said than done. By now, I was on a heightened state of alert for whenever an incident of this sort happens, I always find myself unable to turn a blind eye. Instead, I'll invariably remain in a state of agitation with my mind going into overdrive, running through all the worst possible scenarios and outcomes. I knew full well that there would be more to come in this particular case; the problem was trying to guess what. Yet after an hour, maybe an hour and a half, calmness looked to have been restored. Most people had settled back into their seats; the majority of Indians avidly watching the video on the overhead screens, the foreign tourists snoozing or reading books. Thinking to myself that maybe all of what had passed had just been a storm in a teacup, I reached into my pack and pulled out the remaining postcards I'd been unable to finish writing at breakfast. Just as I was fumbling around for a pen, though, I heard: 'Stop the bus! I need to get out here! Stop the bus please! Please, stop the bus!'

God, what now? I thought. Maybe he just wants the toilet. This assumption, however, was quickly dispelled, when with the bus slowing down, the man promptly reached up for his bags from the overhead luggage rack. The passengers who'd previously shown most concern for the man's plight quickly got up from their seats.

'Are you feeling alright?' said one.

'Please tell me,' he said, throwing back his head in the middle of the aisle, 'is my tongue red?'

Standing on tiptoe, three or four people peered into his mouth. It looked quite long as far as tongues go, but colourwise, no different than anybody else's and this seemed to be the general consensus. He closed his eyes and leaning on the seat in front of him with his hand on his forehead, sat there trembling as four or five western tourists crouched down in the aisle.

'Please, if you're not feeling well, then we need to know,' said a middle-aged woman.

'We want to help,' said her husband. 'Are you travelling in India?'

The man shook his head and muttered something under his breath.

'Can you say that again,' said the husband. 'We couldn't hear you.'

The man, sighing again, finally looked up. 'I've been working in primary health care in Varanasi. I've already tried to get out of India twice.'

'What do you mean?' said the woman, 'What's stopped you? Is it because you're ill?'

He shook his head again. 'I'm short of funds.'

The woman asked if there was a doctor on board and, a few seconds later, an Indian man duly made his way down the aisle. Peering into his face, the doctor asked the man if he was feeling unwell but he continued to stare vacantly into the back of the seat.

'What is the problem?' enquired the driver, who'd now left his seat and was glancing over the circle of people gathered around the man in the middle of the bus.

'Please,' said the doctor, 'can you give us a few minutes?'

The driver, looking rather concerned, nodded his head understandingly.

By now, the man was being inundated with offers of help: the two Swedish girls volunteered to help him book a flight home from Kathmandu, another Canadian guy offered to contact the British embassy on his behalf when he got to Calcutta whilst the middle-aged couple said they'd be willing to accompany him to a local hospital. I, however, blatantly refused to be drawn into the perplexing discourse and remained firmly in my seat, perfectly content to watch the drama unfold from the row behind. Having secured these various promises to get him out of India, the man, to everyone's relief, eventually agreed to take the bus all the way down to Siliguri. Keeping my eyes peeled on him, I spent the remainder of the journey debating in my mind whether or not his plight was genuine. I ran through the possible scenarios:

1. He actually had been mentally disturbed or traumatised by his work in India.
2. He was on medication or was suffering from an illness or disease that he might not have even been aware of.
3. He'd taken too many drugs.
4. He'd simply been in India too long.
5. He was a highly convincing con artist skilfully acting out some elaborate scam.
6. He was Finnish.

The more I thought about it, the more suspicious I became. There were two things in particular which caused me to doubt the man's integrity. The first was a blunder I was sure I'd detected in his conversation with the two Swedish girls when he'd stopped the bus. When they were offering to help him book a flight back to the UK, one of the girls had asked the man if he had a Nepalese visa. His reply had been that he could pick one up at the border and it was the speed of his instant response more than the accuracy conveyed in his reply that started me thinking. This knowledge of visa regulations seemed to demonstrate that he knew a lot more than he was perhaps letting on. The second was remembering a couple of backpackers' messages that had been posted on a noticeboard in the Broadlands in Madras. Both had warned travellers to be very wary of highly elaborate and convincing con artists currently operating in the Georgetown area of the city. If these kinds of people were plying their trade in one Indian city, the chances were that the same kind of deception was happening in other parts of the country as well.

By the time we reached Siliguri, I sensed that the Swedish girls were beginning to regret their offer to help MacGregor (for this, they informed me as we left the bus, was the name written on the piece of paper he'd given them.) In the searing midday heat of the crowded bus depot, they tried to persuade him that it would be much more sensible for him to travel with the Canadian guy back to Calcutta. MacGregor began to remonstrate, though, insisting that he wanted to go to Kathmandu. The girls tried to reason with him, and the Canadian, realising their increased agitation, was doing his utmost to convince him that Calcutta was, indeed, the best option.

'For a start,' he said 'there are far more flights back to England from India than there are from Nepal. And you won't even have to worry about a visa, either,' he added.

We all stood around for a while exchanging nervous glances but MacGregor remained unmoved. The girls, who were travelling on the same bus as me to Kathmandu, began to peer down at their watches, for a jeep was already waiting to drive us the short distance to the Nepal border. With MacGregor's back temporarily turned as he fiddled with one of his bags, I whispered to the girls it was time to make a run for it. After making a quick thumbs-up signal to the Canadian, who nodded back in acknowledgement, we hauled our rucksacks onto our backs and dashed off into the crowds. Twenty minutes later, as the jeep snaked its way back through the throngs of waiting passengers, the three of us ducked our heads when we passed MacGregor and the Canadian. They still hadn't moved from the spot where we'd left them. Peering up a couple of seconds later, I could just make out in the distance the Canadian, standing with his arms outstretched, shaking his head, as an increasingly agitated MacGregor stamped his feet and banged his fists in the air in protest.

Largely due to the tremendous amount of traffic in Siliguri, it took over three hours to travel the 20kms to the border. After completing the arduous documentation at both sides of the border, we then finally boarded our bus that would take us all the way through to Kathmandu. And horror upon horrors, who did I spot in the corner of my eye as I clambered aboard? No, not MacGregor, but 'Rhododendron Woman' whose irritating voice I could already hear starting up in my head. I counted my blessings, though, as if I'd got on the bus just a few seconds later, it would have been me and not the Israeli-born Russian I'd been sitting next to in the jeep who would have been subject to a tormentful night of her endless babble. After two scrapes with oncoming vehicles in the first fifteen minutes (the second ripping off the bus's wing mirror resulting in yet another delay) I reached for my Walkman in the hope it would finally settle me down. For the rest of the journey to Kathmandu, though, I couldn't get the whole MacGregor episode out of my head, and even today, I still sometimes find myself idly gazing out of a window wondering what lay in wait for the noble Canadian on their journey down to Calcutta that fateful day.

CHAPTER 29

KATHMANDU

FRIENDS REUNITED

27th–29th March 1991

'Karom,' said a small, wrinkled-faced man standing next to me, pointing at the table. I'd been following the progress of one of the games with a crowd of venerable onlookers for over ten minutes, nodding my head with them each time a counter disappeared.

'Karom?' I replied.

He grinned at me, revealing a set of yellow stained teeth, then wandering off to an empty table nearby, waved me over and motioned for me to take a seat.

It was late afternoon and I was stood in a large barren park in the centre of Kathmandu. I'd been walking back to my guesthouse when I'd first noticed these groups of old men. Dressed in grubby dark jackets, woollen pullovers and *topis* (the traditional Nepalese hat, similar to in appearance to a fez), they

374

were gathered around a series of square wooden tables, positioned in a long line along one side of the railings. With my curiosity getting the better of me, I'd wandered over to find out what it was they were doing. All of the tables, perhaps a metre square and surrounded by a slightly elevated wooden border, had markings etched onto their surfaces; a large square with an inner and outer ring decorated with an elaborate lattice pattern in the middle. In each corner were netted pockets, similar to those on a snooker table. Two men at every table sat opposite each other on stools and, using their own coloured disc, were taking it in turns to flick small black and white draught-like counters into the pockets.

I knew very little about Nepal and, consequently, even less about 'karom.' Unlike the previous countries I'd visited, I'd done very little in the way of reading up prior to my arrival. Instead, I was relying on Gibbo and Caroline who I'd assumed would come armed with guidebooks and plans already established on respective places to visit. They, however, weren't arriving until the following afternoon and my bus had pulled into Kathmandu early that morning. As soon as I'd stepped off it, a young boy had approached me, promising he could get me a room for just 40 rupees (80 pence) a night. Shattered from the arduous journey and unable to face the thought of traipsing around the city looking for somewhere to stay, I'd wearily followed him to a nearby guesthouse. The room, when we got there, was sparsely furnished, there was no hot water and the toilet was filthy dirty, but I nodded my head nonetheless; it would do for a night.

After a couple of hours' sleep, I'd gone for a quick recce before stopping for some lunch at the splendidly named Yak and Yeti Hotel where I'd sat for a while dunking biscuits into a mug of hot chocolate, trying to gauge my first impressions of the city. Although surrounded by mountains, Kathmandu certainly wasn't the sort of quaint alpine village I'd been expecting. Typified by clusters of ornate and intricate wooden temples and pagodas that dominated the skyline, it was, if anything, a large sprawling medieval looking city nestled in the bowl of the Kathmandu Valley alongside two other legendary cities, Patan and Bhaktapur. And in spite of the fact that the narrow cobbled lanes had been hopelessly congested with tuk-tuks, rickshaws and a seemingly endless flow of bodies, it had a certain calm and relaxed feel after the frenetic hustle and bustle of India. Even though I'd been here just a matter of hours, I was already beginning to unwind.

The old man was now setting up the counters in the middle—nine black, nine white, in a preordained pattern with a mysterious red counter at the centre. Sprinkling a talcum-like powder onto the surface of the table, he handed me an orange counter, then placing a green one between the inner and outer square at his end of the table, took aim with his forefinger and deftly flicked it. The counter skimmed across the surface like an ice hockey puck, wildly dispersing the 'pack' and sending two blacks into the pockets. Picking up the green, he placed it back between the lines of the two squares, flicked it again and pocketed another black. And then another one. And another. When he missed with his next attempt, he gestured for me to place the orange anywhere I wanted between the two lines at my end of the table. After a couple of practice flicks, I aimed my counter at the seven or eight that remained in the middle. Remarkably, when I flicked it, a white counter disappeared into one pocket and the red dropped into another. As I let out a triumphant exclamation, the man stood up and, shaking his head, proceeded to re-set all the counters. I looked at him quizzically, and sensing my confusion, he picked up the red and muttered something. All I could fathom from his gesturing was that potting the red had effectively cost me the game. Then, much to my bewilderment, he opened his outstretched palm. I hadn't, for one minute, realised we'd been playing for money, but I took out some coins from my money belt nevertheless. Thankfully, he only took six rupees (12 pence) from my hand and with that, we started another game as a small crowd gathered around.

It didn't take long to realise that to accurately hit the counters at precisely the correct angle and speed required intricate skills. Fortunately, I had an added advantage here because, as previously mentioned, I used to play 'Subbuteo,' a game that relied on very similar finger-flicking techniques. I'd taken to the game so well, in fact, that at the age of sixteen, I'd been selected to represent my country in a Home International tournament against Scotland in the prestigious Park Hotel in Cardiff, so it didn't take me long to bridge the gap and the games became increasingly closely contested. By the end of the ninth, I'd also managed to pick up many of the finer details surrounding the rules of the game, such as discovering the red counter was the equivalent to the black ball in pool in that it had to be saved to penultimate shot of the game. When I finally got up, I thanked the man for his time and the old man, now a lot better off than when we'd started, gleefully thanked me back in turn.

Back in my room later that evening, I pulled out the last letter I'd received from Gibbo in order to check their flight details. It ended with the following line:

A resume tells me that by 1500 hrs on the 28th March 1991, (five minutes after their flight was due to land) we should be on the beginning of the biggest piss up the Himalayas has ever seen—we're gonna bring down Everest!

Considering I'd hardly touched a drop of alcohol since leaving Sydney two months ago, this was slightly disconcerting, but maybe it was time I let my hair down.

I'd first met Gibbo at Bournemouth in 1986. It was that nervous first day that marks the start of any student's first course away from home. Nine o'clock Monday morning, congregated in a packed lecture theatre with two or three hundred other fresh-faced freshers, I reached for my pencil case, pulled out a Bic pen and carefully placed it horizontally on the virgin pad of A4 paper in front of me. Finally, the door at the side of the room swung open and in marched our course principal. In an instant, the murmurings that had been echoing around the room for the last thirty minutes were replaced with a deathly hush. A bronze-faced Peter Elliot, making the most of the stony silence his mere presence had signalled, placed his hands flat down on the podium and, studiously surveying his audience, waited for a few more moments. Just then, the door to the lecture theatre swung open again and in bound a tall, red-faced, scruffy haired youth, dressed in bright red jogging trousers, a faded yellow T-shirt and a pair of tattered trainers that had clearly seen better days. With a shiny black crash helmet in one hand and a cigarette in his other, he futilely glanced around for an empty seat and then stepping directly in front of a large 'NO SMOKING' sign, joined the long line of lecturers stood against the wall. Peter Elliot, visibly irritated by the interruption, scowled at the youth and spotting the trail of blue cigarette smoke rising behind his back, calmly said: 'When you have a minute, perhaps you'd be good enough to observe the message on that large white sign behind you.' As a few people around me started to snigger, the latecomer glanced over his shoulder, then placing his crash helmet down on the floor, raised his outstretched hand apologetically and peered around in vain for an ashtray.

'I'd suggest you get rid of it somewhere outside!' bellowed Elliot.

Rolling my eyes, I stared down at my pad and sighed.

Nine months later, Gibbo and I had become inseparable drinking buddies and we went on to forge a friendship so strong that it culminated in me travelling over to Thailand three years later to meet up with him, Caroline and Pat in the middle of *their* round the world trip. Now, what's all that rubbish about first impressions! Indeed, if it weren't for that course, Gibbo would never have met Caroline either. When I first heard they were courting, I couldn't quite believe it. They were so much like chalk and cheese: Gibbo, the rebel, a boozer, Mr Popular, the reckless optimist; Caroline, so quiet, calm, sensible and demure. But then so many successful partnerships are founded on the principle of opposites attract.

After checking out of the run-down guesthouse late morning, I jumped into a taxi. Travelling on Bangladesh Airlines, Gibbo and Caroline were scheduled to land at 1455hrs, so arriving at the airport in good time, I made my way up to the viewing gantry on the roof of the terminal building. The first plane that came hurtling in to land was a Royal Nepal Airlines 757. The second, just after midday, was a Biman jumbo. A little bit miffed, I ran back downstairs to the airline's check-in counter to find out whether this could be their flight. The girl behind the desk confirmed that it was, indeed, the only flight due in from Dhaka that day, so after paying another five rupees to re-enter the viewing enclosure, I charged back up the stairs. Inside my bag was a large Union Jack flag, which I'd bought back in January to take along to the Sydney Test, and all morning I'd been contemplating whether I'd had the nerve to unfurl it at the airport to attract their attention. Timidly, I removed it from the bag and, doing my utmost to ignore the curious looks I was receiving from other spectators, hung it over the balcony fence. Then I waited. Just why it takes so long for planes to reach terminal buildings is something I've never fully understood but this jumbo took an absolute eternity. For twenty interminable minutes, I paced up and down, waiting for it to approach. They bloody well better be on it, I kept thinking. Please don't tell me there's been a last minute hitch. Reaching down for a cigarette, I began to think of a contingency plan in case there had. If I was going to stay in Nepal, then the first thing I'd need to do was pick up a guidebook. Gibbo was supposed to be staying for three weeks although Caroline was going back after two, but if I was here by myself, would I really need to stay here that long? Maybe I'd be better off heading straight back to India. But there again, now I was here, it would seem silly not stay for at least a couple of days.

'From England?' said a voice, interrupting my train of thought. I glanced up. A young man in a white *kurta*—a long collarless shirt—was pointing to the flag.

'How d'you guess?' I replied, smiling.

'That's very good,' he nodded, but his next words were quickly drowned out by the deafening roar from the approaching plane, inching its way across the tarmac in front of us. The flag, caught up in the slipstream of the engines was now violently flapping up and down against the fence whilst my fingers were well and truly lodged into the deepest waxy recesses of my ears. As the big metal bird finally came to a standstill, the stairwells were quickly manoeuvred into position and, just moments later, the two side doors of the aircraft popped open. Squinting down in the bright sunshine, I tried to make out Gibbo and Caroline amongst the two lines of passengers filing down each of the steps. Another ten minutes passed and after a couple of false alerts, I was truly on the verge of despair. Then, at last, I spotted them. They were the final two passengers to emerge from the plane and as they made their way across the tarmac ducking under the wing and clutching onto their hats, I could see them pointing up and laughing. I shouted back down to them, but the jet's engines were still screaming away and although I waved my arms in the air, they didn't wave back. Quickly removing the flag, I bundled it back into my bag and legged it down the stairs again.

Back in the terminal building, the passengers from the earlier flight were already streaming through to the arrivals hall though it was another thirty minutes before the first Biman label appeared on a suitcase. As I stood behind the barrier amongst a crowd of waiting relatives and taxi drivers holding up placards, another traveller appeared beside me.

'Family or friends?' she asked in a strong Scottish accent.

'Aw, friends,' I replied. 'And you?'

'My sister, actually. I haven't seen her for six years.'

A couple of seconds later, she picked out her face from the arrivals and as her hand went up to her mouth, tears welled up in her eyes. Jumping up and down, she waved to her frantically. After a few agonising moments, her sister finally spotted her. Running towards each other, their bodies locked together and, as they hugged in emotional embrace, a big lump formed in my throat. Suddenly I become nervous and apprehensive, wondering what emotions I'd feel when I first cast eyes on my pals.

Then, without warning, they appeared.

'Jim! Oh my God!' screamed Caroline. 'Look at your hair!'

'Hey baldy!' cried Gibbo.

Momentarily lost for words, I stood there staring incredulously. Their faces were shockingly pallid from the British winter; compared to the swarthy skins of the locals, they looked like ghosts. 'Hey, good to see you,' I said, still trying to contain my shock. 'What took you so long? I thought you'd left me in the lurch.'

'No chance of that,' retorted Gibbo. 'We've been looking forward to this for months.'

'So, did you see the flag?' I asked, after we'd shaken hands and hugged.

'Was that you?' said Caroline excitedly. 'We saw it from the plane.'

Gibbo was shaking his head. 'I said to Caroline, I bet that's Fordy.'

'Yeah, thought you'd like that,' I said flashing them a broad grin. 'I got it for the test match in Sydney.'

'I can't believe your accent, Jim,' said Caroline. 'You sound so Australian.'

'Do I?' I said, somewhat taken aback.' So how was the flight, then?'

'Long,' said Gibbo. 'Bloody long. Whatever you do, don't go to Dhaka on your travels.'

'Why?' I asked.

'We'll tell you all about it later,' said Caroline.

'Yeah, come on,' said Gibbo, tilting his head to the concourse, 'let's get out of here.'

Jumping into a taxi, we talked non-stop on the way back from the airport and when we arrived in Thamel, the city's new backpackers' quarters, Gibbo insisted we dive straight into a bar. We ended up staying there for over three hours, chatting incessantly as I traded in many stories of my travels for various snippets of news and gossip from back home. Eventually, early evening, after stopping off for some dinner at a Tibetan restaurant, we staggered off to find ourselves a guesthouse. Ten minutes later, with Caroline already crashed out on the bed, Gibbo reached for his bag. 'A-ha Fordy, guess what we've got in here?' Before I had chance to answer, he'd pulled out a bottle of duty free whisky and a couple of huge King Edward cigars. It looked like we could be bringing down Everest after all.

It was well after eleven when we finally surfaced the next morning.

'Come on sleeping beauties!' I shouted across from my bed. 'Time for some breakfast.'

'Cags,' groaned Gibbo from beneath his pillow, 'did you bring any of those Resolves?'

'Yeah,' she yawned, 'they're in the toilet bag.' Sitting up and rubbing the sleep from her eyes, she peered vacantly around the room. 'God, what time did you two get to bed?'

After finding myself somewhat restricted in India, Kathmandu was a culinary heaven. There were eateries specialising in the cuisines of the region: Nepalese, Tibetan, Indian and Chinese, as well as many more from other parts of Asia—Japanese, Korean, Thai, Malaysian, Indonesian and the like. There were also menus listing mouth watering dishes such as Irish stew, toad-in-the-hole, and fruit pies served with custard, dishes I hadn't had for so long, I'd virtually forgotten they existed. Choosing where and what to eat, therefore, became a real quandary, but we eventually opted for a popular backpackers' haunt where, just for the record, I wolfed down a sublime chicken Stroganoff accompanied by an obscenely large helping of mashed potato. Suitably replenished, we wandered around the narrow lanes and cobbled streets of Thamel briefly before I took them back to the park and introduced them to karom. After whiling away a few leisurely hours sitting in the sunshine taking on the locals, we returned to our guesthouse late afternoon and as soon as the others jumped into the shower, I quickly rummaged around in my rucksack for the brown underpants I'd bought in Calcutta. 'Got you both a little something from India,' I grinned, waving them in the air as they emerged from the bathroom in their towels, and seconds later, I was subjected to the inevitable and rather unglamorous fashion parade in the room.

We ate that evening at a Nepalese restaurant, and then toddled along to a bar where Gibbo and Caroline had arranged to catch up with an English guy they'd met on their flight. The prearranged meeting time of 9pm came and went and it soon became clear that, for whatever reason, he wasn't going to turn up, so Gibbo, clearing his throat, glanced nervously at Caroline, then told me he had a proposition.

For the last two or three years, Gibbo had been working for a mutual friend in the jewellery trade and, by all accounts, was doing rather well for himself. So well, in fact, that he now wanted to open a shop; a shop that would break with tradition by specialising almost exclusively in silver. His proposition at this stage, and it was a very loose one, was for me to join him in the business. Doing what, exactly, I wasn't too sure and nor, for that matter, was he. But for the time being, he just wanted to sound me out. The subject of the conversation, however, caught me completely off guard. Even though I'd only got a few months' travelling left, all thoughts of what I'd do when I got back home had, up until now, been put firmly to the back of my mind. Perhaps sensing this incursion, Gibbo quickly tried to make light of it all, and suggested it was probably better I forget about it for the time being. Yet now the subject had been broached, my mind was racing. What exactly *was* I going to do when I got back home? I knew there was no way I'd work for another bank again, or any large company or organisation for that matter, whatever the field. And at the moment, the proposition—and let's be honest, it was the only one I'd currently got—sounded pretty good, so I told him I'd think about what he'd said and that perhaps we could chat about it again in his final week. (Gibbo had arranged to stay on for a third week in order that he could spend some time trying to source some silver wholesalers in Nepal.)

When we eventually returned to our room, the whisky bottle came out again so that we could toast our first business discussion, although I'm sure this wasn't the subject that we were chuckling about a couple of hours later when Caroline got up from her bed to tell us to keep our noisy laughter down.

CHAPTER 30

POKHARA & CHITWAN

RIP-OFFS, RAKSHI AND RHINOS

30th March–4th April 1991

The town of Pokhara, used by many as a starting point for Annapurna treks, is situated next to Lake Phewa some 400 feet above sea level. Like many hillside resorts, it was renowned for being a particularly relaxing and peaceful place, which was more than could be said for the first few hours of the journey there. After hauling our rucksacks onto our backs at 5am, we'd wandered through the quiet dark streets towards the Immigration Office, our pre-designated departure point. Setting off at such an early hour, all three of us had assumed that the bus would be virtually empty, but we'd been lulled into a false sense of security: it was already packed with locals. As we showed our tickets to the driver's assistant on the pavement, a young mother, openly breast-feeding her child, peered down from a dusty window. Glancing away quickly, I followed the others up the steps. 'Quick, down the end!' cried Gibbo, pointing to five empty seats at the back. Making our way through strutting chickens, bleating goats and soot-faced kids playing in the aisle, we quickly commandeered the back row. Bagging one of the window seats, I sat down next to Caroline, whilst Gibbo, stacking our rucksacks up on the two remaining seats in the corner, took the middle. Any hopes we had of spreading out, though, were instantly dispelled by the arrival of another couple of backpackers just seconds later. Dressed in singlets, shorts and bushrangers hats, they gestured towards the corner seats. As Gibbo grudgingly removed the rucksacks, the bus set off, initially following the same endless winding mountain roads that had brought me into Kathmandu just a few days before. Before long, the two couples were happily chatting. About what, exactly, I couldn't tell you, for my eyes were ominously glued to the harrowing drops of the steep-sided ravines below, and even when we finally passed onto flatter terrain, there was still little respite because for the next couple of hours we were constantly tossed up in the air from our seats as the bus careered along bumpy mountain passes at breakneck speeds. Gibbo, by contrast, didn't appear unduly bothered. In fact, he seemed to be thoroughly relishing the journey. Every so often, he'd glance over, tilting his head as if he had some uncontrollable twitch. Each time, I'd stare back inquisitively, and he'd frown back and smirk. It was only later, when we stopped for lunch and Caroline wandered off to the toilet, that I realised he'd been trying to draw my attention to the particularly well-endowed Australian girl sat next to him. 'My God, Fordy, did you see her?' he enthused. 'I swear, the sight of those bouncing breasts is one I'll take to my grave.'

Back in Kathmandu, the night before Gibbo and Caroline had arrived, I'd ventured out for some food in a restaurant just off the main square where I'd happened to meet Max, an Australian traveller, and his Nepalese friend, Birung. Max had been in Nepal for three months and was travelling back to Sydney in a couple of days; Birung was hoping to travel with him. When I'd mentioned I was meeting friends the following day and that I thought we'd probably be heading off to Pokhara, Birung had excitedly informed me that he owned a guesthouse there with his brother.

'Please, please, you must stay there!' he'd implored.

I'd asked him what it was called.

'The Lake View. It's at the north end. My brother's name is Kesh. Please, when you get there, tell him you met me in Kathmandu.'

So when we arrived in Pokhara late that afternoon, we headed straight for the Lake View and as soon as I mentioned Birung's name to the little man behind the counter, his face lit up in an instant.

'Birung? Birung is my brother!' he exclaimed.

'I know,' I replied. 'I met him the other night. He told us to come here. And you must be Kesh.'

He nodded his head excitedly.

'Well, we'd like to book a room, if that's okay.'

'Yes, please, please,' he replied, placing his hands flat together in front of his mouth and bowing before us.

After filling in the registration documents, Kesh led us up the stairs to the first floor and showed us to a light and airy room containing three single beds. The accommodation wasn't particularly cheap, but the others were here on holiday and the fact I'd be paying more for accommodation whilst they were here was an eventuality I'd already prepared myself for.

There was no restaurant attached to the guesthouse so, after a wash and freshen up, we headed out to find somewhere to eat. Just as we were about to leave, though, the skies turned black and the heavens literally opened. We sheltered under the porch for a while, but twenty minutes later, there was still no sign of a let up; the rain was falling in torrents and, if anything, the storm seemed to be getting worse—great claps of thunder were booming around the mountains and the spectacular forks of lightening flashing across the valley seemed to be getting closer and closer.

'Come on,' said Gibbo eventually. 'It's only a passing shower.'

By now, though, my tummy was starting to rumble. 'Okay, then,' I said, peering out into the dark, 'are you ready?'

He nodded his head unconvincingly.

'Right, after three, then,' I beckoned. 'Three, two, one,' and with that, we made a dash for it. With the rain beating down so hard, I could barely hear the shouts coming from behind but I carried on running regardless, desperately trying to keep my feet on the slippery streams of chocolaty mud and rainwater cascading down the path. Glancing back over my shoulder a few seconds later, as the first tantalisingly ice cold droplets trickled down my spine, I could see Caroline clasping onto her striped woollen hat. Hopping across the vast puddles of water that had already formed on the ground, she was screaming at the top of her voice. Soaked to the skin, we stopped at the first restaurant we came to and wiping our faces down with towels handed to us by the staff, proceeded to wolf down our meal under the sheltered balcony as the rain continued to lash down into the night.

We spent breakfast the following morning studying the guidebooks, trying to plan what we were going to do with our time over the forthcoming days. When I muttered that, unlike most visitors to Nepal, I really wasn't too bothered about trekking—especially after my escapades in New Zealand—they both seemed visibly relieved. So, for that matter, was I, because I'd thought a two or three-day trek would be high on their agenda, but thankfully, it turned out they felt exactly the same way. We did, however, concede, mainly out of guilt, that we should at least set aside one day to embark on some kind of climb up into the mountains.

Although not a practising Buddhist, Caroline was a devout follower of the religion and took a great interest in the plight of the exiled Dalai Lama. Consequently, she'd been just as excited as Gibbo about coming to Nepal in the first place. So, after mapping out a rough itinerary for the rest of the fortnight, we hired out some mountain bikes and later in the morning, headed up to Hyangja, four miles out of Pokhara, to visit a Tibetan refugee self-help centre.

DON'T WORRY, BE HAPPY

It was an arduous climb up the mountain road and we spent much of the two-hour journey walking our bikes up the gradual incline in steady drizzle. On our arrival at the monastery, three young women, dressed in traditional homespun aprons and sandals, emerged from the swirling mist and with beaming smiles, came over to greet us, raising their hands in prayer and bowing their heads in unison as seemed to be the custom here. Ushering us through to the settlement, our saintly hosts proceeded to take us on a short tour, firstly around a temple and then to a carpet-weaving centre before, somewhat to our surprise, we were split up and taken off in all different directions, each with our own individual guide. After being shown into my escort's hut, I was served a cup of tea. I say 'tea' but although the warm brown liquid looked like the tea I knew, it was sour in taste like gone off milk whilst on the surface of the drink was a filmed layer of honey-coloured fat and I couldn't help wondering if somebody had inadvertently dropped a tablet of butter into it. With the best will in the world, I knew there was no way I'd be able to finish the foul tasting drink, but then I didn't want to offend my host either, so I tentatively put the cup down on the stone floor and when she wasn't looking, 'accidentally' kicked it over.

The tea, though, was just the pre-amble, for a couple of minutes later, I was shown into another room crammed full with Tibetan wares and artefacts: turquoise pendants, terracotta pots, boxes of old coins, scroll paintings, packets of incense sticks, papier-mache masks, prayer wheels, purple and crimson coloured stone necklaces, block prints and a mind boggling array of Buddha statutes. The woman systematically began picking up the various objects on the table making it abundantly clear I was expected to buy something. Realising this was probably the real reason we'd been split up, I eventually opted for a set of brass statuettes depicting three ancient Tibetan men dressed in robes, each measuring about six inches in height. The first, she said, represented wisdom; the second, good luck, and the third, faith and these three tiny, intricately carved men set me back a whopping 450 rupees. When I was reunited with the others soon after, Gibbo and Caroline recounted very similar stories to my own and we stood around trying to contain our laughter as, one by one, we ceremoniously unveiled our newly acquired antiques. When he found out how much I'd paid for my so-called 'three kings,' Gibbo was aghast but then his very dodgy looking cumbersome ink-printing contraption at 400 rupees wasn't exactly sale of the century either. (Well, it was for his escort.) It was Caroline, however, who'd topped the bill with a set of 600 rupee brass Tibetan bells. Maybe these Buddhists, for all their humble demeanour, weren't so incorruptible after all.

Eventually, after bidding our hosts' farewell, we jumped back on our bikes and as we freewheeled back down the mountain road, a funny thought passed through my mind. Indeed, as I began to envisage myself sat at a table with Hugh Scully on *Antiques Roadshow* discussing the value of my newly acquired antiques, I found myself chuckling out loud:

'Good afternoon, and what do we have here, sir?'

'Ah, well, I picked up these delightful little characters at a Tibetan monastery twenty years ago. I'm told that these wonderfully crafted ornaments depict the three characteristics so inherent to the Tibetans beliefs.'

'Oh, I see, sir, and what might they be?'

'Well, now this one here with the head-dress and scroll represents wisdom.'

'Right, okay, and how about the portly fellow with the belt?'

'Well, this one stands for faith.'

'And what about this cheeky chappie with the goblet and cloth?'

'Ah, this one is the bringer of good luck.'

'And may I ask how much you paid for these endearing little men?'

'Oh, I'd say about four hundred and fifty rupees, which back in 1991, would have been about nine pounds.'

'Well, this may come as a bit of a disappointment, but I'm afraid to say that it looks like you've been stitched up good and proper here. These statuettes are not antiques at all. I'm afraid they're nothing more than cheap reproductions cast in base metal and sprayed with a bronze lacquer. Just two words of advice I can give you here, sir.'

'Oh, and what might they be?'

'Car boot.'

A couple of days later, returning to the Lake View after our evening meal, we were greeted by a highly excitable Kesh. Stood by the front door with a huge grin on his face, he was jabbing an outstretched finger towards a bottle of clear liquid he was holding up in his other hand. We'd asked him earlier in the morning if he could get us a bottle of *rakshi* (pronounced *ro-xy*), the local spirit distilled from millet, in order that we could celebrate the fact our trekking days were now behind us. (Although quite frankly, as far as I was concerned, there could be no adequate recompense for what we'd had to put ourselves through.) We'd started our dreaded hike early the previous morning with a pleasant enough one-hour taxi drive along the Yamdi Khola river valley to the foot of the mountains. Indeed, by the time we'd arrived at a place called Phedi just after 8am, it seemed a great shame to have to get out of the car in the first place, and if it hadn't been for the others virtually pulling me out of the vehicle, I would have quite happily remained in the back seat and let the car take the strain instead. But we were in Nepal and people who came to Nepal trekked so, reluctantly climbing out, we braced ourselves for the ascent.

Our guide for the day was a small but sturdy character called Don, who cheerily informed us at the foot of the mountain we would be climbing 1600-feet to a village called Dhampus. It sounded a bloody long way to me. And so it turned out. For four and a half interminable hours, we slowly huffed and puffed our way up twisting hillside paths, stopping every few minutes to guzzle down the bottled water we'd brought with us, and each time we did, we'd look on bewilderingly at the parties of tiny *sherpas* dashing past, each and every one dwarfed by the ridiculously large loads on their backs. Then, after repeatedly badgering our smiling guide with the same question ('Don, are we nearly there yet?'), we'd wearily set off again toiling and sweating in the hot morning sunshine. When we finally reached the top early afternoon we were, I have to confess, rewarded with some fantastic postcard views of the lush green-terraced paddy fields on the opposite side of the mountain, but even then, as I peered back down at the glaciated valley below, I still failed to understand why nobody had thought of a chair lift. After Don had taken the mandatory photo of the three of us standing in front of the Union Jack to mark our moment of triumph, we then trudged all the way back down again, and eventually arriving back at Pokhara early evening thoroughly exhausted, retired to our room and promptly crashed out. So now, after a day of rest and recuperation, it was time to celebrate.

Sitting ourselves down around a table under the porch of the guesthouse, Kesh duly poured us each a glass of the local firewater and as Gibbo invited him to join us, I quickly brought out the pocket-sized Ludo game the three of us had been playing for much of the afternoon. Whilst I hastily set up the pieces, Caroline began explaining the rules to Kesh, but it seemed to make little difference, for struggling to grasp the tactics, he came a resounding last in each of the games we went on to play. He did, though, find the concept of having to swig, back a shot of the drink if another player landed on one of your colours highly amusing. Before long, the bottle was finished, so Kesh disappeared and a short while after, returned with another.

An hour or so later, with the alcohol taking effect, Kesh, quite unexpectedly, got rather emotional. In fact, he started to sob. Looking at each other for a few seconds not knowing quite what to do, Caroline eventually reached over and clutching onto his arm, asked him what was wrong. Fighting back the tears, he said he was worried about his brother, Birung.

'He's gone off with Max to Australia, and I don't think I'll ever see him again,' he snivelled.

As we sat there exchanging worried glances, he told us that three of his other brothers had previously died and he now thought something terrible was going to happen to Birung. I asked him if his brother was ill as, for a horrible moment, I wondered if he had some kind of incurable disease. Maybe he was going to Australia in order to get some specialised medication or treatment, but Kesh shook his head. Then, another and altogether more chilling thought crossed my mind: drugs. Could it be his brother was setting off on a drugs run? Was this why Kesh was so worried? Maybe he knew of the plan but was too frightened to divulge it. Perhaps it was just my imagination beginning to run away with me. Either that or the drink was kicking in. I knew that certain spirits were known to contain substances that induce a state of paranoia and I was beginning to wonder whether *rakshi* was one. This could easily explain why Kesh was getting so upset. By now, though, my mind was racing. I suppose it all boiled down to just why his brother should be going to Australia with Max in the first place. The only other explanation I could think of was they were lovers. If they were, though, it certainly hadn't been that obvious when I'd met them back in Kathmandu that night. As much as I tried to dismiss it, my mind kept returning to the drugs notion. Kesh came from the Gurung ethnic group from where the majority of Gurkhas originated (unfortunately, poor old Kesh was only four foot eleven, which had made him too small to sign up.) Earlier in the evening, he'd told us that there were 36 of these 'tribes' in Nepal, and that the Gurung were traditionally one of the of poorest. So this begged the question where could they have got the money to afford their guesthouse in the first place? I knew the Gurkhas were extremely well paid by Nepalese standards, so perhaps his brothers had financed the project but I still felt I was clutching at straws. Whatever the reason, though, Kesh was clearly very worried. We tried to comfort him and assure him that his brother would be all right, but just as we managed to stop him crying by reminding him we should all be having a good time, he started sobbing again.

'You are my good friends, my very good friends and in a couple of days you will be leaving. I don't have any real friends here, in the hotel or in Pokhara.'

So maybe this was it: perhaps he was just lonely. We eventually suggested to Kesh we'd all probably had a bit too much to drink and that it was time to call it a night. Rubbing his eyes, he slowly nodded his head so we hastily packed up the Ludo and took all the glasses back inside. Up on the landing, we said goodnight to Kesh, but as he stood forlornly down the corridor watching us unlock the door to our room, his eyes filled up with tears again. Wandering over, I put my arm on his shoulder and told him not to worry but, to my embarrassment, he took this as a signal to start hugging me. I tried to move away, but he wouldn't let go, much to the amusement of Gibbo who was standing behind him and having a real job to contain himself. Finally managing to prise Kesh away, I told him that we'd see him in the morning but back in our room, Gibbo was still beside himself.

'What could I do? He just grabbed onto me!'

'Ah, just wait 'til the lads hear about this back home. That was so funny!'

I suppose it was. So was the whole evening, really, in a 'funny' kind of way.

Back in the days of the Raj, the Royal Chitwan National Park was renowned as an exclusive hunting reserve. More recently, though, in 1984, largely due to the efforts of the late King Mahendra, it was designated a World Heritage site and as a result, many of the rare species of mammals such as the Indian rhinoceros, the Bengal tiger and the striped hyena had been allowed to survive. The park was also home to an abundance of bird life—over 400 different species in fact—so after bidding Kesh an emotional early morning farewell, we headed off on the bus to Chitwan feeling quite excited. It was late afternoon by the time we eventually arrived at the Evergreen Camp, and after being shown to our thatched roofed huts and a quick bite to eat, we, along with a couple of lively Dutch girls and a lone Japanese traveller, were whisked off for a whirlwind jeep trip through the park. Tired and weary from the five-hour journey and still a little hungover, we needed a second wind, but it didn't come and as our heads began to loll, all we could do from the back of the truck was struggle to stay awake, but after returning to our hut for a good night's sleep, the next morning certainly made up for it.

After breakfast, we were introduced to our young guide, Manu, who, we were informed, was going to take us on a canoe ride down the Rapti River. Tall and spindly and dressed in jeans and a long combat shirt, his quiet, almost aloof manner didn't exactly inspire confidence, which was probably just as well really because by the time we got down to the riverbank, we quickly realised it wasn't going to be the thrill-a-minute white water rafting experience we'd all been expecting. Indeed, so shallow and still were the reed-filled waters that this stretch of the Rapti looked more like a half-dredged canal than a river. However, not long after we'd set off, we couldn't help noticing our boat was slowly filling up with water. Gibbo, who rather comically was sitting at one end with his ankles virtually submerged in brown cloudy riverwater, eventually pointed this out to Manu. Not looking particularly concerned, he handed him a plastic cup with which Gibbo, somewhat bemusedly began to use to shovel the water over the side of the boat. It soon became clear, though, that the hole at the bottom of the boat was bigger than our guide had initially thought and with the water continuing to fill up, he finally steered us over to the bank of the river where we abandoned ship. Undeterred, he then told us that he'd take us on a trek into the Park instead.

For the first hour we saw nothing at all in terms of wildlife and after the canoeing fiasco, I got the feeling Manu was beginning to feel a little embarrassed. Spotting another party in the park, he ran over to chat with a colleague for a couple of minutes and returned in a state of excitement with the news that a rhino had been spotted in the last few minutes somewhere in our vicinity. Glancing down to the ground, he fervidly pointed at some hoof prints that were embedded in a muddy path and quickly ushered us up a small tree.

'What happens if we see one?' I asked a couple of seconds later, peering down from a decidedly rickety branch.

He put his index finger over his lips. 'Just stay very still,' he whispered, 'we don't want it charging at us.'

'What do we do if it does?' I whispered back.

'Try and get up another tree. If you can't, then run away as fast as you can in zigzags.'

'Zigzags?' frowned Gibbo.

'Sssssh!' whispered Manu again. 'Rhinos move very fast when they charge, but they can only run in straight lines. You can throw something at them to distract their attention. If you don't have time to get up a tree, hide behind the trunk.'

'Are they really that dangerous, then?' asked Caroline in a hush voice.

'Each year, between five and ten people are gored to death in this park by rhinos,' he replied almost nonchalantly. 'Most are tourists unaware of the dangers. They walk in the park without proper guides.'

The three of us exchanged nervous glances and, still perched precariously on the creaking branches, sat in silence for a few more minutes before Manu, suddenly putting his hand to his ear, began to look very serious. Scouring out across the plains, we saw nothing: there was no movement coming from the dense thickets of grass, the bare frail trees were all totally still, and there were certainly no sounds of charging hooves in the distance, so we looked down at our guide again, hoping for some clue as to what the impending danger could be, but wedged between two of the lower boughs, he just stood there rolling his eyes. And then, at last, came a faint sound of rustling. I wasn't sure at first if it was just my imagination, but the look of concentration on Caroline's face said it all, and whatever it was, it seemed to be getting closer. Just then, Manu animatedly pointed to something in the distance.

'Look! There! Rhino! Over there!'

We peered over to our left and, sure enough, standing no more than twenty metres away was a rhinoceros, and a truly fearsome looking beast it was too. It's grey armour plated skin was wrinkled and rubbery looking, its torso was sturdy and comfortably big enough to accommodate the four of us all in one go, whilst between its beady shifting eyes protruded an ominously large spiked horn. It was also staring intently straight at us. I peered down anxiously at the flimsy tree and the full extent of the threat that this primitive looking creature posed quickly sank in. Quite simply, if it wanted to, the rhino could charge our trunk at any given moment and in one fell swoop, we'd all be unceremoniously unseated from our lofty vantage point, hurled into the air and sent scattering down into the undergrowth like flies. The consequences of this didn't bear thinking about. Glancing down at Manu, I suddenly realised he wasn't even armed. In fact, he'd only been carrying a bamboo stick, and a fat lot of good that was going to do if ol' grisly guts over there hadn't taken breakfast yet. For a few seconds, we sat there transfixed, not daring to move and unable to take our eyes off the scavenging predator. As it continued to stare back at us for what seemed like an eternity, I spotted Gibbo out of the corner of my eye, rubbing his nose, and then another horrible thought crossed my mind: he's bloody asthmatic! As the excruciating eyeballing continued, all I kept saying to myself was: 'Gibbo, if you sneeze now, mate, I'll never forgive you.'

But just as my foot, uncomfortably tucked under my buttock, started to go numb through an untimely attack of pins and needles, our fat-faced friend finally turned around and slowly lumbered off into the undergrowth. Clutching onto the overhead branches, we swung our heads around and gawping at each other wide-eyed, simultaneously puffed our cheeks. Even Manu seemed somewhat relieved, for he was busily wiping away the beads of sweat that had formed on his brow with a hanky. Five minutes later, when the coast was finally clear, we tentatively climbed down from the tree and, now far more fearful for our safety, frantically bombard Manu with questions about the dangers from the other wildlife in the park. He didn't seem overly concerned; if anything, I think he found our heightened state of anxiety mildly amusing. Walking much closer to him now, we continued on our trek looking around nervously like the soldiers on the opening scene of *Dads Army*. Although there were no further scares, the three of us were mightily relieved just to get back to the camp an hour or so later still in one piece.

When, the following night, we arrived back in Kathmandu

after a seemingly never ending seven-hour bus journey, we returned to the Langtan, the guesthouse we'd stayed at on our first night, deposited our bags and then headed straight out again for some much-needed food, this time Japanese. It was the first time I'd ever eaten sushi, and perhaps because my stomach was unaccustomed to raw fish, I hurriedly dashed off to the toilets as soon as we'd finished eating and promptly threw up the entire contents of the meal along with the numerous glasses of saki that had accompanied it. In hindsight, this was probably quite a good thing, for after walking Caroline back to the room, Gibbo and I stopped off for a couple of nightcaps. Suffice to say, a couple of hours later, we were still sat there shooting the breeze although by now, he was in a decidedly worse state than me: his eyes were bloodshot, he was mumbling incoherently and sat on a stool with his head in his hands, he was slumped across the bar with his elbows on the counter. By the time we eventually returned to the Langtan just after midnight, the temperatures had plummeted and I needed my bed quickly. Gibbo, though, was lagging behind. Glancing back disconcertedly, I could see him staggering back and forth across the deserted streets with his arms outstretched in front of him as if he were sleepwalking. 'C'mon, Gibbo!' I shouted from further up the street. 'We're not in bloody Chitwan now!'

CHAPTER 31

KATHMANDU

BURNING THE CANDLE BOTH ENDS

8th–22nd April 1991

I didn't sleep well the following night, which might have had something to do with our scheduled early start the next day. Our sole mission on our first day back in Kathmandu had been to book ourselves on to the daily morning flight over the Himalayas. The one-hour sightseeing flight was by no means cheap at $96 per person, but it's not every day you get the chance to fly over the world's highest mountain. So, after being woken at 6am by a knock on the door from Hari, the friendly young boy running the Langtan, we took a taxi to the airport where I was both pleasantly surprised and somewhat relieved to see a big Royal Nepal Airlines aircraft waiting on the tarmac. In my ignorance, I had mistakenly assumed that the plane which was going to take us on our flight over the Himalayas was going to be a small twelve or fifteen seater, and I suppose my fear of flying had been the *real* reason why I'd slept so fitfully. Even more encouragingly, there only happened to be twenty or so passengers on board which meant we were all able to secure window seats, Gibbo and Caroline on one side of the aisle, me on the other. As we fastened our seat belts, I picked up the complimentary information wallet that was sitting on my plastic table:

R.N.A.C.'s daily 'Mountain flight' allows you to enjoy a unique experience indeed: to admire the breathtaking range of the eastern HIMALAYA from a distance of less than 14 miles, while comfortably seated on board of this pressurized aircraft.

The flight will take approximately 40 minutes. On the outward leg of the journey (eastbound), the mountain range will of course unfurl itself on the left side of the plane. But on the return trip (westbound), it will be, at the same distance and perfectly clear again, visible to the passengers seated on the right side. Thus, all seats being equally 'good', we would request you, for safety reasons, not to move from one side to the other during the flight.

Our plane took off just after 7am and because I was sitting on the right hand side, I did, indeed, see very little for the first twenty-five minutes. Whilst it was only natural that the passengers on the other side should be continually exclaiming how magnificent the great Himalayas looked out of their windows as the aircraft slowly crept its way along the Eastern divide, it still didn't make it any easier. It felt like they were all opening their Christmas presents a day early, and as the captain, talking over the address system, proceeded to point out all the respective summits, I sat in my seat getting increasingly frustrated, constantly leaning over desperately trying to capture a glimpse of the views. Finally, though, the plane circled and my patience and that of all the other passengers sitting on the starboard side was duly rewarded. Mercifully, the running commentary from the cockpit didn't let up and virtually the first mountain pointed out to us was Everest itself. In truth, it wasn't difficult to miss because, as it was so much higher, it was the only peak shrouded in light cloud.

'Bet you didn't know it was named after a Welsh surveyor,' I shouted across the aisle.

'Oh, God,' groaned Gibbo, nudging Caroline's arm. 'I think Fordy's been on the rakshi again.'

Thankfully, we'd been blessed with a relatively clear day and the contrast between the dazzling virgin white snow beneath us and the deep dark blue of the early morning skies was almost blinding. Glued to the window, I squinted down thousands of feet below in the vain hope I'd spot a few struggling climbers. Of course, it was a fruitless search but the fact that somewhere down there lay the frozen remains of those two British climbers, Mallory and Irvine, didn't escape me. Shaking my head, I wondered whether their bodies would ever be found and after all the fuss with Tenzing and Mallory over who had made it to the summit first, I couldn't help feeling how ironic it would be if one day it was discovered that they had, in fact, been beaten to the post. Before I knew it, though, the snow on the rugged Himalayan peaks had given way to gentler bare brown mountains and the plane was already beginning its descent back down into Kathmandu. Fifteen minutes later, we were back on the ground, and even after we'd taken a taxi back to Thamel and stopped off for a king-sized breakfast, the three of us were still buzzing with adrenaline.

The previous evening, we'd whiled away a couple of pleasant hours sat outside our guesthouse sipping beers and chatting to three enterprising Israeli guys staying in a room down the corridor. Amongst other things, they'd proceeded to tell us all about the holy men and Sadhus that hung around the grounds of Pashupatinath, one of the most sacred temples in Nepal, and they spoke, much to our incredulity, about one man in particular whose party trick was to lift up boulders with his penis. Of course, such a feat sounded totally preposterous but they seemed a genuine lot so, later in the morning, we took another taxi a few miles east of the city to check it out for ourselves. Discovering on arrival that only Hindus were allowed to enter the main temple, we had to make do with climbing the steps on the other side of the Bagmati River to get a proper view of things and even then, I was a little circumspect. The river itself was highly sacred to the Nepalese and apparently, on certain days, dead bodies were cremated on the ghats (the steps leading down to the river) before their ashes were scattered in the murky water. Luckily for us, because I wasn't entirely sure I wanted to see such a gruesome spectacle, it looked like no such ceremonies were taking place that morning as the ghats on the opposite side of the river remained strangely empty, so we wandered around for a while in the sweltering morning sunshine, peering over instead at the packs of screaming monkeys leaping across the crimson temple roofs, scurrying up and down trunks of towering palms and defiantly hanging from branches by one hand whilst gorging themselves with nuts with their other. But in spite of the fact it was a holy site, Pashupatinath seemed to attract a whole host of the city's 'undesirables', and before long, we found ourselves being constantly hassled by beggars, drunks and dreadlocked rogues purporting to be holy men. (I still got the impression from my time in Goa that becoming a Sadhu simply gave you free licence to get off your face smoking ganga and then cash in on your claim to spirituality through begging, and from what I saw here, it was an opinion I was unlikely to change.) Becoming increasingly irritated by the continual badgering, we were just about to head off when Caroline stopped abruptly.

'Ooh, look!' she cried, shielding her eyes from the sun. 'What's going on over there?'

We followed her gaze a few hundred yards further along the river, where a small crowd was converging.

'I wonder what's happening?' she added, thoughtfully.

'Hey, maybe one of these guys has got his just deserts!' I grinned, envisaging an enraged tourist trading blows with one of the miscreants.

'C'mon,' cried Gibbo, 'let's go and take a look.'

We hurried over and, after a couple of minutes, managed to push our way to the front of the crowds. Squatting on his haunches in the middle of a large circle, five or six deep with curious onlookers, was a skinny gangling man with a long dark beard. Perhaps in his forties, he was dressed in a light blue sarong and shirt with a huge navy turban and, crouching with his eyes closed, seemed totally oblivious to all around him. We asked a couple of female travellers what was happening. The two girls, Scandinavian I think, started to giggle.

'The man in the middle,' said one, 'lifts rocks with his...you know...willy.'

So it was true! The Israelis had been right after all. We waited around for ten or fifteen minutes whilst a couple of young boys went around the crowd collecting money. When the turbaned man was finally happy there were enough rupees in the two buckets, he stood up and removing his garments, revealed a spindly beanpole frame. Standing in the centre of the circle, now wearing just a tiny pink loincloth and turban, he tied a bright saffron-coloured piece of material to a large slab of white rock, perhaps the size of a car wheel, that lay on the ground. Then, pulling his loincloth to the side, he fastened the material to his semi-flaccid penis and with the help of his hand, lifted the rock about three inches off the ground. Instantaneously, the large crowd started to whistle and cheer. Why, I don't know, as it was patently obvious that all of the leverage required to lift the rock was made through his wrist and not his donger. For a few moments, I stood there staring in astonishment. Gibbo and Caroline were also shaking their heads and chuckling but everyone else was still in raptures, wildly cheering and applauding the man as he put on his shirt and sarong again. And once fully dressed, he promptly walked off, waving his hand behind his head, his day's work seemingly all but done.

'Party trick, indeed!' I exclaimed to Gibbo as the crowds began to disperse. 'Bloody hell, even I could have done that.'

'Go on then, Fordy,' he replied, pointing to the rock on the floor, 'let's see you try, then.'

'Yeah, well, maybe not,' I muttered, turning around and slinking off in the other direction.

Seeing as Caroline only had one more full day left, we got up early the next morning and spent a couple of hours shopping. In fact, the others embarked on a buying frenzy. Nine T-shirts, a couple of tea cosies, a carpet, a cardigan and three black and white photographs later, they were done so we took a taxi over to Patan and explored the area around the Durbar Square, quintessentially the heart of old Kathmandu. The square itself, surrounded by a cluster of red-bricked three-tiered pagodas, was a hive of activity. In one corner, street sellers laid out their wares of antiques, handicrafts and jewellery on blankets for the hundreds of tourists milling about. In another, a party of schoolchildren immaculately dressed in sky blue and navy uniforms were playing hopscotch and jacks in their lunch break. And amidst the hubbub, as cyclists and porters continually darted back and forth across the square before disappearing off down winding cobbled streets, the touts were also out in force with their never-ending unscrupulous offers of hashish, good exchange rates and cheap rickshaws. Mercifully others, simply content to use the square as a place to come and meet with friends, were sat on the temples' steps, happy to while away a few hours chatting, catching up on all the latest gossip and putting their worlds to right. The whole scene had a kind of surreal feeling to it, like a medieval bazaar plucked from the pages of some magical fairy tale.

Sitting outside the guesthouse again later in the evening, we had the dubious pleasure of meeting Ali, a moustachioed jeweller from Jaipur. As soon as Gibbo told him of our tentative plans to open a shop, he immediately offered to accompany me back to his home city where he said he could train me up on gemstones and other aspects of the jewellery trade. The offer seemed genuine but his manner was arrogant and not particularly endearing. He didn't speak; he bragged, he didn't talk; he lectured and whenever we tried to speak, he constantly interrupted or sat in his seat leering and gloating. Finding myself questioning his motives, I politely declined his offer and quickly changed the subject to cricket. Even then, I could still see Gibbo getting visibly irritated next to me.

'Of course India will win the World Cup,' proclaimed the Langtan's new arrival. 'There is no doubt about it. In Sachin Tendulkar, we have the best cricketer in the world.'

'So you don't hold much hope for England, then?' I said.

'England?' he scoffed, waving his hand dismissively across his face. 'Don't make me laugh.'

'Not even with Botham coming back?'

'Listen, my friend, I am telling you, England don't have a chance.'

'What about Australia and the West Indies, then?' said Gibbo, sitting back with his arms folded.

'The West Indies are past their best now. The Aussies are good but they're still not in the same class. Come on, I'll bet you. Give me your odds.'

'I don't want a bet, thanks,' retorted Gibbo, 'and certainly not with you.'

'Very well, that means you know I am right. India will triumph. Admit it.'

Gibbo, rolling his eyes, flicked his head in the direction of our room and, not wanting to listen to any more of the man's boastful claims, we promptly got up from our chairs and rather prematurely bade him a curt goodnight.

After seeing Caroline off at the airport the next morning, we returned to the Langtan and waited for Dinesh to arrive. Dinesh was a man who Hari had put us in touch with who was going to introduce us to some jewellers in the city, so when he still hadn't turned up an hour later, we walked over to the hotel where he worked. We met him in the reception and, to our relief, discovered he was able to show us around straight away. The first shop he took us to wasn't, by all accounts, really what we were looking for, as they didn't stock the kind of jewellery that Gibbo was hoping to buy. The second one, however, owned by a rather lethargic character called Ram, was apparently much better and Gibbo decided to place an order on the spot. Realising that his services were no longer required, Dinesh got up from his seat and we duly thanked him for his help. I meanwhile, sat on, watching in fascination as Gibbo picked out an assortment of rings, some plain silver, and others with stones all with wonderful exotic sounding names such as moonstone, tiger's eye and black star. Just an hour or so later, all the buying had been done. The order was totalled up and came to just over £500, a little more than what Gibbo had been expecting, although he seemed mightily relieved that the whole thing had been so straightforward. We got up, shook hands with Ram, and arranged to pick up the stock a couple of days before Gibbo was due to leave.

By now, it was mid-afternoon, and to celebrate the fact that the buying was done, we treated ourselves to a slap-up meal in the restaurant of the five-star Annapurna Hotel. No doubt buoyed on by the thrill and excitement of being able to conduct your very own business deals, I decided to give Gibbo the go-ahead for us to open a jewellery shop together, and we immediately began to go through the names of prospective towns in the South that he believed were crying out for the new and unconventional kind of store he had in mind. It was all heady stuff, and for the first time since I'd been away, I actually had something I could look forward to when my trip was over.

On the way back, we bought a few bottles of beer to take back to Langtan and then spent a couple of hours playing karom with Hari in the garden. Later on, the three Israeli guys, who happened to be heading off the next day, arrived back from a final shopping spree. After depositing their many bags of goods in their room, they came back out and joined us and we all sat around again exchanging travel stories well into the evening. As soon as Ali, now in the company of a sidekick, turned up at the end of the night, however, the whole atmosphere changed. Pulling up a seat, the Indian turned to Hari and clicking his fingers, grunted: 'Hey you, a couple of beers.'

Hari duly got to his feet and wandered inside.

'Haven't you heard of the word 'please',' said Gibbo, a few seconds later.

Ali shrugged, and pulling out a packet of cigarettes, muttered something to his partner and smirked. Spotting the karom board, he then peered around the table and cocked his head back. 'So, who's been playing this?'

Nobody replied. Just then, Hari returned with a couple of beers and, placing them on the table, handed him a docket. The Indian looked at it for a couple of seconds and screwing the piece of paper up in his hand, said, 'Put them on my bill.' Then, quickly glancing around the table again, he threw down the gauntlet. 'Come on,' he beckoned, 'who's going to challenge us to a game of doubles.' Gibbo leapt to his feet in a flash and with a look of fierce determination in his eyes, said: 'We will.'

As Ali's accomplice set up the counters, I flicked a coin in the air and, catching it in my palm, flipped it on to my wrist.

'So, what's it to be, then?' I said to Ali.

'Heads,' he called, rather unwisely.

'Bad luck,' I chirped, 'Looks like we're breaking, then.'

With that, Gibbo took aim but instead of cannoning into the pack and dispersing the counters all over the table, as was his custom, he flicked our disc gently into the side of the pack, barely dispersing any of the assembled pieces. Not only was it going to be a intense tactical battle, it was a game we simply had to win in order to put one over on the exasperating Indian, and I sensed that an awful lot more than pride was at stake here. Fifteen incredibly tense minutes later, the match was still evenly poised; black and white counters had been pocketed with startling regularity, but three or four shots later, Ali was presented with the first opportunity to win the game. If he pocketed the red and their last remaining white in successive shots, then it was curtains. As Gibbo reached for my cigarettes, I sat there for a few nail biting moments holding my breath. After confidently despatching the red into the centre of a pocket, the game looked all but over but when his counter connected with the final white just inches from the opposite pocket, it miraculously cannoned off both edges of the corner back into play. Gibbo quickly clenched his fist. I looked up to the skies. The red was replaced in the centre of the table and, seizing on the mistake, Gibbo then pocketed our penultimate black and the re-spotted red in successive shots and now *we* had a chance to win the game. After an agonising wait as he prepared to shoot, Gibbo flicked the disc at our last remaining black. Almost as soon as the counter moved, I realised that his finger hadn't connected properly and that the shot wouldn't have nearly enough power to push the final black into the pocket. I looked on open-mouthed as the counter, almost in slow motion, was nudged up the side of the table ever closer to the pocket. But it was slowing down too quickly. Or was it? OR WAS IT? The black reached the edge of the hole where it hovered momentarily. And then, a couple of seconds later, it magically disappeared.

'Yesss!' I hissed, as Gibbo, leaping up from his seat again, unashamedly punched the air in delight. It was a sweet tasting victory and although Ali begged us to play again, we turned down the offer, knowing this would infuriate him even more. After mockingly shaking hands with our opponents across the table, we then smugly returned to our room leaving them to wallow in defeat.

'Yep,' said Gibbo when we got up the next day. 'How do you fancy that, Fordy? An early morning round of golf. We can call it the 'Tuborg Challenge.'' (Tuborg, by no strange coincidence, just happened to be one of the two locally produced beers in Kathmandu.)

'Sounds good to me,' I replied.

The Royal Nepal Golf Course was situated right next to the airport. We'd spotted it the previous day sitting in the taxi after seeing Caroline off, and had promised ourselves that before we left, we'd have to go along and have a game. Because the jewellery buying had been done, we'd found ourselves with a lot more time on our hands than anticipated, so a nice leisurely round of golf seemed like the perfect idea. Arriving at the course an hour later, we discovered the charge for a round was 350 rupees (£7). This, we were informed, included green fees, caddies, ball boys, club hire, and golf balls. Scratching my head, I wondered to myself quite what the 'ball boys' were for and when the Tuborg Challenge commenced a few minutes later, I duly found out. My caddie pulled out a three-wood and handed me the club. As I stood on the tee desperately trying to adopt a suitably professional looking stance, two small kids tore a couple of hundred yards up the fairway. Casting a quizzical look at my caddie, he informed me that they would stand there to spot my ball. Surprisingly, after a couple of mandatory practice swings, I stuck the ball quite sweetly and quickly glanced up to see it shooting up the fairway. One of the boys watchfully followed my shot, ran over to where the ball had landed and stood there with one hand raised proudly in the air. What a great idea! And the way I played golf, I suspected our little friends were going to be in for a busy afternoon. We proceeded to make our way up and down the course with our respective entourages in tow, basking in the glorious warm sunshine as free roaming ducks, cows and monkeys served as spectators. The first six holes on the nine-hole course were pretty straightforward, characterised by long wide fairways strewn across an undulating terrain which led up to the airport on the horizon. So, as we tramped up holes one, three and five, we could visibly monitor the planes in the distance hurtling in or soaring up into the clear skies ahead whilst on holes two, four and six, we could only hear the noise of the roaring jet engines behind us. Holes seven, eight and nine, by contrast, were set amongst steep hillocks and clusters of thick bushes and trees and, as a result, had far less margin for error, as we ultimately found out to our cost.

Since we were playing 'matchplay,' where a point is won by whoever completes a hole in the least number of shots, we finished the first nine with Gibbo one ahead. By the time we'd reached the eighteenth, after playing the same nine holes again, the score had remained unchanged, which meant I needed to win the last to tie the match. But alas, disaster struck and I took eight shots to make the hole, three more than Gibbo and the Tuborg Challenge had effectively been surrendered. Totting the scorecards up as we made our way back to the clubhouse, Gibbo had finished on 132, and I'd ended up eight shots back on 140. Par for the course was a paltry 67. Thanking our troops for their help, we rewarded them with over-generous tips, then retired to the clubhouse for a well-earned drink.

A few days later, we were back on the course for the big rematch, the San Miguel Open, though it turned out to be nowhere near as close as the Tuborg Challenge. Indeed, by the time we'd reached the fourteenth, I was five holes down, not helped by a catastrophic 15 at the twelfth. Yet surprisingly, in spite of my woeful performance, I wasn't unduly concerned. In fact, I couldn't stop smiling to myself and I had good reason to be happy, for the previous evening, something quite dramatic had occurred. For the first time on my travels, I'd experienced my first genuine holiday romance. No, let me qualify that! For the first time on my travels, I'd experienced my first holiday romance with a girl I'd genuinely fancied.

It had all happened by pure chance. After spending another afternoon playing karom with Hari in the garden of the Langtan, we'd wandered along to a bar called Tom and Jerry's after dinner, where we'd bumped into Helma and Ella, the two bubbly Dutch girls who'd accompanied us on the jeep trip at Chitwan. Typical to their nationality, they were both tremendously laid-back and game on for a laugh, so before long, the Ludo board was brought out and the drinking forfeits had begun in earnest. An hour or so later, we were all completely sozzled and this is where my recollections get a bit hazy. What I certainly *do* remember is finding myself, some time towards the end of the night, standing outside the bar locked in a passionate embrace with Helma under a street lamp. A few minutes later, she asked me to walk her back to her guesthouse. Convinced that this could only mean one thing, we set off with my heart beating nineteen to the dozen. Unfortunately for me, though, I was to be sadly mistaken. Our drinking frenzy had finally caught up with her and all she wanted to do was get back to her bed to crash out. I still tried to persuade her to let me come back to her room but my advances were all in vain, and after one last snog in the courtyard beneath her guesthouse, she returned to her room alone. For the next fifteen, twenty, perhaps even thirty minutes, I stood out on the street with my hands in my pockets, peering up at her window desperately hoping that she'd change her mind and come running back down the stairs, but the wait was a futile one. Finally conceding defeat, I headed back to the bar and further up the street, bumped into Ella. Gibbo, she told me, was still in Tom and Jerry's. Dashing up the road, I saw him stumbling around outside the bar.

'Gibbo, what are you doing?' I yelled.

'Dunno,' he mumbled, rubbing his eyes, 'Think I'm lost.'

'Hey, you'll never believe what's just happened to me!'

'Yeah, where did you get to?' he asked, squinting at his watch. 'I was waiting for you for ages.'

'Come on, let's go back upstairs, I'll tell you all about it.'

So back on the course, I was putting my poor performance down to the fact that my mind was on other things, namely Helma and last night's impetuous fling that had come so completely out of the blue. Gibbo, though, cited her voluptuous breasts as the real distraction.

'You can't stop thinking about them, can you, Fordy, you dirty little man.'

I suppose I'd be lying if I said I hadn't.

So virtually resigned to the fact that the San Miguel Challenge had already been forfeited, I stood on the fourteenth preparing to tee off again, fearing the worst. All morning long, my driving had been poor, even by my own shocking standards. Hole after hole, I'd either sliced or hooked, consistently sending my ball careering off wildly in all different directions and my poor spotter no longer knew which way to look. I glanced up despairingly for a couple of seconds wondering if I was ever going to make the fairway again. The fourteenth hole was 174 yards long and shielding my eyes from the blazing midday sun, I spotted, at the edge of the green, the figure of an elderly man sheltering under a large black umbrella. Squatting on his haunches with his outstretched arms resting on his knees, he was staring at the dozen or so cows wandering indiscriminately across the course. Odd place for a shepherd to sit, I thought. Gibbo jokingly warned me not to hit him.

'No fear of that!' I replied. 'Not the way I'm playing today.' I tried to compose myself again. 'Now keep your head still, just remember to keep your head still,' I said to myself over and over again.

Raising the three-iron above my head, I held it there for two or three seconds and then, in one swift movement, swung the club down towards the ball. I knew straight away by the sound of the swish that I'd finally made a sweet connection and, with my follow through completed, raised my head to see the white ball disappear high into the blue unblemished sky. For a few seconds, we followed its path up the fairway and then it dropped, perilously close to the old man. Gibbo stared at me wide-eyed.

'Bloody Hell, I think you've hit him!'

Bloody Hell, I thought. I think I may have too.

Whilst our caddies started giggling, I looked on rather concerned, urging Gibbo to hurry up with his drive. When he finally teed off, I didn't even look to see where his shot had gone; instead, I was already marching up the fairway. A minute or so later, with Gibbo running behind, I reached the old man. Unbelievably, it appeared that my ball had landed right on top of his umbrella, for there was now a gaping wide hole where it had penetrated the nylon. Turning to my caddie, I asked him to find out if the old man was okay. Thankfully, it seemed that the ball hadn't hit him on his head, which had been my main concern. When Gibbo turned up, realising what had happened and that the man had remained unharmed, he was beside himself. The caddies were chuckling also and so too the ball spotters, and looking at the grimacing old man still squatting there and squinting behind the thick lenses of his black framed spectacles, I finally began to see the funny side. As Gibbo rummaged around in his bag for his camera, I asked the caddie to inform the man that I'd gladly pay for a new umbrella. A price of 60 rupees was hastily agreed and, reaching into my money belt, I duly handed over the money. Then, shaking hands with the old man, I stood on the fairway pointing my club to the hole in the umbrella and as Gibbo prepared to take a picture of the comical scene, I could already hear him reciting the story to his children in years to come: 'Well, you see that fellow there, boys? He was a harmless old shepherd, and a long time ago, when daddy was on holiday in Nepal, your Uncle Jim struck a golf ball clean through the top of his umbrella. Nearly hit him full on the head, you know.'

Gibbo eventually went on to win by seven holes, completing the course in a much more respectable score of 116, whilst I finished way back on 138. Stopping off at the clubhouse again early afternoon for some much-needed refreshments, we came across Alf and John, a couple of middle-aged British ex-pats. (In fact, we didn't actually catch 'John's' real name, though this is how we later referred to him as he reminded us both so much of John Noakes, the ebullient 1970s *Blue Peter* presenter.) They told us they were here in Nepal training Gurkhas, and almost instinctively, as we pulled up another couple of bar stools, we began to interrogate them on the various aspects of their work, asking them things like: how strong in combat the Gurkhas *really* were; if, for example, they could overcome the SAS in a battle; what they were like as a people, and how the two of them got on living in Nepal. The Gurkhas, they told us, were very easy people to work with and all the stories about their ferocity and deadliness in battle should not be taken lightly. Whether they'd prove a match for the SAS remained highly debatable and as for living in Nepal, 'it's just like living in any other country, you learn to adapt and just get on with it.' As the afternoon wore on, it emerged that the two men were extremely well travelled, both having lived in other parts of Asia and we listened on intently as they recounted one wonderful story after another from their full and colourful pasts.

'So, where would you say was the best place you were posted,' I asked them eventually.

They looked at each other for a few seconds.

'I know mine,' said Alf. 'But go on, you say yours.'

'Well, I suppose it's gotta be Hong Kong,' said John.

'I'm glad you said that,' said Alf, smiling as he glanced down to the floor.

'Cor, we had some right good nights in that place!'

'My God, didn't we just! Either of you two been there?'

Gibbo, shaking his head, blurted, 'Jim has, though.'

'And what did you think?' asked Alf.

'Don't ask,' I said, puffing my cheeks. 'It's a long story. I can tell you all about Chunking Mansions, though.'

'The Mansions?' cried Alf. 'You've got a few stories about the Mansions, haven't you John? Isn't that where you met those Korean acrobats?'

'Blimey, so it was,' mused John, scratching his chin and smiling. 'Just thinking about that lot makes my eyes water.'

Before we knew it, over three hours had elapsed and having made the mistake of buying rounds with our fellow countrymen, who'd set a frighteningly quick drinking pace throughout, Gibbo and I were beginning to flounder. Drinking for so long on empty stomachs after four hours on the golf course was not, in hindsight, a particularly clever idea, but the afternoon chat had been so entertaining we didn't regret it for a minute. Almost reluctant to bring the thoroughly engaging conversations to an end, we eventually decided it was time for us to head back. Wobbling about precariously on our feet after we'd finally managed to prise ourselves off our stools, we called for a taxi, which arrived minutes later, and shaking their hands, bade Alf and John a fond farewell.

I felt truly awful when I woke up the next morning. After treating ourselves to a slap-up steak and chips after we'd left the golf club, we'd then made the foolish mistake of carrying on drinking so by the time we'd returned from a local casino just after two in the morning, my teeth were chattering, my head was pounding and I was shivering uncontrollably from head to toe. I knew things still weren't right when I couldn't even stomach breakfast. On previous days, hangovers had been successfully quelled with a huge early morning plate of fried food, but not that morning. Gibbo insisted I should try to eat something and ordered me a bowl of porridge. It sat on the table in front of me going cold, and while I knew his sentiments were right, the porridge remained untouched. Ten minutes later, we very slowly and fragilely made our way back to Ram's to pick up the rings,

413

only to discover there'd been complications. It looked like the order still wasn't ready which meant Gibbo wouldn't be able to take them back with him when he flew back the next day. Taking a time-out to work out what to do, we came up with a contingency plan. If the rings weren't ready by the morning, then I'd hang around in Kathmandu for a couple more days to pick them up. Walking back into the showroom, Gibbo asked Ram if he could complete the order by the end of the day. Ram, apologising for the delay, nodded his head unconvincingly. Gibbo then asked him if he knew of a place where he could buy a large terracotta rhino, something I seemed to remember Caroline admiring a few days ago. Keen to make up for his embarrassment with the delay of the rings, Ram, getting up from his seat, said he could take us to a place immediately.

'Oh,' said Gibbo, seizing the opportunity to cash in on another favour, 'we're also looking to buy a couple of karom boards too.'

Ram was already on his way out of the showroom.

By the time we'd eventually returned to the Langtan early afternoon, I'd developed a soaring fever and to make matters worse, as I sat on the toilet, I heard the all too familiar rumblings of my stomach that could only mean one thing: my bottom was about to fall apart. A few debilitating minutes later, I collapsed on my bed and didn't stir until early evening. Even though I didn't remember suggesting it, I'd apparently arranged for us to meet up with Helma and Ella for a bite to eat later in the evening, but when 8pm arrived, all my strength had been sapped and, regrettably, I knew there was no way I'd be able to make it. Not wanting to stand the girls up, Gibbo went along to tell Helma that I'd been struck down with a fever. When he returned a short while later and said that they hadn't even shown up, all I could manage was a groan, and as I turned over and buried my head under the pillow, he went back outside to play karom with Hari. I didn't get much sleep after that. In between regular visits to the toilet to throw up or splatter the pan with liquid diarrhoea, my temperature constantly changed. One minute, I was reaching for my bedclothes to wrap around my trembling body; the next, I was kicking the same bedclothes off as I found myself burning hot and soaked in sweat. It was a long, long night.

After fourteen hours in bed, during which I'd somehow managed to get through half a dozen bottles of water, I did feel a little better when I woke up the next morning, so much so that I managed to shovel down a bowl of cornflakes for breakfast. Just after eight, we returned to Ram's. The good news was that most of the rings were ready. The bad news was that the rings that weren't, wouldn't be ready for another couple of days, so after I'd arranged to pick these up on Sunday, we hastily rushed back to our guesthouse where I sat on the bed with my head in my hands watching Gibbo pack. Half an hour later, we jumped in a taxi to the airport, and shaking hands in the departure hall, made our farewells. Then, hauling his rucksack onto his back, Gibbo bent down and with a full-sized karom board under each arm, passed through the gate and was gone.

Taking another taxi straight back to Thamel, I returned to the Langtan and sat outside for a while chatting with Hari in the garden. Late afternoon, starting to feel hungry again, I went out and ordered myself another steak and chips. Encouragingly, I managed to polish off nearly the whole plate. When I returned to my room, though, I started to think about Helma. By pure coincidence, Ella also happened to be travelling back that morning, though on a different flight, whereas Helma wasn't leaving for another couple of days, and before long, I began to picture her sitting alone in her room just like me. I knew the name of the guesthouse she was staying at and toyed with the idea of giving her a call. I even contemplated just marching around there, but the nagging doubt as to why she didn't show up the previous night stopped me from doing either. In desperation, I got up and started to walk the streets of Thamel in the vain hope I might bump into her but it wasn't to be and I returned to my room an hour or so later in despondent mood. If only I could call her up, I kept thinking, if only, if only, if only, although deep down, I knew that I simply hadn't got the courage to do so, and for the rest of the evening, I just lay on my bed staring up to the ceiling wondering whether my failure to act was something I was going to end up regretting for the rest of my life.

I woke up the next morning feeling 100% better. I called in at the Singapore Airlines office and, because of my increasingly dire financial situation, brought forward my flight home by a month, and then booked a bus ticket to Varanasi for the following evening. I even managed to dispel any more thoughts of Helma from my mind. When I arrived back at the Langtan, though, poor Hari was in a terrible state. Apparently, earlier that morning, Ali had done a runner from the hotel. As well as not paying his bill, he'd also ripped off a number of other guests, running off with a cassette recorder, a couple of Walkmans and a substantial sum of money. And to think that this was the bloke who was trying to talk me into travelling back to Jaipur with him! The whole episode left me seething.

Late afternoon the next day after I'd picked up the remaining rings, I packed, settled the bill, and then shook hands with Hari, assuring him that I'd stay in touch and vowing to keep a promise I'd made to send him an English dictionary to help him with his studies. Wishing him well, I lugged my rucksack into the back of the waiting taxi and waved goodbye. It was quite a moving moment, as he'd become a good friend to us over the past few weeks and as the taxi pulled away, I told myself that, come what may, I'd make sure I would fulfil my promise to him. It was the very least I could do to repay him for his kind hospitality.

CHAPTER 32

VARANASI

AN ODD PLACE FOR DOLPHINS

23rd–27th April 1991

After a virtually sleepless night—made only slightly more bearable by the large proportion of backpackers on board who, judging from the huge black rings under their eyes, were all suffering from insomnia too—our overcrowded bus arrived at the border town of Sunauli just after daybreak. Having passed through customs and immigration relatively quickly, however, we were then inexplicably left sitting in our seats for over two hours. The wait was all the more infuriating because there was no obvious reason for the delay. Well, if there was, then we were being kept firmly in the dark. With nothing better to do, I sat in my seat reflecting on the last few weeks in Nepal, realising just how much we'd packed into the relatively short time we were there: mountain biking, jungle treks, mountain treks, flights over Everest, rounds of golf, jewellery buying, karom and to top it all off, a little romantic fling thrown in for good measure. With my mind drifting, I then started to think about the numerous people we'd met: Helma and her travelling partner Ella, Hari, Kesh, Ram, Manu, the two terrifically entertaining ex-pats, Alf and John, even that thieving bastard, Ali. These were all characters who, in one way or another, had contributed to making my time there so memorable and without them and, of course, Gibbo and Caroline, Nepal wouldn't have been half as enjoyable. Indeed, it began to dawn on me that if it hadn't been for Gibbo and Caroline, I would probably never have met half of these people in the first place and this in turn begged another question: how many more people might I have met over the last couple of months if I'd been accompanied by trusted pals in India as well? Ever since I'd left Basir in Goa, I thought I'd been perfectly happy in my own company but now the doubts had started to creep in again. My ongoing debate over the respective merits of travelling alone or with others had seemingly taken another twist.

Just then, our driver re-boarded the bus, started up the engine and, at long last, we were on the move again. With the spectacular mountain scenery of Nepal now behind us, I stared blankly out of the window at the drab flat dusty terrain, trying to gather my thoughts and focus again on what lay ahead. Nepal had been great fun, but it was, in effect, a holiday and it was time to get back to 'travelling' again. And returning to India a second time around wasn't going to be easy. The temperatures would be getting increasingly oppressive before the monsoons arrived, shortening tempers and tolerance levels alike; there was much talk of sporadic violence breaking out in the lead up to the Indian elections at the end of May, with Delhi being cited as one of the likely hotspots and, on top of this, my credit card debts were mounting by the day. I had, as expected, ended up spending a small fortune in Nepal so I really needed to get back to scrimping and saving. From hereon in, it would be second-class train journeys all the way. Sod the luxury!

Reaching for my guidebook, I tried to map out a rough itinerary for my last month. First stop had to be Varanasi, the most important pilgrimage site in India, where every day, thousands of Hindus flocked to immerse themselves in the sacred waters of the Ganges. Without exception, every person I'd spoke to who'd been to Varanasi had raved about the place and its proximity to Kathmandu made it the obvious first port of call. Agra, home to the Taj Mahal, the very icon of India, was another one of those sights I just had to go to see for myself and, after a brief stop in Delhi, it was on to Rajasthan, one of the most vibrant and colourful states in India. Whether I actually stopped in Jaipur, the capital, however, was little more debatable. Dubbed by many as 'hassle city,' the countless stories I'd heard about travellers getting ripped off there made me highly dubious. The mere fact it was also Ali's hometown did nothing to dispel this circumspection either. In contrast, the lakeside town of Pushkar, described as 'one of those travellers' centres where people go to for a little respite from the hardships of life on the Indian road,' sounded far more appealing. And Udaipur, also situated on the side of a large lake, looked like another good place to while away a few days. I was also intrigued by the exotic old fortress city of Jaisalmer, situated in the far west of Rajasthan, close to the Pakistan border, and in particular, the chance to spend a couple of nights in the surrounding Thar Desert on a camel safari. My only fear was that the temperatures there this time of year would be reaching 40°C, which may just prove to be too hot, so I'd keep that one on the back burner for now. And then, after returning to Delhi, it was back down to Bombay, then home.

A number of other Westerners and backpackers had boarded the bus at Sunauli—three Australian lads, a couple of Israelis and a few more Europeans, including an extremely attractive German girl with tightly cropped peroxide hair. Sat on the other side of the aisle, she was sultrily smoking a cigarette, and for a while, I found myself constantly gazing at her. But before long, with my head beginning to loll, I dozed off in my seat. When I woke a couple of hours later, I realised I happened to be sitting next to not one, but *two* particularly striking females, for the young dusky woman now sat quietly

DON'T WORRY, BE HAPPY

next to me against the window was, in fact, an angel in disguise. By the time she got up to remove her bag from the overhead rack at the next stop, I was completely overwhelmed by her consummate grace and femininity. Her olive coloured skin was smooth and unblemished, her hands were long and slender and an array of thin brightly coloured bangles adorned both her wrists. A long peach-coloured scarf covered her hair whilst a couple of beaded necklaces hung tantalisingly close to her bosom. Yet it was her huge wide brown eyes that were most alluring, making me think that she must come from mixed parentage, perhaps Indian and either Nepalese or Tibetan. But who cared, what did it matter? She was just about to get off the bus and I was worrying about her genealogy! With one knee on the seat and an arm leant on the backrest, I stood there transfixed for a few moments, watching her as she glided down the aisle exuding serenity. Then, she disappeared down the steps and was gone. Looking down at the empty seat next to me, scratching my head, I wondered for a moment if my vision of this resplendent goddess had been nothing more than just that: a vision, a wild apparition, a pure figment of my imagination. It had, as I said, been an exceptionally long and sleepless night.

A short while later, we pulled in again, this time at a roadside-eating house to stop for a late morning breakfast. Not feeling especially hungry, I stood outside the bus, chatting to one of the Israeli guys. Like his three compatriots we'd met back at the Langtan, he was very open and forthright, so much so that I felt compelled to ask him if he could clear up a little mystery that had been baffling us over the last few weeks; namely why there were so many Israelis currently in Kathmandu. I'd noticed it, Gibbo and Caroline had noticed it, even Alf, one of the two fellows we'd met at the golf course had picked up on it and we'd all been at odds as to the reason. He finally put me out of my misery. Apparently, every year, the Israeli embassy designated a particular city in the world for many of its younger generation to travel to, and this year, Kathmandu happened to be the chosen place. Consequently, over a thousand Israelis, he reckoned, had descended on the mountain kingdom over the Easter period. Why on earth the Israelis, of all people, should feel a need to go around in packs, however, was something I failed to comprehend. Of all the nationalities I'd come across, they seemed the most perfectly equipped; they were plain spoken, they were worldly wise and they possessed bargaining powers that could reduce a peddler to tears. (I'd seen one Israeli girl back in Kathmandu walk off, after an hour of particularly vociferous haggling, with a Nepalese coat acquired for a tenth of the original asking price.) Still, I told him the concept sounded like a good idea. He didn't look too convinced and admitted that he felt somewhat uncomfortable to see so many of his countrymen congregated in such a relatively small place all at one time. Although I didn't tell him so, I couldn't have agreed more.

Eventually arriving in Varanasi early evening, I grabbed my rucksack from the luggage hold, jumped into an auto-rickshaw and headed off to the old part of the city to find myself somewhere to stay. Finding many of the popular hotels full so late in the day, I eventually decided to book into the Kumiko Lodge, a place frequented by many of the Japanese backpackers, simply because I found them so unobtrusive. I continued to be fascinated by the Japanese travellers, especially here in India. It was a difficult enough country to travel through in any case but to do so, as many of them seemed to, without a proper grasp of the English language, which could only present insurmountable problems, was all the more remarkable. And yet, whenever I came across them, they always seemed so calm and unfazed, appearing to take all that India threw up at them fully in their stride and I couldn't help but admire them for this.

I put my alarm on for 7.30 the next morning but woke up two hours before to go to the toilet. Worryingly, my diarrhoea had returned and I was beginning to wonder if I *had* now, in fact, contracted the dreaded dysentery. Unable to get back to sleep, I eventually pulled on a T-shirt, stepped into a pair of shorts and wandered down to the river to get my first glimpse of the Ganges. Even at this time of morning, the ghats were already a frenzy of activity. Converged knee deep in the shallow waters—seemingly unperturbed by the uncleanliness of the river that was littered with floating waste—hordes of happily chatting washerwomen were busily scrubbing away at their soap-sudded laundry, repeatedly immersing the garments in the brown murky water before wringing out the sopping wet clothes and laying them out in neat tidy rows on the terraces ready to be dried by the sun. Further along, scores of males of all ages and builds—tall, podgy, lean and small—splashed and frolicked about in the same dirty water. Many were dressed just in pants, and most were the same unflattering brown coloured pants I'd bought for Gibbo and Caroline back in Calcutta. Beyond the bathers, lines of boats bobbed about on the water, ready to take tourists up and down the river, whilst up on the top of the ghats, the chai vendors were busily positioning their carts and unfurling their parasols in preparation for another day's trade.

'Boat trip?' enquired a kindly faced man in a white shirt and sarong, ambling up the steps towards me.

'How much?' I asked, somewhat circumspectly.

'Ten rupees half an hour, twenty rupees an hour,' came the reply. This was much cheaper than I'd been expecting, so I quickly nodded and followed him down to the water's edge. As soon as I stepped into the boat, a little kid hopped aboard and proudly held out his hand. Reaching into my pocket, I handed him a twenty-rupee note.

He shook his head. 'No, eighty rupees.'

'Eighty? He said twenty!' I exclaimed, pointing to the boatman.

'Twenty rupees when boat is full. Just you, eighty rupees.'

I got up and shaking my head, told him he could forget it.

'Okay, okay, forty rupees,' he cried.

'No way,' I snapped, sitting back down defiantly. 'The man told me twenty rupees, so twenty rupees is what I'm going to pay.'

The boy didn't budge from his seat and continued to ask for forty rupees, whilst I continued to wave a hand across my face. A few minutes later, he muttered something to the boatman, and then the three of us set off upstream. It still wasn't long after dawn and the calm waters were now bathed in early morning sunshine. An array of looming temples and shrines lined one side of the river whilst the other remained strangely barren with virtually no buildings at all. I wanted to ask the boatman why this was, but feeling a bit inhibited with the pesky little kid on board, I kept quiet. After fifteen minutes, the boatman turned around and headed back down the river. When we reached the steps, the boy, holding out his hand again, asked for twenty rupees.

'No way,' I said again, with another shake of the head. 'We agreed twenty rupees for an hour. That was only half an hour so I'll pay ten.'

The placid boatman, who up until now had remained silent, finally intervened, indicating with his fingers that the boy had told him thirty rupees.

'Okay, how about we go back out this way,' I suggested, pointing downriver.

With that, the boy jumped off and the boatman started rowing again. This time, the trip was much more enjoyable and relaxing. Even the boatman seemed somewhat relieved. His English, however, was as limited as mine of Hindi, so I was unable to ask him about the various temples and we continued to sit there in silence, smiling and nodding at each other. On the way back, though, he did point to one of the temples on the shore which, after consulting my guidebook, I took to be one of the infamous burning ghats where dead bodies were ceremoniously burnt. As it happened, the steps were empty which might not have been such a bad thing. Back on the shore, I nodded my thanks to the boatman and happily paid him his thirty rupees.

Sitting on my bed later in the morning, I spent a couple of hours revising my travel plans for the next few weeks. I struck Jaipur off my itinerary and decided that I'd try to get to Jaisalmer come what may. Hari had warned me back in Kathmandu how hot and unbearable Varanasi would be, although it was nowhere near as uncomfortable as I'd been expecting, so I decided I'd been worrying too much about the heat. Without further haste, I took a rickshaw straight to the train station and made a surprisingly straightforward reservation to Delhi for Saturday. On the way back to my guesthouse, though, I got lost. I'd already struggled to find my way back to my accommodation the previous evening after I'd gone out for some food, and although my sense of direction is normally very good, the old town of Varanasi, a complex labyrinth of never-ending back streets and winding narrow alleyways that all looked the same, appeared to be a law unto itself. There also happened to be more cows present here than any other city I'd visited. All across the streets they idly lay, front legs tucked under their bodies casually watching with their big fond eyes the world pass them by. Not that they had too much choice, for these poor creatures hadn't got a hope in hell of finding their way out and had clearly resigned themselves to spending their lives trapped in a perpetual cocoon.

Back in China, I described how people can react when faced with something that's claimed to be notorious. On that occasion, my curiosity had gotten the better of me, and I'd been fully prepared to suffer the consequences of seeing animals locked in cages and dogs being butchered in front of my very eyes. Sat on my bed again later that afternoon, I found myself toying with the idea of wandering down to one of the burning ghats. This time, however, I wasn't so sure. Many travellers had told me if I visit Varanasi, I must go to see one of the burning ghats, though the thought of intruding on what was, after all, a very private ceremony, was one that turned me cold. But then again, when, as they say, in Rome... My heart and my head, it seemed, were still in conflict. An hour later, I tentatively, almost reluctantly, made my way down to the Manikarnika Ghat but halfway there, stopped in my tracks. What was I doing? If a foreign tourist turned up uninvited at one of my relative's funeral, I'd be bloody livid. How could I be even contemplating being so insensitive? And with that, I turned around and marched straight back up the street, this time fully content in the knowledge I'd buried my head in the sand.

With my stomach still playing up, I returned to a Chinese

restaurant I'd visited the previous evening, and as I was eating, overheard an Australian couple chatting on a nearby table. Spotting the *Lonely Planet* guide on my table, the girl quickly got to her feet and came striding over.

'Mind if I have a quick look?

'No worries,' I instinctively replied. A few minutes later, she came back over with her partner to return the book and introducing themselves as Fiona and Darren, they pulled up a couple of seats and we got chatting.

'Have you been to see the burning ghats yet?' said Fiona, after we'd recounted many of the places we'd visited.

I shook my head. 'Funnily enough I was gonna go this morning, but...'

'We went yesterday,'

I quickly sat up. 'Did you? I nearly went earlier on. So what was it like?'

'Well, we couldn't see much but I felt really uncomfortable.

'What, you mean seeing the body being burnt?'

'No, not so much that, it was the men.'

'How do you mean?'

'They were all staring at her,' said Darren, interrupting. 'Even I found it a bit unnerving.'

'We've got a *Lonely Planet*,' continued Fiona, 'but it's an earlier edition, so we were wondering if there'd been some update about women being prohibited from watching the ceremonies.'

'But there's nothing in there?' I asked.

'No,' replied Fiona. 'But jeez, it still gives me the creeps just thinking about it.'

I woke up again at five the next morning, made my way straight back down to the ghats and took a boat up the river with exactly the same boatman. People often say this is such a typically British trait, although I'm not entirely sure this is the case. Personally, I think it all boils down to personality and while some adopt the 'grass is always greener' approach, I (if you haven't already guessed) am more of the 'if it ain't broke, don't fix it' variety.

Besides, the boatman was such a calm and unassuming man, which was more than could be said for many of his more overly pushy counterparts. Anyway, this time we headed further downstream where the activities were no less frenetic. The washerwomen continued to thrash their laundry against the steps, bathers still splashed about in the water, the beggars were out in abundance, tourists sat on the ghats shielding themselves from the sun with umbrellas, whilst the ever-industrious chai sellers ran up and down the steps collecting glasses. Indeed, so fervent were the sounds of frolicking and splashing coming from the water that if I closed my eyes for a few seconds, I could have easily been mistaken for thinking I was at the seaside.

Late afternoon, back on the steps, I noticed a middle-aged Israeli guy remonstrating with the same pesky little kid from the previous day over the price of the trip he'd just been on. The boy was trying to get the man to pay him more, but the Israeli was having none of it. Eventually conceding defeat, the boy sauntered off and the Israeli, spotting me looking on, came over and promptly launched into a ranting tirade about all the beggars, touts and boatmen trying to rip off tourists. As he was babbling, I spotted in the distance something splashing about in the river. I'd seen the same thing on the boat trip earlier that morning when I'd been momentarily startled by something that had jumped out of the water just a few yards in front of us. At first, I'd thought it might have been the remains of a cremated body floating to the surface, but a couple of seconds later, there'd been another splash. I'd asked my man what it was and he'd indicated it was a fish. Well if it was a fish, it was a bloody big one! Pointing out to the river now, I asked the Israeli if he knew what it was.

'I think you'll find that's a dolphin,' he replied.

'A dolphin?' I exclaimed. 'You've got to be joking?'

'It is, I swear.'

'A dolphin?' I said again. 'Are you sure?'

'I tell you, it's true. Varanasi actually happens to be only one of three inland places in the world where dolphins can be found.'

For a few seconds, I was floored. Why in heaven's name these supposedly highly intelligent creatures should choose the filthy stinking waters of the Ganges as one of them was something that remained quite beyond me.

I couldn't find my boatman the next morning. For over an hour, I sat on the steps peering down at the boats each time they returned, searching in vain for his face. My other friend, the annoying little kid did, however, spot me and came charging up the steps. Before he said anything, I told him I didn't need a boat and that I'd happily wait for my man to show up. Surprisingly, he sat down quietly next to me, rubbing his eyes and yawning. A few minutes later, he still hadn't uttered a word and as he crouched over his knees, carefully checking his hair for nits, I began to wonder if I'd been a bit too harsh on him. Feeling a little guilty, I eventually asked him if he wanted a cup of chai, the sweet tasting spiced tea that I'd really taken to in the last three or four days. He nodded sombrely so I wandered over to one of the chai vendors and returned a minute or so later with a couple of half-full glass cups.

'You know James Bond?' he asked some minutes later.

'James Bond?'

'He came to Varanasi a few years ago,'

'Oh, you mean Sean Connery?'

He nodded again. 'He came out on my boat.'

'So, what was he like?'

For a few seconds he just sat there staring out towards the river and smiling. Once he'd finished his drink, I asked him about the argument he'd had with the Israeli man the day before. He muttered something and sleepily shook his head. Israelis, it seemed, were not his favourite customers.

Back in my room later, after reading up on Rajasthan for a while, I caught up on some letter writing. The beginning of the latest aerogramme to my parents perfectly encapsulated the profound effect the city of Varanasi was having on me:

Like Calcutta and Nepal, I'll be leaving Varanasi tomorrow with very fond memories. The incredible frenzy of activity on the ghats leading down to the river every sunrise and sunset, the number of boats laden with tourists that ply the river every hour of the day, the hundreds of Indians bathing and swimming in the filthy waters, the amazing sight of dolphins diving about in the same waters, the daily early evening power cuts, the masses of cows that inhabit the cobbled pavements of the long and winding alleyways of the old city and the cow dung that every day without fail, I manage to tread in on the way back from the Chinese restaurant I frequent. It really is such a wonderful place. I have never seen so many people celebrate religion with so much fervour and rejoicement and for once, all the religions are worshipped in harmony side by side. Each morning, I get up at 5am and for a few hours, just sit and watch from the steps just trying to take it all in.

There's been a marked increase in temperatures since I left Nepal, and I've noticed that my daily intake of fluids has risen dramatically. Yesterday, I got through no less than nine 1000ml bottles of mineral water and at 35p a bottle, this is no laughing matter. A quick calculation tells me that if I continue drinking water at that rate, I'll end up having to pay over £90 for water alone between now and 24 May. Maybe I should try to bring my flight forward by another couple of weeks!

A few days in Varanasi had mellowed my mood. In fact, I couldn't have felt more at peace with the world. Returning to the ghats again late afternoon, I was joined on the steps by a toothless old Sadhu. Dressed in a vest and long raincoat, with rubber gloves on his hands, he carried a stick. His hair was matted, he had a long white beard and he smelt of damp, but he was a chirpy and chatty fellow and he'd soon talked me into helping his cause. Up until then, with the possible exception of Calcutta, I had resolutely refused to donate to beggars and the like, so when he asked me for money, I shook my head. A couple of minutes later, though, I asked him what he wanted the money for. He told me food.

I asked him what kind of food.

'Rice or dhal,' he replied.

'Okay,' I said, 'I'm not gonna give you any money but I'll certainly buy you some food.'

'You will?'

'Sure, why not.'

He led me through the back streets and five minutes later, emerged from a shop holding a kilo bag of rice and lentils with a big beaming smile across his face. This set me back 26 rupees (75 pence) which was quite a lot of money by local standards, but my conscience had been eased somewhat. For the first time since I'd been in India, I felt I'd actually given something back.

Wandering back down to the ghats for the last time the following morning, I sat on the steps for a while watching one of the chai vendors walking around collecting empty glasses. When he spotted a couple of Indians urinating by the side of a temple, he marched over, gave them a good ticking off, and then shooed them away. It was funny, because he bore an uncanny resemblance to a cockney barman who'd been working on Magnetic Island last Christmas. It seemed that I was increasingly meeting people on this trip who possessed remarkably similar features and characteristics of other people I knew. What I found strange about this phenomenon, and it had happened an awful lot in China as well, was how people of completely different races could look so similar to particular friends and relations back home, in spite of all the obvious differences in the respective facial traits. This discovery was especially pleasing as it effectively meant that somewhere in the world there would be a Billy Connolly double, a Tom Selleck look-alike and a Kylie Minogue clone, three of my most celebrated idols. And indeed, in just a couple of weeks' time, I'd discover that Robin Williams had a bus-driving twin who lived in Bombay.

After returning to my Chinese haunt for a final breakfast, I was quietly reading up on Delhi when I was joined again by Darren and Fiona. The last time we'd met, they'd been telling me about their tentative plans to buy some Indian clothes to try to sell back home, although I have to admit, I'd suspected it was nothing more than a spur of the moment whim. But much to my surprise, it looked like they'd now finally taken the plunge. They told me that they'd spent all the previous day making their first purchase of 160 lunghis—the Indian version of a sarong—and by all accounts, it sounded like bloody hard work. They had started at 9am and spent the whole day walking around comparing quality, designs and prices. It was gone 10pm when they'd finally emerged with their newly acquired merchandise and later that morning, they had the thankless task of traipsing up to the post office to try to send them all back to Australia. Shaking their hands, I wished them good luck, thinking to myself that they were really going to need it, and then set off for the station to catch my train to Delhi.

CHAPTER 33
DELHI
JUST GOTTA GET OUT OF THIS PLACE
28th–30th April 1991

My preconceptions of New Delhi were that it was a dull, drab, sterile place. These were largely borne out of the fact that not a single person I knew who'd been to India's capital had had a particularly good word to say about it. So, for the first time in India, and perhaps even on my travels, I found myself heading to a place I wasn't specially looking forward to visiting. This was not to say such a preconceived notion would actually be corroborated — Fiji was probably the most notable example of a place that had turned out to be significantly different to how I'd imagined — but even though I'd been trying to keep an open mind, the signs weren't good. When Gibbo, Caroline and Pat had fallen ill during their travels, it was in New Delhi, so their abiding memories of the city were understandably tarnished, and more recently, Gary described it as... Well, it's probably best not to say how he described it, but the following story he recounted after his troublesome journey to India will give you a clearer idea of just what he'd thought about the place.

To put the story in full perspective, I need to tell you a bit about Gary. Gary was a work colleague from my banking days who, when I was promoted to supervisor, was assigned to work on my department. He was a cheery little fellow, slightly pompous perhaps, but always up for a laugh, and given that he was in his late twenties and still living at home, I likened him to the Timothy Lumsden character played by Ronnie Corbett in the BBC sitcom *Sorry*. (Much, I hasten to add, in the same way an erstwhile colleague gratuitously afforded me the nickname 'Jimothy Tiddler' many years later.) He also happened to wear the same dufflecoat and thinking about it, he wore glasses too but now I'm digressing again. To work with, Gary was a complete nightmare because he was a terrible shirker and I'd often find piles of uncompleted documents sitting at the bottom of his drawers long after he'd gone home, even though he'd sworn blind during the day that the same papers had been completed. Socially, though, he was great company and we spent many a memorable Friday night sitting in the work bar at the end of the week, discussing office politics and getting progressively sloshed. So it came as something of a surprise when, on one such night, he casually informed me he wouldn't be around for a few weeks.

'That's strange,' he frowned, rocking back and forth on his barstool. 'I'm sure I told you I was going away next month.'

'Nope,' I replied, shaking my head, 'you definitely didn't. Holiday?'

'Yep, how d'you guess?'

'So, where're you going?'

'I'm off to India.'

Hearing him utter these immortal words, I nearly choked on my beer.

'India? You're going to India? Are you mad? Do you know what you're letting yourself in for?'

'Oh, don't worry, it'll be a doddle,' he said, nonchalantly

waving his hand across his face.

Although he went on to tell me he was travelling on an organised tour, I was still shocked and waited with great interest to hear how he'd fared upon his return.

When he got back to work the following month, he spent the whole of his first week slagging off just about every aspect there is of Indian life to everybody who enquired how his holiday had gone, so as the week wore on, I was looking forward with increasing anticipation to our regular Friday sojourn when I could hear the full unabridged version of his trip up in the bar. Predictably, when the night arrived, he launched into another scathing verbal attack on the subcontinent. This was hardly surprising, as I knew from previous accounts from people who'd been to India that Gary would be totally unprepared for the culture shock. But this one particular story he recounted left me in hysterics.

'Every morning,' he told me, 'I'd leave the hotel and each time I stepped onto the street, I'd look down and there be a piece of shit on my shoes. It was bizarre. I didn't know where the hell it was coming from, I didn't know how the hell it was getting there, but I swear, every morning without fail, I'd look down and there'd be this bloody crap on my shoes. And do you know, it took me four days before I realised what was happening and when I did, I couldn't believe it.'

'Go on,' I said, twirling an outstretched hand.

'Well, standing over the other side of the road was the very same small kid who unfailingly came bounding up every morning to clean off all the crap for a few rupees, and it was this little shit who was catapulting the muck onto my shoes in the first place. I tell you, if I'd managed to get my hands on him, I would have throttled him, the little bugger. Can you believe it!' he chortled. 'Typical bloody India.'

Rather ominously for me, this classic story had also happened to take place in Delhi, so by mentally preparing myself *not* to enjoy the couple of days I planned to spend there, I figured it would be virtually impossible to be unduly disappointed by Delhi accordingly.

The overnight journey from Varanasi passed relatively peacefully and the train pulled into New Delhi station right on time at 5.45am. After booking into a cheap hotel in the Paharganj district, close to the station, I called in at a local restaurant and, over an early morning bowl of porridge, decided to celebrate my birthday the next day by taking a day trip out to Agra to see the Taj Mahal. So a short while later, upon returning to the station, I headed straight for the special foreign tourist booking office, described as 'a calm, quiet and efficient place to buy tickets and make 1st and 2nd class reservations in one go.' What the guidebook failed to mention, however, was that the office was closed on a Sunday. Although the normal booking office was located just a little further down the station, it was, when I got there, hopelessly overcrowded. And to make matters worse, the Indian Railway authorities had decided — presumably in an attempt to make the reservation system more orderly — to adopt one of those highly annoying booking systems where you take a docket on arrival and then sit in your seat waiting for your designated number to be called. So you can imagine my indignation when, after picking up a sticker marked 87, I quickly glanced up at the screen and saw they were still only on 23. Fifty benumbing minutes later, I finally made it to the counter, duly made the reservation and then emerging into dazzling sunlight, wandered along in the sweltering heat of the morning to Connaught Place, Delhi's main shopping district.

Characterised by three concentric circular streets, the inner of which surrounded a small park and fountain, the crescents and long avenues that bisected Connaught Place were occupied by a plethora of hotels, shops, airline offices and fast food restaurants. On first sight, it reminded me a little of the area around Piccadilly Circus and Regent Street. Many families were out strolling around the streets and the atmosphere felt relaxed and informal, and very Sunday. Spotting a Wimpy joint on the other side of one of the crescents, my eyes lit up and I made an immediate beeline towards it, drooling over the thought of burger and chips, but when I approached, my relaxed frame of mind was replaced with a certain feeling of unease, as housed right next to the restaurant was the Iraqi Airlines office. Given the current tensions that still existed after the Gulf conflict and the recent spate of bombings here in the capital, I hastily decided to opt for a takeout and as soon as the food arrived, quickly retreated to the park to wolf down my meal.

Almost begrudgingly, I then took a taxi to the old part of Delhi to indulge in a spot of sightseeing. Ten minutes later, though, casting my eyes on the city's two main tourist attractions, the Red Fort and the Jami Masjid, the largest Mosque in India, I realised that I simply didn't have the inclination to go in and explore them. As I'd previously suspected, 'templeitis' had by now well and truly set in, so I decided to cut my losses and head back to my hotel instead. I made this hour-long journey on foot in the searing heat of the afternoon, passing through bustling back streets and alleyways and stopping every ten minutes or so for a bottle of Pepsi or Gold Spot (Fanta). It was on one of these refreshment breaks that I found myself being kept waiting for what seemed like an age. I had, as I said, already stopped a few times at a succession of roadside kiosks and, on each occasion, I'd paid for a drink, drunk it on the spot and quickly moved on. This particular stall, however, doubled up as a small restaurant, so whilst the Indian kid who'd served me went around collecting plates, I stood at the bar for ten minutes mopping my brow and impatiently drumming my fingers on the counter, waiting to pay. When he eventually returned, I handed him a five-rupee note, expecting to receive back 50 or 75 paise in change. After studying the note for a few seconds, he thrust out an open hand and seeing me frowning, held up all his fingers.

'Naaaaah,' I remonstrated. 'Five rupees, that's what I've been paying.'

Much to my dismay, he just held his fingers up again.

'Look,' I said, raising my voice, 'I've stopped four times already and...' but it was no use. My protests were seemingly falling on deaf ears for the kid just stood there shaking his head. 'Shit,' I muttered, rubbing my brow. I really wasn't in the mood for this, especially in this heat. Looking around, I wondered if the prices of drinks could, perhaps, have been a little more. It was, after all, a restaurant. Reaching into my money belt, I fished out a 50 paise coin and grudgingly handed it over, but this only served for the kid to launch into a lengthy and unintelligible tirade. By now I was really beginning to get irate, especially when hearing the commotion, a number of onlookers gathered around. Travelling alone, this kind of thing can be very intimidating because as a foreigner, you're instantly made to feel like an outsider who's committed some kind of hideous crime against one of their fellow citizens. Finding myself surrounded by faces staring intently at me as if I was a crazed, axe-wielding lunatic was something that had already happened to me a number of times on my travels, notably in China and, without fail, it had always been a very unnerving experience. But when a couple of young blokes pulled up on a motorbike, and one of them informed me, after speaking to the kid, that I should be paying for two drinks, I went berserk.

'Two! Why two?' I hollered. 'I had one drink, not two! Tell him I only had one!'

He translated this to the kid. 'He says you had two drinks,' came the reply.

'No way!' I bellowed, 'No fuckin' way!' If I'd been sitting at one of the tables for fifteen minutes, I could have begun to understand such a mistake, but I'd come in, asked for a bottle of Gold Spot, or whatever the bloody stupid drink was called, drank it on the spot and then waited to pay. The little shit of a kid was blatantly trying to rip me off and I was having none of it. If this was what he was accusing me of, then he could...

'Look,' I yelled at the kid, looking him square in the eye and jabbing a pointed finger in his direction as I did. 'I had one drink and one drink only which I've already paid for. End of bloody story!' And with that, I picked up my bag and boldly pushed my way through the gathering crowd, swearing and spitting at the ground, (which I only do when I'm really livid) totally unconcerned about the ensuing furore I was leaving behind. Indeed, as I continued to march up the street, I was so incensed, I even contemplated going back to demand my 50 paise change.

A few minutes later, still frothing at the mouth, I spotted a silver wholesaler's sign above a shop. With my curiosity eventually getting the better of me, I decided to go in and have a mooch around to see what kind of jewellery they stocked. As I was about to enter, two men followed me up the steps. Instinctively, I put one hand across the pocket of my daypack and as I did, found another hand there. In a flash, I swung round. One of the men raised his hand apologetically and indicated that he'd tripped into me up the steps. The gesture, though, was far from convincing. Inside the shop, I glared at the two men. They stood there for a couple of minutes, furtively examining a tray of rings, although I was sure it was only a charade. But what could I do? I was sure one of them had definitely tried to reach into my bag. Confronting them, however, was probably not a wise move. Pushing open the door, I quickly made my way back down the steps and scurried off down the main street, peering back over my shoulder at regular intervals to make sure I wasn't being followed. After the last half-hour, just getting back to my hotel in one piece was a huge relief and I spent the rest of the day in the confines of my room. Delhi! I needed to get out of this place as soon as possible.

Sitting opposite me on the Taj Express to Agra were a mother and her two children. The daughter was quiet and well-behaved, but her brother, in contrast, was a hyperactive nightmare. He leapt about in the carriage for the duration of the three-hour journey, repeatedly treading on my feet and diving over my lap. When he inadvertently kicked my bag on the floor, I tutted out loud, but his mother just looked away, seemingly untroubled by his unruly behaviour. When his sister tried to calm him down by reading him a story, he continued to fidget incessantly in his seat opposite me. And when he began to flagrantly pick his nose in front of me, I stared back at him wide-eyed. This seemed to only encourage him to do it even more and, to make matters worse, it seemed as if he was deriving inane pleasure from my obvious discomfort. He was, without doubt, one of the most irritating specimens of children I've ever come across although later in the morning, I got my chance to exact a little revenge. Because they'd been swapping seats at regular intervals, I returned from a visit to the toilet to notice that the kid was now sitting in the seat next to me. With his mother dozing, I planted myself back down next to him, squashing the boy into the corner, and each time he started to fidget, I quickly dug my elbow into his ribs. It seemed to do the trick for he eventually nodded off and as he slept for over an hour with his head leant against my arm, I began to think that perhaps he wasn't such a bad kid. It was only later, when I got out onto the platform at Agra, that I noticed he'd left a long trail of dribble down the side of my T-shirt. The little shit had seemingly got the last laugh after all.

A number of fellow travellers had warned me about the 'aggro of Agra'. I gathered it had a notoriously bad reputation, a place where tourists and travellers alike could expect to be constantly hassled by touts, hawkers and rickshaw drivers alike. So when, towards the end of the three-hour journey, a guard came into our compartment selling tickets for an all-inclusive day trip to the Taj and accompanying attractions around Agra, I didn't hesitate in reaching for my money belt. Battling my way through the scores of peddlers that came running up as soon as I got off the train, I set off in search of my allocated bus for the start of the tour. Our first stop, an hour or so's drive out of Agra, was the deserted city of Fatehpur Sikri. The story had it that the Emperor Akbar had transferred his capital here after meeting a Sufi saint nearby who had foretold him about the imminent birth of his son. Under the Emperor's command, work had begun on the construction of a dramatic new city in 1569 and for the next fifteen years, Fatehpur Sikri became the capital of the Moghul Empire. But partly due to a problem with the city's water supply, it was suddenly abandoned in 1584 and the Moghuls moved their capital to nearby Agra. It was now a vast complex of surprisingly well-preserved palaces, mosques, tombs and gardens, yet walking around in a perpetual daze, I struggled to take it all in. Just like the visit to Ming Tombs before the Great Wall, it seemed this was just the pre-cursor to the main event, and the suspense of waiting to finally cast my eyes on the Taj Mahal lingered throughout the morning.

After stopping for lunch, our bus, passing hundreds of other empty coaches in the adjoining car parks, pulled up outside the Taj just after 3pm, not that we could actually see it, because the entrance was through a turnstile gate set into a high surrounding wall. We were told that we would be spending just over an hour here, which, for one of the sights of the world, hardly seemed long enough so, following my fellow passengers, I eagerly rushed off the bus to join the lengthy queues of Indian tourists. Once inside, I got my all-important first glimpse of the monument and my reaction was somewhat perplexing. I suppose I'd been expecting that it would stop me in my tracks and take my breath away but it didn't. At first, I thought this was because it looked exactly as I had imagined. Perhaps a little smaller maybe but almost exactly as I'd imagined. This was not to detract from its obvious beauty, for the white-marbled building was incredibly soothing on the eye, especially in the heat of the afternoon, and its perfect symmetry struck a bewitching chord. After a while, though, I began to realise that it wasn't just this. No, I'm afraid to say that when it came to the iconic sights of the world, I'd simply become rather blasé. I'd already been fortunate enough to cast my eyes on the Great Wall of China, the Hong Kong skyline, Ayers Rock, the Sydney Harbour Bridge and Opera House and, more recently, Mount Everest, and so by the time I'd passed through the turnstile gates, it felt as if I was ticking off another place on a treasure hunt. Maybe this was what travelling for so long does to people. This rather hollow feeling, however, was soon to be replaced with one of total and utter wonder for as we wandered around the grounds, the full story behind this extravagant monument to love, the most famous of all India's buildings, was told to us by our guide. And it truly was a heart-breaking tale.

It began in 1592 with the birth of Prince Khurram, the third son of the fourth Great Moghul leader, Emperor Jahangir. The young prince, who without doubt quickly became his father's favourite, first set eyes on Arjumand Banu—the girl who would later turn out to be the true love of his life—at the Meena Bazaar. The Bazaar, introduced by his great grandfather, was an annual event held at court where the emperor and his entourage of fawning courtiers could indulge themselves by wandering around and audaciously flirting with the haggling ladies and wives of nobles who stood behind the stalls. The prince, by all accounts, a handsome young man himself approached her stand. She was fourteen, he fifteen. Drawn to her stunning beauty, he pointed to a piece of glass and asked her its worth. 'It is a diamond, not glass,' she was reported to have replied and boldly added 'and its value is ten thousand rupees, a sum that not even you could afford.' The prince picked up the piece of glass, duly paid her the sum asked and walked away. Completely awestruck, he presented his case the very next day before the emperor seeking Arjumand's hand in marriage. His father granted him permission but then rather bizarrely, the prince promptly married a Persian princess by the name of Quandari Begum instead. Most historians agree the reasons for the hastily arranged ceremony were largely political but what exactly caused this marriage to end after only five years and, indeed, what became of the princess after are far from clear, although rather pertinently, perhaps, she bore him no children during this period.

In 1612, however, the prince was finally united with his beloved Arjumand in a grand wedding celebrated with nobles, musicians, dancers and priests. Over the next few years, he was sent by his father to other parts of the surrounding country where he embarked on a series of missions to further secure the Moghul frontiers. His early campaigns, generally secured more through diplomacy than epic sieges, brought him spectacular success and in his father's eyes, he could simply do no wrong. The emperor announced that from now on, the prince would be known as Shah Jahan, 'King of the World.' Arjumand remained inseparable from her husband, accompanying him on all of these journeys and military campaigns, and became his true soul mate. She was said to be a compassionate and generous woman who actively encouraged the prince to help the weak and needy and stories of her virtue quickly spread across the empire. The prince's successes in the field continued although many of these were still hollow victories where the enemy was not actually defeated but merely contained. Meanwhile, back in Agra, his father's health was quickly deteriorating, not helped by his joint addiction to alcohol and opium, and news was reaching the prince from back home that his mother, Nur Juhan, was beginning to favour Sheriyar, one of his brothers, to succeed the emperor when he died. In 1622, with Persia's great Shah Abbas advancing on the strategically important city of Kandahar, the ailing emperor assembled a huge army to prevent the city from being taken and ordered the prince to rush west from the Deccan with his troops to help in the battle. Wanting to be sure that he would have sufficient strength to march for the throne if his father perished, the prince replied by stating that he would only return if he were given sole command of the army. This was seen as confirmation that the prince was in rebellion and when it was learnt that he was heading towards Agra, his father redeployed his troops to confront him accordingly. The prince fled and for nearly three years, the imperial forces pursued him all around the country. Still accompanied by Arjumand and their children, he continually managed to stay one step ahead and evade their clutches. Eventually, though, the prince, tired of being on the run, sought reconciliation with his father, and whilst not exactly welcomed back with loving arms, he escaped punishment for his actions. His two young sons, however, were placed under the permanent care of his mother, Nur Juhan, as a means to keep any more rebellious ideas he may have had firmly at bay.

Two years later, the emperor finally died. When the prince learnt of the news he headed straight to Agra, sending out orders for his brother, Sheriyar, to be killed and these were duly carried out. In January 1628, reunited with his two sons, the prince was coronated and he declared that from now on, his beloved Arjumand would be known as Mumtaz Mahal, 'Chosen One of the Palace.' By now, she had borne him thirteen children, although seven of these had died in infancy. Just two years later, though, in 1631, tragedy struck when Arjumand, shortly after giving birth to her fourteenth child, a healthy baby girl, died. According to one account, the empress had had a premonition of her death a few months earlier when she'd heard the unborn child cry out from her womb. 'When a child dies before its birth,' she told the emperor, 'the mother always dies; therefore I must prepare to take leave of this world.' And so one of her last wishes was for Shah Jahan to build her a monument that would symbolise the beauty of their love. After her death, the new emperor was inconsolable. For a week, he remained locked behind closed doors refusing to eat. When he finally emerged, it is said that his black beard had turned white, his back was bent and his face was worn with despair. The court was ordered into mourning for a period of almost two years, although work on the construction of the Taj Mahal commenced in early 1632 on the banks of the River Yamuna in Agra. How long it finally took to complete is another mooted point. Some say it was finished in 1648, others say 1953, but whatever the date, the sheer scale of work involved was astounding.

Along with the masses of labourers flocking to Agra once news of its inception spread, materials for the construction had also began arriving: red sandstone from local quarries in Fatehpur Sikri and marble dug from the hills of far-off Makrana in Rajasthan. In order to transport the marble, a ten-mile long ramp of tampered earth was built through Agra on which an unending parade of a thousand elephants and bullock carts continually dragged the blocks of marble to the building site. Meanwhile, caravans were despatched to all corners of the empire and beyond to bring back the precious stones—jade, turquoise, amber, sapphire, lapis lazuli and chrysolite—required for the intricate inlay work known as *Pietra Dura*. A project as ambitious as this also demanded talent from many quarters. As well as the many master craftsmen from neighbouring states, renowned experts in their respective fields were also brought in: sculptors, lapidaries, calligraphers, stonecutters, a man who specialised in building turrets as well as another who carved only marble flowers. To this core was added a labour force of twenty thousand workers recruited from across North India, all housed in a makeshift village hastily erected next to the site.

The first buildings constructed were the tomb proper and the two identical mosques that flank it, followed by the four minarets, the gateway and, last of all, the auxiliary buildings. It was instantly acknowledged as a masterpiece and its unsurpassed beauty would go on to astound the world for centuries to come. But although the emperor finally got his wish, there was to be one final and cruel twist of fate. In 1658, he was deposed by his son, Aurangzeb, by now a recurring theme of the Moghuls, and was forced to spend the last eight years of his life imprisoned in a section of Agra's Red Fort. It was his eldest daughter, Jahanara, who cared for him in this time, much of which he spent studying the Koran and staring out for hours on end at the view he had from his window of the Taj Mahal along the river. He died peacefully in January 1666 and the very next morning, his body was taken by water to the marble mausoleum where he was buried beside his wife. It was, as I say, a truly heart-breaking tale, and just why no Hollywood producer has ever seized on the opportunity to make the story into a blockbuster movie still, to this day, remains a complete mystery to me.

The Taj Express back to Delhi was due to leave at 6.30, but didn't pull into the station until an hour later. When it did, I found an elderly man occupying my reserved seat. Thoroughly exhausted after a particularly long and trying day (all the Agra scaremongers had been dead right in their assertions), I was not in charitable mood, so I asked him to produce his ticket with the seat number on it. He couldn't, so I told the man the seat was mine. I had booked it, I had paid for it, he hadn't and it was as simple as that. As the old man reluctantly got up and left the carriage, two men sitting opposite me glared at me disdainfully.

Although I'd barely picked up a word of Hindi in the time I'd been in India, it didn't take long to realise that their resulting animated and prolonged conversations were over their disapproval over my actions.

'Excuse me,' one of them eventually asked. 'Please can you tell us why you have not booked into first class?'

'Because I'm quite happy here in second class,' I replied rather curtly. In fact, I felt like jumping out of my seat and telling them if they felt so strongly about it, why hadn't they given up one of their seats for the old man in the first place. As they sat there shaking their heads, a young woman came into the carriage with another uncontrollable young child. By a stroke of good fortune, I'd picked up another Maugham book in Delhi, so I quickly reached into my daypack.

The Gentleman in the Parlour, an account of a journey made by Maugham in the late 1920s from Rangoon to Haiphong, was one of the author's best works. One of the stories, and a compelling one at that, concerned a chance meeting he made towards the end his travels with a character called Grosely, an old fellow student from medical college. Grosely had spent over twenty-five years working in China as tide-waiter—a sort of official employed by the Chinese customs whose duty it was to board vessels at various ports in an effort to clamp down on opium smuggling. In his time there, he'd made a small fortune by investing in curios, often given or sold to him at cheap prices by the Chinese, which he would go on to sell for handsome profits. As soon as he'd amassed enough money, he was able to fulfil his only true ambition to return to England and live a rich and comfortable life. When he arrived back in London, though, things were different than he'd remembered and he soon longed to be back in China. He booked a passage back to Shanghai but on the last two-night stopover in Haiphong, he told his rickshaw boy that he wanted a woman. The boy took him to a tenement where he found an old woman and a girl. The old woman asked him if he wanted to smoke and Grosely, never having tried it before, was introduced to opium. It made him restful and thoughtful. Maugham was clearly intrigued by his story. Later that day, Grosely invited him back to his place. It was the very same tenement, and there he found the old woman and the girl, who was now the mother of Grosely's child. Maugham reckoned that after England, Grosely, at the very last moment, had suddenly become afraid to return to China, fearing another disappointment and so had remained in Haiphong where he'd finally found contentment. I now only had four weeks left before I returned to the UK myself, and when I finished reading this story, I couldn't help thinking about it, wondering if, when I arrived back, I'd suddenly want to head off again like Grosely had.

Before I left the capital later the next day, I was hoping to make an advance train reservation from Delhi to Bombay for when I returned from Rajasthan. It was supposed to be one of the busiest routes in India so I wanted to be sure of both confirming a seat and paying for the ticket before I departed. Returning to the much-vaunted special foreign tourist booking office the following lunchtime, I discovered, to my dismay, that payment was only accepted in US dollars. Because I'd changed my last one hundred dollar note literally just a few hours earlier, I no longer had enough in dollars to pay, so cursing to myself, I made my way again back to the main booking office where I had to wait a full two hours before I could get even get to the counter. When my allotted number finally appeared on the screen, I trudged up to the glass window and told the man I wanted to book a ticket on the Delhi to Bombay Express. The man calculated the fare in dollars.

'No, no, I'll be paying in rupees,' I said.

'No, sir, payment on this service can only be made in foreign currency.'

'But I want to pay in rupees.'

'No, sir, the train is fully booked. Unless you pay in foreign currency, you must join the waiting list.'

'You've got to be joking!' I cried, taking two steps back.

'No, sir, this is no joke.'

'I don't believe this,' I said, pacing up and down like a caged animal.

'This train, very busy train, sir.'
'So, how many people are on the waiting list?'
'Ninety-nine.'

I was so outraged I was speechless. Abruptly turning around, I marched out, effing and blinding, barging into people that happened to cross my path. Outside the station, I screwed up several pieces of paper from my guidebook and threw them high into the air. Then, after five minutes of reflection, I solemnly vowed never to return to Delhi again and set about trying to work out if I could get down to Bombay via Rajasthan and Gujarat. Earlier that morning, I was beginning to think that maybe I had judged the city of Delhi and its people too harshly, but now, I'd never return to Delhi, my bogey city of India.

CHAPTER 34

JAISALMER

DESERT DELIGHT

1st–5th May 1991

Dear All,

India continues to astound. Just when I think I've seen all that can be seen of the country, I come across another place that defies all similarities to any other previously visited. Each new place seems to invariably possess a character, atmosphere and appearance unique to itself and will also be inhabited by a brand of people that again differ from all others I've come across in terms of dress, culture and looks. This time, the place in question is Jaisalmer, right on the Pakistan border and my guidebook is spot on with its description of the city. 'This desert fortress is straight out of *The Tales of the Arabian Nights* and you could easily be forgiven for imagining that you'd somehow been transported back to medieval

Afghanistan. Exotic, remote and beautiful—Jaisalmer.'
    The fortress is indeed imposing and spectacular, situated on top of a hill and commanding fantastic views of the surrounding desert. And the local people are immaculately dressed, men with twirly moustaches in turbans, baggy trousers and pointed slippers and women in either brightly coloured or dark saris and veils covering their faces, while hundreds of camels replace the cows that are so commonly found idly wandering the streets of other Indian cities.
    Today I head off on a three-day jeep and camel safari into the desert...

This was the first part of the latest postcard I wrote to my parents on top of the fort overlooking the city, from where the views of the hundreds of sandstone houses below were, indeed, impressive: a vast sea of beige that blended into an equally beige sky, completely obscuring the horizon. I had arrived in Jaisalmer late the previous night, suitably pleased by my first impressions of the city.

Early afternoon, my mood had changed. I was stood outside the guesthouse I'd booked into, staring down at the cobbled pavement and shaking my head. Standing alongside me was a lean, young, po-faced Frenchman who, smartly dressed in designer hiking gear, happened to be staying in the same establishment. We were just about to embark on a three-day camel trek into the Thar Desert, and we'd been waiting in stony silence for over twenty minutes for our driver to show up. As the minutes continued to tick by, I couldn't help wondering what had happened to the two other Australian and Japanese travellers I'd been told were coming along with us. Presumably, they hadn't been prepared to move the trip forward a day like we had, so it looked as if the two of us would be heading into the desert alone, which was rather disconcerting. As far as I was concerned, when it came to the size of the party on a trip such as this, it was definitely a case of the more the merrier, and the fact that my travelling companion was standing there with a face as long as a fiddle didn't exactly bode well.

By the time we'd arrived at the edge of the desert a couple of hours later, after being whisked off on a whistle-stop jeep tour around half a dozen local villages, my housemate still hadn't uttered a single word. Having already tried to pull him out of his shell without success, I didn't see the point of voluntarily engaging in conversation with him again, so likewise, I'd kept quiet. Climbing out of the vehicle, our driver informed us that our two Rajput guides would soon be arriving with the camels. With nothing else to do but wait for them to show up, I lay down on one of the rolling soft powdery sand dunes and looked up to the sky in salvation, praying they'd turn up with some more backpackers. Alas, though, it wasn't to be.

After introducing us to Mohan and Haji, our somewhat bemused driver quickly jumped back into his jeep and headed off back to Jaisalmer. He'd probably never been on such a quiet trip before and was probably, by now, feeling as paranoid as myself. Still, our guides were all smiles so maybe there was hope yet. Mohan was unquestionably the more animated of the two. Sporting a long handlebar moustache, he was dressed in a T-shirt, sarong, and a bright purple turban and, with a knowing, almost mischievous twinkle in his eyes, I warmed to him in an instant. By contrast, his clean-shaven companion was lanky and quieter, and given his detached air of nonchalance and somewhat docile manner, I couldn't help but liken him to a Rajput version of Rodney Trotter in *Only Fools and Horses*. Encouraging us to familiarise ourselves with the camels straight away, they quickly hoisted us up onto their backs, and as Mohan began to wrap a piece of cloth around my head to protect me from the sun, I glanced across to the Frenchman and saw the faintest of smiles appear on his face. A few minutes later, Haji led us over some tussocky grass to a nearby clump of thorn bushes and informed us that this was where we'd be spending the night. Jumping down from the camels, we planted ourselves down on the sheltered sand, and as we sat there watching our guides preparing a meal of rice, vegetables, dhal and japattis, my companion finally found his tongue. In broken

English, he introduced himself as Pierre, then apologising for his quietness, tentatively pointed at his stomach. So that was it! The poor sod wasn't well. But why hadn't he told me so earlier? Over food, with the ice now broken, we bombarded our guides with questions: How far would we be travelling over the next couple of days? Would we get sore sitting on the camels for so long? What time would we be setting off in the morning? What happens if we run out of water? How long can the camels go without a drink? So, after eventually discovering we'd be leaving at daybreak to travel twenty to thirty tiresome miles with more than adequate supplies of water on creatures that, if it came to it, could go for days without, the four of us sat around the fire happily chatting in the twilight. Later on, I brought out the Ludo and introduced our guides to the game, which passed another hour or so and then our hosts treated us to some Rajput folk singing. But although it was all quite pleasant and relaxed, I still couldn't help feeling how much more enjoyable the evening could have been with a few more people, especially a couple of girls such as the two particularly dashing brunettes I'd spotted in a Jaisalmer restaurant earlier that morning.

Around nine, Mohan and Haji laid out the mattresses and blew out the fire. Then, after a few more final renditions of some local songs, there was silence. Complete and utter silence. As the others shuffled around in their sleeping bags, I lay there for a while staring up at the stars thinking how romantic this could be if only...and then, eventually reaching for a jumper, bundled it into a ball and tucking it under my head, finally closed my eyes. A couple of hours later, the wind picked up causing me to stir from my slumber. The desert sand was being blown everywhere; it was in my eyes, my ears and up my nose and had somehow found its way into my sleeping bag too. Peering up, I saw that Pierre had wisely covered his head in a shirt. I did likewise and turned over again to try to get back to sleep.

I was woken at daybreak by the movement of Mohan and Haji preparing for the day ahead. After helping them collect some wood for the fire, we sat around for some toast and tea, and then headed off on the camels across the vast sea of sand surrounding us. My camel was called 'Tatoo', and surprisingly, given my notoriously poor record of pony trekking (of three separate outings, I'd been unceremoniously dislodged from my horse on each occasion), I took to riding quite well, which was more than could be said of Pierre who, clutching onto his reins for dear life, looked decidedly uncomfortable. The camels themselves, though, were real characters. Whenever they looked at you, they had a knowing, almost condescending look in their heavily-lashed eyes. In fact, they somehow always managed to appear to be sneering down at you, even if you were standing right over them. And adding to their quirkiness was their incredible repertoire of bodily noises. Every now and again, without warning, they'd suddenly pull up and stand there for a few seconds expelling terrifically noisy farts or making boisterously loud burping and gurgling noises.

Just after eleven, with the day really hotting up, we stopped at a particularly parched piece of sunbaked land close to a remote settlement and took shelter under the shade of three large acacias. After serving up lunch, our guides got up and started chatting with great fervour to a group of locals nearby who'd rushed over as soon as we'd arrived. Judging by the way he'd been greeted, Mohan, the older and more experienced of the two, seemed to be regarded as something of a local folk hero in these parts and these conversations went on for a couple of hours with much animation, gesticulation and laughter. Eventually, Haji came bounding back over with a couple of friends.

'Jim, please can you bring out the game?' he asked excitedly. I frowned at him for a few seconds.

'You know, the one we play last night.'

'Oh, the Ludo you mean,' I said. 'Yeah, of course.'

He introduced me to his colleagues, a young lad and a water seller, and after explaining the rules, the four of us sat down to play. Haji, I'm afraid to say, was undoubtedly the worst Ludo player I'd ever seen. He simply didn't appear to have grasped any of the tactics of the game from the previous night and insisted on bringing as many of his counters out on the board as he could, only to see them being landed on and sent back home again a few goes later. It was a good job we weren't playing for rakshi like we had in Pokhara, for Haji would have been well and truly legless by now. Predictably, he finished the game exactly where he'd started, with all four of his counters still at home. Leaving the three of them to play again, I moved over and following Pierre's lead, lay down next to the gurgling and chomping camels and took a siesta.

We set off again mid-afternoon and rode for just two more hours before stopping for the night by cluster of bushes in a virtually desolate area of sand. After another meal of vegetables, rice and japattis, we sat around chatting for a while and then,on a pitch-black moonless night, settled down for another night's sleep. Some time later, I was disturbed from my slumber for a second consecutive night by some strange rustling noises, interspersed with the occasional hiss. Sitting up in my sleeping bag, I peered across to see Pierre running around in a pair of underpants desperately trying to shoo away one of the camels that was nosing about in his bags. Sometime later, I woke up again, this time to the sinister sound of crazed laughter. Tilting my head, I sat up again and put my hand to my ear, but suddenly everything was quiet again. I waited for a few more moments and then thought better of it. Perhaps it had just been my imagination. I couldn't for the life of me believe that anyone else would be out at this time of night and, besides, if there *were* some other people lurking out there, there'd surely be a light from a torch or lantern. But just as I settled back into my sleeping bag, I heard it again, and whoever it was, they were very close. Now sat bolt upright, I grabbed the cover of my sleeping bag and waited for the sound to return. A couple of seconds later it did. It was Pierre, chuckling to himself. At first, I assumed he was just having a bad dream, for he was now tossing and turning in his sleeping bag, but when the macabre laughter started again, I began to wonder if the sun had gone to his head and he was now succumbing to the first signs of desert madness. 'Pierre,' I whispered, but he muttered something and then turned back over. I lay back down again, trying to convince myself he must have been doing it in his sleep although, at the back of my mind, I really wasn't too sure.

Mohan, shielding his eyes, squinted up to the sky. 'A hundred and ten today,' he said. 'Maybe a hundred and fifteen.' It was only just gone nine, but the scorching sun was already unbearable. Pierre, leading the way, was still setting the same infuriatingly slow pace that he had been all morning. Much to my annoyance, he adamantly refused to kick his camel with any force to encourage it to trot. The most he'd do was sort of dainty little flick with the back of his hand, which the camel probably couldn't even feel, and a couple of times, I felt severely tempted to rush up behind him on Tatoo and give his camel a good whack on the back of his leg. Maybe that would teach Pierre not to scare the living daylights out of me in his sleep too!

The four of us were undecided to as to what time we should return to Jaisalmer. The choices were to return at midday or, failing that, take another longer route that would mean not getting back until late afternoon. Haji wanted to get back for noon, Pierre was quite happy to go on, whilst Mohan and I weren't really bothered either way. We ended up opting for the longer route, so with midday already fast approaching, we stopped soon after by a sandstone temple. After unsaddling the camels under the shade of a tree, our guides slowly removed all the pots and pans from the bags in preparation for lunch, whilst I was despatched to a nearby well to fetch a bucket of water. This simple task should have taken a couple of minutes but when I reached the oasis, it was surrounded by fifteen to twenty Rajput women dressed in elaborately bright coloured saris, all waiting to fill their own containers. Out in the desert, the fact I was a foreigner mattered for little, for they clearly weren't prepared to do me any favours by letting me into the queue, not that a queue actually existed. Each time a gap appeared around the well, I'd gingerly edge towards the vacated space, and each time, another girl would quickly jump in and I'd find myself being unceremoniously pushed out of the way. After a quarter of an hour, a young Indian lad sporting a Man United top came to my rescue. Spotting my predicament, he wandered over and grabbing hold of my bucket, stepped in and promptly filled it up with water. Just then, Haji turned up. 'Jim, what took you so long?' he cried. 'We thought you fallen down the hole.' For a few seconds, I just stood there rather pathetically, shaking my head.

Returning to the sound of farting camels, lunch was waiting, and relaxing for another hour or so under the shade of the trees after we'd eaten, I brought out my Dictaphone to record the sound of Mohan and Haji singing. When I first played the tape back to them, they both looked at me incredulously, especially Mohan, who asked if he could keep the recorder as a gift. It was difficult to say no, but I knew I had to. Undeterred, the two of them quickly burst into the rendition of another song, and then, with their eyes swelling with pride, sat there like two little kids, listening open-mouthed to the sounds of their own warbling voices again.

Late afternoon, they loaded up the camels again for the final time, though the last two hours of the journey back to Jaisalmer, made under the unforgiving glare of the sun, were excruciatingly torturous. The blistering afternoon heat was energy sapping, my inner thighs were aching like crazy and becoming increasingly dehydrated, my throat was so parched it felt like sandpaper. By now, the smooth rolling sand dunes were long behind us and crossing over arid scrubland and rocky terrain, the desert suddenly seemed a much more dispiriting place. So when, way out in the distance, the stupendous walls of the Jaisalmer fort finally appeared in front of us like a mirage on the horizon, I shouted ahead to Mohan and, flashing him a broad grin, ecstatically waved a fist in the air. Indeed, such was the relief to realise we were now on the home straight that even Pierre was having a job to contain himself for I could now hear him behind me cheerily whistling the 'Marseillaise'. Arriving back just after six, Mohan and Haji hoisted us down off our camels and we duly thanked them for the wonderful experience and their kind hospitality. Shaking their hands, I presented

Mohan with a 100 rupee tip and Haji with my Ludo game as a token of my appreciation, before dashing off to pick up a bottle of mineral water that I greedily gulped down on the spot.

As I followed Pierre into the reception of the guesthouse a couple of minutes later, quite a few members of staff rushed over to warmly greet him. In fact, much to my bemusement, two or three even got down on their hands and knees. I'd noticed this the first day I'd arrived too and I was beginning to wonder if he was some kind of unbeknown royal dignitary travelling around India incognito. But even if he was, I was by now too tired to care, so after agreeing to meet up later for a bite to eat, I wearily climbed up the steps to my room and, exhausted from the long trip, collapsed on my bed. It was a full hour before I could even find the strength to take a shower although it was still was a mighty relief to finally wash off all the sand ingrained in every nook and cranny of my body.

I met Pierre back down in reception later. As per usual, he was surrounded by more of the staff. Now clean and refreshed, I felt it was time to get to the bottom of this.

'Pierre, is there a Royal Family in France?' I asked on our way to a restaurant just down the road.

He shook his head. 'Only in Monaco. Why do youz ask?'

'Aw, just wondering.'

Changing tack, I then said, 'And Pierre, what is the word in French for celebrity?'

'Celebrity? Er, it ees célébrité.'

Twenty minutes later, I was still none the wiser. Over the meal, though, he casually confided he'd just invested in the purchase of a carpet.

'Oh right,' I said, 'so how much did you pay?'

'Fifteen zhousand rupees,' he whispered.

'How much?' I shrieked. 'Fifteen thousand rupees?'

'Ssh. Don't say zis too loud.'

'Fifteen thousand rupees? Pierre, that's nearly four hundred quid!'

'Oui, but it ees top quality.'

'I should bloody well think so too at that price!'

A few more seconds later, I was still sitting there open-mouthed. No wonder all the staff were pandering to him; they were probably all on commission. We went on to discuss a wide range of subjects—sleep-talking, travels, tummy bugs, French films, music and the beauty of Indian women, especially the women here in Rajasthan—and by the end of the meal, I wondered if I'd initially judged him too harshly. Anyway, he was moving on later that evening to Bikaner, another desert town some 200 miles northeast from Jaisalmer so, returning to the guesthouse, we shook hands and went our separate ways.

Jaisalmer itself had a very relaxed feeling to it, particularly inside the old city walls where there existed an alluring maze of winding cobbled streets. I spent an hour or so the next morning happily wandering up and down these narrow lanes and alleyways, trying to imagine what it would have been like here all those centuries ago. Jaisalmer then was a thriving and prosperous trading post that flourished for over six hundred years, and its wealth was significantly aided and sustained by the levies imposed on the caravans that passed through the region by the town's feudal chiefs, the Bhatti Rajputs. Situated on the main trade route that linked India to Egypt, Persia, Arabia and Central Asia, traders laden with precious cargoes of spices, silks, carpets and precious stones would often stop here en route to Delhi, Gujarat and places far beyond. Nowhere did the city's prosperity of this time exude this more than in the havelis, the magnificent mansions intricately carved from sandstone, built by the wealthy locals and merchants in the 18th and 19th centuries. Many of these had been beautifully preserved and, with no entry fees, they'd now become popular places for people to wander around to marvel at the resplendent murals, balconies and facades. And although Jaisalmer's strategic importance had ultimately faded when the sea trade went on to replace the old land routes, the city remained relatively unchanged and, mercifully, the authorities here appeared committed to keep it that way.

Later in the morning, I bumped into Mohan walking up one of the main streets. His face lit up when he saw me, and he insisted we stop for a drink so we dived into a roadside bar. Up until then, I had purposely stayed clear of lassis, the drinks made out of iced curd preferred by all the 'okay yah' backpackers. So many conversations I'd had with these fellow travellers had evolved around this pretentious drink, which simply because of my obstinacy, I'd become even more determined not to try:

'Have you had a lassi yet?' someone would ask.

'No,' I'd snap.

'Oh you have to, they're so refreshing.'

'But I don't want to.'

'Steve, Steve, tell him how cool a lassi is.'

'Yeah, they're good. You should try one.'

'I know, why don't you let us treat you?'

'No, no, I'm fine thanks.'

'Steve, which flavour shall we get him? What d'you think? Banana? Mango?

'No, honestly, water is fine. Yep, err, yes, a bottle of Bisleri please.'

But Mohan insisted I try one and since he was an Indian friend, I was prepared to give one a go. And when our lassis were brought over a couple of minutes later, I was in for a pleasant surprise. The drink, served in a long glass, was like a cross between milk shake and yoghurt and it was, it has to be said, wonderfully refreshing. Taureans, I gather, are supposed to be notoriously stubborn people and sometimes, I have to admit, I take this trait to extremes. But as I wandered back down the narrow streets after bidding Mohan farewell, I was still damned if I was ever going to down a lassi within a 100 mile radius of another backpacker dressed in embroidered sandals, pyjama trousers and a Fred Perry T-shirt.

CHAPTER 35

PUSHKAR & UDAIPUR

CHUNGLEE SINGH

6th–11th May 1991

'Another puncture?' I said to the man sat next to me, his face now glued to the window.

'No,' he replied, wobbling his head, 'that smoke is coming from the engine.'

Three hours into the journey to Pushkar, and it looked liked we'd broken down again. As always seemed to happen in India, (and Nepal for that matter) everybody quickly piled out of the bus to inspect the damage and throw in their two pennies' worth. Peering down at all the Indian men stood around gravely nodding, some with their arms folded, others with hands on hips, I sat in my seat shaking my head. If this had been a National Express bus broken down on the M4, the driver would have got out and all the passengers would have remained firmly rooted in their seats. And three hours later, they'd probably still

458

be sat there indignantly waiting for the driver to get back on board to inform them what had happened. Maybe this just said more about us British being so reserved. We are, I suppose through tradition, a nation of people only too happy to be waited upon, whereas other nationalities are far more inclined to take matters into their own hands. On this occasion, though, the delay was not a long one, and twenty minutes later the engine spluttered back to life.

I'd decided to come to Pushkar as it was supposed to be another one of those laid-back places where groups of travellers tended to congregate. It was for Hindus, however, a very important pilgrimage centre, and as I wandered down to the lakeside ghats early the next morning, the abundance of Sadhus and holy people out on the streets briefly brought back memories of Varanasi. At the same time, though, I couldn't help sensing amongst the vast numbers of hippies and backpackers sitting outside the restaurants on the main square, the same kind of clickiness that I'd noticed in Goa. Not withstanding this, the overriding feeling was that the pace here in the town was very unhurried, and after an hour I hadn't been approached by a single hawker. There was also a very nice garden in the grounds of my hotel and I guessed these factors would probably keep me here for two or three days at least.

After spending a couple more hours exploring the town, however, I began to feel restless. I'd been told there was some kind of festival taking place here later on Friday, yet in spite of this, later in the afternoon, I decided to book a ticket to Udaipur for Thursday night. It seemed that the feeling I'd get from time to time of needing to keep on the move had returned. Heading back to my room, I came across two young boys sitting on a balcony at the top of the steps. They were keen to chat and after the usual interrogation of where I was from, how long I'd been in India and so on, I asked them their names. They glanced at one another for a few seconds before one of them blurted out: 'Chunglee Singh.'

I looked on slightly bemused as they proceeded to collapse into fits of uncontrollable laughter in front of me. When they finally stopped, I asked 'Chunglee Singh' what his real name was.

'No, it's Chunglee Singh,' he replied, before the rather predictable giggles started again. Despite my subsequent efforts to be let in on the joke, they refused to tell me what it meant or what their real names were and I could only guess they either didn't know how to translate it or it was too rude. Still rather intrigued, I scoured my guidebooks when I got back to my room to see if I could find any reference to 'Chunglee Singh', which would give me some clue to its meaning, but half an hour later, I was still none the wiser.

My next day in Pushkar was much more enjoyable. Perhaps it had taken me twenty-four hours to acclimatise to the town's easy going pace. After breakfast, I'd sat out in the garden for a couple of hours basking in the sun and then spent the afternoon washing clothes and writing a few letters. Late afternoon, I wandered down to the Sunset Café overlooking the lake and spent another relaxing hour drinking lemon tea and writing some more postcards with the dulcet tones of Astrud Gilberto playing in the background.

On my way back, as I climbed the steps to my room, I bumped into the two boys again. This time I played along and shouted out 'Chunglee Singh!' much to their delight. We spent another twenty minutes chatting on the balcony. The good-natured banter was all harmless fun and the two enterprising lads were actually quite entertaining, so it was quite a nice way to while away another half an hour. It also beat the hell out of chatting to pretentious travellers and hippies. 'Chunglee Singh,' indeed! One day, I'd find out.

Later that evening, I was feeling rather chuffed with myself. I was, in fact, feeling ten feet tall, for at long last, it seemed I'd finally acquired that elusive 'I've-been-in-India-a-long-time' look. I guess the telltale signs were my worn and faded clothes and the colour of my browning skin, but it wasn't just this. I felt that I'd now gained a certain confidence. All of a sudden, it seemed that I could play along, laugh, chat and banter with the good Indians I met and feel naturally at ease at the same time. And likewise, I'd also learnt how to differentiate the good from

460

the bad, how to quickly recognise the money-grabbing locals, the not-so-savoury type and the people to be wary of and, when called upon, how to be abrupt and dismissive accordingly. Two things in particular had brought all this to my attention. One was another backpacker I'd met earlier in the afternoon whose first off the cuff comment was: 'Looks like you've been in India a while.' This could just have been the ultimate compliment that you could possibly pay a fellow traveller in this country. The other was a group of young backpackers I'd seen earlier that evening, who'd clearly only just arrived in India. I could tell this not only because of their pale skin, but also by the way they found themselves immediately surrounded by touts and peddlers eager to make a quick killing from these naïve travellers. And to think, I must have looked just like them when I'd arrived in Bombay just a couple of months back.

Around 6am the next morning, I was awoken by the sound of chatter. Crawling over to my window, a party of Indian day-trippers dressed in sun hats and shades were congregated in the hotel garden below. Back in my bed, as I lay there wondering where they were heading, I had that horrible feeling in my stomach that could only mean one thing: TOILET! Leaping up, I grabbed a roll of tissue from my bag, darted across the room, and pulled open the door only to see a large Indian woman walk straight into the toilet and slam the door closed behind her. Pacing back and forth across the landing, waiting for the sound of the flush, I was beginning to feel decidedly uncomfortable, for the pains in my stomach were becoming more and more intense by the second.

'Come on,' I muttered, grimacing to myself. 'What are you doing in there?' I knew I couldn't hang on for very long. Another few minutes passed and I was now so desperate that my fingers were literally clenching into my buttocks. Looking around the landing in hope, I knew I couldn't hold out much longer, so I had to think on my feet. But what was I going to do? I hadn't seen any other toilet in the building, and now was probably not the time to start looking for one.

'Come on, in there!' I grunted again. 'Hurry up! Please, come on!' But it was no good. I could already feel it coming. Just as I was about to resort to Plan B, the only one I could think of, which was to squat over yesterday's newspaper back in my room, the toilet flushed, the door to the bathroom opened and out strolled the obliviously nonchalant 'Queen of Plop Plops'. Unashamedly, I ran straight in and, seconds later, with tears of relief rolling down my cheeks, deposited my splattering load into the pan.

After such an auspicious start to the day, I decided to capitalise on the fact I'd been woken so early and, taking advantage of the cool temperatures, set off to climb up to a nearby hilltop temple. The views from the top over the lake and town were supposed to be magnificent so it seemed there was no time like the present. The size of the mountain was deceiving, though, and after an hour, I realised that getting to the top was going to take much longer than expected. Indeed, not only was I wondering if I was ever going to make it to the temple; I was beginning to think this whole thing had been a bad idea. As the sun beat down relentlessly, I found myself repeatedly stopping for breath every five minutes. My pants, clinging between my legs were badly chafing my skin, my calf muscles were aching so much they were throbbing, flies swarmed incessantly around my head, beads of perspiration dripped into my eyes and all the while, the long meandering path just went on and on.

Greeting me at the top, after two hours of toil and sweat, were a couple of snarling dogs and although not quite the size of Alsatians, they possessed the same kind of wolf-like faces and colourings. Exactly what they were doing up here was anybody's guess, but given that they weren't wearing collars, they clearly weren't pets. As the menacing little creatures snapped at my feet, I desperately wanted to kick them away but, so painful were the blisters already forming around my ankles, I'd already been forced to remove my trainers, so I growled back at them as loudly as I could. It seemed to do the trick for they eventually loped off with their tails, quite literally, between their legs. Fearing they'd just gone off to get reinforcements, I quickly staked my claim on top of the peak and peered down below. To my delight, the views over the town, in spite of the early morning haze, were so impressive they suddenly made all of my efforts seem worthwhile. In the distance, nestling under a couple of volcanic looking mountains, I could just about make out the glistening lake which, encircled by the whitewashed houses of Pushkar, now looked more like a fishpond. Meanwhile, leading all the way up the hill like the never-ending yellow brick road, was the confoundedly long and meandering zigzag path I'd just climbed. But the most surprising thing of all was the starkness of the barren terrain surrounding the town; miles and miles of nothingness, just flat and desolate arid land as far as the eye could see, with this little glowing oasis in the middle. I'd read that Pushkar was situated right on the edge of the desert and I could now see this all too clearly for myself.

On the way down, I passed a procession of people making the climb up. Greeting them all with a smile or a nod , I couldn't have felt more relieved that I'd now been woken when I was. Although it wasn't much after eight, the humidity was already sweltering and, consequently, the climb back down was just as uncomfortable as the long trudge up. I arrived back at my guesthouse an hour or so later thoroughly exhausted and desperately in need of water. As I quickly gurgled down another bottle of Bisleri in the town square, I glanced up again at the mountain out of the corner of my eye. Infuriatingly, it just looked like a small hillock once more, the proverbial mountain I took to be a molehill.

The excitement of arriving in a new place can often be too much. Almost without fail, my first inclination on this trip after finding somewhere to stay had always been to rush out and check out the surrounding area, primarily to get my bearings, but also to try to get a feeling for the place, to see how it came up to prior expectations, to gauge if it was all it was cracked up to be. The most sensible thing to have done when I arrived in a still dark Udaipur the next morning would have been to find a room and crash out for a few hours. The seven-hour bus journey from Pushkar had passed slowly and after a virtually sleepless night, I felt exhausted. So given that I'd now been away for getting on eighteen months, I should have perhaps known better, which is why I only had myself to blame for what followed. After some protracted negotiations in order to procure a room I deemed cheap enough, I set off for a highly acclaimed restaurant at the top of the town, hoping to enjoy an early morning breakfast overlooking the lake. Before long, though, I found myself lost in the vast labyrinth of lanes of the old city. Quickly deciding to abandon that idea, I stopped at another restaurant for some breakfast. Eating something, I hoped, would put me on track again. This plan, however, backfired; the prices in the restaurant were overly expensive and my food, when it finally turned up, was not particularly inspiring, a bland dish of colourless trudge purporting to be porridge.

After battling to do up the faltering zips on my daypack, I got to my feet and wearily made my way up a long steep hill towards the City Palace. When I arrived, though, more troubles awaited. All I'd somehow managed to do was mistake the whitewashed walls of a large hotel for the side entrance to the palace grounds. Disconcertedly, I asked one of the staff how I get into the palace. He gave me a set of long and complicated directions, something along the lines of: 'Down this street, up the next, take the third right, then the second left, cross a park and it's down the hill.' It couldn't really be that far away? I thought. Well, one thing was for sure and that was I certainly couldn't get to the palace through the hotel. Great! I had no alternative other than to walk back out into the stifling heat of the hot morning and trudge all the way back down the hill again. As I set off again, I began to wonder if I should just cut my losses and hire out a bike for the day. Try as I did, though, I couldn't even decide on this. I mean, I could get a bike for the day, but surely I'd be better off leaving it until the following morning? There again, cycling around all of these bewildering lanes now would undeniably enable me to get my bearings of Udaipur once and for all. How on earth could I be so incapable of making such as simple decision? It was pathetic, and this very inability to act decisively was simply adding to my frustrations. Completely dispirited, I finally decided to forget about bicycles and proceeded to try to retrace my steps back to my guesthouse. And to my growing despair, this turned out to be another lost cause. As I wandered up and down sidestreets like a lost sheep, kids came running up to me continually asking me for my name and country, and hawkers, hell bent on ushering me into their shops, repeatedly tried to grab my arm. My patience, yet again, was being pushed to its very limits.

Twenty minutes later, I finally stumbled across the palace and as always seemed to happen on these occasions, I found a pleasant surprise lying in store. The spectacular, vast white-marbled and granite exterior, surmounted by medieval balconies, cupolas and octagonal towers was, in itself, worth the entrance fee alone, whilst inside was a museum of great variety. In one room, I came across a collection of delightful miniature paintings of a fabled and tragic young princess who'd nobly chosen suicide over marriage in order to preserve the family dynasty; in another some beautiful inlaid mosaics of dancing peacocks, the favourite bird of the region; and in a third, an impressive display of old Rajput weaponry including the suit of chain armour used by Maharana Pratap, one of Udaipur's great heroes, and a huge artificial elephant's trunk worn by his equally famous horse into battle. Most stunning of all, though, was the mesmerising Moti Mahal, a small dark temple embellished ceiling to floor in stained glass mirrors of amazingly bright and vivid hues of scarlets, violets, azures, ambers and sky blues.

After the museum, things took a turn for the better—well, they couldn't have really gotten much worse after such a troublesome morning. I took a short boat trip out onto Lake Pichola and then made my way to the Natural Attic, a renowned eating-place especially popular with budget travellers. It didn't take very long to discover why, when, just ten minutes later, I was treated to a delicious potato and spinach curry. I'd now gone four days without a meat dish, which for me, must have been some kind of record, but the vegetarian food so prevalent in this region had been consistently nourishing and tasty.

After lunch, I managed to book a bus ticket on a direct service to Bombay for the following afternoon. This came as a huge relief as it effectively meant I wouldn't have to return to Delhi again after all. Returning to my guesthouse, I then made my way out to the courtyard, sat in a wicker chair amongst the bougainvilleas for a while and, watching a couple of amorous geckos tangoing up and down the whitewashed walls, decided to abandon the idea of going over to the Lake Palace Hotel later that evening. The Lake Palace, to all intents and purposes, was a palace in its own right. Well, it certainly looked like one! Situated on an island in the middle of the lake, it was one of India's most luxurious hotels and they apparently ran an excellent buffet for non-residents in a separate restaurant. Earlier in the morning, a few other backpackers I'd met on the bus here had been talking of going over that evening for some dinner but, on reflection, I really didn't think I could justify the 250 rupees it cost. I mean, in just two weeks, I'd be back in Wales gorging myself on home-cooked dishes such as roast lamb, spaghetti bolognaise and toad in the hole, so I decided I'd try to save what little money I had left on my credit cards and treat myself to one final splurge in Bombay if the opportunity presented itself. I was, by now, really looking forward to Bombay. After the highs of Jaisalmer, both Pushkar and Udaipur had been pleasant enough, but I found myself yearning to return to the hustle and bustle of another big city. I'd initially only been planning to spend a week there, although I'd now have getting on twelve days, and I suppose that if I'd got some time to kill, then I'd far prefer to do so in a big city like Bombay.

Hiring out a bike the next morning, I set off to explore Udaipur in earnest. Situated on the east side of Lake Pichola was the picturesque old part of the city, whilst further to the north was a second lake, Fateh Sagar. But being a creature of habit, my first stop of the day took me back to the Natural Attic for a hearty breakfast of baked beans on toast topped off with a pot of Earl Grey. Then, after circumnavigating part of the northern lake for an hour or so, I set off again in pursuit of the Hilltop Restaurant.

Reaching the foot of a long road that led up to the top of the town, I noticed some kind of commotion ahead. Fifty yards further on, an overturned auto rickshaw lay on the side of the road. Beside it, with his hands on his head, stood the distraught driver of the vehicle, looking on forlornly at the hundreds of smashed bottles of Limca, Thums Up and Pepsi that lay strewn across the side of the road. Without hesitation, I jumped off my bike and, together with a three or four other passers-by, ran over to rescue the few bottles that remained unbroken. The hapless driver, mopping his brow with an oily rag, looked inconsolable, and I couldn't help fearing what the consequences would be for the poor fellow when he eventually summoned up the courage to break the news to his employers. How would they react? Would he have to pay for the broken bottles himself? Could the accident ultimately cost him job and, if so, what repercussions would this have on his family? Crawling around on my hands and knees, I kept peering across to the driver and the more I thought about it, the worse it got. He couldn't have been older than thirty and judging by his betel stained teeth and clothing—he was dressed in a grubby white vest, navy lunghi and flip-flops—he probably lived in a remote village somewhere out in the sticks and was working his fingers to the bone just to keep his young wife and kids in food. I even began to envisage him staggering across a field with tears in his eyes as he prepared to tell them what had happened, and I could just picture his sobbing wife hugging him outside their hut as their children crawled by their feet. Feeling totally helpless, I desperately wanted to offer him a 20 rupee note for his troubles, but feared that this would put the man in a compromised position. In his predicament, I was sure he could gladly do with the money, although the impression I'd got from the Indians I'd met was that they were a fiercely proud people and such an offer could equally be construed as deeply insulting. So, after eventually shaking hands with the driver who, nodding his head gratefully, thanked me for my help, I headed off, still somewhat distressed by the poor man's plight. Oh, and by the way, when I finally found the Hilltop Restaurant, the views weren't that great and the food was awful.

Later that evening, as I was tucking into another spinach and potato curry at the Natural Attic, I started scribbling down various categories for a little scheme I'd been hatching in my mind over the last few days. I'd decided that on my last night in Bombay, I would host my very own Oscars ceremony. It would comprise all the things that had happened on my travels, things like best places visited, worst journeys taken, nicest hotels stayed in and so on. If I could agree all the categories now and draw them up, it would give me ample time to dwell over the respective shortlists for nominations over the next week or so, before deciding on the definitive winners of each category on my final night.

Because I got so carried away with this, it was probably one of the reasons why I failed to realise I'd been short-changed. My bill for the meal had come to 25 rupees. Since I only had a 20 rupee and a 100 rupee note, I'd paid with the hundred. A short while later, on the way back to my guesthouse, I stopped off to buy a bottle of water but when I opened my money belt, I discovered I only had 45 rupees in total, the original 20 rupee note and the 25 rupees they must have inadvertently given me in change. I was, therefore, 50 rupees short.

Carrying on back to the guesthouse, the first thing I did when I returned to my room was sit on the bed, light up a beedi (one of the small hand-rolled Indian cigarettes that I'd taken to smoking of late) and think about what I should do. Fifty rupees might not sound like a lot of money, but it was when I'd been budgeting so hard over the last few weeks and fifty rupees would easily pay for a good lunchtime meal before I left for Bombay the following afternoon. However, it wasn't just the money, it was also my stupidity in not realising the mistake at the time, and I just knew that I wouldn't be able to get to sleep if I let it go. So with that, I jumped up and marched straight back to the restaurant. It was a good twenty minute walk and on the way, I psyched myself up for a long drawn out argument. Walking into the restaurant, I spotted the owner sitting at a table, bobbing his baby son up and down on his lap. As soon as he saw me, he reached straight into his shirt pocket and brought out a 50 rupee note. Strolling over, I took the money from his outstretched hand, thanked him and smiling, turned around and walked back out. From his reaction, my gut feeling was that the mistake had, in fact, been genuine, although I'd never really know for sure.

The lesson I learnt from all this was not to get too complacent, especially so near to the end of my trip. Just earlier that morning, I'd heard a startling story about an Aussie backpacker who, on virtually his last sightseeing tour of the country, had accepted a cup of tea from a local on the way back from the Taj Mahal on the Agra to Delhi Express, only to discover when he'd woken up a couple of hours later that most of his belongings, including all the gifts and souvenirs he'd been frantically buying for family and friends, had disappeared. After hearing this, I'd quickly reflected how lucky I'd been on my travels; I'd not lost or had anything stolen of value, I'd never really found myself threatened or in danger and, although I'd had my fare share of scares along the way, I'd somehow managed to stay clear of illness. This could only be the timely wake up call I needed before Bombay.

CHAPTER 36

BOMBAY

MAUGHAM HEAVEN... AND THEN I
SEE THE HEADLINES

12th–24th May 1991

Boarding the bus the following afternoon, I asked our driver
what time we could expect to arrive in Bombay.

'Bombay?' he replied. 'This bus go to Delhi.'

'What?' I retorted. 'But the boy down there said this was
the...'

The driver now was grinning. 'I joke, I joke, my friend,' he
said, waving a hand across his face. 'This is Bombay bus. We
should be in Bombay by lunchtime.'

'Lunchtime?' I stammered, still failing to see the funny side.
'Are you sure?'

This time, though, he was deadly serious and as I stood on
the steps rolling my eyes, I felt like running back to the ticket
office to throttle the ticket seller, for he'd sworn blind that the

bus would get in at 7am, four or five hours before all the other Udaipur to Bombay services. This, after all, was the only reason I'd booked this ticket. Adding to my consternation, as I stared down the dusty aisle at the rigid plastic seats, was the realisation that this rather battered looking vehicle was anything but a deluxe service and that my prized no.2 ticket, the one that usually guaranteed the most legroom, happened to be on this bus the seat directly behind the driver. Consequently, all hopes I had for stretching out my legs over the next twelve hours evaporated in an instant. Even more disconcerting, however, was the sight of the video and television set positioned just above my head. I'd yet to travel on a bus in India that hadn't played music or videos at full volume, so this would have serious repercussions on the amount of sleep I'd get. So, all in all, not a particularly good start to the long journey, and all this before we'd even set off!

When we eventually did, though, I had something far more important to worry about, namely our irreverent bus driver. Dressed casually in slacks and a short-sleeved white shirt, his moustache, unshaven chin, long nose and twinkling eyes made him a dead ringer for Robin Williams. He even had that very same madcap expression to boot and he started off driving just as you'd expect Robin Williams to drive a bus—like a man possessed. For the first thirty minutes, I stared wide-eyed out of the front window, fearing for my life, constantly turning my head away as he recklessly swerved our bus at breakneck speeds in and out of vehicles we were overtaking on the outside lane. Reaching for my Walkman, I rummaged around for my Tracy Chapman tape in the hope a few renditions of *Talkin' Bout a Revolution* would calm me down, but after a while something quite strange happened: I found myself cheering our driver on, urging him to go faster. Each time, he'd turn around grinning crazily and each time, I'd sit there grinning back, giving him the thumbs up. If he carried on at this rate, it looked like we might even end up in Bombay at 7am after all.

A couple of hours into the journey, our animated driver, finally bowing to the numerous requests from the other passengers, turned on the dreaded video. The first thing that appeared on the screen was like an Indian version of *Top of the Pops*. The quality of the recording, however, was very poor and before long, more ranting and raving from the back of the bus followed. The tape was soon replaced with a Hindi feature film, and although this still didn't satisfy many of the passengers, who continued to complain about the volume and the picture throughout, it turned out to be eminently watchable. The video, filmed I'd guess in the 1970s, was a love story evolving around a young couple who'd met in university. At first, the girl hadn't been attracted to her admirer so when he started to follow her around the campus and pester her, she reported him to the principal. He was severely punished, so she then felt guilty for her actions and tried in vain to intervene to get him off the hook. The principal wasn't going to change his mind, though, so the pair escaped from the compound and eloped to the mountains where they fell hopelessly in love. But not being the agreeable sort, our confounding hero continued to tread on people's toes, so somebody decided to cut the brake cables on his car. He was then blinded by the resultant accident and this, sadly, was as far as it got, because after the bus went over a series of bumps, the video seemingly stopped on its own accord and the screen went blank. Much howling and banging on the windows followed from behind which, in turn, woke up the driver's assistant. Still half asleep, he got up and managed to restore the picture, but even this still didn't satisfy the passengers who now wanted the tape to be rewound to where the story had left off. This was the final straw for our highly revered driver, for he promptly reached up, turned the video off and not a subsequent word was heard. As soon as the overhead lights were turned off shortly after, I sheepishly reached for my blow-up neck cushion I'd bought specifically for the trip (but eighteen months later, had still yet to use) and, under the cover of dark, proceeded to inflate it. My embarrassing little travel aid seemed to do the trick, though, for the next thing I knew it was daylight.

When I looked up, Robin Williams was wearing a turban. Strange, I thought, mad, but not that mad, surely? A couple of seconds later, I realised my stupidity: Robin Williams was, in fact, standing in the corner by the door, ridiculing and patronising all the drivers of the trucks and buses we were overtaking whilst sitting in the drivers seat was a new Sikh driver. With his flamboyant hand movements and verbal gestures, our original driver now bore an even more striking resemblance to his illustrious Hollywood look-alike, and I continued to gaze on as he chatted incessantly to his colleague. The likeness really was uncanny and for the remainder of the journey, I just couldn't stop smiling.

I crammed an awful lot into my first few days in Bombay and it truly was delightful to find myself based in one place at last and no longer on the move. I shopped 'til I dropped for souvenirs and presents in the city's numerous state-run emporiums, I called in at the UK consulate each morning to read the latest copies of the British broadsheets, I dined almost exclusively at Leopold's, a large, popular, open-fronted restaurant on the Colaba Causeway and every night before I went to sleep, I'd sit on the bed in my room trying to complete the ridiculously easy crossword in the local tabloid, *Mid-Day*.

It was on one of these evenings that I came across a feature in the newspaper that caught my eye. It was an advert for an expo of consumer durables and household items taking place in the rather grandly named Sundaby Hall. Seeing the word 'expo' instantly conjured up in my mind pictures of an international Earls Court-type trade show, teeming with businessmen and exhibitors' stands, and given that one of the things I was hoping to invest in here in Bombay was a pressure cooker, a kitchen utensil that Basir the Bold had convinced me I shouldn't be without, it seemed foolish not to check it out. So the next morning, I pulled out the paper again and buoyed on by the offer of 'Heavy Discounts on Exports,' quickly consulted my map. Discovering that Sundaby Hall was located only twenty minutes away in the Churchgate area of the city, I reached down for my trainers and decided to take a stroll up there, but even though it was only just gone nine, it was already stiflingly hot, and before long, as I passed through the bustling arcades of shopping stalls that lined the crowded streets, my T-shirt was soaked in sweat. The dry heat of Rajasthan, which I'd only just become accustomed to, had now been replaced with a pre-monsoon humidity so suffocating and oppressive it made even a walk as short as this almost unbearable. In fact, the only thing that stopped me turning back was the prospect of whiling away a few hours wandering up and down the aisles of the vast arena in the relative comfort of air conditioning. It was probably about fifteen minutes into this journey when a young man, emerging from the crowded pavements, came bounding up and, after firing of all the predictable barrage of opening questions, decided to tag along. He claimed he was a student although I wasn't so sure. If he was, then why wasn't he studying, for a start? Not particularly in the mood for conversation, I carried on weaving my way between oncoming pedestrians, blatantly ignoring his persistent questioning. When, ten minutes later, I still hadn't shaken him off, I began to wonder if I was going to have a repeat of the Calcutta Museum debacle on my hands especially, when approaching the Churchgate area, he grabbed hold of my arm and pointed excitedly to a side road. For two or three seconds, I looked at him quizzically.

'Down there,' he said, 'a building collapse last night. Over hundred people killed. Come, I show you the dead bodies.'

I shook my head, one, because I didn't really want to see a pile of dead bodies and, two, because the last thing that anybody on the scene would have wanted was people coming along to have a look. With that, my friend quickly disappeared, and letting out a huge gasp of relief, I quickened up my pace. Sundaby Hall, though, was proving to be elusive, and another ten minutes later, after aimlessly walking up and down half a dozen side streets, I was really beginning to flounder. So when, by chance, I looked up at the large building in front of me and saw it was none other than the Government of India tourist office, I rushed inside to ask for directions. Sundaby Hall, I was informed, was only two blocks away, but when I found it a couple of minutes later, my jaw dropped to the floor. Pushing open a creaking wooden door, I peered into a dimly lit room no bigger in size than a tennis court. Inside, I could just about make out half a dozen trestle tables full of what appeared to be nothing more than bric-a-brac, whilst stood idly chatting alongside one of the walls, with a cup of tea in their hands, were two silver-haired men in glasses and safari suits, and a rather large woman in a bright yellow sari. Expo indeed! It looked more like a village jumble sale, and there was, needless to say, not a pressure cooker in sight.

Making my way along the harbour later in the afternoon, I called into the Taj Mahal Hotel. The Taj, a huge and imposing seven-storey building, lavishly decorated with crimson Moorish domes, was one of the most luxurious hotels in India, and with the FA Cup Final only a few days away, it seemed worthwhile dropping in to see if they had satellite television and if so, how much the rooms cost. It turned out they did have cable, but the rates started at $110 a night for a standard suite, which was way out of my price range, so much so that I wasn't even tempted to say 'to hell with it' and just whack the bill on one of my credit cards as I'd done at the Peace Hotel two Christmases ago. Fifty dollars and I might have even considered it, so I'd just have to make do with listening to the game on the radio instead.

Looming in front of me, when I stepped back outside, was one of the city's most famous landmarks: the Gateway of India. On first sight, the large thickset concrete gateway—a carbon copy of the Arc de Triomphe—didn't appear that inspiring but the crowded waterside promenade that surrounded it, the Apollo Bunder, was a hive of activity. With the light beginning to fade as the sun disappeared behind the hotel, snack vendors, fruit sellers, photographers and all kinds of performing acts—jugglers, clowns, men on stilts—abounded, all busily plying their trades to the hordes of locals and sightseers strolling around the esplanade. And amidst these crowds, groups of ragged little urchins ran amok, begging tourists for money and following guests back towards the hotel before they inevitably found themselves shooed away by the hotel staff. And, as always, there were the other kinds of sellers, constantly whispering offers of 'hashish' and 'shansh maanee' into the ear.

One of the more heartening sights I'd seen quite regularly in India was that of families out with their children. The place I'd first noticed this was on the beaches of Madras six or seven weeks ago. There were so many parents out with their children, some playing on the sand and others seemingly content just to be out strolling with their loved ones. And then, the same thing just last month in New Delhi, when I headed downtown to Connaught Circus on that Sunday morning. Families who just appeared glad to be out and about, happy to be spending time with the people they cared for, and now, here at the Gateway of India, exactly the same thing again. The family bond here in India seemed to be particularly important and I found this quite touching.

On my way back to Colaba Causeway, a busy shopping avenue thronged with shops, market stalls, restaurants and cheap hotels, I picked up a short wave radio for the princely sum of 100 rupees, and then, after treating myself to another gorgeous stir-fried meal at Leopold's, got up and battled my way back to my hotel. As usual, the streets were rife with touts and peddlers, predominantly the large black African men who seemed to congregate in this part of the city, and finding these people forever blocking your path and approaching you with all the usual offers was becoming a real hassle. The best way I found to deal with this was to totally ignore them, pretend they simply weren't there and completely blank them. To me, if I was in their position, this would this even more insulting then being told by a passer-by where to go. That said, the continual badgering was still wearing me down. As I was walking along the street dodging all these miscreants, though, I suddenly recalled a night in Nepal when Gibbo and I, on our way back to our guesthouse a little worse for wear, had effectively turned the tables on the touts. I wasn't too sure how it had actually come about but what I did remember was the immensely satisfying hour we spent stealing their thunder by running up to all the peddlers we passed, imploring them with offers of 'hashish' and 'shansh maanee,' before they had chance to do so. To our increasing delight, this unfailingly left them utterly bemused and bewildered. Indeed, some were so startled they lost their tongues completely. I really wanted to do it again now, but to carry it out successfully, you really needed an abundance of Dutch courage and a sparring partner who could gee you along, and right now, I had neither.

Back in my room, I fiddled about with my new radio, trying to tune into the BBC World Service. Later that evening, Man United were playing Johan Cruyff's mighty Barcelona in the European Cup-Winners' Cup Final, and whilst not a great United fan myself, I'd read in the paper there was to be live radio commentary on the match. Still dearly missing my beloved game, I simply couldn't let this opportunity pass me by, especially as this was the first season English clubs had been allowed back into Europe following the five-year ban imposed after the Heysel tragedy. It took a while, but I eventually managed to find the station and my ears pricked up a few minutes later when they crossed over to Rotterdam for a pre-match report. The game, by all accounts, was a huge sell-out and thousands of fans were apparently roaming the streets of the city in search of tickets for the final. Earlier in the day, I'd been wondering whether two of my old flatmates in Bournemouth, both huge United fans, would have gone over to watch it; hearing this, I suspected not. The lucky buggers would probably be sitting in front of the television with a lounge full of friends and fridge full of beers.

I set my alarm for eleven, an hour before kick-off Bombay time, though trying to get some sleep before it went off proved to be a lost cause. Lying in bed with my mind racing, I eventually got up, turned on the light and spent some time reading. When the alarm eventually did go off, I then made the foolish mistake of twiddling about with the tuning dial again, so when I tried to pick up the World Service half an hour later, I couldn't find it and consequently spent forty totally frustrating minutes desperately trying to get the signal back. Then, just as I was about to hurl the radio out of the window, I picked it up again and, hearing they were crossing back over to Rotterdam in twenty minutes' time for full second half commentary, hastily gathered a couple of satsumas along with a bag of Bombay mix from my bag and crept along the corridor to listen to the game on the hotel balcony. The radio reception outside was much clearer and discovering the first half was goalless, I pulled up another chair and, placing the radio down on the table beside me, braced myself for a nail biting forty-five minutes. And this was exactly how the second half turned out, especially when with United 2-0 up, Ronald Koeman pulled a goal back for the Catalans in the 79th minute. Alex Ferguson later went on to describe the reminder of the game as the worst ten minutes of his life, with the United defence coming under increasing pressure as the men in claret and blue surged forward in search of a late equaliser. Sitting outside some 4000 miles away in the early hours of a balmy Bombay morning, just listening to all this drama unfold was quite a surreal experience in itself, though. Down on the silvery moonlit sidestreet below, bodies of the homeless were curled up in doorways, glistening rats scurried along the gutters, the smell of rotten vegetables hung in the air and every now and then, the lights of a passing aircraft blinked overhead. It was eerily quiet, and this tranquillity was only disturbed once in a while by the howling of a roaming dog or the slamming of a door from the brothel opposite as a prostitute or client entered or departed. Well that, and a Welshman sat in his boxers leaping up from his seat and hissing 'Yesssss,' when the Swedish referee finally blew the full-time whistle.

The following day, in the relative cool of the late afternoon, I took a stroll along to Chowpatty Beach and, on the way there, happened to pass by the Oval Maidan. The long and flat rectangular park, surrounded by tall swaying palms and many of the city's old Gothic buildings, was one of my first memories of Bombay when I arrived here in February, for it was alongside this park that all the Goa buses departed. As a result, I felt quite sentimentally attached to the area. A cricket match was taking place out on the scorched grass so, delving into my bag, I quickly pulled out my camera only for the game to end just a couple of balls later. Bloody typical, I thought, a picture of all the fielders in their whites, congregating around the uneven clay wicket with the bowler charging in from the clock-tower end would have easily merited a place in my photo album. As the players filed past me towards the hospitality tent, a couple of them saw me standing there forlornly with my camera still in hand and, I can only assume out of sheer sympathy, promptly invited me to join them for a drink.

Under the shade of the canopy, we discussed, over an ice cold glass of freshly squeezed orange juice, the upcoming World Cup in Australia: how strong the hosts would be playing in front of their home crowds, the recent demise of the great West Indies side, the current state of the English and Indian teams—whether for instance an ageing Botham would make the final squad—and, of course, their expectations of how the emerging and gifted local hero, Sachin Tendulkar, would perform on the world stage. The banter was all good-natured and before long, many other players had gathered around, all seemingly keen to hear the English stance on the respective chances both countries had of winning the competition. After an invigorating and enlightening twenty minutes of chat, I thanked the players for their hospitality and, with a new spring in my step, moved on.

Crossing over to Marine Drive, I followed the long, arcing promenade around the bay for a while, the cool breeze blowing in from the Arabian Sea providing a welcome respite from the stiflingly airless city streets. Twenty minutes later, as if marking the start of the beach, a series of snack stalls and performing acts began to spring up on the side of the walkway. A few yards further on, a particularly large crowd of people had gathered and, standing in a semi-circle four or five deep, were blocking the entire promenade. Many of those at the back were chatting excitedly amongst themselves, gesticulating and pointing towards the sea; one of these acts was clearly causing a stir. Wandering over to see what all fuss about, I slowly managed to push my way to the front. Sitting in a row on the promenade wall were three men. They weren't dancing or juggling, they had no works of art at their feet, they didn't even have a snake around their necks or a couple of monkeys at their feet; they just sat there in silence. When I got closer, I had to rub my eyes to make sure I could actually believe what it was I was seeing. Bodily, they were normal. The three of them, clothed only in shorts, were perfectly round, a little plump perhaps, but nothing particularly out of the ordinary. It was their tiny pin-sized heads, however, which were completely out of proportion to the size of their bodies, that made their deformities so shocking. It looked as if somebody had come along with a syringe and literally sucked out the entire contents of their heads. Their faces were all covered in what seemed to be an unnaturally healthy growth of facial hair, and when they each in turn covered their eyes, ears and mouth with their hands, their act became all too clear; these freaks of nature were plainly being masqueraded as the three monkeys, 'see no evil,' 'hear no evil' and 'speak no evil.' Shocked to the bone, I could now see only too clearly why they should be attracting so much attention yet, sitting there grinning at the crowds, they didn't seem to mind this at all. Noticing that the bucket in front of their dangling feet was brimming with notes and coins, I couldn't for the life of me work out if this was a good thing or not. Still in shock, I abruptly barged my way back though the crowds and shaking my head, staggered off.

The beach itself was another one of those great gathering places for families. I'd first seen pictures of Chowpatty on an episode of *Rough Guides,* the travel show in which two young presenters were sent off each week to report on far-off exotic locations. All of the activities going on here with the entertainers, snack sellers, amusement rides, musicians and horse rides were exactly as I had remembered on the programme. I hung around for around half an hour or so, just content to see so much delight and happiness etched on the children's faces as they ran about playing on the sand. Then, with my tummy beginning to rumble, I headed back for some food, though when I made my way back up the promenade, I was somewhat surprised to see the 'monkey men' had already packed up and gone. Although this should have come as something of a relief, I have to admit I'd secretly been hoping to steal another look at them, just to convince myself that my eyes hadn't deceived me.

By now, I'd been in Bombay a week and I was really warming to the city. I looked forward especially to my daily visits to Leopold's. Quite often, I'd wander over to the restaurant, pull up a seat under one of the twenty or so revolving fans and just sit there sipping lemon tea, quietly watching the world go by. It even seemed as if the touts outside on the streets were hassling me less as well. I was also becoming quite attached to my hotel. The Carlton was an old fashioned colonial building with about twenty or so rooms. It was quite dark and dingy but it had a lot of character. Dilapidated was probably too strong a word to describe it, perhaps rickety summed it up better. Downstairs, there was an overly large hall with a floor lined with small black and white diamond shaped tiles that felt more like a reception for an old Victorian doctors' surgery. My room was at the top of these stairs, and at the end of the dimly lit corridor was the long communal balcony that overlooked the busy sidestreet below. Staying in a couple of rooms further along were two old Chinese men, and every morning and every evening without fail, it seemed, I'd pass them on the corridor shuffling along with just towels around their waists towards the shower. I was sure that they must be living here in the hotel, although what they actually did every day remained a mystery. And besides these two rather intriguing old guys, there were just a handful of other backpackers staying here while all the rest of the guests were Indian.

The next morning, I laid out all my newly acquired purchases on my bed and, after ticking them off one by one against a long list of names of various family members and friends, packed them all away again. It looked like I still had a few things to get but I'd broken the back of it. Feeling rather pleased with myself, I picked up a copy of *Mid-Day* from the newspaper stand outside the hotel and wandered over to Leopold's for some lunch. The news on the front page took me by surprise. A Prohibition order had been imposed all over Bombay by the city council. It would start immediately and last until midnight on the 26th May, the polling date here in Maharashtra. Not even the big hotels, it seemed, were exempted. How ironic, as for the first time since I'd arrived in Bombay, I'd actually been looking forward to treating myself to a beer later on. With the Cup Final being broadcast on the radio that evening, a couple of bottles of amber nectar whilst listening to the commentary would have gone down a treat. Consoling myself with the fact I'd still got some whisky left in my hip flask, which I could look forward to on my final night, I glanced around the dining hall and, whether by coincidence or not, it did seem a lot quieter today. Normally, it was difficult just to find a seat, especially over the busy lunchtime period but, surprisingly, several of the tables at the back of the restaurant remained empty. Casting my eyes on the large banquet-sized table in the middle of the hall, I then remembered the boisterous party of Americans, Aussies and Brits who'd been knocking San Miguels back by the dozen the previous evening, and I couldn't help wondering how they were going to react when they heard this news.

Early evening, after taking my seat on the balcony again and listening on intently to what turned out to be one of the most dramatic FA Cup Finals in years, I was buzzing with adrenaline from all the frenetic action. The game had seemingly had it all: Gascoigne's reckless tackle, Pearce's controversial goal from the resultant free kick, Lineker's harshly disallowed effort, Crossley's dramatic penalty save, Stewart's deserved second-half equaliser and Walker's disastrous extra-time own goal that effectively cost Forest the cup. Knowing I'd be unable to get to sleep straight away, I stayed out on the balcony for a while, and then made a comeback of my own by completing the crossword, thus reducing the deficit to 2-5 in the little ongoing competition I'd been having with the *Mid-Day* newspaper. Still feeling restless, I decided to take a late night stroll around the block, and passing by Leopolds ten minutes later, dropped in for a cuppa. Pulling up a seat, I happened to spot—sitting over the other side of the dining hall—my group of rowdy drinking friends from the other night and, boy, oh boy, they didn't look very happy at all. I could only assume from the startled looks on their faces that they'd only just found out about the Prohibition order. They were plainly not impressed and sat in their seats chewing the cud or, as the Aussies so aptly call it, 'spewing'. Right on cue, one of the group made his way to the bar, presumably to try to have a word with the owner, but he was clearly going to be wasting his time. And, sure enough, when the manager was called out I could see straight away from his body language he was in a helpless position. In spite of the remonstrations, he continued to hold up his hands and shake his head while the group negotiator, digesting the sobering news, screwed up his face in disbelief. They'd obviously all been looking forward to another night of partying but it wasn't gonna happen now. For a few intensely gratifying moments, I sat in my seat quietly sniggering.

I felt strangely subdued when I woke up the next day. I tried writing some postcards but each time I put pen to paper, the words wouldn't come, I repeatedly reached for my guidebooks only to find myself reading the same passages over and over again, and every time I put my trainers on, I found myself kicking them off again a few seconds later. Overcome with lethargy, I whiled away the remainder of the morning lying on my bed staring vacantly up at the overhead fan. By early afternoon, though, I was feeling really down in the dumps. Whether it was after all the euphoria of listening to the Cup Final the previous night, I don't know, but all of a sudden, it felt like that there was very little to look forward to between now and my flight home in two days' time. Deciding to shelve my plans to finish the remainder of my shopping, I designated what was left of the day for rest and recuperation. A few hours later, my mood had changed. Firstly, I'd managed to complete the crossword and so had pulled back the score to 3-5 in the *Mid-Day* Challenge, and then, I'd picked up my latest Maugham book.

So taken had I been by the works of Maugham over the last twelve months since first discovering his books in Sydney, I now treated him with almost guru status. The book I was currently reading, *A Writer's Notebook,* contained extracts from the great man's manuscripts from a period beginning in 1892 (when he was just eighteen) through to 1944. In his own words, he had described these notebooks as 'a storehouse of materials for future use and nothing else.' It contained hundreds and hundreds of scribblings, some just a few words long, and others, lasting pages. There were quotes, aphorisms, theories, anecdotes, questions, sayings, phrases, remarks, opinions, reflections, parables, characterisations, observations, portrayals, descriptions, tales, accounts, stories, even yarns, and I quickly realised they would provide an invaluable and revealing insight into both Maugham's life and mind. I sat on my bed for hours in seventh heaven, ticking, circling and scribbling comments such as 'how true,' 'favourite so far' and 'spot on' next to all of the notes and narratives that particularly struck a chord. And the more I read, the more I scribbled and, try as I did, I just couldn't put the book down. It was, quite simply, a revelation, a monumental kind of 'greatest hits' anthology of my newly acquired hero. It was gone 2am by the time I finally finished the book, but when I did, I felt totally and utterly invigorated. And as for discovering more about Maugham, well I could only conclude that he clearly possessed a totally unsurpassed twofold ability: firstly, to be able to sit and quietly watch, listen and observe all around him to the tiniest detail as he patently must have done and, secondly, to be able to transfer all of these findings so evocatively, so coherently and so eloquently onto paper.

I felt mentally replenished when I woke up the next morning and, buoyed on by such an enriching evening, went out and completed virtually all my remaining souvenir shopping in just a couple of hours. I even managed to buy a pressure cooker—a gleaming top of the range stainless steel Hawkins, with a massive 20-litre capacity. Arriving back at the Carlton mid-afternoon, I lay on my bed for a while and, after completing another crossword, began leafing though the rest of the newspaper. The preceding day was the first day of elections in India, and it seemed to have gone quite smoothly: only 47 people killed, which apparently was quite low.

I went to bed just before eleven, but was woken not long after by the sound of shouting out in the street. It sounded like some kind of altercation and, turning over in my bed, I tried not to think any more of it. The unrest, however, seemed to go on and on and as a result, I slept fitfully for the rest of the night.

Eight-thirty the next morning, I sleepily grabbed onto my toilet bag and unlocked the door to my room, thinking about all the things that I needed to do on my penultimate day. First port of call was the Singapore Airlines office where I'd reconfirm my flight and make some enquiries about transport to the airport, after which I'd call in at the post office for the final time (just to make sure no more mail had turned up) before spending the rest of the morning leafing through all the newspapers at the UK consulate. There were still a couple of final presents to purchase, so the afternoon had been set aside for some last minute shopping. Then, after dinner at Leopold's, I'd spend the evening in my room going over once more the final nominations for my travel awards ceremony the following night. Well, that was the plan. Half way down the corridor, one of the hotel staff, standing with his back to the wall, was reading a newspaper. As I walked past, I stopped dead in my tracks. What did those headlines say? Turning on my heels, I took a couple of steps back. Emblazoned across the front page of *The Indian Express* in large thick black letters were three words: Rajiv Gandhi Assassinated.

Rooted to the spot, I gaped at the headlines again. The young man appeared remarkably calm but it took just a couple of seconds to realise the gravity of this news and its harrowing implications. When his mother, Indira Gandhi, was assassinated in 1984 by her Sikh bodyguards, the repercussions had been devastating, as racial violence erupted across India on a truly horrific scale. The huge backlash began in Delhi. Innocent Sikhs were indiscriminately dragged off the street, off carriages of trains and buses, and brutally massacred by Hindus hell bent on revenge. Sikh neighbourhoods became the subject of barbarous raids by rampaging mobs, Sikh houses, shops and gurdwaras (temples) were looted and burned down, Sikh women were raped and hundreds more Sikh men were beaten, burned and hacked to death over the days that followed. The carnage quickly spread to neighbouring states, and in the week that proceeded her death, it was estimated that over three thousand Sikhs lost their lives as a result of the sickening violence.

I peered into the face of the hotel worker again for clues. His expression was not one of anger, but of quiet resignation. Catching my glance, he lowered his eyes to the floor, sighing disconsolately. I desperately tried to think of something to say to offer my condolences, but I was totally lost for words. He looked so forlorn and helpless, I almost wanted to hug him or, at least, put my arm around him to comfort him in his moment of grief but, instead, I just stood there for a few seconds hanging my head before shuffling back to my room in silence.

Five minutes later, dashing down the stairs, I threw open the hotel door. The streets were deserted. It felt like a ghost town. Placing a ten rupee note firmly into the palm of the old man at the bottom of the steps, I indiscriminately grabbed a handful of the early editions and, rushing back to my room, laid all the papers on my bed, frantically trying to find out what had happened. The headlines were numerous. *'A Heinous Murder'*, *'A Nation Mourns'*, *'Third Tragic Death In Nehru Family'*, *'Blood Stained Politics'*, *'Red Alert As Violence Erupts'*, *'Elections Put Back To June'*, and perhaps most poignantly *'What Hope Now?'*

The former Prime Minister, it emerged, had been killed by a powerful bomb that had exploded just seconds before he was due to address a public meeting on the outskirts of Madras. At least nine others had also been killed in the blast, including a couple of his security personnel. It had happened around 10.30pm the previous evening, which now explained the strange disturbances I'd heard outside on the street late last night. The shocking and gruesome account of the events in *The Indian*

Express read as follows:

'Mr Gandhi arrived at the meeting venue around 10.15pm, about 90 minutes behind schedule after garlanding a statue of his mother Indira Gandhi at a nearby junction a few hundred metres away. After the garlanding he got back into his car and was driven up to the pathway to the dais.

He alighted from the car and was walking down towards the dais about 10 metres away as local partymen lined up on one side shouted slogans and started garlanding him. He was about 10 metres away from the dais when fireworks signalling his arrival were set off in the background. Seconds afterwards, an explosion rent the air. A few moments later, when the smoke cleared, only a tangled mass of bodies were seen at the spot. The bomb ripped off parts of Mr Gandhi's head and decapitated some of the others near him.

Mr. Shaki Vikraman, our staff reporter, who was an eyewitness to the incident, counted at least ten bodies, including that of Mr. Gandhi. A couple of the bodies were torn asunder in the explosion, which sent mutilated limbs flying all round.'

World leaders had been quick to pay tribute. Back home, John Major described the killing as *'a great loss for India and for the world'* and George Bush declared to reporters in Washington *'I do not know what the world is coming to.'* Bush said that he and his wife had a personal friendship with Gandhi and so his death was a personal loss. *'When you look at his contribution to international order and think of his decency,'* said Bush, *'Rajiv Gandhi's assassination is a real tragedy. And when people will resort in a democratic country or anywhere to violence of this nature, it's just appalling. It's sad that this young man should have lost his life in this way. It is a tragedy.'*

A theory in one newspaper suggested that the bomb had been contained in a bouquet of flowers presented to the Congress leader although others claimed that the explosives had been placed in the flowerpots lining the pathway. Gandhi's body had already arrived in Delhi, accompanied by his daughter Priyanka and wife, Mrs Sonia Gandhi, who the newspapers were already widely predicting would take over the post as party president. As yet, no one had claimed responsibility for the attack although, pertinently, police had not ruled out the involvement of Sri Lankan militants, in spite of the claims of the Tamil Tigers' leader denying his group's involvement. Another paper carried a chilling quote and one that was hardly helpful in the circumstances. It read: *'I suspect that as soon as it emerges who exactly was behind the assassination we can expect the large scale repercussions and acts of horrific revenge and retaliation that have so far been successfully kept bubbling away under the surface.'*

I had never underestimated the volatility of this county and its capacity to shock and surprise. Notwithstanding this, though, there was no way I could have contemplated that an incident of *this* magnitude would occur whilst I was here and, now that it had, I was totally shell-shocked.

In spite of the impending dangers of violence breaking out, I still had to eat so, after peering down from the balcony to make sure there were no angry mobs rampaging the streets, I crept down the stairs again and tentatively walked back out of the reception hall. It didn't take long, just a few seconds in fact, to realise that Leopold's was out of the question, because every shop, every stall and every eating-house was closed. The streets were empty, there was hardly any traffic and the few people I did see were slowly shuffling along the pavements with their faces buried in newspapers. With no other alternative, I wandered over to the Taj.

The foyer was much busier than usual, which given the circumstances, was hardly surprising whilst the Shamiana Bar was doing a roaring trade, presumably because it was the only restaurant open in the vicinity. Consequently, the hotel staff, running around with trays of food and drinks, were being worked off their feet. What I certainly didn't expect, however, was the odd sense of indifference amongst the hotel guests. Many of them, predominantly dressed in blazers and cravats, were stood around in the lobby casually chatting and sipping tea, some were even openly laughing and joking, apparently oblivious to the tragic killing, and since I didn't want to associate myself with these people for a second more than I had to, I quickly bought a sandwich and left. Back outside, the silence that prevailed on the streets was eerie. Other than the faint wailing sound of a siren in the distance, there were no blasts of fog horns echoing around the harbour, no revving car engines, no beeping horns, no policemens' whistles, no crunching of gear sticks, no sounds of canned sitar music resonating from shops and, for once, no cries of 'hashish' or 'shansh maanee.'

I ended up spending the remainder of the day cooped up in my room, trying to pick up any news of what was happening around India on the BBC World Service. Mercifully, although some violence had broken out, it seemed to have been quite sporadic, and certainly not on the scale I'd been fearing. Late afternoon and early evening, I made a couple more dashes over to the Taj, where an increasing number of ashen-faced backpackers had congregated to seek refuge. Sitting around their rucksacks on the floor of the lobby—many in faded T-shirts, cut-off jeans and flip-flops—the contrast between them and the affluent guests, nonchalantly sipping their gin and tonics on the raised platform of the tearoom, couldn't have been more marked. Still, their sneering looks at seeing their beloved foyer overrun with riffraff more than made up for the thirty minutes it took to get another sandwich and, after making a quick phone call home to reassure my parents I was okay, I gladly returned to my room and radio.

The next day normality seemed to have been restored a little and the city felt like it was slowly getting back to business. There was much more traffic on the streets, there were more people crowding the pavements and many of the shops and restaurants were opening up again. The newspapers all now carried the story that preliminary investigations into the assassination indicated that the explosive device had, after all, been strapped to the body of a woman. It was claimed she had probably been a member of a suicide squad, and it appeared that a Sri Lankan Tamil militant group was still thought to be behind the blast. The cremation and funeral would take place the following day and would be broadcast live on state television. The government, as a mark of respect to Mr Gandhi, had also declared a seven-day period of state mourning, and the second and third rounds of polling had been put back until the 12th and 15th of June respectively. Thankfully, it appeared that the violence that had so far broken out had only claimed ten lives, although the country's police and security forces remained on high alert.

Still a little warily, I wandered over to the Singapore Airlines office later in the afternoon to re-confirm my flight. Fortunately, there were no complications. After a couple of hours packing and re-packing, trying to fathom out what I should put in my rucksack and what I should carry on board, I settled down to do the final crossword, which I successfully completed, so levelling the series 5-5. The fact it had ended in a tie couldn't have pleased me more.

There was just one thing left to do now and that was a final recording, recounting in detail my defining thoughts on the last eighteen months. Maugham had written a book called *The Summing Up*. This final recording would be mine.

Over dinner, I was already in reflective mood. I asked myself the all-important question—if I could have done it all again, would I have done anything significantly different? And the honest answer was no, I didn't really think I would have. Maybe I could have taken less with me, perhaps I shouldn't have relied on guidebooks so much and, in hindsight, I probably should have made a greater effort to travel to a few more places off the beaten track. As regards the respective merits of travelling alone or with others, however, the jury was still out. On many occasions, I'd rued the fact I had no company, but then some of the best times I'd had, notably in Australia and Nepal, were spent with friends, both old and new. Oddly enough, though, this no longer seemed to matter, or at least not nearly as much as it had at the outset. Maybe the trick was just getting the balance right. Either way, I was keen to travel again. The Middle East, Pakistan, Japan and Mongolia were all places that quickly sprung to mind, even a visit to the States was no longer beyond the realms of possibility. Finland, though, remained firmly out of bounds. One thing I certainly didn't want to do was to return to any of the places I'd just visited as I simply couldn't see the point. Second time around, I maintained that I'd be on a perpetual loser as I now had comparisons formed in my mind to judge these places by. Consequently, my expectations would never conceivably come up to scratch. Places change, people change and perceptions change, and more often than not, these changes were not likely to be for the better. But no, overall, if I was to have done it all again, I wouldn't have done much different, and I guessed this signified two things: firstly, that all my meticulous preparations had been finally worth it and, secondly, that my overriding decision to come away and see only the parts of the world that I had genuinely wanted to see had now been fully vindicated.

So, my flight home the following morning beckoned and all I could do now was prepare myself for my return. I had really mixed feelings about this. Of course, it would be great to see all of my family and friends again, but there was a certain degree of poignancy over the unavoidable fact my long venture was now drawing to an end. In my favour I at least had something to get my teeth stuck into with my plans to go into business with Gibbo. Nearly everybody I'd spoken to who'd gone off travelling had complained how depressing it was when you got home, although I was determined not to let this get me down. Sure, I was going to have a lot of money to pay back on my credit cards but it seemed the mistake too many people made was to dwell too long on the great time they'd had. Fortunately, this last week in Bombay had already given me the chance to do this and take stock. Now I had to look straight ahead and not behind. That was then, this was now. Notwithstanding this, these past eighteen months had literally flown by and it only seemed like yesterday that I was working in London and dreaming about setting off. The check-in time for my Singapore Airlines flight was 11am. I still had a little packing to do first thing in the morning and then, after one last breakfast at

Leopold's, I'd jump on the bus to the airport. And as for India itself, well, it had far surpassed all my expectations and I doubted I'd ever come across another country that was so vibrant, so diverse and so colourful. I'd be leaving here with a great deal of affection for the people, especially after the events of the last few days, and I could only ponder what its uncertain future held.

An hour later, the time had come. It was just gone seven and, after wolfing down my dinner, I was sitting in my room back at the Carlton. In spite of the tragic news two days ago, I had something very special planned for my final night and I felt reluctant to abandon it now. As I previously mentioned, the idea to host my very own travel awards ceremony had been hatched a few weeks before in Pushkar, and ever since then, I'd been busily jotting down various categories and nominations in my notebook. Now that this moment had finally arrived, I could hardly contain my excitement. Trying to settle myself down, I poured myself a drink from the whisky that had been swimming around in my hip flask for the last three months, and then lit up one of the huge King Edward cigars Gibbo had left me in Nepal. Opening my notebook, I glanced at the first category—Most Memorable Country Visited—and then began talking into my beloved Dictaphone recorder for the very last time.

AFTERWORD

I arrived back in the UK two days later, and whilst it was wonderful to see my family and friends again, the novelty soon wore off and for a while, all I found myself doing was wishing I were still travelling. Very little seemed to have changed back home and my active mind, deprived of its constant eighteen month diet of learning, awakening and stimulation, was becoming increasingly restless. The first six months, in particular, were the most difficult but almost a year to the day after I returned, Gibbo and I managed to find a suitable location for a shop and before we knew it, found ourselves preoccupied with all the unfamiliar complexities and nuances so inherent to the peculiar world of retail. Twelve years later (touch wood) our business is still going strong and whilst it'll never make us millionaires, it still beats the hell out of 'Avoir Fiscal.'

I kept all of the promises I made to keep in touch with people I'd met: I sent off copies of photographs, I wrote to Lu Xiao, David and Reilly, Slim, Basir and Bob, I even sent Hari a huge concise dictionary but, in time, all the letters dried up. My Dutch friend, Rob, moved back with Madeline to the Netherlands for a short period, so I popped over to visit them for a weekend. Indeed, a few months later they returned the compliment but when they eventually moved back to Australia, I lost touch with them as well. Gibbo and Caroline, for their part, finally got married and I was bestowed with the thankless task of being his best man. I still don't think Caroline's fully forgiven me, though. It wasn't so much that anything untoward happened on the stag weekend, but more the small matter of the photographs of their fashion parade in Nepal wearing the hideously unflattering brown pants, which went on to figure so prominently in the after dinner speech.

And did my venture change me in any way? Well, it made me a more tolerant person, that I am certain, especially when it comes to other races and religions; 'Live and let live' became my adopted motto. It also helped me to curb my impatience. Now, whenever I'm stood at the back of a long queue at the post office or supermarket checkout, sighing like everybody else, I think back for a few moments to the crowded train stations of China and India, and then, breathing a deep sigh of relief, start to count my blessings.

Another thing I discovered about myself on the trip was my love of writing. It subsequently came to light I'd sent no less than 380 letters to friends and family in the eighteen months I'd been away, and a huge cardboard box in our spare room still contains all the replies I received. These, along with my tapes, provided me with all the invaluable material I needed to reconstruct my venture. Initially, I was going to leave it a lot longer. I had this kind of romantic notion to store the tapes away for fifty years and then, in my old age, sit in a rocking chair, reminiscing as I played them back one after the other. And just before I popped my clogs, I'd hand them down to my grandchildren as family heirlooms because by then, of course, they'd be worth a fortune. I could even picture them running around the schoolyard telling all their friends their grandfather was some kind of fabled, intrepid explorer.

But over time, I began to get impatient and when my father-in-law suffered a series of silent strokes, tragically robbing him of his memory, the need to transcribe the tapes while all *my* faculties remained intact overtook me. It turned out to be a thoroughly enjoyable project, although it was—it has to be said—not without difficulties. Sitting in front of a computer screen every night after work and most weekends is a huge strain in itself, whilst trying to break into the world of publishing, as many an aspiring writer can attest, is an immensely difficult and frustrating process and to this, I really have to thank the Literary Council and Alan Wilkinson, in particular, for providing me with the invaluable criticism I needed at a time when I was all but ready to pack it all in. Without his help, I simply wouldn't have had enthusiasm to persevere. And on the subject of acknowledgements, I must also say a big thank you to Huw, Simon, Caroline, and especially Lisa, for all her encouragement and feedback.

Funnily enough, I never did back pack again, and this was largely down to the constraints of the business. The only places I have returned to are New Zealand and Goa and, nice though they were, they still weren't the same second time around. But when one door closes another one opens, for if it hadn't had been for our first little shop, I'd probably never have met Sam, the soon-to-be mother of our first child. The girl I'd subconsciously been longing to meet on my travels had, rather ironically, been living just down the road all the time!

As regards my trip, I still look back at it with a great deal of affection: each time a news item, a travel programme or a documentary on one of the countries I visited comes on the television, I always look on with interest; whenever friends or family happen to be stopping over, the good ol' pressure cooker is unfailingly hauled out from the cupboard a couple of days before and dusted down in preparation, whilst my tattered beloved Reeboks are still serving me well twelve years on. Indeed, as I type these very words into the computer, a certain three Tibetan characters stare sagely down at me from the top of the monitor. They say there's a time and a place for everything and, all said and done, those eighteen wonderful months were unquestionably mine.

PS. I never did find out what 'Chunglee Singh' meant so, if you want to finally put me out of my misery or, indeed, if you have any other comments—good or bad—about anything else you may have read, please feel free to contact me at

www.jimford.net